Gender in Management

Sixth Edition

Gary N. Powell
University of Connecticut

Sage

Sage

FOR INFORMATION:

2455 Teller Road
Thousand Oaks, California 91320
E-mail: order@sagepub.com

1 Oliver's Yard
55 City Road
London, EC1Y 1SP
United Kingdom

Unit No. 323–333, Third Floor, F-Block
International Trade Tower
Nehru Place, New Delhi—110 019
India

18 Cross Street #10–10/11/12
China Square Central
Singapore 048423

Acquisitions Editor: Lauren Gobell
Product Associate: Izumi Sunada
Production Editor: Vijayakumar
Copy Editor: Erin Livingston
Typesetter: Tracy Buyan
Cover Designer: Janet Kiesel
Marketing Manager: Jennifer Haldeman

Printed in Germany
Libri Plureos GmbH
Friedensallee 273
22763 Hamburg

Library of Congress Control Number: LCCN 2023045819 | ISBN 978-1-0719-1035-1 (paperback)

This book is printed on acid-free paper.

24 25 26 27 28 10 9 8 7 6 5 4 3 2 1

Gender in Management

Sixth Edition

To Laura Graves for her love and support
and
to the memory of my grandmother, Edna Powell, for all the quarters and much more.

Sara Miller McCune founded Sage Publishing in 1965 to support the dissemination of usable knowledge and educate a global community. Sage publishes more than 1,000 journals and over 600 new books each year, spanning a wide range of subject areas. Our growing selection of library products includes archives, data, case studies, and video. Sage remains majority owned by our founder and after her lifetime will become owned by a charitable trust that secures the company's continued independence.

Los Angeles | London | New Delhi | Singapore | Washington DC | Melbourne

BRIEF CONTENTS

DETAILED CONTENTS

FOREWORD

Much important history has been made in the three and a half decades since the first edition of *Women and Men in Management*. Yet, the COVID-19 pandemic feels like a uniquely distinct and defining event for individuals who have lived through it and for the organizations they belong to. While first and foremost a public and global health emergency that took innumerable lives, the pandemic revealed itself as an unescapable mirror to our gendered world, reflecting both a despairingly deep entrenchment of problematic gendered patterns and uplifting possibilities for more gender equity from new work arrangements.

As the pandemic forced employees around the world to work from home and their children to attend school and preschool virtually, families adjusted to these dramatic and sudden shifts by reverting to traditional childcare schemas that disproportionately increased women's time spent in childcare (Grantham et al., 2021). In part because of these issues, women dropped out of the workplace in larger numbers than men. Moreover, because jobs continue to be segregated not only by gender but also by race and because sectors most affected by COVID-19 were female-dominated (and, specifically, more likely to employ women of color), women and women of color lost their jobs at higher rates than men during the global health emergency (Barua, 2022; Martin-Caughey, 2023).

Businesses responded to COVID-19 by experimenting with new and creative work arrangements, adopting remote work on an unimaginably wide scale. Some companies have incorporated these arrangements as a more permanent feature of work, while other firms are increasingly requiring employees to come back to the office (Liu, 2023), especially now that COVID-19's emergency status has ended. Whether remote work helps or hurts women's careers is not yet clear. To a degree, it provides relief as women spend less time on the home–childcare/school–work commute, the length of which is exacerbated by an infrastructure that was historically developed for men moving to and from the suburbs (rather than for people commuting within suburbs). Yet, other experts caution that working from home reduces women's access to two promotability-enhancing factors: networking opportunities and visibility (Ibarra et al., 2020).

Contrasting with the pandemic-induced regression toward traditional gendered patterns in childcare and in workplace outcomes, alternate gender identifications to the man/woman binary have burgeoned worldwide, especially among young people (Kenney, 2020). A growing number of adults know someone who is transgender or goes by gender-neutral pronouns. In many countries, new legislation has supported these developments (Konotey-Ahulu, 2023). At the same time, organizations and workers are grappling with backlash against transgender rights, which still vary greatly and often conflict from place to place.

The pandemic also reinvigorated the debate around the so-called gender leadership advantage, as several women heads of state (and in other leadership roles) were profiled for prioritizing the health outcomes of their citizens over economic considerations (Friedman, 2020).

Against this backdrop that shows both retrogression and progress at the intersection of gender and the workplace, the sixth edition of *Gender in Management* is timely and valuable. It cuts through the noise and helps make sense of the sometimes confusing and often contradictory evidence from thousands of research studies. It provides honest and actionable advice for those seeking to defeat gender biases in employment decisions, for teams striving to leverage the potential of their gender diversity, for organizations pursuing equity and inclusion, and for individuals and couples working toward work–life balance. Most refreshingly, it provides recommendations to help organizations move beyond the limiting assumptions about who is most effective at leading; instead, it explains what organizations can do to help leaders of all genders be successful in their roles.

We need more books like this one, not only to stay up to date on the ever-changing roles and experiences of women, men, and those for whom this binary distinction does not apply. The knowledge and advice provided here also equip us—as individuals and as organizational actors—to make changes in our lives and in our organizations for greater diversity, equity, and well-being.

Corinne Post
Villanova University

REFERENCES

Barua, A. (2022, January 21). *Gender equality, dealt a blow by COVID-19, still has much ground to cover. Deloitte. Insights*. https://www2.deloitte.com/us/en/insights/economy/impact-of-covid-on-women.html

Friedman, U. (2020, April 19). *New Zealand's prime minister may be the most effective leader on the planet. The Atlantic*. https://www.theatlantic.com/politics/archive/2020/04/jacinda-ardern-new-zealand-leadership-coronavirus/610237/

Grantham, K., Rouhani, L., Gupta, N., Melesse, M., Dhar, D., Mehta, S., & Kingra, K. J. (2021). *Evidence review of the global childcare crisis and the road for post-Covid-19 recovery and resilience*. International Development Research Centre. http://hdl.handle.net/10625/59915

Ibarra, H., Gillard, J., & Chamorro-Premuzic, T. (2020, July 16). *Why WFH isn't necessarily good for women. Harvard Business Review*. https://hbr.org/2020/07/why-wfh-isnt-necessarily-good-for-women

Kenney, L. (2020, April 8). *Companies can't ignore shifting gender norms. Harvard Business Review*. https://hbr.org/2020/04/companies-cant-ignore-shifting-gender-norms

Konotey-Ahulu, O. (2023, January 16). *Where change is coming for LGBTQ rights around the world. Bloomberg.* https://www.bloomberg.com/news/features/2023-01-17/lgbtq-rights-around-the-world-changes-in-2023

Liu, J. (2023, January 20). *Bosses are increasing RTO requirements, but experts say it won't stick: 'We're at an inflection point.'. CNBC.* https://www.cnbc.com/2023/01/20/bosses-hope-fresh-rto-requirements-will-stick-experts-arent-so-sure.html

Martin-Caughey, A. (2023, March 13). *Women and men both experienced changes in occupations during COVID-19.* United States Census Bureau. https://www.census.gov/library/stories/2023/03/women-and-men-occupation-changes-during-covid-19.html

PREFACE

This book has an interesting backstory. Early in my career in the management department of the School of Business at the University of Connecticut (UConn), I was given the opportunity to teach an ad-hoc graduate elective on any topic I wanted. I decided to teach a course with a unique title: Women and Men in Management. The title was carefully chosen.

First, the words "and men" were included in the title in part to legitimate my teaching such a course. The first courses on this topic mostly had titles such as Women in Management and were typically taught by women to a class composed entirely or nearly entirely of women. My course title might make its having a male instructor seem less strange and increase its appeal to male students.

Second, the words "women and men" were included in that order in the title to call attention to the order of words typically and unconsciously used. When a male colleague at UConn heard about the course, he asked me, "Why 'women and men' in that order rather than 'men and women' like everyone is used to saying?" Before I could reply, someone within earshot said, "If you need to ask a question like that, you need to take the course!"

Finally, the words "in management" were included in the title simply because I was a professor in a management department. However, the course was intended to apply to women and men in all types of positions in organizations—managerial and non-managerial—and might as well have been titled Women and Men in the Workplace.

My business school's dean heard about the course and saw an opportunity. He knew that the primary business school accrediting agency, now called the Association to Advance Collegiate Schools of Business (AACSB), had a committee on women's issues in business schools that gave an annual course innovation award. The dean asked me to write up the course and apply for the award. In the application, I stated the course objectives as (1) to increase understanding of the interactions between women and men in work settings and (2) to encourage both women and men to recognize the stake they have in addressing female–male issues that occur in the workplace. The course won the AACSB Committee on Equal Opportunity for Women Innovation Award, which pleased my dean, helped me get the course officially in the UConn graduate catalog, and got me thinking further.

Buoyed by winning the award, I decided to write a proposal for a book of the same title. Ideally, the book would serve as a resource for scholars as well as a text for courses on the topic, including my own. I anticipated that my being able to say that it was based on "an award-winning course" would be a selling point for the book. SAGE expressed interest in the book but was initially wary about its having only a male author. However, by this time, I had served as chair of the Women in Management Division of the Academy of Management, the primary professional association in my field, becoming the first man to do so. Several of my female colleagues in the division told SAGE representatives at my request that they thought I would do a good job on the book, even though I am a man. To my good fortune, SAGE agreed to publish the book, and what became the first edition was published in 1988.

However, while the book title of *Women and Men in Management* was more inclusive than the titles of earlier books in the field, it did not acknowledge the workplace experiences of people for whom this binary distinction does not apply. Hence, the updated book title.

So here we are, with the sixth edition of Gender in Management in your hands or on your electronic device. The book has been updated along the way and from the fifth edition in several ways:

1. To reflect the explosion of research on this topic since the first edition was published, this edition now includes references to more than 1,200 sources, ranging from classics in the field to more recent research and almost half of which are new to this edition.

2. Increased attention is devoted to issues of sexual orientation and the unique workplace experiences of LGBTQ+ (lesbian, gay, bisexual, transgender, and self-described queer) employees.

3. Increased attention is devoted to issues of intersectionality, examining how multiple identities of individuals overlap to affect their workplace experiences in many ways. In particular, increased attention is devoted to the intersection of individuals' sex and race and the unique workplace experiences of women of color.

4. All statistics pertaining to labor force participation, educational attainment, occupational attainment, managerial advancement, earnings, family structures, and so on have been updated to reflect the most current statistics available.

5. Public events and trends since the fifth edition (e.g., the #MeToo and Black Lives Matter movements, the COVID-19 pandemic, the increased use of artificial intelligence systems in organizational hiring decisions, the increased prevalence of virtual teams and of working at home) have been incorporated into this edition as it was being written as fast as I could keep up with them.

Enjoy your reading!

ACKNOWLEDGMENTS

Many people contributed to the preparation of this sixth edition of Gender in Management. I wish to express my deepest gratitude to the following:

1. Laura Graves for being a terrific collaborator on Chapters 4 and 5 of this edition as well as coauthor of an earlier edition;
2. Tony Butterfield for being my great mentor, collaborator, colleague, and friend;
3. the School of Business of the University of Connecticut for giving me the opportunity to teach the course that won the American Assembly of Collegiate Schools of Business (AACSB) Committee on Equal Opportunity for Women Innovation Award and inspired the writing of this book;
4. my many colleagues in professional associations—the Diversity, Equity, and Inclusion Division (formerly Women in Management Division) and the Careers Division of the Academy of Management, the Gender in Management Special Interest Group of the British Academy of Management, and the Work and Family Researchers Network—for providing both a forum for the sharing of research findings and a stimulus for creative thinking on this topic;
5. the following reviewers:
    - John L. Hudgins, Coppin State University
    - Konnie Kustron, Bay College
    - Liesl H. Eberhardt, University of Colorado at Colorado Springs
6. Mosey the cat for unlimited love, affection, and play; and
7. again, and most of all, Laura Graves, my wife and favorite colleague, for standing by me all the way.

1 INTRODUCTION

LEARNING OBJECTIVES

After reading this chapter, you should be able to do the following:

1.1 Identify trends that promote an optimistic versus pessimistic view of the future of gender equality at work.

1.2 Define key terms used in gender studies.

1.3 Distinguish between primary and secondary dimensions of diversity and provide examples of each.

1.4 Define *stereotyping, prejudice,* and *discrimination.*

1.5 Distinguish between alpha and beta bias in considering sex similarities and differences.

OPTIMISTIC AND PESSIMISTIC VIEWS OF GENDER EQUALITY AT WORK

> There is perhaps no field aspiring to be scientific where flagrant personal bias, logic martyred in the cause of supporting a prejudice, unfounded assertions, and even sentimental rot and drivel, have run riot to such an extent as here.[1]

> Psychologists love dichotomies. They love to slice and dice a broader population into two categories.[2]

Our story begins with a pithy word from the first psychologist to undertake an extensive and systematic examination of the psychological characteristics of women vis-à-vis men.[3] In 1910, Helen Thompson Woolley issued a stinging indictment of research about the topic that is quoted at the beginning of this chapter. Since then, many thousands of studies on the topic have been published by scholars around the world. Has anything changed?

Exactly one century later, Susan Fiske, a prominent modern-day psychologist, offered the humorous take on psychologists that appears in the second quote above. When psychologists consider the characteristics of two groups such as men and women, they tend to view members of the two groups as opposite in traits. This tendency in turn influences the psychologists' research, including the topics studied, the labels assigned to traits, and the interpretation of results and conclusions reached. However, even if psychologists and other observers are predisposed to believe that differences in women's and men's personal traits are prevalent, this does not necessarily mean that such differences are absent. Moreover, even if differences in personal traits that men and women bring to the workplace are minimal, their experiences in the workplace may differ dramatically.

Gender in Management, sixth edition, examines the evolving roles and experiences of women vis-à-vis men in the global workplace as well as the experiences of individuals to whom this binary distinction does not apply. Although research over the past several decades on the topic of gender in management has overwhelmingly focused on comparing the experiences of women and men at work, research that has focused on the experiences of transgender, nonbinary, and LGBTQ+ employees at work (terms to be defined later in the chapter) is incorporated into the book in detail.

Significant changes have been documented over time in the status of women and men and in their interactions at work. However, sharply differing views have been offered about the implications of these changes for the workplace of the future. Some believe that all of the needed changes have taken place and remaining gender inequalities in the workplace, if any, will continue to erode. According to an **optimistic view** of trends toward gender equality, the inevitable consequence of egalitarian values among parents to provide their daughters and sons with similar opportunities, among citizens to fully support and comply with laws banning discrimination on the basis of sex, and among organizations to offer family-friendly programs (such as on-site childcare) will be equal opportunities and pay for women and men. In short, the day will come when a person's sex no longer matters at work.[4]

What has been called a **postfeminist sensibility** at work captures the optimistic view. According to this sensibility, gender inequalities existed in the past (not in the present); gender inequalities occur elsewhere (not in my place of work); being a woman is an advantage (not a disadvantage); and, if any gender inequalities exist, that's simply the way the workplace is and it needs to be accepted. In short, a postfeminist sensibility suggests that "the problem of gender has been 'solved'" as much as it ever needed to be solved.[5]

However, others believe that needed changes have stalled and remaining gender inequalities are now entrenched. According to a **pessimistic view** of trends toward gender equality, although men are doing more housework, they are not exactly embracing the opportunity to take on equal responsibility with their female partners for childcare and other household demands; people will continue to value gender equality at work more than gender equality at home.[6] Also, although women have sought access to male-intensive occupations (those in which two-thirds or more of the workforce is male) in greater numbers, fewer men have sought access to female-intensive occupations (those in which two-thirds or more of the workforce is female). Further, the legal mandate of equal opportunities for women and men at work is not equivalent to a societal commitment to ensure that they will be similarly oriented to take advantage of such opportunities.

Worldwide, in a survey of 34 countries, most people say that gender equality in their country is very important (e.g., 96% in Sweden, 93% in Canada, 92% in the United Kingdom and the Netherlands, 91% in the United States and Australia, 90% in France and Germany). However, men are seen as having more opportunities than women in gaining high-paying jobs, and women are less optimistic than men about whether gender equality will ever be achieved in their country. Not surprisingly, employed women and men tend to see the workplace differently, with women leaning more toward the pessimistic view and men more toward the optimistic view.[7]

Both female and male university students tend to embrace the optimistic view and postfeminist sensibility, believing that they will be personally unaffected by or witness any sex discrimination when they enter the workplace. Moreover, female students are more likely to believe that other women will experience discrimination on the basis of sex than they will experience themselves, suggesting that they see themselves as personally immune from workplace forces that disadvantage other women. In contrast, older women are likely to believe that younger women are kidding themselves in adopting such beliefs.[8]

Although we do not know whether the future will offer greater support for the optimistic or pessimistic view, the evidence about the present state of affairs in the workplace offers more of a mixed picture. The role of women in the workplace has expanded considerably in recent decades. In the United States, the proportion of women in the labor force (i.e., the proportion of all adults employed or seeking employment who are women), which was 43% in 1982, has risen to 47%. Although the current proportion of women in the labor force varies widely across countries, the trend in almost all countries has been in the same direction—toward the increased employment of women.[9]

Similarly, although the proportion of women in management in different countries varies widely due to differences in national culture and definitions of the term *manager*, the trend in almost all countries has been toward the increased representation of women in the managerial ranks. However, female managers remain concentrated in lower management levels and hold positions with less status, power, and authority than men. The higher the level of the organization, the fewer women are found. Around the world, a **glass ceiling** appears to restrict women's access to top management positions solely because they are women. Women are not allowed to advance in managerial hierarchies as far as men with equivalent credentials.[10]

Evidence about the gender composition of the top management ranks has been interpreted in sharply different ways. For example, in 1996, one (i.e., 0.2%) of the chief executive officers (CEOs) of *Fortune 500* corporations was female. At the time of writing, 53 (10.6%) of the *Fortune 500* CEOs are female. What should be made of this trend? It depends in part on what statistic is used to describe it. On the one hand, the increase in the proportion of female CEOs of *Fortune 500* corporations since 1996 has been 5200.0% (from one to 53), certainly a large proportion. On the other hand, the decrease in the proportion of male CEOs of such corporations over the same period has been only 10.4% (from 499 to 447). Observers have disagreed over what this trend actually means. When the proportion reached 4.0% for the first time, one observer declared "the dawn of the age of female CEOs" and a real breakthrough for women. However, commenting on the same trend, others argued that it represented "delusions of progress" and the real story was that there are still too few female CEOs. Thus, the same trend in the status of women in top management may be interpreted both optimistically and pessimistically.[11]

In addition, the economic status of women in the global workplace remains lower than that of men. The average female full-time worker continues to be paid less than the average male full-time worker. This gap is partly due to the lower average wages of workers in female-intensive occupations than that of workers in male-intensive occupations. Also, women are paid less than men in the same occupation and often in the same job. The ratio of female-to-male wages for similar work is below 100% in all nations for which the World Economic Forum reports data.[12]

Further, the global labor force remains sharply segregated on the basis of sex. In recent years, women have shown more interest in entering male-intensive occupations than men have shown in entering female-intensive occupations, which is not surprising because workers in male-intensive occupations are paid more. However, women continue to be crowded into a lower-paying set of occupations than are men.[13]

Overall, differences in workplace status according to biological sex remain strong, even though there have been considerable changes. Although progress toward global gender equality has been made, it has been estimated that it would take 132 more years to close the global gender gap entirely at the current rate of progress.[14] You may interpret this estimate optimistically (global gender equality will eventually be achieved . . .) or pessimistically (. . . but not in my lifetime, if it is ever achieved at all).

Is it only a matter of time until the proportions of women and men in all managerial levels and all occupations become essentially equal, until women and men are paid equal wages for equal work, and until individuals' work experiences are unaffected by their biological sex? As we shall see, it will depend on actions that organizations and individuals take.

TERMINOLOGY

Terminology has expanded in the field of gender studies and in the world at large in recent years. Although there is not complete agreement on the terms to be used, definitions of these terms, and descriptions of the phenomena to which they are applied (there never is), it is useful for us to review some of the terms and definitions that may be applied to the topic of gender in management.[15]

Psychologists have long distinguished between the terms of *sex* and *gender.* The term **sex** (or *biological sex*) has historically been used to refer to the binary categories of male and female, which are determined by biological characteristics of individuals such as their physiological properties and reproductive apparatus. In contrast, the term **gender** has historically been used to refer to the psychosocial implications of being male or female.[16] These implications include *gender stereotypes*, defined as beliefs about the psychological traits that are characteristic of males vis-à-vis females; *gender roles*, defined as beliefs about the behaviors that are appropriate for males vis-à-vis females; *gender socialization*, defined as the processes by which individuals learn gender stereotypes and roles beginning in childhood; and so on.[17]

However, you can probably see the limitations of the historical definition of sex. Not all individuals are captured by the binary categorization of being either male or female in biological characteristics. **Intersex** individuals have biological characteristics that do not fit the typical characteristics that are associated with females or males; that is, they possess physical characteristics associated with both females and males. Also, **transgender** individuals, who identify with a sex different from the one assigned to them at birth, may go through a physical transition such that they become members of the sex with which they identify. Thus, biological sex is best regarded as a continuous rather than binary variable. Categorizing individuals as either female or male does not cover all people, and being female or male is not necessarily a stable category.[18]

In the same vein, phenomena such as gender stereotypes, roles, and socialization should not be regarded as exclusively applying to females vis-à-vis males; they also may be associated with intersex and transgender individuals. That is, gender-related phenomena as well as biological sex are best characterized as falling on a continuum.[19] Cognitive and behavioral phenomena associated with gender are discussed in greater detail in Chapter 3.

As transgender individuals have received more attention from scholars as well as the mass media in recent years, greater attention has also been devoted to **gender identity**, defined as an individual's personal identification with the sex assigned at birth. **Cisgender** individuals feel a match between the sex they were assigned at birth and their gender identity, whereas transgender individuals do not. **Nonbinary** individuals are those whose gender identity is neither exclusively female nor exclusively male.[20]

It should be noted that gender identity is not the same as sexual orientation. For transgender, cisgender, and nonbinary people alike, *gender identity* refers to "who they feel themselves to be" whereas *sexual orientation* refers to "whom they are attracted to."[21]

Some umbrella terms are used by individuals to describe themselves and others. For example, the term **queer** is often used to describe a gender identity, sexual orientation, or other form of expression that does not conform to traditional societal norms; that is, anyone who is not cisgender and heterosexual. Although this term has historically been used as a slur, some people proudly embrace it as a self-descriptor. Also, the term **LGBTQ+** (or variations of the term such as LGBT+) is used to refer to lesbian, gay, bisexual, transgender, and self-described queer people as well as all individuals who live or express themselves outside traditional societal norms regarding sexuality and its expression.[22]

In the bulk of research to be reviewed in this book, studies of **sex differences** generally examine how males and females actually differ; intersex individuals are rarely included in such studies. In contrast, studies of **gender differences** generally focus on how people believe that males and females differ. For example, a sex difference in leadership style would exist if female leaders were more considerate of subordinates than male leaders were, whereas a gender difference in leadership style would exist if people believed that female leaders were more considerate of subordinates than male leaders were. However, there could be a gender difference in leadership style without a corresponding sex difference and vice versa.

As we consider the effects of sex differences on work-related behavior, we also need to consider the effects of gender differences. Sex differences influence how people are disposed to behave in work settings. Gender differences influence how people react to others' behavior in such settings. Further, gender differences can *cause* sex differences. For example, if parents believe that the developmental needs of their sons differ from those of their daughters, they may raise their children in ways that reinforce that belief. In the same vein, if supervisors believe that the skills and interests of their female and male subordinates differ, they may assign tasks to their subordinates in ways that reinforce that belief. In each case, the result is a **self-fulfilling prophecy**—when expectations cause behavior that makes the expectations come true. We identify many workplace situations in which self-fulfilling prophecies are likely to occur.[23]

DIMENSIONS OF DIVERSITY

People differ in many ways, some of which are changeable, while others are less amenable to change. **Primary dimensions of diversity** are unchangeable or difficult-to-change personal characteristics that may exert significant lifelong impacts. Sex is typically classified as a primary dimension of diversity (although it may be changed), along with race, ethnicity, age, sexual orientation, and physical abilities/disabilities. Primary dimensions of diversity affect our early learning experiences, which in turn exert an impact over the course of our lives.[24]

Secondary dimensions of diversity, on the other hand, are more readily changeable personal characteristics. These characteristics are acquired and may be modified or abandoned throughout life. Education, income, marital and parental status, religion, political affiliation, and work experience are some secondary dimensions of diversity of importance to many people. People also distinguish themselves in many other ways, such as in their choices of collegiate fraternities or sororities, hobbies, activities, voluntary associations, clothing and grooming style, and music preferences. People do not completely determine their secondary dimensions of diversity. For instance, educational background, work experience, income, and marital status are also affected by other people's decisions. However, people generally exercise more control over secondary than primary dimensions of diversity in their lives.

Dimensions of diversity, both primary and secondary, may affect your basic self-image and sense of identity. To illustrate this point, try the following exercise:

> Draw a pie chart that identifies group affiliations that have some importance in your self-identity. These affiliations may be based on any of the primary or secondary dimensions of diversity mentioned above or on some other personal characteristic that is particularly important to you (e.g., cat or dog lover, fan of a particular sports team or musical act). Indicate the approximate importance of each group affiliation by the size of the slice of pie that you assign it.[25]

Now review your pie chart. It indicates the specific group affiliations with which you most identify; these are likely to be numerous and unique to you. As Jaye Goosby Smith put it, "We are all messy mashups of identity!"[26] Taylor Cox concluded from his experiences with using this exercise in diversity workshops that people tend to be highly aware of the group affiliation that most distinguishes them from the majority group in a particular setting. For example, women in male-dominated settings are more likely than men in such settings to emphasize their sex in their pie charts, and Blacks in White-dominated settings are more likely than Whites in such settings to emphasize their race. Thus, your pie chart and the identities it displays may be influenced by the setting that provides your frame of reference when you draw it.[27]

Dimensions of diversity pertain to group memberships that may be visible or invisible to other people and sometimes present individuals with choices to make. For example, people with a **visible disability** face a decision about whether to acknowledge it to others and, if so, how. Acknowledgment strategies vary from claiming the visible disability (i.e., accentuating its positive aspects and making it part of one's identity) to downplaying it (i.e., minimizing its negative aspects and redirecting attention from it); these decisions are likely to be based on anticipated reactions to the form of acknowledgment (if any). People with a visible disability also vary in whether they request a workplace accommodation for the disability.[28]

In contrast, sexual orientation represents a dimension of diversity that is not visible to others at work, although it may be inferred. In work environments in which heterosexuality is assumed unless information is provided to the contrary, LGBTQ+ individuals face decisions about whether to "come out" by disclosing their sexual orientation or gender identity to others and, if so, to whom. Their disclosure decisions may be influenced by anticipated reactions of coworkers and whether they work in organizations with supportive LGBTQ+ practices in place that they trust. When LGBT+ individuals disclose their sexual orientation or gender identity at work, they feel more authentic about sharing their "true self" (or at least "authentic enough" to be accepted by others), which contributes to their feeling more positive about their work environment. On the other hand, when they conceal their sexual orientation or gender identity at work, they feel less authentic and more negative about their work environment.[29] In general, people with any invisible dimension of diversity may face a difficult choice about whether to disclose (stand out) or conceal (blend in) this aspect of themselves at work, especially if disclosing it would expose them to potential negative reactions from coworkers.[30]

Visible or inferred dimensions of diversity may have a greater impact on how others see and react to you than on how you see yourself. For example, sex is a highly visible personal characteristic that is important to most people when forming their impression of someone.[31] Even if sex is not important to a person's own sense of identity (i.e., left out of their pie chart), other people are often influenced by their beliefs and expectations associated with that person's sex.

Intersectionality refers to the notion that multiple dimensions of diversity, with which individuals may or may not identify, intersect, or overlap to shape their experiences in unique ways. Thus, the intersection of sex and other personal characteristics such as race, ethnicity, age, sexual orientation, national origin, religion, socioeconomic class, and so on assumes importance. However, researchers often ignore the ways in which individuals' sex combines with other dimensions of diversity to influence their experiences at work.[32]

For example, many studies of sex or gender differences have not examined the influence of the racial and ethnic group of the individuals who were the focus of the study. By ignoring issues of race and ethnicity, such studies reflect an underlying assumption that sex and gender similarities and differences in work-related phenomena are similar across all racial and ethnic groups. However, the intersection of sex with race and ethnicity may influence group stereotypes, occupational choices, hiring decisions, leadership perceptions, career experiences, and other work-related phenomena. Factor in other dimensions of diversity that might have been reported and examined in studies but were not (e.g., socioeconomic class, sexual orientation, national origin, religion, etc.), and the list of assumptions about the similarity of sex and gender differences across members of different groups grows.[33] We need to guard against making such assumptions ourselves.

STEREOTYPING, PREJUDICE, AND DISCRIMINATION

People may engage in stereotyping, prejudice, and discrimination according to how they literally see others in terms of dimensions of diversity. **Stereotyping** consists of having a set of beliefs about the personal attributes of a group of people. It is a cognitive activity, related to thinking, learning, and remembering distinctions among groups of people. Stereotypes may be accurate or inaccurate and positive or negative in their depiction of the average group member, but they seldom fully characterize a particular individual within a given group. In contrast, people who display **prejudice**, or a negative attitude toward members of other groups, are engaging in an emotional activity. Being a target of prejudice is similar to being stigmatized, as both prejudice and stigmatization entail a negative social reaction based solely on an individual's group membership.[34] Stereotyping and prejudice may both be learned in childhood, which we discuss in Chapter 3. Finally, **discrimination**, regarded as a behavioral activity, is exhibited in how people treat members of other groups and in decisions they make about others. Discrimination may vary from overt or blatant to subtle or difficult to detect, with subtle and overt discrimination being just as detrimental to targets. Negative stereotypes and/or prejudice may lead to discriminatory behavior.[35]

Given today's technology, discrimination may also be a digital activity. For example, Apple Card was accused of using an algorithm that engaged in sex discrimination after Steve Wozniak, Apple's co-founder, complained that he received ten times the credit limit as his wife, although they had no separate bank or credit accounts and no separate assets. In an experimental study, Google was found to exhibit sex discrimination in the ads it showed to men versus women. When simulated men visited employment-related web pages, Google displayed ads for a career coaching agency that promoted jobs with high salaries more frequently than when simulated women visited the same web pages. A different study found that online ads for providers of arrest records were more likely to be displayed when searches were conducted for real names that were most associated with Black people than for real names that were most associated with White people, even if the searched-for individuals had no actual arrest record. Thus, discrimination may be exhibited by computer software and algorithms as well as people.[36]

We have reason to be concerned about stereotyping, prejudice, and discrimination in the workplace. All of us may be targets of these phenomena as well as engage in these phenomena, whether consciously or unconsciously. In this book, we focus on stereotyping, prejudice, and discrimination on the basis of sex, but sex represents only one of many personal characteristics that may intersect with other characteristics to influence individuals' experiences in the workplace.

People may be subjected to "isms" on the basis of visible dimensions of diversity such as sex, race, and age. *Sexism* refers to prejudice displayed toward members who belong, or are perceived to belong, to a particular sex. Although women are most often the target of sexism, it may be exhibited toward members of any sex, including intersex individuals.[37] **Racism** refers to prejudice directed by members of any race toward members of any race. However, what *race* exactly means is debatable, and how it is used to distinguish members of one racial group from another is questionable. As Audrey and Brian Smedley stated, "Race as biology is fiction, racism as a social problem is real."[38] Sexism and racism are discussed in greater detail in Chapter 3.

Ageism may be directed toward both older workers and younger workers, subjecting members of either group to negative stereotypes, prejudice, or discrimination. Curiously, discrimination against older workers is illegal in most countries, but discrimination against younger workers is perfectly legal. As a result, younger workers report experiencing more discrimination than older workers.[39]

People may also be subjected to "isms" according to whether they disclose less visible dimensions of diversity (such as sexual orientation) or this information is revealed or inferred about them by others. **Heterosexism** refers to negative stereotyping, prejudice, and discrimination on the basis of sexual orientation specifically directed toward LGBTQ+ individuals. When it occurs, it provides a less welcoming and inclusive environment for LGBTQ+ employees that may affect workplace matters ranging from whether family photos are displayed in an office setting to who gets rewarded and by how much.[40]

Ableism refers to stereotyping, prejudice, and discrimination directed toward people with disabilities that are either visible (e.g., physical, sensory) or invisible (e.g., mental health disorders, chronic health conditions). Ableism may be benevolent, such as by providing unwanted help and praising people with disabilities as inspirational for performing everyday activities. However, it may be hostile, such as by treating people with disabilities in degrading or humiliating ways, or ambivalent, such as by exhibiting feelings of discomfort in their presence.[41]

People often compare the effects of stereotyping, prejudice, and discrimination on the basis of different dimensions of diversity and offer conclusions about which "ism" (e.g., sexism, racism, ageism, heterosexism, ableism) has worse consequences. This oversimplifies the complex issues involved and ignores how "isms" may intersect. It seems more reasonable to acknowledge that sex (as well as a host of other dimensions of diversity, solely or intersecting with each other) may be used as the basis for stereotyping, prejudice, and discrimination. We need to guard against all "isms" in the workplace and not be distracted by comparisons of their strength.

WATCHING OUT FOR BIASES

People tend to have strong beliefs about whether there are fundamental differences between the capabilities of females and males. In fact, speculation about such differences is a universal phenomenon. People seldom wonder whether children who differ in eye color or height also differ in personality, abilities, and behavioral tendencies. However, they do care if there are such differences between girls and boys.

Researchers may bring either of two types of bias to the consideration of sex similarities and differences: alpha bias and beta bias. **Alpha bias** consists of the tendency to exaggerate sex differences. **Beta bias** consists of the tendency to minimize or ignore sex differences. Either type of bias can lead to a distortion of how the researcher sees reality. If alpha or beta bias prevails regardless of the research evidence, Helen Thompson Wooley's quote at the beginning of the chapter may not seem so far-fetched.[42]

Such biases may be the result of the personal prejudices of researchers. On the one hand, if the researchers' goal is to disprove traditional gender stereotypes and to prove that females and males are essentially equivalent in their personalities, abilities, and behavioral tendencies, they are likely to demonstrate beta bias by concluding that any sex differences that are found are trivial and claims of widespread sex differences are inflated. On the other hand, if the researchers' goal is to confirm gender stereotypes or to justify a status quo in which women and men are seen as naturally suited to different roles and thereby deserving of different treatment, they are likely to demonstrate alpha bias by concluding that sex differences in personal characteristics are large and fundamental to human functioning.[43]

For example, one critique of modern neuroscience (the study of the structure and functioning of the nervous system and brain) is that it engages in what may be labeled as **neurosexism**. That is, neuroscience is inappropriately used by neuroscientists with alpha bias to advance the notion that female and male brains are essentially different in ways that justify gender stereotypes. Neurosexism has historical roots. Early craniologists believed that brains were analogous to muscles, with larger size resulting in increased strength; to them, the fact that women's skulls tended to be smaller than men's skulls (with skull size closely related to brain size) provided an explanation for women's supposedly inferior intelligence—a notion that seems preposterous now. However, some neuroscientists are reluctant to acknowledge any sex differences that exist because they fear being inappropriately labeled as neurosexists by other neuroscientists with beta bias.[44]

Also, as Susan Fiske suggested in the opening quote, the mere presence of a two-category system leads psychologists as well as other people to view the two categories as opposites. For example, parents with two children tend to describe each in contrast to the other (e.g., "Tom is more of a leader and Joe is more of a follower"). However, parents with three or more children tend to focus on the unique aspects of each child (e.g., "Kristin enjoys rooting for her favorite baseball team, Melissa likes to produce school plays, Rob likes camping, Will enjoys photography, and Nate likes to bang the drums"). Similarly, anthropologists who have done fieldwork in only two cultures tend to emphasize the differences between these cultures, whereas anthropologists with a wider field of experience are more aware of the diversity of human experience. The same phenomenon may occur for sex. Because most (but not all) people fall into one of two categories on the basis of sex, there is little opportunity for researchers to gain "a wider field of experience" with a third or fourth sex. As a result, people tend to focus on the differences between males and females, thereby reinforcing alpha bias. Also, almost every researcher of sex similarities and differences belongs to one of the two groups being examined. Researchers may be more likely to report sex differences that reflect favorably on members of their own sex. Moreover, the popular media tend to exhibit alpha bias in their choice of which research results to publicize. Findings of sex differences are glamorized and magnified, whereas findings of sex similarities receive much less media attention.[45]

Fundamentally, people may be naturally inclined to focus on information or opinions that support their particular worldview, which explains why biases arise but not what to do about them. People may adopt cognitive strategies to reduce or eliminate their biases, such as by asking themselves to consider the opposite point of view before acting or reacting; this strategy encourages them to consider contrary evidence they would otherwise ignore. However, they first need to recognize that they are biased and then work toward becoming "debiased"—tendencies that do not appear to be present in many commentators on sex similarities and differences.[46]

Overall, it seems realistic to expect that some sex differences will be small to nonexistent, others will be moderate, and still others will be large. However, we need to be aware of the possibility of biases, both in researchers and in media accounts of research on sex differences, that affect what research findings are reported and how they are interpreted. We also need to guard against two dangerous assumptions that may be made about the results of research. First, if a sex difference is found in some aspect of human behavior, this does not mean that all males do something and all females do something quite different. Second, sex differences that are found are not necessarily biologically based or immutable. Indeed, the behavior of females and males is highly subject to social influences, as we shall see throughout the book.[47]

ORGANIZATION OF THE BOOK

The book begins its analysis of issues pertaining to gender in management by looking back in time. Chapter 2 provides a historical perspective on the economic roles of women and men. It examines influences such as the occurrence of two major world wars, the passage of equal employment opportunity laws, and social developments such as the women's liberation movement, LGBTQ+ civil rights movement, #MeToo movement, and Black Lives Matter movement. It considers the impact of the COVID-19 pandemic on individuals' work and family lives. The economic status of women and men in today's workplace is described in terms of sex differences in labor force participation, occupation, and pay.

Chapter 3 examines sex and gender differences that affect the behavior of women and men in the workplace. This chapter reviews some of the major findings of psychological research on sex differences. Key concepts such as gender stereotypes, gender roles, gender role identity and androgyny, sexism, and gender socialization that are critical to understanding interactions are examined. The ways in which parents, schools, and media convey gender role expectations to children, as well as the limitations of strict adherence to gender roles in adults, are explored.

Chapter 4, coauthored with Laura Graves, considers how individuals and organizations make decisions about establishing employment relationships. For individuals, these decisions entail choosing which job opportunities to pursue and which job offers to accept; for organizations, they entail choosing which applicants to hire. The chapter describes how differences in men's and women's job search strategies and reactions to specific jobs and organizations lead them to seek and obtain very different employment opportunities. It also examines sex discrimination in organizations' hiring decisions, including how and when sex discrimination occurs and who and what, including artificial intelligence (AI) systems, discriminates against whom. Recommendations are offered for reducing sex and gender effects on the employment decisions of individuals and organizations.

Chapter 5, also coauthored with Laura Graves, considers the effects of sex and gender on behavior in diverse teams. The chapter analyzes differences in how men and women behave and are evaluated in mixed-sex teams. It also examines how the sex composition of the team influences the experiences of male and female team members and the team's effectiveness. It suggests that mixed-sex teams are susceptible to a host of problems, the severity of which depends on a number of situational factors. It examines the impact of the increased use of virtual teams. The chapter concludes with recommendations for actions that team members and leaders may take to facilitate the functioning of mixed-sex teams.

Chapter 6 examines the effects of leader preferences and stereotypes in relation to gender stereotypes on how leadership is exhibited in organizations. It reviews how leader stereotypes have historically reflected the beliefs of "think manager—think male" and "think manager—think masculine" as well as recent evidence supporting a "think manager—think androgynous" perspective on leader stereotypes. Sex differences in actual leader behavior and effectiveness are examined to determine whether there is any basis to leader stereotypes. Glass ceilings—barriers to women's attainment of top executive positions—are also discussed. Organizations are urged to take actions to ensure that leaders with equivalent credentials—regardless of their sex—have equal chances to be chosen for leader roles at all levels and succeed in these roles.

Chapter 7 explores issues pertaining to the presence of social sexual behavior in the workplace, including sexual harassment (unwelcome sexual attention directed toward others at work) and workplace romance (mutually desired relationships between two people at work). It examines the causes and consequences of both types of social sexual behavior. It discusses the legacy of the #MeToo movement. Actions are recommended for both organizations and individuals to deal with sexual harassment and to minimize the disruption caused by workplace romances.

Chapter 8 considers what it takes for individuals to achieve a sense of work–family balance in their lives. It examines sex differences in how people define and measure personal success. It reviews the increasing diversity of family structures. It describes how individuals' experiences of the work–family interface may be both positive and negative, depending on the extent to which they segment or integrate these two roles. It considers sex differences in how individuals take family factors into account in making important work decisions. It also considers how different types of dual-career couples make decisions about each other's involvement in work and family activities.

The chapter concludes with actions that organizations may take to enhance employees' work–family balance as well as actions that individuals and couples may take on their own behalf.

Chapters 1 through 8 identify numerous issues related to sex and gender that arise in today's workplace. Chapter 9 offers solutions to these problems. It argues that organizations gain from promoting nondiscrimination, diversity, and inclusion on the basis of sex as well as other job-irrelevant personal characteristics. It details the laws and regulations with which organizations must comply to avoid legal charges of discrimination as well as the costs of discrimination whether illegal or not. It also presents the business case for promoting diversity (i.e., representation of members of different groups in all jobs and levels) and inclusion (i.e., acceptance of members of all groups in the organizational culture). Numerous actions are recommended for organizations to take in promoting nondiscrimination, diversity, and inclusion.

In summary, *Gender in Management*, sixth edition, covers a wide range of topics. It describes work roles in the past and present. The effects of sex and gender on childhood development and adult behavior are considered. It examines how sex and gender influence individuals' experiences as job candidates, team members, managers, and family members. Issues associated with the expression of sexuality in the workplace are explored. Finally, this book offers concrete recommendations for individuals and organizations to ensure that all people feel successful according to their own definition of success, whatever their sex and gender identity may be.

2 YESTERDAY AND TODAY

LEARNING OBJECTIVES

After reading this chapter, you should be able to do the following:

2.1 Understand the impact of the advent of a market economy and the Industrial Revolution prior to the 20th century on the household distribution of economic roles.

2.2 Describe the impact of World Wars I and II in the first half of the 20th century on the sex distribution of economic roles.

2.3 Discuss the impact of women's increased educational attainment and the women's liberation movement in the second half of the 20th century on the sex distribution of economic roles.

2.4 Recognize the influence of social developments in the 21st century on workplace dynamics.

2.5 Discuss the impact of the COVID-19 pandemic on gender roles in the workplace.

2.6 Describe current trends in labor force participation and educational attainment.

2.7 Define the sex segregation of occupations and describe its current status.

2.8 Identify factors that influence the sex gap in pay.

Young people are entering a very different work world from past decades, with new expectations of what they will encounter as well as new expectations of others that they will have to meet. How different are the current roles that women and men play in the workplace compared with those of the past? Gender roles have traditionally suggested that men's proper place is at work and women's proper place is at home. These norms for behavior have had a profound impact on relations between women and men in all spheres of society—the family, the educational system, the legal system, and the workplace. However, they have been increasingly flouted over time. If traditional gender roles have been tossed aside, what has replaced them (if anything)?

In this chapter, we first provide a historical perspective by considering the evolution of the economic roles of women and men in American society since the nation was founded. We trace the impact of diverse historical events, such as the advent of industrialization, two world wars, the women's liberation movement, the LGBTQ+ civil rights movement, and the COVID-19 pandemic. Second, we look at current roles played in the workforce, considering sex differences as well as differences among racial and ethnic groups. Finally, we consider the impact of the changes in workplace roles over time on current economic realities and their implications for work relationships among different-sex individuals today.

SOCIETY PRIOR TO THE 20TH CENTURY

Throughout the recorded history of Western civilizations, a **patriarchal social system** in which the male has authority over the female has almost always prevailed or at least has been the public norm. Early American society was no exception. Puritan New Englanders, who were prominent in the founding of the American colonies, believed in a hierarchy within the family, with the man as head and the women and children as subordinates. Man's role in the home was seen as similar to God's role in the universe—that is, in charge. However, Puritans weren't the only group to endorse the concept of patriarchy. Members of other religious groups who were early American settlers shared the same attitudes regarding male supremacy. These attitudes were in force as the colonists wrested control over their affairs from Great Britain in the Revolutionary War and formed their own government.

The decision to rebel against Great Britain was made by men. The Preamble of the U.S. Constitution referred only to men. In the conferences that led to the formation of the new nation, it was never considered that anyone other than men should have the same rights and privileges that men had bestowed upon themselves. The right to vote was not granted to women until 1920, long after it was theoretically granted to men who were former slaves and only then after a half-century of resistance. As far as the conduct of public affairs was concerned, women played little direct role in the early shaping of the American republic.[1]

Although disenfranchised, women played a considerable role in the economic system of early American society. Prior to the 1800s, society was predominantly agrarian, with most work taking place in or around the home. Women and men were engaged in different activities. For example, men were responsible for tasks that called for lifting heavy burdens and women were responsible for matters related to clothing and food preparation. However, the activities of all household members, children included, were essential to the family economy, as all who were able to do so worked at productive tasks.

Women became managers of shops, businesses, plantations, or farms only through the early deaths of their husbands. According to English Common Law, which governed the colonies until the Revolutionary War, a woman could not appear in court, enter into a contract, or inherit from heirs without the approval of a male relative or guardian. Nonetheless, economic needs took precedence over legalities. Women were too skilled a resource to not be fully utilized in preindustrial America.[2]

The slow rise of a **market economy** altered the relationships between married women and men markedly. Better production and distribution methods began to allow the sale in the marketplace of farm produce and crafted goods that were not needed by the family. Because of the types of activities that men and women had performed, the products that men made were more likely to enter the marketplace than those produced by women. For example, milk, wheat, and wool, produced by men or both women and men, could be sold to townspeople. Butter, bread, and cloth, produced by women, could then be readily manufactured within most of those families. As a result, men, more often than women, received and thereby controlled the money coming into the family. Their control was legitimized by the religious and social doctrines that had been paid lip service but had been effectively dormant for some time.

During the same period, the American legal system was refined and tightened, and previously unwritten laws were codified. The cultural doctrines supporting male supremacy that had been unofficial since English Common Law had become no longer applicable. They were now formalized in a manner compatible with the new market economy in which men dominated economic life. Wives became legally obligated to serve the wishes of their husbands, and husbands were legally elevated to the position of almost total dominance and responsibility.

The labor of wives was still valuable after the advent of the market economy, but it could not be sold as easily. Its value depended on the use the family could make of it. When piecework manufacturing methods were later developed, women who worked in their homes could also earn wages outside the home. However, by this time, the laws formalizing women's subordinate position to men were already in place. Had the laws been codified earlier, the de facto equality between the sexes then in existence might have been recognized. Had they been codified later, men and women might have been accorded equal status.

Despite its apparent rigidity after the advent of the market economy, the economic system in America ordinarily would have been expected to continue changing to allow for the most efficient division of labor. However, the **Industrial Revolution** temporarily suspended the need for further changes by allowing economic superiority to be achieved through the superior organization of production. With surplus production, it became possible for more affluent husbands to keep their wives at home rather than allow them outside work. Thus, the stay-at-home wife became a status symbol for men in American society. This division of labor outwardly copied the earlier fashion of life among European nobility, allowed the conspicuous demonstration of affluence, and reaffirmed the legally defined superior/subordinate relationship between the husband and the wife. Growing general affluence allowed the practice to spread gradually until it became institutionalized as an ideal, the standard against which other allocations of roles between the sexes were judged. However, this ideal was largely based on the experiences of White middle-class families, which differed greatly from the experiences of other families. Men of color tended to hold agricultural, mining, or service jobs that were considered too low-paying, insecure, dangerous, or degrading by most White men. The impact of historical forces was similar in other Western cultures.[3]

Unmarried women, who were relied upon as workers in the early days of the Industrial Revolution, were subject to a different set of economic forces but the same social norms. To avoid the miserable working conditions and abuse of female and child labor that had taken place in British factories, Francis Cabot Lowell introduced the **Waltham system** of large-scale manufacturing to the New England textile industry in the 1810s. Factory communities built by Lowell and his associates in mill towns throughout New England were designed with adult females in mind as the workers. Primarily single and from farming families, these women were required to reside in boardinghouses under the direction of a matron employed by the company. The matron enforced regulations regarding proper behavior, including a 10 o'clock curfew and mandatory church attendance. These arrangements were intended to assure Yankee farmers that their daughters would not be working in places of sin and corruption and the community that the invasion of a large number of young women would not drastically alter its social fabric.

The women mainly tended the roving and spinning frames and minded the looms in the mills. Men were employed primarily as overseers, as machinists, and in other heavy occupations or in those requiring a definite skill, such as printing. Men's wages were typically set at the prevailing wage rate for the appropriate skill or trade. Women's wages were set at a level high enough to induce them to leave the farms and stay away from other forms of employment, such as domestic service, but low enough to offer an advantage for employing females rather than males and to compete with the wages of unskilled workers in British textile factories.

Female factory workers, whose ranks gradually came to include widows and wives from poorer families as well as single women, did not conform to the female gender role that was being developed in White middle-class families. They had no choice about whether to work. Instead, their wages often made them the primary wage earners in their families, which became all the more important when New England's farming economy began a long period of decline in the 1830s. As a lifestyle of genteel leisure became the ideal for all women, those in the growing female workforce were looked down upon for having to work. A "cult of true womanhood," led by middle-class reformers such as Catherine Beecher, encouraged women to guard their natural place—the home—with their virtues of "piety, purity, submissiveness, and domesticity." Thus, the spread of industrialization was affecting women throughout society. For some, it meant long hours in the factory. For others, it meant isolation in the home.[4]

The Industrial Revolution also greatly affected the lives of men. Toward the end of the 19th century, men were required to work in factories in increasing numbers due to the rise of heavy industry, for which women were regarded as too frail. The shift from an agricultural to an industrial society changed the ways in which men made use of their abilities and assessed their self-worth. In much earlier days, men proved their worth by demonstrating their physical prowess at killing animals for food. More recently, men had been admired as craftsmen for their skills at making things. Now, the role of strong provider and skilled artisan was being replaced by the role of keeper of the machines. Even though the Industrial Revolution provided mass-produced goods and a less strenuous way of life for most, it also robbed many men of their opportunity for creativity and accomplishment and of their sense of purpose.[5]

With the rise of the market economy and then the Industrial Revolution, both husbands and wives realized that the husband was providing the major economic support for the family. Attitudes changed to conform to this new economic relationship. Wives changed their attitudes to make themselves more subordinate to their husbands' desires. Husbands' attitudes changed in the direction of feeling more superior to their wives than they did before, even though they weren't as fulfilled by their factory work. Whereas social doctrine had been declaring for some time that men were already superior to women, it had been expressing the official and unofficial norms of American society rather than the economic reality. Now, at least for the more affluent, reality had caught up with the norms.

Thus, we have identified the source of what have come to be known as traditional gender roles in American society. These roles, developed within White middle-class families that could afford to have the woman not earn wages outside the home, provided an ideal that was supposed to apply to all families. However, the label of "traditional" is misleading. It implies a constancy in the actual economic roles of women and men that simply has not been present, although public norms about economic roles have varied less. Why did these particular traditions become cast as ideal rather than traditions based on the greater equality in women's and men's economic roles that had prevailed before? It's probably because they most agreed with the doctrine of a patriarchal social system, which had been brought to America by its original settlers. It's certainly not because they were adhered to by all social classes and not because they reflected the economic roles that were to emerge in the years to come.

FIRST HALF OF THE 20TH CENTURY

As the 20th century began, the United States (U.S.) labor force was clearly differentiated by sex. Census statistics regarding **labor force participation rates** showed that 19% of women and 80% of men were in the labor force (see Table 2.1). In other words, four of every five women *were not* engaged in paid employment, whereas four out of every five men *were*.

In the decades between 1900 and 1940, labor force participation rates for men and women remained essentially unchanged, despite the occurrence of several major

TABLE 2.1 ■ Labor Force Participation Rates

	Percentage in the U.S. Labor Force	
Year	**Women**	**Men**
1900	19	80
1910	23	81
1920	21	78
1930	22	76
1940	25	79
1950	31	80
1960	35	79
1970	42	78
1980	51	77
1990	58	76
2000	60	75
2010	59	71
2020	56	68
2023	57	68

Sources: **1900-1970**: U.S. Department of Commerce, Bureau of the Census. (1975). *Historical statistics of the United States: Colonial times to 1970* (pp. 127–128, Series D11-25). Government Printing Office; **1980–2020**: U.S. Department of Labor, Bureau of Labor Statistics. (2022). *Labor force statistics from the Current Population Survey,* Table 2. Retrieved October 19, 2022, from https://www.bls.gov/cps; **2023**: U.S. Department of Labor, Bureau of Labor Statistics. (2023). *Labor force statistics from the Current Population Survey,* Table A-3. Retrieved May 4, 2023, from https://www.bls.gov/cps.

Note: **1900-1930**: data for persons 10 years old and over; **1940-1960**: data for persons 14 years old and over; **1970-2023**: data for persons 16 years old and over.

events. A garment workers' strike at the Triangle Shirtwaist Company in New York from 1909 to 1910, led and carried out by women, became the largest women's strike in American history. It contributed to support for the unionization of the garment industry, which was the largest employer of women at the time. However, the strike yielded mixed results for the predominantly immigrant women who carried it out, and women's subsequent acceptance as members of male-dominated labor unions was begrudgingly slow.[6]

During the same time, women as well as men were immigrating to the U.S. in large numbers. Women's immigration tended to be highest from nations in which they had high autonomy and relatively low prospects for both marriage and employment. Immigration was largely unrestricted and unregulated until the passage of the National Origins Act in 1924, which instituted nationality-based quotas. After then through 1965 (when nationality-based quotas were repealed), female immigrants were more likely to be married to men who had immigrated earlier on their own and become American citizens before calling for their wives to join them.[7]

World War I (1914 to 1918) created new jobs for women at higher wages than previous levels as large numbers of men went off to war. However, no sustained change in the employment of women resulted. In fact, the labor force participation rate of women in 1920 (21%) was slightly lower than it had been in 1910 (23%). Labor unions, government, and society in general were not ready for more than a temporary change in the economic role of women. Men received first priority in hiring when they returned from the war, and many women were driven from the labor force.

The Nineteenth Amendment to the U.S. Constitution, which gave women the right to vote, was passed in 1920 after a seven-decade-long women's suffrage movement that had begun with the Seneca Falls Convention of 1848, the first women's rights convention. Its backers hoped that ending sex discrimination in the right to vote would lead to the dismantling of sex discrimination in other areas and usher in a new era of gender equality. However, women's suffrage brought about little change in women's economic status and roles.[8]

The Great Depression, extending from the U.S. stock market crash in 1929 to the Japanese bombing of Pearl Harbor in 1941, threw millions of Americans out of work. The unemployment rate rose considerably, peaking at 25% during 1933. These conditions contributed to an identity crisis for unemployed men of all races. In the book *Puzzled America*, published in 1935, Sherwood Anderson concluded,

> The breaking down of the moral fiber of the American man through being out of a job, losing that sense of being some part of the moving world of activity, so essential to an American man's sense of his manhood . . . can never be measured in dollars.[9]

The Great Depression caused great strains in family relations as unemployed men suffered a loss of status in their families. Those who relied upon holding an authoritative role in the family and society felt humbled and disgraced. In addition, it triggered resentment toward working women, especially working wives. The attention being expended on the problems of men intensified the attitude that working women were depriving male breadwinners of employment. However, these dynamics were not reflected in the labor force participation rates of women and men shown in Table 2.1 because unemployed workers were still counted in the labor force.[10]

World War II (1941 to 1945 for the United States), which closely followed the Great Depression, marked a turning point in the distribution of economic roles between women and men, although it did not necessarily cause the massive changes that were to follow. Similar to World War I, World War II created what was expected to be a temporary high demand for female labor. Women were attracted to war-related industries by a "Rosie the Riveter" recruitment campaign appealing to their patriotism, and they were given access to the more skilled, higher-paying jobs usually held by men. Rosie was a fictional character created for the campaign, and her image appeared on posters and magazine covers during the war. However, she was typically portrayed as White except for in news photographs; there were no posters of Black Rosies.[11]

Spurred by the recruitment campaign and war needs, the number of employed women increased by 50% in the U.S. between 1940 and 1945. However, after World War II was won in 1945, the labor force did not quickly "return to normal" as it did after World War I. Instead, a new sense of what is normal emerged.

SECOND HALF OF THE 20TH CENTURY

Changes in the economic roles played by women and men in the second half of the 20th century took several forms. The labor force participation rate of women rose steadily from 31% in 1950 to 60% by 2000, with the largest increase in labor force participation seen among non-Hispanic White women. In contrast, the labor force participation rate of men declined from 80% in 1950 to 75% in 2000. Although the gap between men and women remained at 15% in 2000, it had narrowed considerably over the 20th century.

This was the result of a significant change in the composition of the female labor force. In 1900, 6% of married women and 44% of single (never-married) women worked. In 1950, 24% of married women and 51% of single women worked. However, in 2000, 62% of married women and 65% of single women worked. Thus, the gap between the labor force participation rates of married and single women virtually disappeared over the century. In 2000, 53% of the female labor force was married, close to the 59% of the male labor force that was married.[12]

Postwar changes in the female labor force demonstrated increasing disregard for the idea that the woman's proper place was in the home. In 1900, the women most accepted into the workplace were single, making up two-thirds of the female labor force. Employment of single women required the least adjustment to public opinion; the notion that the *mother's* proper place was in the home could still be held as a standard when single women worked. The next group to enter the labor force in large numbers was older married women. Between 1940 and 1960, the proportion of 45- to 64-year-old women who worked went from 20% to 42%. These women were past their peak child-raising years. Their increasing presence in the workplace could be accepted begrudgingly by defenders of the status quo as long as *young* mothers stayed at home. The final group of women to increase its labor force participation consisted of younger, married women with preschool or school-age children. By 2000, 81% of mothers with children between 14 and 17 years old, 78% of those with children between 6 and 13 years old, 74% of those with children between 3 and 5 years old, and 63% of those with children 2 years old or under were in the labor force. The employment of a majority of mothers of children of all ages in 2000 effectively signaled the end of adherence to the belief that women belong at home.[13]

The **educational attainment** of women also changed considerably in the postwar years. In the United States, the proportion of college degrees earned by women increased between 1950 and 2000 from 24% to 57% at the bachelor's level and from 29% to 58% at the master's level. As Table 2.2 indicates, these increases were exhibited among members of the major racial and ethnic groups. Moreover, the proportion of college degrees in business earned by women increased between 1960 and 2000 from only 7% to 50% at the bachelor's level and from only 4% to 40% at the master's level. These trends reflected a major societal shift toward the enhancement of women's academic credentials as well as an increased commitment of women to managerial and professional careers.

TABLE 2.2 ■ College Degrees, Proportion Earned by Women

	1950	1960	1970	1980	1990	2000	2010	2020
Bachelor's Level								
All disciplines: Total	24	35	43	49	53	57	57	58
White	-	-	-	50	54	57	56	57
Black	-	-	-	60	63	66	66	64
Hispanic	-	-	-	50	56	60	61	61
Asian	-	-	-	46	50	54	55	55
Business: Total	-	7	9	34	47	50	49	46
Master's Level								
All disciplines: Total	29	32	39	49	52	58	60	61
White	-	-	-	51	56	60	62	64
Black	-	-	-	63	64	68	71	70
Hispanic	-	-	-	52	55	60	64	66
Asian	-	-	-	40	43	52	54	58
Business: Total	-	4	4	22	34	40	46	49

Sources: U.S. Department of Education, National Center for Education Statistics (2022). *Digest of education statistics*, computed from Tables 318.10, 322.20, 323.20, and 325.25. Retrieved October 21, 2022, from https://nces.ed.gov.

Note: Dash indicates data not available.

These changes may in part be attributed to the power of "the pill" (female oral contraceptives), regarded by *The Economist* as the most important advance in science and technology in the 20th century. The pill was approved for use by U.S. women in 1960 and was dispensed rapidly first to married women and, after several federal and state court actions, to single women. The pill greatly increased the reliability of contraception and reduced uncertainty about the consequences of sexual activity. Women could invest in a lengthy education without fearing that it would be interrupted by an unplanned pregnancy. By 1964, about a quarter of married women under age 45 were "on the pill." Further, because the pill led to the postponing of marriage by most young women regardless of their educational aspirations, single women could delay marriage until completing their initial career preparation without being forced to choose from a reduced pool of eligible bachelors. As a result, the pill facilitated women's preparation for managerial and professional careers regardless of their marital status.[14]

The increased employment and educational attainment of women coincided with a rise in the proportion of **white-collar jobs** in the economy. White-collar jobs are those that do not require manual labor, including managerial jobs, professional jobs (e.g., engineers, teachers, lawyers, computer scientists, and health care practitioners), sales jobs (e.g., sales representatives and proprietors), and administrative support jobs (e.g., administrative assistants and clerical workers). In 1950, 36% of all jobs were white-collar and women held 40% of these jobs. By 2000, over half of all jobs were white-collar and women held more than half of these jobs.[15]

The women who entered the U.S. labor force after World War II came increasingly from the non-Hispanic White middle class. The growth in white-collar occupations created jobs that were compatible with middle-class status. Aspirations for a higher standard of living, consumerism, the desire to send children to college, and inflation made it necessary for some middle-class women to work to maintain a middle-class standard of living.

However, traditional attitudes concerning women's proper place in society persisted. During the 1950s, the mass media promoted an image of family togetherness that defined the mother's role as central to all domestic activity. According to Betty Friedan's *The Feminine Mystique*, women were supposedly finding true fulfillment in this way:

> Their only dream was to be perfect wives and mothers; their highest ambition to have five children and a beautiful house, their only fight to get and keep their husbands. . . . They gloried in their role as women, and wrote proudly on the census blank: "Occupation: housewife."[16]

Women were expected to revel in this role and happily surrender control of and participation in economic and public life to men. According to opinion polls, both women and men accepted such gender roles. Yet the statistics that have been presented show that something else was actually happening in the workplace. As one observer put it, "A visitor from another planet who read the magazines and newspapers of the 1950s would never have guessed that the women portrayed as being engaged exclusively in homemaking activities were also joining the job market in unprecedented numbers."[17]

During this period, women workers were not perceived as crusading to achieve economic equality with men. Instead, their increased economic activity could be interpreted as consistent with their primary role as helpmates to their spouses. Most women who worked were citing economic need as the reason for their employment, even when the family income was solidly in the middle-class range. If women had not been portrayed, or portrayed themselves, as working temporarily to help meet immediate needs, male resistance to their entry into the labor force might have been greater.

Nonetheless, the contradiction between traditional attitudes and actual behavior could not last, especially when that contradiction became greater each year. What eventually changed was the public perception of traditional gender roles. In the late 1960s and early 1970s, a **women's liberation movement** emerged that had a major impact on the attitudes of women and, indirectly, men about their roles. This change was spurred both by the experiences of women in the civil rights movement of the 1960s and by the increasing resentment of middle-class business and professional women toward the barriers that held back their progress. This discontent found an early voice in Friedan's *The Feminine Mystique*, but mere recognition of the limits on women's achievements placed by society's attitudes was not enough. A full-fledged push for legislative and economic action ensued that would bring closer the goal of equality—or at least of equal opportunity—for men and women.[18]

The National Organization for Women (NOW), the first avowedly feminist organization since women gained the right to vote, held its inaugural meeting in 1966 with Betty Friedan as the chief organizer. Its statement of purpose expressed concerns about discrimination in employment, education, and the legal system. It also called for a true partnership between women and men to be brought about by equitable sharing of the responsibilities of home and children and their economic support. Women's groups such as NOW were successful in promoting change in many areas. Through lawsuits or the threat of legal action, large corporations were pressured into initiating "affirmative action" programs to increase their hiring and promotion of women. The federal government was pressured into investigating sex discrimination in federally funded contracts and federally sponsored programs and then devising programs to end it. Women's studies courses were added to the curricula at many colleges and universities. Pressure from the women's liberation movement reduced the emphasis on gender stereotypes in children's books, stimulated the opening of day care centers, and contributed to the elimination of sexist language in professional journals and of separate advertising for "women's jobs" and "men's jobs" in newspapers. *Ms.*, a magazine founded in 1972, declared the 1970s as "the decade of women." The women's liberation movement had an impact in many ways, large and small, and a whole generation of women became aware of the possibilities that could be open to them if they did not follow traditional norms.[19]

Starting in the 1960s, **equal employment opportunity (EEO) laws** were passed in many countries to restrict sex discrimination as well as other types of discrimination. In the United States, Title VII of the Civil Rights Act of 1964 prohibited discrimination on the basis of sex, race, color, religion, or national origin in any employment condition, including hiring, firing, promotion, transfer, compensation, and access to training programs. Title VII was later extended to ban discrimination on the basis of pregnancy or childbirth and to ban sexual harassment. The Equal Pay Act of 1963 made it illegal to pay members of one sex less than the other if they are in equivalent jobs. All organizations with 50 or more employees and federal contracts exceeding $50,000 per year were required to file affirmative action programs with the federal government detailing the steps they were taking to eliminate discrimination. In addition, Title IX of the Education Amendments of 1972 banned sex discrimination in educational institutions receiving federal funds. Among other benefits, Title IX led to an enormous increase in opportunities for women to participate in college athletics.[20]

Ironically, the Title VII ban on sex discrimination in the United States was proposed as a last-minute amendment by a civil rights opponent as a strategy to prevent passage of the bill. Opponents felt the male-dominated Congress would be more reluctant to pass the legislation if the ban on sex discrimination was included. Indeed, one representative justified his opposition with the phrase, *"Vive la difference!"* However, women's rights advocates joined civil rights opponents to pass the amendment and then joined civil rights advocates to pass the entire bill, amendment and all. Thus, Title VII opened the door for significant gains for women in the workplace despite the intent of the representative who offered the amendment.[21]

The women's movement and EEO laws elicited mixed reactions from men. The men most threatened by these social and legal developments were those most committed to traditional roles in the family, the workplace, and public affairs. They were alarmed because their power in a patriarchal social system was being challenged. Other men were concerned about the impact on their job security and future advancement as more women entered the workplace. These men were inclined to dismiss newly mandated affirmative action programs as "promoting reverse discrimination." Most men, however, viewed the women's movement and EEO laws with ambivalence and anxiety. They took these developments seriously, but they did not know what to make of them or how to respond to them.[22]

Many women, on the other hand, complained of a backlash against the women's liberation movement and were frustrated at the incomplete achievement of its goals. One woman characterized feminism as the "Great Experiment That Failed," with its perpetuators as the casualties. Younger women, however, tended to see such complaints as tales from "the old days when, once upon a time, women had trouble getting into the schools or jobs they now hold."[23]

A **LGBTQ+ civil rights movement** emerged in 1969 and gathered strength in the 1970s after a police raid and ensuing riots at the Stonewall Inn in New York City. At the time, homosexuality was classified as a mental disorder by the American Psychiatric Association and American Psychological Association, state laws against sodomy were prevalent, and police raids on gay bars were common. However, patrons of the Stonewall Inn, most of whom were transgender, fought back against a police raid on June 28, 1969, and riots continued for several days. The LGBTQ+ community was galvanized by the Stonewall riots and activist groups soon formed. On the first anniversary of the riots, gay pride parades took place in several major cities, an annual tradition that has continued. By the end of the 1970s, both associations had removed homosexuality from their official lists of mental disorders, and sodomy laws had been repealed in many states—policy changes that were attributed to the movement.[24]

In the last decade of the 20th century, tensions between women and men over public issues and events repeatedly emerged. **Sexual harassment**—the directing of unwelcome sexual attention by one workforce member toward another—became a matter of considerable public discussion due to several highly publicized incidents. For example, female sportswriters experienced rampant sexual harassment and blatant sexism as they entered locker rooms for male sports teams in which there had previously been no female presence. Sexual harassment in the military became recognized as a major problem as revelations emerged of its being experienced by female aviators, Army recruits, and cadets at U.S. military academies training to be future officers. The first woman to complain of sexual harassment in a particular setting was typically subjected to a public smear campaign after reporting the incident.[25]

In the public arena, issues of sexism and racism were raised when Clarence Thomas, a Black nominee for the U.S. Supreme Court who was eventually confirmed as a justice, was accused by Anita Hill, a Black law professor and former subordinate of Thomas, of sexual harassment. In televised hearings, Hill's graphic charges were dramatically aired and vehemently denied by Thomas, who claimed he was a victim of racism. Battle lines were drawn over the merits of Hill's charges. Polls suggested that White women, who were less sensitive to racism, were most favorable to Hill, whereas Black women, who were more sensitive to racism, were most favorable to Thomas. Publicity from the Thomas–Hill hearings increased public sensitivity to the issue of sexual harassment. In the first half of the next year, sexual harassment charges filed with the U.S. Equal Employment Opportunity Commission were up by more than 50% over the same period the year before.[26]

Workplace romance—the sharing of welcome sexual attention by two workforce members—also became a public issue after it became known that U.S. President Bill Clinton had engaged in sexual activity with a White House intern, Monica Lewinsky. Clinton was impeached by the U.S. House of Representatives but was not convicted of the impeachment charges by the U.S. Senate, which would have forced him to leave office. Clinton claimed that the investigation of the affair infringed on his private life. However, the fact that the incidents occurred on White House premises and placed a burden on his office staff made it a very public affair.[27]

Even the merits of flirting by professional women in the workplace were hotly debated. After *The Wall Street Journal* reported that younger women were more inclined to "let their femininity show" and use it to get ahead professionally than their mothers had been, readers took sides. A female reader complained that giving the impression that young women were using their sexual appeal to compete in the workplace perpetuated the stereotype of women as sex objects and harmed women perceived as less attractive who were working hard to get ahead based on merit. A male reader complained that if he risked a sexual harassment complaint by flaunting his sexuality in the office, professional women should not be allowed to flaunt their feminine lures either. The only people who seemed to be happy about the situation were the women who enjoyed and benefited from flirting and the men who welcomed their attention.[28]

In summary, our review of key events and trends in the 20th century and before suggests that (1) changes in reproductive technology, a women's liberation movement, and civil rights laws contributed to women's enhanced educational attainment and workplace status; (2) social concerns emerged about issues such as sexual harassment and workplace romance that had received little attention before the increased status of women in the workplace; and (3) the economic roles played by women and men became more similar over time, especially during the 20th century's second half. Sex differences in U.S. labor force participation, educational attainment, employment in white-collar occupations, and the marital status of labor force participants all decreased dramatically over the course of the century.

SOCIAL DEVELOPMENTS IN THE 21ST CENTURY

Corporations have displayed increased concern in the 21st century about sexual harassment and workplace romance in their midst, including their executive suites. Many chief executive officers (CEOs) of major corporations have lost their jobs for engaging in one or the other or for fostering an overly sexualized work environment through their actions or inactions. Powerful men below the CEO position in many companies have also lost their jobs for having sexually harassed women in positions of less power. Prominent politicians continue to be called out for inappropriate social sexual behavior, both sexual harassment of and romantic relationships with staff members. Sexual harassment, as well as workplace romance when relationships are consensual but seen as inappropriate by others, remain issues of heightened public concern. Chapter 7 discusses issues associated with social sexual behavior in the workplace in detail.

After allegations that Harvey Weinstein, a movie studio CEO, had engaged in rampant sexual harassment, assault, and rape over three decades became public knowledge in 2017, the **#MeToo movement** was launched by victims of sexual harassment and resulted in hundreds of thousands of women sharing their experiences. (Weinstein has since been convicted of some of these allegations and is serving prison time at the time of this writing.) As a result of the #MeToo hashtag movement, Twitter became a major platform in the 21st century for sharing experiences of sexual violence in the workplace and raising awareness of the prevalence of the phenomenon.[29]

Increased attention has been directed in the 21st century toward issues faced by LGBTQ+ (lesbian, gay, bisexual, transgender, and self-described queer) individuals in the workplace and society. The LGBTQ+ civil rights movement has continued to foster positive developments. For example, the United Nations passed its first resolution supporting LGBTQ+ rights. In the United States and many other nations, same-sex marriage was legalized and anti-LGBTQ+ discrimination laws passed. Gender health centers were initiated to offer health services to LGBTQ+ people in particular. Many corporations have adopted policies fostering inclusion of LGBTQ+ employees and tangible supports such as health care benefits for same-sex partners and have seen corresponding benefits in LGBTQ+ employee commitment and engagement. Overall, although not uniformly, acceptance of LGBTQ+ individuals in the workplace has increased during the 21st century.[30]

Workplaces were affected by protests over the killings of George Floyd, Breonna Taylor, and Ahmaud Arbery (all Black people) by current or former police officers in 2020. The **Black Lives Matter movement**, which arose to address issues of police violence against Black people, has been described as the largest social movement in U.S. history. At the peak of months of protests, half a million Americans protested in over 500 locations on June 6, 2020. The **#SayHerName movement**, which gained strength after Taylor's death, raised issues of the intersection of victims' race and sex in responses to such incidents. It sought to increase awareness of Black women who had been victims of police violence and to address what was seen as their marginalization in the media and the Black Lives Matter movement.[31]

Many companies responded to these social movements by pledging support for Black employees and programs to eradicate racial discrimination. Statements from CEOs denouncing racism and media ads supporting the Black Lives Matter and #SayHerName movements were common. However, companies exhibited varying levels of commitment to making actual changes to reduce racial inequities in their midst. Corporate responses varied from no commitment to no new commitment to token commitment (e.g., social media posts claiming support but no substantive internal changes) to true commitment. For their part, Black employees said that they saw some positive changes in their places of work after the Black Lives Matter protests, but not enough.[32]

During the 21st century so far, trends toward gender equality in the workplace and society fostered by social developments have received mixed reviews. On the 50th anniversary of the founding of *Ms.* in 1972, Gloria Steinem, a co-founder of the magazine and prominent figure in the women's liberation movement, said, "I feel proud, and I feel mad as hell. We are still dealing with the same issues." On the 100th anniversary of passage of the Nineteenth Amendment to the U.S. Constitution in 1920, which guaranteed women the right to vote, about two-thirds of all women and half of all men said that the nation had not gone far enough when it comes to giving women equal rights with men, although most believed that progress had been made. The World Economic Forum, which issues an annual global gender gap report focusing on workplace and societal trends, estimated that it would take 132 years to close the gap entirely. This estimate may be viewed either optimistically ("Hey, we're getting there. It's just a matter of time") or pessimistically ("Yea, right. And if the gap is ever closed, why will it take so long?").[33]

THE COVID-19 PANDEMIC

The **COVID-19 pandemic** led to widespread lockdowns by workplaces and schools starting in 2020 to try to reduce the spread of the coronavirus.[34] At one point, about half of the world's population was under some form of lockdown due to the pandemic, having been asked or ordered by their governments to stay at home.[35] Simultaneous work and family lockdowns had different but overlapping implications for employees.

Work lockdowns that were imposed on employees not deemed as "essential workers" led to a considerable increase in virtual work. During a two-week period in March 2020, because of work lockdowns, the proportion of the U.S. labor force that was working from home increased from 33% to 61%. Being conducted in a predominantly virtual manner changes the nature of work in fundamental ways. During the pandemic, an increased level in virtual work influenced the nature of gender issues in mixed-sex teams, issues that are discussed in detail in Chapter 5.[36]

Female employees who were not essential workers were disproportionately affected by the pandemic. Women were highly represented in some of the industries that were hit hardest by the pandemic, including travel, childcare, personal care and services, and education. In contrast, men were more likely to be employed in jobs that were preserved during the pandemic by a shift to virtual work. As a result, women suffered more from pandemic-related job losses than men.[37]

Further, the majority of essential workers in the U.S. were women, with one-third of all jobs held by women designated as essential. Female-dominated essential jobs included health care (e.g., nurses and nursing assistants, respiratory therapists), social work (e.g., home health aides checking on older clients), and critical retail jobs (e.g., pharmacists and pharmacy aides, cashiers at grocery stores). Although other types of essential jobs were male-dominated (e.g., transportation, handling of hazardous materials), the numbers of essential workers in male-dominated jobs were smaller than in female-dominated jobs.[38]

Essential workers faced the risk that ill health derived from their work role would affect their ability to maintain family finances and spill over into the health of family members. For example, a registered nurse in the coronavirus ward of a local hospital had the following experience: In caring for patients with the coronavirus, she contracted the virus herself, stayed home to receive medical attention for it while fearing that she would pass it along to her husband, and then went back to work while still experiencing symptoms because she was so concerned about her family's income. Her holding a black belt in martial arts did not protect her from this kind of risk at all.

Family lockdowns resulted in increased family responsibilities for parents of school-age children as schools closed and shifted to online instruction. Homeschooling or assisting children with distance learning became the primary mode of childhood education. Theoretically, having both parents working at home during a family lockdown provided the opportunity for an approximately equal division of household labor in dual-career, heterosexual households. This was not exactly the case. The gendered division of unpaid domestic labor roles, with women performing or being responsible for most of the housework, has been an enduring feature of such households over time, even when women earn more than their male partners. This division continued during the pandemic, with women tending to spend more time on homeschooling their children while simultaneously working virtually than their husbands, who might pitch in on occasion. However, some less gendered, egalitarian strategies for dual-career couples' coping with family lockdowns were exhibited during the pandemic.[39]

Overall, the COVID-19 pandemic was, as one observer put it, "a disaster for feminism." Traditional gender role expectations as described in Betty Friedan's *The Feminine Mystique* appeared to be reinforced during the pandemic. Contrary to the dream that Friedan said that married women were supposed to have in the 1950s ("Occupation: housewife"), most working mothers were not happy about and were extremely stressed out by simultaneous work and family lockdowns in response to the pandemic.[40]

ECONOMIC ROLES IN THE 21ST CENTURY

In the 21st century so far (i.e., since 2000) as Table 2.1 indicates, the proportion of men in the labor force decreased from 75% to 68%, and the proportion of women in the labor force decreased from 60% to 57%. As a result, the sex difference in labor force participation rates decreased from 15% to 11%. However, the proportion of labor force participants who are female has held steady since 2000 at 47%. The COVID-19 pandemic did not appear to affect labor force participation rates, as unemployed workers were still regarded as being in the labor force.

Also since 2000, as Table 2.2 indicates, although the proportion of bachelor's degrees earned by women essentially held steady (57% vs. 58%), the proportion of master's degrees earned by women increased from 58% to 61%. Further, although the proportion of bachelor's degrees in business earned by women decreased from 50% to 46%, retreating from gender equality and reversing direction from the late 20th century trend, the proportion of master's degrees in business earned by women rose from 40% to 49%, approaching gender equality and continuing the late 20th century trend. Thus, trends in women's preparation for managerial and professional roles as exhibited by their earning college degrees, especially in business, have differed at the bachelor's versus master's levels in the 21st century so far.

There are sex differences in the employment status of members of different racial and ethnic groups. First, a note on the terminology used to represent race and ethnicity in this book: The terms *White, Black*, and *Asian* are used to designate racial groups and *Hispanic* to designate an ethnic group, because these are the terms most frequently used in U.S. government reports and employment statistics; employment statistics for other racial and ethnic groups are not reported in this chapter. However, terms such as *Caucasian, African American, Pacific Islander*, and *Latino/Latina/Latinx* might be used just as well. Also, note that U.S. employment statistics are not reported for LGBTQ+ individuals.

The three largest racial groups in the U.S. labor force according to government data are Whites (77%), Blacks (12%), and Asians (7%); other racial groups (e.g., Native Americans) represent a combined total of about 4% of the labor force. Hispanics represent the largest ethnic group in the labor force tracked in government data (18%). Hispanics as an ethnic group may be classified according to race; 89% of Hispanics in the labor force are classified as White, 5% as Black, and 1% as Asian. For purposes of comparison, we will examine the employment status of White, Black, Asian, and Hispanic men and women.[41]

However, each of these groups may be divided into multiple subgroups. For example, Asians in the U.S. labor force are 25% Indian, 22% Chinese, 14% Filipino, 9% Vietnamese, 8% Korean, 5% Japanese, and 17% other (e.g., Pakistani, Cambodian, etc.), including those who belong to two or more Asian groups. Hispanics in the labor force are 60% Mexican, 11% Central American, 9% Puerto Rican, 8% South American, 4% Cuban, 4% Dominican, and 4% other; some of these categories (e.g., Central American, South American) may be further divided into individuals from different nations. U.S. employment statistics do not recognize subdivisions of the major racial and ethnic groups. Further, these statistics do not acknowledge that many labor force participants consider themselves multiracial.[42]

Table 2.3 reports the percentage of women and men in the labor force for each of the four examined racial and ethnic groups. The sex difference in labor force participation rates favoring men varies considerably across racial and ethnic groups, ranging from 5% for Blacks to 19% for Hispanics. As we shall see, there are other significant differences in the employment status of women and men as well as members of different racial and ethnic groups.

TABLE 2.3 ■ Labor Force Participation Rates by Racial/Ethnic Group

	Percentage in the U.S. Labor Force		
Racial/Ethnic Group	**Women**	**Men**	**Difference**
White	55	68	13
Black	59	64	5
Asian	57	72	15
Hispanic	56	75	19

Sources: U.S. Department of Labor, Bureau of Labor Statistics (2022). *Labor force statistics from the Current Population Survey*, Tables 3 and 4. Retrieved November 3, 2022, from https://www.bls.gov/cps/tables.htm

THE SEX SEGREGATION OF OCCUPATIONS

If the workplace were completely integrated with respect to sex, the percentages of the male and female labor force in each occupation would be equal. For example, if 5% of all males were engineers, 5% of all females would be engineers, and the same would hold true for all occupations. Occupations may be characterized as segregated with respect to sex when females and males are *not* similarly distributed across occupations. The level of **sex segregation of occupations** has dropped in most countries since the 1970s, primarily due to the increased employment of women in male-dominated occupations. However, it has been stable during the 21st century so far and remains very high. In fact, the sex segregation of occupations is one of the most enduring features of the global economy.[43]

The nature of sex segregation in the U.S. workplace may be understood best by examining the employment of women and men in major occupational categories. As Table 2.4 indicates, women hold 47% of all jobs in the labor force. Occupations are classified as male-intensive, female-intensive, or sex-neutral based on the proportion of women in the occupation. **Male-intensive occupations** are defined as those in which one-third (33%) or less of the workforce is female. **Female-intensive occupations** are defined as those in which two-thirds (67%) or more of the workforce is female. **Sex-neutral occupations** consist of occupations in which women hold more than one-third and less than two-thirds of the jobs (34% to 66%).

Taking into account the size of the labor force in these occupations, only 11.4% of women work in male-intensive occupations, and only 14.4% of men work in female-intensive occupations. In contrast, 45.7% of all men work in male-intensive occupations, and 47.5% of all women work in female-intensive occupations. Overall, slightly less than half of the labor force works in occupations numerically dominated by members of their own sex, whereas less than 15% of the labor force works in occupations numerically dominated by members of a different sex.[44] The experiences of workers may differ substantially depending on whether they are employed in occupations that are sex-neutral, dominated by members of their own sex, or dominated by members of a different sex.

Details about the level of sex segregation in specific occupations are masked by the fact that employment statistics for about 800 different occupations are combined into 22 major occupational groups in the U.S. government data reported in Table 2.4. For example, although production occupations are classified as male-intensive overall (28.3% female), they include female-intensive occupations such as sewing machine operators (71.1% female) as well as male-intensive occupations such as machinists (3.4% female). Also, although healthcare practitioner and technical occupations are classified as female-intensive overall (74.3% female), they include male-intensive occupations such as chiropractors (24.2% female) as well as female-intensive occupations such as dental hygienists (95.1% female); note the large difference in the proportion of women for two types of jobs in the same occupation. Finally, although

TABLE 2.4 ■ Employment of Women and Men in Occupations

Occupation	Percentage of Female Employees	Occupation Type
1. Management	40.9	
2. Business and financial operations	54.8	
3. Computer and mathematics	26.2	M
4. Architecture and engineering	17.4	M
5. Life, physical, and social sciences	47.4	
6. Community and social services	67.5	F
7. Legal	53.5	
8. Education, training, and library	73.7	F
9. Arts, design, entertainment, sports, and media	50.0	
10. Healthcare practitioner and technical	74.3	F
11. Healthcare support	85.1	F
12. Protective services	23.8	M
13. Food preparation and serving	54.6	
14. Building and grounds cleaning and maintenance	41.7	
15. Personal care and services	78.7	F
16. Sales	49.8	
17. Office and administrative support	72.2	F
18. Farming, fishing, and forestry	24.2	M
19. Construction and extraction	3.9	M
20. Installation, maintenance, and repair	4.3	M
21. Production	28.3	M
22. Transportation and material moving	21.6	M
TOTAL	**47.0**	

Source: U.S. Department of Labor, Bureau of Labor Statistics (2022). *Labor force statistics from the Current Population Survey,* Table 11. Retrieved November 4, 2022, from https://www.bls.gov/cps.

Note: Occupation type equals M for a male-intensive occupation (33% female employees or less) and F for a female-intensive occupation (67% female employees or more); no symbol indicates a sex-neutral occupation (between 34% and 66% female employees). The table includes both full-time and part-time employees.

food preparation and serving occupations are classified as sex-neutral overall (54.6% female), they include male-intensive occupations involved in food preparation such as chefs and head cooks (22.8% female) and female-intensive occupations involved in food serving such as wait staff (68.2% female). We shall discuss sex differences in the status of food servers in Chapter 4.[45]

Management occupations, classified as sex-neutral in Table 2.4 (40.9% female), deserve special attention because they include workers with power and authority over others. These occupations include managers (also called *supervisors*) who work in different types of functions (e.g., marketing, finance, public relations, human resources, purchasing, etc.) as well as different types of industries (e.g., lodging, funeral services, medical, construction). As for other occupational groups, the combining of management occupations into one occupational group masks sex segregation within specific types of managerial jobs. For example, some managerial jobs such as computer and information systems managers (26.7% female) are male-intensive, whereas other managerial jobs such as human resources managers are female-intensive (80.8% female). However, although management occupations as a whole have shifted over time from once being male-intensive to now being sex-neutral in composition, the *top* ranks of management occupations remain male-intensive.[46]

The **racial and ethnic segregation of occupations** also warrants attention. If the U.S. workplace was completely integrated with regard to race and ethnicity, the percentage of the Black labor force in every occupation would be about 12%, the percentage of the Asian labor force would be about 7%, and the percentage of the Hispanic labor force would be about 18%. Table 2.5 displays the percentage of Black, Asian, and Hispanic employees in each of the major occupational groups; it does not include percentages for White employees because these percentages are overwhelmingly larger than those of the other groups. The proportion of Black employees is highest in healthcare support (e.g., nursing, psychiatric, and home health aides), protective services, and transportation and material moving occupations. The proportion of Asian employees is highest in computer and mathematics; life, physical, and social sciences; and architecture and engineering occupations. The proportion of Hispanic employees is highest in farming, fishing, and forestry; construction and extraction; and building and grounds cleaning and maintenance. Overall, occupations are segregated with regard to race and ethnicity as well as sex and the intersection of sex with race and ethnicity.[47]

THE SEX GAP IN EARNINGS

Not only do women and men tend to work in different occupations, but they also differ in earnings. The ratio of female-to-male earnings (F/M ratio) for full-time U.S. employees across all occupations is 83%.[48] Although this ratio has risen since the 1970s, when it was about 60%, the **sex gap in earnings** is another enduring feature of the global economy.[49]

TABLE 2.5 ■ Employment of Members of Racial and Ethnic Groups in Occupations

	Percentage of Employees		
Occupation	**Black**	**Asian**	**Hispanic**
1. Management	8.6	6.5	11.1
2. Business and financial operations	10.5	8.6	10.3
3. Computer and mathematics	8.5	23.3	8.3
4. Architecture and engineering	5.8	14.6	9.9
5. Life, physical, and social sciences	7.4	15.2	8.3
6. Community and social services	19.7	3.8	12.5
7. Legal	8.1	4.8	10.4
8. Education, training, and library	9.9	5.6	10.8
9. Arts, design, entertainment, sports, and media	8.2	5.7	11.1
10. Healthcare practitioner and technical	12.0	9.5	9.4
11. Healthcare support	24.5	6.8	20.9
12. Protective services	20.3	2.7	14.9
13. Food preparation and serving	13.4	6.3	27.8
14. Building and grounds cleaning and maintenance	14.2	3.4	38.3
15. Personal care and services	12.5	10.1	18.0
16. Sales	11.2	5.4	16.7
17. Office and administrative support	15.0	4.8	17.7
18. Farming, fishing, and forestry	4.4	2.3	43.9
19. Construction and extraction	7.1	1.7	38.9
20. Installation, maintenance, and repair	8.3	3.3	22.0
21. Production	13.3	5.5	24.0
22. Transportation and material moving	20.1	4.2	23.6
TOTAL	**12.3**	**6.6**	**18.0**

Source: U.S. Department of Labor, Bureau of Labor Statistics (2022). *Labor force statistics from the Current Population Survey*, Table 11. Retrieved November 4, 2022, from https://www.bls.gov/cps.

Note: The table includes both full-time and part-time employees.

The sex gap in earnings exists within each of the major racial and ethnic groups.[50] It also exists within all of the 22 major occupational groups reported in Table 2.4, including male-intensive, female-intensive, and sex-neutral occupations. To cite a few examples for specific occupations within the major occupational groups, the F/M ratio for full-time workers is 92% for civil engineers, 77% for lawyers, 90% for college and university teachers, 87% for elementary and middle school teachers, 89% for registered nurses, 87% for waiters and waitresses, 83% for janitors and building cleaners, 85% for customer service representatives, and 80% for administrative assistants and secretaries. In management occupations, the F/M ratio is 77% for managers overall and 70% for CEOs. In rare examples of occupations in which women earn more than men, the F/M ratio is 107% for business compliance officers, 106% for graphic designers, and 104% for pharmacists.

The wages earned in female-intensive occupations are typically lower than those earned in male-intensive occupations. The reduction in the earnings gap since the 1970s has been primarily due to the increased employment and retention of women in occupations that were previously male-intensive (e.g., management and law) or are still male-intensive (e.g., architecture and engineering). When women enter a male-intensive occupation, they are likely to remain in it to keep the higher pay. In contrast, when men enter a female-intensive occupation, they are more likely to be "stopgappers" and leave soon after their entry to avoid the lower pay. However, women's entering an occupation in greater numbers tends to suppress wages in the occupation itself, especially for occupations that are highly paid and male-intensive, such that these women find themselves "moving up the down staircase."[51]

Among women, there is a wage gap between mothers and women without children. A **motherhood penalty** in earnings exists for women at all pay and skill levels. This penalty is greatest in women's starting salaries and in their salaries when they resume paid employment after bearing and raising a child. In contrast, among men, there is no fatherhood penalty in earnings. In fact, fathers tend to be offered higher starting salaries than men without children, suggesting the presence of a **fatherhood bonus** in earnings.[52]

The sex gap in earnings does not diminish with educational attainment and actually becomes larger for the more highly educated. Although education has a strong positive effect on earnings for both women and men, it yields greater economic benefits for men. The earnings gap exists at every educational level—for workers with less than a high school education, a high school diploma, a bachelor's degree, and even an advanced graduate degree. For college graduates, the sex gap in earnings is influenced by the choice of major. Because women major more than men in fields that prepare graduates for female-intensive occupations and less than men in fields that prepare graduates for male-intensive occupations, we can see that the sex gap in future earnings originates before college students even interview for jobs. Sex differences in preemployment experiences are examined further in Chapter 3.[53]

The sex gap in earnings tends to increase with age, providing an example of intersectionality between two primary dimensions of diversity—sex and age—in accounting for individuals' wages in ways in which adding separate effects of sex and age would not explain. For example, a study of Hollywood movie stars (defined as actors and actresses who have played a leading role in a movie) found that actresses' salaries per movie increased until age 34 and then decreased rapidly, whereas actors' salaries per movie increased until age 51 and then remained at about the same level. In the study, the authors noted, "Men's well-worn faces are thought to convey maturity, character, and experience. A woman's face, on the other hand, is valued for appearing young." In an interview, Tim Judge, one of the study's authors, said, "This is a microcosm of what happens in society. . . . We are such an appearance-based society."[54]

The sex gap in earnings is also influenced by weight, providing another example of intersectionality between sex and a personal characteristic. The U.S. has been described as "one of the most weight-conscious societies in the world while simultaneously being one of the most obese." In other words, it is an appearance-based society on the basis of weight (even though many of its citizens are overweight) as well as age. A study using health data from the same individuals over a 25-year period found a sex difference in the effect of weight on earnings: Women were penalized in earnings for gaining weight, especially if they started with being thin, whereas men were rewarded in earnings for gaining weight until they reached the point of obesity. Overall, the sex gap in earnings appears to be highest for individuals who are at high weight levels relative to the average member of their own sex.[55]

Thus, there is a "cost of being female" (especially for mothers) that prevails within occupations as well as across occupations, racial and ethnic groups, and educational levels. The magnitude of the cost of being female is influenced by other factors such as age and weight. The gap between male and female earnings is a long-standing attribute of the global economy, and it is not likely that this gap will disappear anytime soon.

In conclusion, women and men tend to play different economic roles in the workplace today. Employment and compensation patterns send a powerful message to young people entering the labor force today and to current labor force participants. The message is that although all occupations are theoretically open to all individuals, (1) some occupations are more appropriate for members of one sex than other occupations, (2) the lower-paying occupations are more appropriate for women, (3) the higher-paying occupations are more appropriate for men, (4) work in male-intensive occupations is worth more than work in female-intensive occupations, and (5) work performed by men is worth more than equivalent work performed by women.

LOOKING FORWARD

Traditional gender roles have less to do with present-day economic realities than at any previous time. The changes experienced by women in the labor force through the 20th century were striking. Women entering male-intensive organizations went from being the only woman holding a particular job to being a member of a small group of women in the midst of a larger group of men in the job, sometimes to being a member of the majority group and increasingly more often to being in charge. The changes experienced by men during this time were less dramatic. However, men were required to adapt to the presence of more women as their peers, superiors, and subordinates. Since the 20th century, changes experienced by women and men in the workplace appear to have stalled.

As a result, significant differences between the economic roles played by women and men remain firmly in place. Men continue to hold most top management positions in organizations. Even when organizations consist predominantly of female employees, the leaders are typically male. The gap between male and female wages persists. Among full-time workers, women consistently earn lower wages than men. Even with the same job in the same occupation, women's average earnings are typically lower than those of men. The highest-paid occupations are those with predominantly male workers.

Even though work and its rewards are not distributed equally between women and men, traditional gender roles are no longer appropriate guidelines for workplace behavior. However, new standards of behavior have not replaced the old standards. Whether consciously or unconsciously, people often are influenced by their own sex and others' sex in their work behavior.

What *does* it mean to be a woman, a man, or an LGBTQ+ person in today's workplace? How *should* people take into account their own sex and others' sex in their workplace interactions, if at all? Widely accepted answers to these questions, promoting either a unisex standard of behavior or separate sex-based standards of behavior, have not emerged.

Due to the substantial increase in women's labor force participation rate in the second half of the 20th century (from 31% to 60%; see Table 2.1) and the sustained proportion of labor force participants who are female in the 21st century so far (47%; see Table 2.4), more workplace interactions are occurring between women and men than in earlier times. One of the few advantages of adhering to traditional gender roles was that men and women knew how they were expected to treat each other. That advantage is gone. Instead, in today's workplace, different-sex individuals need to develop and act on their own norms for how to work together effectively.

3 SEX, GENDER, AND SOCIETY

LEARNING OBJECTIVES

After reading this chapter, you should be able to do the following:

3.1 Discuss your reactions to issues of sex and gender in society such as those raised by examples in this chapter.

3.2 Recognize sex differences in children's interests and activities and adults' social behavior.

3.3 Understand the potential influence of gender stereotypes on workplace dynamics.

3.4 Define *gender role identity* and *androgyny*.

3.5 Identify different types of sexism and racism.

3.6 Describe the arguments for the influence of nature, nurture, and their intersection on human behavior.

3.7 Discuss key influences of parents, schools, and media on the gender socialization of children.

3.8 Identify limitations associated with strict belief in gender stereotypes and strict adherence to gender roles by adults.

ISSUES OF SEX AND GENDER

Issues of sex and gender arouse considerable controversy and debate in society. Consider the following examples:

On the labeling of children's shoes: British shoemaker Clarks put new children's shoes with gendered names on sale. The company labeled its shoe for girls, which had a Mary Jane style with a pink, heart-shaped insole, the "Dolly Babe." It labeled its shoe for boys, which had a lace-up style imprinted with a soccer ball, the "Leader." Ten types of Dolly Babe shoes for girls and eleven types of Leader shoes for boys were for sale on amazon.co.uk. A public outrage triggered by publicity about the shoe names immediately followed. In response, Clarks issued a statement: "We are working hard to ensure our ranges reflect our gender-neutral ethos. We apologize for any unintended offense caused." When I asked a colleague about her reactions, she said she was "beyond distressed" at Clarks's actions and added, "Did no one think this was a bad idea when it was proposed to the product team? Unbelievable that this could still happen!"[1]

On the labeling of children's products: British department store chain John Lewis eliminated sex-specific labels from its store brand of children's clothes. Instead, it placed "boys & girls" or "girls & boys" tags on these items. It also removed "girls" and "boys" signs from the children's clothing department in its stores. A public outrage triggered by publicity of its actions immediately followed (e.g., "What a load of PC crap!"). In response, a spokesperson said, "We do not want to reinforce gender stereotypes within our John Lewis collections and instead want to provide greater choice and variety to our customers, so that the parent or child can choose what they would like to wear." United States (U.S.) retailer Target acted in a similar manner by removing "girls" and "boys" labels from its stores' signage in children's toy displays; in response, some applauded Target's decision as a way to reduce gender stereotyping of toys while others argued that sex differences in children's toy interests are natural rather than a result of gender stereotyping. Further, the state of California passed a law requiring retailers with at least 500 employees in the state to have sex-neutral sections of children's childcare items and toys regardless of whether the products were traditionally marketed as for either girls or boys.[2]

On permissible attire for athletes: Norway's women's beach handball team was fined by the European Handball Federation for wearing banned attire (shorts instead of bikini bottoms) in a European championship. At the time, International Handball Federation (IHF) rules mandated that women must wear bikini bottoms "with a close fit and cut on an upward angle toward the top of the leg;" the sides of the bikini bottoms could be no more than four inches. In contrast, men were allowed to wear shorts as long as four inches above their knees as long as they were not "too baggy." International outrage immediately followed. The Norway team gained support from female beach handball players from other nations, including Germany, Sweden, Denmark, France, and the Netherlands. A German women's beach handball player raised the question of whether spectators in international competitions were there to see them play or to gawk at their bodies; that is, were she and her teammates being watched as athletes in competitions or merely as girls in bikinis? In addition, concerns were raised about sexism and double standards affecting female athletes in other sports, including gymnastics and tennis. In response, IHF rules were changed to allow men to wear "tank tops and shorts" and women to wear "body fit (i.e., tight) tank tops and short tight pants." The message now being sent about attire was, "Men, wear loose and baggy uniforms if you want, but women, you must wear tight uniforms." Even though standards had changed, a sex difference in permissible attire for beach handball players remained.[3]

On the hazards of masculinity in males: The American Psychological Association issued its first-ever guidelines for counselors on the hazards of expecting males to be highly masculine. The dominant ideal of masculinity in Western culture as being rugged and self-sufficient was depicted as limiting males' psychological development, constraining their behavior, and negatively affecting their mental and physical health. A debate over the guidelines immediately arose among scholars and in the media. Some praised the guidelines as "reimagining boys in the 21st century," while others criticized the guidelines as defining masculinity as an illness. A poll of British young men found that although most had a negative view of masculinity, they felt pressured to "man up" by conforming to the male gender stereotype.[4] The city of Bogotá, Colombia, initiated a hotline for men over 18 called the "Calm Line" to teach men to understand their emotions and be in control of their actions. In doing so, the hotline is intended to fight violence against women and also its root cause of "machismo," the ingrained belief that men must be dominant in societal status and social interactions.[5]

On the inclusion of LGBTQ+ athletes in athletic competitions: Considerable public debate arose over whether individuals who have transitioned from being male to being female should be allowed to compete in women's sports events against individuals whose sex assigned at birth is female, with many U.S. states passing laws banning their participation. In response, major marathons around the world in cities such as Boston, Berlin, San Francisco, London, and New York City began to allow runners to compete without having to register as men or women by adding a nonbinary division to their existing women's and men's divisions. A leader of the grassroots movement to allow LGBTQ+ (lesbian, gay, bisexual, transgender, and self-described queer) runners to compete in marathons in a nonbinary category said to a marathon organizer, "I want to register as myself." Once they were allowed to do so, other major marathons soon followed suit with little public controversy to date.[6]

Consider *your* reactions to these examples. Do you believe that Clarks had a "gender-neutral ethos" at the time as it claimed or was it trying to sound politically correct? Were John Lewis, Target, and the state of California trying to ensure greater choice and variety to customers and reduce gender stereotyping of children's products or were they trying to be politically correct? Were the IHF standards for beach handball attire—both old and new—appropriate or inappropriate? Is a hotline for men such as Bogotá's Calm Line good for municipalities to offer? If so, why not also offer hotlines for women and LGBTQ+ people? Have major marathons worldwide moved in a good direction with their addition of a nonbinary division, and if so, should other athletic competitions follow their lead? Do you find these examples unbelievable in this day and age or very believable? And finally, why is there so much controversy and debate raised over the issues of sex and gender in such examples?

Collectively, these examples set the stage for the questions to be addressed in this chapter: Are there sex differences beyond physiological ones that exist for individuals who fall into the categories of female and male? What do people believe sex differences to be? How are beliefs about sex differences conveyed? What causes sex differences when they exist, and what effects do they have on individuals' well-being?

Sex differences influence how people are disposed to behave in work settings. In contrast, gender differences influence how people react to others' behavior in work settings. In this chapter, we make particular use of the concepts of gender stereotypes, roles, and socialization, which were introduced in Chapter 1. **Gender stereotypes** represent beliefs about the psychological traits that are characteristic of males and females. According to gender stereotypes, males are high in "masculine" traits such as independence, aggressiveness, and dominance, and females are high in "feminine" traits such as gentleness, sensitivity to the feelings of others, and tactfulness. **Gender roles** represent beliefs about the behaviors that are appropriate for women and men. According to gender roles, men's proper place is at work, and women's proper place is at home. **Gender socialization** consists of the processes by which individuals learn gender stereotypes and roles beginning in childhood.[7]

As we discuss later in the chapter, the nature of gender stereotypes has been generally stable in recent decades, although they have exhibited some signs of change. However, both men and women have been less likely to endorse or express belief in gender roles in recent years. The drop-off has been especially pronounced among men, such that the sex difference in attitudes toward gender roles has essentially disappeared. Also, younger people are the least likely to endorse gender roles, suggesting that further societal changes in norms regarding the proper roles of men vis-à-vis women are likely to come.[8] Gender socialization processes have also evolved over time as younger people become parents socializing their own children.

This chapter examines sex and gender differences in society that influence workplace dynamics. First, selected research evidence about sex differences is presented. Next, gender stereotypes are examined, and concepts such as gender role identity and androgyny are introduced. Different types of sexist and racist attitudes as well as their intersection are examined. The influence of nature and nurture on individuals' behavior is considered. The ways in which gender socialization processes by parents, schools, and media convey gender role expectations to children are examined. Finally, the chapter considers how gender stereotypes and roles influence adult health and well-being and unduly restrict adult behavior.

SEX DIFFERENCES

The study of sex differences has been a preoccupation and source of controversy for more than a century, as the Chapter 1 opening quote about researchers' biases, prejudices, and "sentimental rot and drivel" from a 1910 review of the literature on the psychology of sex attests. A recent search of the PsycINFO database, which compiles scholarly articles in psychology and related fields, on the term *sex differences* yielded about 150,000 items. This topic is not simply "hot" in the sense of being frequently studied; it is also inflammatory. Many people have strong beliefs about sex similarities and differences in basic interests, abilities, attitudes, and behaviors, whatever the research evidence may suggest. That is, alpha and beta biases, which were noted in Chapter 1 as researchers' tendencies to either exaggerate or downplay sex differences, are not confined solely to researchers.[9]

Research methods used in reviews of studies of sex differences have evolved over time. Early reviews used what may be called a **vote counting** technique. That is, they simply tallied the number of studies on a given topic that found significant differences favoring females, significant differences favoring males, or no significant sex differences and then reached conclusions based on the "vote." A statistical method called **meta-analysis** is commonly used now. Meta-analysis uses sophisticated quantitative methods to synthesize statistical evidence from numerous studies. It yields results that are typically more complex and often different from those yielded by vote counting. Sex differences have been examined in many types of psychological traits and behavior using the meta-analysis technique.[10]

In this section of the chapter, we consider sex differences in children's interests and activities and in adults' social behavior.

CHILDREN'S INTERESTS AND ACTIVITIES

Starting at an early age, the interests and activities of boys and girls differ greatly. For example, starting at about 3 years old, children in multiple cultures go through a period of rigidity in their clothing preferences. Girls tend to prefer pink, frilly dresses, whereas boys will refuse to wear any article of clothing that might be seen as feminine.[11]

A sex difference in toy preferences emerges at about 2 years of age. Girls are more likely than boys to choose to play with **dolls** such as Barbie as well as jewelry, play kitchens, and domestic toys such as tea sets and playhouses. In contrast, boys are more likely than girls to choose to play with **action figures** as well as mock aggression toys such as guns and swords, transportation toys such as toy trucks and trains, construction toys, and sports collectibles.[12]

The difference between dolls and action figures may be semantic. Consider the following exchange that actually occurred between two children: Susan (not her real name), a 5-year-old girl, was speaking with a 5-year-old boy who said that he didn't play with dolls. Susan replied, "Yes, you do. They just call them action figures so you don't know you're playing with dolls!" Her tone of voice came across as, "You moron, can't you see what they are putting over you?" We can see from this exchange that Susan, if not her friend, regarded the difference as meaningless.[13]

However, the physical differences between toys described as dolls, marketed to girls, and toys described as action figures, marketed to boys, are very real. Dolls and action figures tend to convey unattainable body images for girls and boys, respectively. Most female dolls have unrealistically thin bodies, and most male action figures have unrealistically muscular bodies (which have grown even more muscular over time). Further, thinner dolls are more likely to be dressed as sex objects, and highly muscular action figures are more likely to have clenched fists and angry expressions, conveying an image of male dominance. That is, dolls convey what may be called **emphatic femininity**, whereas male action figures convey what may be called **emphatic masculinity**.[14]

Barbie, the best-selling doll of all time and subject of a highly popular live-action movie, has been characterized as the primary perpetuator of an unattainable body image for girls. In response to criticisms, Mattel, the doll's maker, decided to introduce a new range of body types called "tall," "petite," and "curvy" as options to what was now called the "original" Barbie. The documentary *Tiny Shoulders: Rethinking Barbie*, streaming on Hulu at the time of this writing, offers an excellent depiction of the history of Barbie and the decision-making process to increase the range of available body types. However, girls ages 3–10 identified Curvy Barbie, who was larger than the other three slimmer options, as the doll they least wanted to play with. Their doll preferences suggested that the emphatic femininity ideal was still being held by young girls.[15]

Playing with toys such as dolls and action figures has very real consequences. Boys' and girls' self-esteem tends to be lower after playing with muscular action figures and thin dolls, and their desire for muscularity and thinness, respectively, tends to increase. Reflecting their toy preferences, more girls want a thinner body shape compared with boys, and more boys want a larger body shape compared to girls. Moreover, playing with childhood toys may even influence perceptions of future career options. Girls who played with Barbie in one study perceived that they had fewer career options than boys, whereas girls who played with dolls that were less emphatically feminine perceived lesser difference between their career options and those of boys.[16]

Live dolls and action figures are seen on doorsteps on Halloween. Girls are more likely to dress as princesses with ruffled dresses (pink, of course) and an abundance of jewelry, beauty queens, and other examples of emphatic femininity. In contrast, boys are more likely to dress as villainous characters, monsters, and symbols of death, with the most emphatically masculine costumes being superheroes with fake muscles and weapons. Younger children are less likely to wear masculine or feminine Halloween costumes than older children, and costumes chosen for children by their parents are less masculine or feminine than costumes chosen by the children themselves. Especially as they get older and have more say in their choice of costume, children are likely to pose as the dolls and action figures with which they play.[17]

Virtual dolls and action figures are seen in video games. Male characters tend to be emphatically masculine (e.g., highly muscular, aggressive, and violent), whereas female characters tend to be emphatically feminine (e.g., voluptuous, thin, and wearing less clothing). Relatively few video games have a central female character, and when they do, the women tend to be portrayed as sex objects. The portrayal of highly sexualized female characters in video game box art, when women are depicted on the box at all, is positively related to sales, which demonstrates the economic motive behind marginalizing and sexualizing images of women in this industry.[18]

Boys prefer a more physically aggressive rough-and-tumble style of play than do girls, including both fighting and mock fighting. They welcome a physically active style of play with both parents. However, due to a sex difference in parental preferences for this style of play, boys engage in it more with their fathers than with their mothers. Also, boys spend more time watching television and participating in sports, whereas girls spend more time reading.[19]

Although there is variation across cultures, boys and girls exhibit a considerable difference in how they spend their time. In Western cultures, it is believed that play is the work of children; play is culturally sanctioned. However, boys have more time to play than girls do because they do not have to devote as much time to household chores. Boys and girls also differ in the types of household chores they perform. Boys perform more tasks outside the home for which they get paid, including yard work and outdoor errands. Girls perform more tasks inside the home for which they do not get paid, including caring for younger siblings, cleaning, and preparing food.

As they move into adolescence, girls and boys in Western cultures devote similar amounts of time to paid labor. Adolescent employment is particularly encouraged in the United States as a way to learn self-sufficiency and responsibility. However, girls and boys are employed in different kinds of activities. Girls are likely to be babysitters, waitresses, and food counter workers, whereas boys are likely to be gardeners, busboys, and manual laborers.[20]

So far, we have focused on mean differences between girls' and boys' interests and activities. However, these differences do not apply to *all* girls or *all* boys. Girls who are interested in activities that are considered more typical of boys than of girls are labeled **tomboys**, whereas boys who are interested in activities associated with girls are labeled **sissies**. These labels have different connotations. A sissy is defined as "an effeminate man or boy"; however, a sissy is also defined as "a timid, weak, or cowardly person"—certainly a negative definition. In contrast, a tomboy is defined as "a girl who behaves in a manner usually considered boyish"—a more neutral definition. Boys labeled as sissies are more negatively evaluated than girls labeled as tomboys, especially by males. Tomboys are seldom rejected by their peers because of their interest in activities associated with boys; they can always return to playing with other girls. However, boys have less freedom of choice and run a high risk of being taunted by other boys for showing any interest in girls' activities.[21]

Identifying as a tomboy may have benefits and risks for girls. For example, tomboys tend to be more accepting of other children's behavior, whether it conforms to gender stereotypes or not, which is a positive trait. Tomboys may suffer from lower self-esteem because they feel different from other girls. However, participation in athletics, which is enhanced by having same-sex athletic role models, can offset this negative effect. Highly athletic tomboys were found in one study to have higher levels of self-esteem than less athletic tomboys. In fact, female undergraduate students who participate in varsity athletics are more likely than nonathletes to describe themselves as having been tomboys.[22]

Thus, as children grow up and progress through adolescence, they exhibit considerable sex differences in interests and activities. However, girls engage more in activities typically associated with boys than vice versa. This is because there are more societally approved ways to be a girl than to be a boy.[23] As discussed later in the chapter, the ways parents socialize girls and boys contribute greatly to these types of sex differences in children.

ADULTS' SOCIAL BEHAVIOR

Sex differences have been examined in many types of social behavior exhibited by adults, including aggression, helping behavior, and nonverbal communications. **Aggression**, or behavior that is intended to hurt someone else, may be physical, verbal, or indirect. According to meta-analyses, males are more likely to engage in physical aggression that produces pain or physical injury than are females, especially when their emotions are aroused. However, this does not necessarily mean that males are the more aggressive sex. Because females are (on average) physically weaker than males, they may learn to avoid physical aggression and to adopt other ways to bring about harm. For instance, they may use their superior verbal skills for aggressive purposes; the sex difference in aggression favoring males is less pronounced for verbal than for physical aggression.[24]

Females may also engage in indirect aggression by trying to hurt others without being identified by their victims. For example, on Bellona Island in the Pacific Ocean, the society was characterized until recent times by extreme male violence and physical dominance. Women were to respond quickly and unquestioningly to the demands of men (especially their husbands) or expect to be beaten. However, women found creative ways to get back at men. One approach was to compose a "mocking song" to humiliate the offending man. As the song was circulated around the island, the subject was stigmatized in the eyes of his fellow men. The mocking song is a form of indirect aggression.[25]

Women and men exhibit similarities and differences in **helping behavior.** Although men are encouraged by society to play the role of "white knight" by helping women, both women and men engage in helping behavior. However, they tend to do so differently. Males are more likely to offer heroic or chivalrous help in areas where they feel most competent, such as helping a motorist with a flat tire at the side of a dangerous highway. In contrast, females are more likely to offer nurturant or caring help in areas where they feel most competent, such as volunteering to spend time with a sick child. These differences are also seen in occupational roles: Women are particularly well represented in occupations that involve some type of personal service, such as nurse and teacher, whereas men are especially well represented in occupations that call for placing one's life in jeopardy to help others, such as firefighter and police officer.[26]

Status differences between women and men play an important role in **nonverbal communications**. Nonverbal communication skills include the ability to express oneself accurately using the face, body, and voice; to assess the meaning of nonverbal cues from others; and to recall having met or seen people. Females have higher skills than do males in all three areas, perhaps because they tend to have lower status in organizations and society. They also tend to smile more than males, especially when they are aware that they are being observed. Overall, compared to males, females may be better able to interpret others' nonverbal cues and more inclined to offer positive nonverbal cues themselves because they are in weaker status positions and constantly have to monitor others' reactions to themselves.[27]

In summary, this is a selective review of some of the major findings about sex similarities and differences obtained from psychological research. It suggests that there are both sex differences and sex similarities. Sex similarities prevail, for example, in helping behavior, but sex differences exist in how it is expressed. Some sex differences, such as those in nonverbal communications, may be attributable to factors other than sex, such as status. Other sex differences, such as those in children's interests and activities, remain strong. However, as for adults' interests as indicated by the occupations they pursue, girls are more interested in activities associated with boys than boys are interested in activities associated with girls.

GENDER STEREOTYPES

Before we discuss gender stereotypes, try the following exercise. Create a mental image of the "typical woman"; then create a mental image of what most people would consider the typical woman. Next, complete these two sentences with five different adjectives or phrases: (1) I think the typical woman is __________________. (2) Most other people think the typical woman is ______________. Now repeat the exercise, this time thinking about the "typical man."[28]

Now consider your responses. You probably feel that most people would answer in a more biased manner than you, invoking gender stereotypes of the two sexes. But have you noticed the bias of the exercise itself? It is likely to have led you to focus on the differences between the sexes, when in fact, there is considerable overlap and similarity between their characteristics.

One of the earliest studies of gender stereotypes was conducted in this manner. Inge Broverman and her colleagues asked a group of college students to list characteristics, attitudes, and behaviors in which they believed women and men differ; these students compiled a list of 122 items. A second group of college students rated the extent to which they agreed that these 122 items were typical of an adult man or an adult woman. Analysis of these results yielded 41 items that were believed to differentiate between men and women. The men and women who responded to the survey were in almost complete agreement on the items, which fell into two clusters. Men were seen as more **competent** (i.e., instrumental or "agentic") than women, rating higher on items such as "very skilled in business," "can make decisions easily," and "almost always acts as a leader." In contrast, women were seen as more **warm** (i.e., expressive or "communal") than men, rating higher on items such as "very aware of feelings of others," "very talkative," and "easily expresses tender feelings." Competence was labeled as **masculine** because it was associated with males, whereas warmth was labeled as **feminine** because it was associated with females.[29]

Stereotypes of people are often represented by the two dimensions of competence and warmth. Individuals and groups may be seen as high or low in each dimension. As individuals' life situations change, stereotypes of them may change as well. For example, childless working women and men are stereotyped as significantly more competent than warm. When working women become mothers, they are perceived as losing competence but gaining warmth. In contrast, when working men become fathers, they are perceived as maintaining their competence and gaining warmth. Such perceptions reflect the effect of the intersection of sex and parental status on stereotypes in the workplace. Given that decision makers are more likely to hire, promote, and develop individuals whom they see as more competent, these stereotypes suggest that becoming a parent leads to discrimination on the basis of sex that hurts women professionally but not men.[30]

Stereotypes of all kinds tend to be durable. People like to categorize themselves and others into groups along primary and secondary dimensions of diversity and then identify ways in which their own group is better than and different from other groups. When these beliefs act as self-fulfilling prophecies, there is little reason for them to change. Also, girls and boys tend to learn stereotypes of different groups in their formative years from parents, teachers, other adults, and media. By the time they become adults themselves, their stereotypes of groups are mostly fixed. People are reluctant to give up a long-held stereotype unless it is thoroughly discredited, and even then, they may still hold onto it. After all, relying on stereotypes saves us mental work in identifying and categorizing others. However, as noted in Chapter 1, stereotyping may also result in prejudice and discrimination.[31]

The nature of gender stereotypes has evolved somewhat over the last five decades. Men continue to be seen as higher in masculine (agentic) traits and lower in feminine (communal) traits than women. However, there is also evidence that these perceived sex differences have diminished over time.[32]

This may be because stereotypes of groups can evolve in response to overwhelming evidence of change in their social roles. One study asked participants to describe the average man or woman either 50 years in the past, in the present, or 50 years in the future. Women of the future were described as more masculine than women of the present, who in turn were described as more masculine than women of the past.

Relatively little change was seen in descriptions of women's femininity or men's masculinity or femininity over time. Stereotypes of women, especially regarding their possession of masculine traits traditionally associated with men, may have been particularly dynamic as a result of considerable change in their societal roles over time (e.g., increased educational attainment, increased labor force participation, and increased pursuit of careers in male-intensive occupations). In comparison, stereotypes of men, who have exhibited less change in their societal roles over time, may have been more static.[33]

Gender stereotypes intersect with stereotypes based on other personal characteristics such as sexual orientation and race. For example, stereotypes of heterosexual men are higher in masculinity and lower in femininity than stereotypes of heterosexual women; in contrast, stereotypes of gay men and lesbians do not differ in either masculinity or femininity. Black women are stereotyped as both angry (or aggressive, a masculine trait) and strong (or self-reliant, also a masculine trait). Asian women are stereotyped as both highly competent (a masculine trait) and submissive (a feminine trait). White women, however, are stereotyped as emphasizing feminine traits over masculine traits, similar to stereotypes of women in general.[34]

Overall, gender stereotypes, and the intersection of gender stereotypes with other types of stereotypes, may contribute to workplace discrimination by serving as the basis for differential treatment of and biased decision making about individuals solely because of their group memberships.[35]

GENDER ROLE IDENTITY AND ANDROGYNY

At one time, psychologists regarded masculinity and femininity as opposites. An individual who was high in masculinity was regarded as low in femininity, and vice versa. Sandra Bem challenged this notion in a series of studies beginning in the 1970s. As others had done, she labeled traits as masculine or feminine based on whether they were typically seen as desirable for men or for women. However, unlike earlier researchers, Bem defined masculinity and femininity as independent dimensions rather than opposite ends of a single dimension. Instead of classifying each trait on a single scale ranging from masculine at one end to feminine at the other end, she classified masculine and feminine traits on two separate scales. Masculine items were evaluated on a scale ranging from "high in masculinity" at one end to "low in masculinity" at the other end, and feminine items were evaluated on a scale ranging from "high in femininity" at one end to "low in femininity" at the other. Bem used data from this procedure to choose items for a new survey instrument to be used in research studies, the Bem Sex-Role Inventory (BSRI).[36]

The BSRI contained 20 masculine items, 20 feminine items, and 20 filler items to disguise the purpose of the instrument. Individuals were asked to rate the extent to which they thought each item was characteristic of themselves. Masculinity and femininity scores were calculated by averaging individuals' self-ratings for the respective items. Thus, rather than measuring beliefs about others, the BSRI measured beliefs about oneself in relation to traditional concepts of masculinity and femininity. Although Bem called these beliefs an individual's "sex role identity," we use the term **gender role identity**, consistent with the distinction between sex and gender (see Chapter 1) that emerged shortly after she developed the BSRI, to refer to beliefs about the extent to which one possesses traits associated with gender stereotypes—that is, masculine traits associated with males and feminine traits associated with females.

Before proceeding, we should note the distinction between two similar sounding terms, gender identity and gender role identity. *Gender identity*, as defined in Chapter 1, refers to an individual's personal identification with the sex assigned at birth; cisgender individuals feel a match between the sex they were assigned at birth, whereas transgender individuals do not. In contrast, as defined above, *gender role identity* refers to an individual's self-perception regarding possession of masculine and feminine traits. The two terms refer to distinctly different phenomena and should not be confused with each other.[37]

Besides pertaining to beliefs about oneself as an individual, gender role identity also pertains to beliefs about oneself in social relationships. Individuals' self-construals capture their sense of self in relation to others. People who see themselves as higher in femininity than masculinity according to the BSRI are more likely to display an **interdependent self-construal** in which people who are important in their lives are included in their representations of themselves (e.g., "I am a loving parent" and "I am a valuable team member"). In contrast, people who see themselves as higher in masculinity than femininity are more likely to display an **independent self-construal** in which others are seen as separate and distinct from themselves (e.g., "I am a strong-willed individual" and "I value my autonomy").[38]

In advocating her notion of gender role identity, Bem introduced the psychological concept of **androgyny**, representing similar amounts of masculinity and femininity; individuals with less of a difference between their masculinity and femininity scores on the BSRI were regarded as more androgynous. The term *androgyny* comes from the Greek words "andr" (man) and "gyne" (woman), meaning both masculine and feminine. An androgynous gender role identity was found in early research to be associated with higher self-esteem, a more flexible response to situations that seemed to call for either feminine or masculine behaviors, and a host of other positive factors. The individual who adheres to gender stereotypes no longer seemed the ideal of psychological health. Instead, the androgynous individual (whose self-image and behavior are less narrowly restricted) was seen as more ready to meet the complex demands of society. In short, androgyny was proposed as an ideal combination of the "best of both worlds."[39]

The revolutionary nature of the concept of androgyny in the field of psychology matched the feminist spirit of the women's revolution movement that prevailed at the time, and its merits became the subject of considerable debate. This debate has subsided over the years but has never been fully settled. Several conceptions of what people should be like have been proposed. One view argues for conformity with gender stereotypes. A second view argues that people should break free from gender stereotypes and pursue an androgynous ideal. However, both of these views are limited. A more reasonable view is that there should be no conception of ideal behavior. Instead, the goal should be the development of an environment in which all people are free to be themselves rather than expected to live up to any standard of psychological health. As Bem later put it, "If there is a moral to the concept of psychological androgyny, it is that *behavior* should have no gender."[40]

The BSRI itself has been used in thousands of studies investigating gender role identity and has overwhelmingly been the "instrument of choice" in research on gender issues. It has received a great deal of attention as a result and has been critiqued on both theoretical and methodological grounds. Theoretically, the primary criticism has been that masculinity and femininity may be further divided into independent dimensions and that it makes no sense to consider masculinity and femininity in themselves. For example, masculinity may be subdivided into an internal dimension (e.g., defends own beliefs, willing to take a stand, and is independent) and a social dimension (e.g., forceful, dominant, and aggressive). However, the terms *masculinity* and *femininity* refer to meaningful concepts for people and are an important part of their **gender schemas** (a multifaceted and internally consistent set of ideas they have about gender) even though the concepts themselves may be broken down further.[41]

Methodologically, the primary criticism of the original (long) BSRI has been that although the average desirability of the masculine items for a man and the average desirability of the feminine items for a woman is similar, the masculine items are more desirable for an adult of unspecified sex than the feminine items. In response to this criticism, Bem developed the Short Bem Sex-Role Inventory (Short BSRI), which has half as many masculine and feminine items as the original BSRI and eliminates most of the items regarded as undesirable for adults in general. As a result, the Short BSRI has been demonstrated to be a sounder instrument, more valid and reliable than the original BSRI to measure gender role identity and androgyny.[42] The linkages of gender role identity and androgyny to individuals' work-related attitudes and behaviors are examined in later chapters.

SEXISM AND RACISM

The term **sexism** refers to prejudice displayed toward members who belong (or are perceived to belong) to a particular sex.[43] Sexism, like prejudice in general, is usually assumed to represent a negative attitude. However, some researchers have distinguished between hostile sexism and benevolent sexism. **Hostile sexism** toward women as a group entails antagonism toward women who are viewed as challenging or usurping men's power. In contrast, **benevolent sexism** puts women on pedestals; it characterizes women as "pure creatures who ought to be protected, supported, and adored and whose love is necessary to make a man complete." One study found sex differences in hostile sexism and benevolent sexism toward women in 19 countries. Men scored significantly higher in hostile sexism than did women in all countries. The sex difference in benevolent sexism was much less than the sex difference in hostile sexism. Overall, women rejected hostile sexism outright but often accepted benevolent sexism, believing that they needed to be protected by men.[44]

Both hostile and benevolent sexism among men pose barriers to women's status in the workplace, particularly in nontraditional roles. Hostile sexists prefer male authority figures over female authority figures, evaluate male candidates for managerial positions more highly than female candidates, and are more tolerant of sexual harassment toward women. Benevolent sexists are likely to support sex-based affirmative action policies but only for the hiring of women in female-intensive occupations and not male-intensive occupations. Thus, benevolent sexism, although appearing to be supportive of women, may contribute to the sex segregation of occupations discussed in Chapter 2. Also, benevolent sexists are less likely to assign challenging tasks to women than to men under the rationale that women need to be protected from the frustrations and difficulties that may accompany such tasks. This way of "helping" women undermines their career progress by denying them the opportunity to learn under fire.[45]

Although they occur less frequently, hostile and benevolent sexism may be displayed toward men as a group. For example, women may exhibit hostile attitudes by criticizing men's greater power and status in society as well as their manner of seeking and maintaining control. In addition, they may display benevolent attitudes of protective maternalism, admiration for men's competence, and appreciation of men's roles in making women's lives complete. Women score higher than men on hostile sexism toward men and lower on benevolent sexism toward men.[46]

A distinction may also be made between old-fashioned sexism and modern sexism. **Old-fashioned sexism**, like hostile sexism, is blatant; it is associated with the endorsement of traditional gender roles in the workplace, differential treatment of women and men, and the endorsement of laws and societal norms that promote adherence to gender roles. In contrast, **modern sexism** is associated with the denial of the existence of sex discrimination, antagonism toward women's demands that alleged sex discrimination be discontinued, and a lack of support for programs designed to help women in the workplace. The old-fashioned sexist says, "Women cause problems in the workplace when they don't stick to their proper roles." The modern sexist says, "Women cause problems in the workplace when they complain too much about nonexistent problems they face." Both statements reflect sexist attitudes but in different ways. The old-fashioned sexist is prejudiced against women who seek to play nontraditional roles in the workplace, whereas the modern sexist is prejudiced against women who claim that there are barriers to their performing such roles. Ironically, modern sexists may personally benefit from their sexist attitudes by relying more on men for work-related advice and in turn gaining more access to resources and receiving more promotions.[47]

The distinction between old-fashioned and modern sexism is similar to one that has been made between old-fashioned and modern racism. **Old-fashioned racism** entails overt expressions of hostility and antagonism. **Modern racism** is a more subtle form of prejudice. Modern racists endorse racial equality and avoid obvious acts of discrimination to maintain their self-images as fair and just individuals. However, they still harbor unconscious negative feelings and beliefs about low-status racial groups. These feelings and beliefs result in subtle bias, particularly when such bias is not obvious or can be rationalized based on factors other than race. Like modern sexists, some modern racists deny the existence of racial discrimination, express antagonism toward the demands of people of color, and resent programs that support people of color. Despite its subtle nature, modern racism is extremely detrimental to people of color. White people may display acts of "microaggression" toward people of color, including avoidance, closed and unfriendly verbal and nonverbal communication, and failure to help, all of which lead people of color to feel devalued and discriminated against.[48]

Sexism and racism differ in basic ways in how they are learned and experienced. Women are not statistically in the minority in most cultures, whereas members of many racial and ethnic groups are in the minority depending on the culture. The socialization of males and females tends to take place in the immediate presence of the other group, whereas races are more separated in society in their schools and neighborhoods. White males may view racism as a problem affecting a group of outsiders with whom they have little contact, whereas they may be more concerned with sexism, especially the hostile or old-fashioned kind, because they can directly observe its effects on their mothers, wives, sisters, and daughters.[49]

The intersection of sexism and racism may result in **gendered racism**, which has negative consequences for women of color above and beyond what would result solely from sexism or solely from racism. For example, Black women may have to deal with being stereotyped as angry and being silenced and marginalized. White women, in contrast, are not subjected to such experiences. As discussed in Chapter 1, sexism and racism are only two of the "isms" that may negatively affect people's experiences in the workplace and society.[50]

NATURE AND NURTURE

Numerous theories have been offered for why sex differences occur in the first place. Researchers tend to focus on one of two competing explanations, biological forces (nature) or social-environmental forces (nurture). What ultimately determines individual behavior: nature or nurture or both? To understand the effects of nature and nurture, we need to consider the basic arguments concerning how biological and social-environmental factors lead to sex differences.[51]

Those who focus on the effects of **biological forces** argue that sex differences in adults and children are mostly hardwired and innate. According to this argument, boys behave the way they do simply because they are male, and girls behave as they do because they are female, although the underlying reasons proposed for biological effects differ. Sex differences in cognitive abilities, social behavior, gender role identity, and other psychological variables have been attributed to sex differences in physiological properties such as genes, hormones, nerve cell activity, and brain structure. The creationist perspective attributes sex differences to distinct acts of creation by God.[52]

A prominent biological view focuses on the effects of **evolutionary processes** on men's and women's genes and subsequent behavior. Evolutionary psychologists, following the famed 19th-century scientist Charles Darwin, suggest that sex differences in behavior reflect adaptations to the differential demands of the environment on males and females during prehistoric times. According to evolutionary theory, men and women coexisted in hunting-and-gathering groups at the beginning of civilization, with men doing most of the hunting of food (being the physically stronger sex) and women doing most of the food gathering. This ancestral division of labor favored men and women who were the most psychologically prepared for their assigned roles. Effective adaptations to these environmental demands were then incorporated into the genetic makeup of humans and inherited by future generations. Thus, different psychological mechanisms evolved in males and females over time, leading to the sex differences that we observe today.[53]

Others argue that **social-environmental forces** such as pressures from family, peers, media, schools, employers, and society cause sex differences in interests, abilities, gender identity, and behavior to be learned in childhood and reinforced in adulthood. According to this view, the present-day environment influences the behavior of girls and boys by rewarding them for engaging in the "right" behaviors (i.e., behaviors consistent with gender stereotypes and roles) and by punishing them for engaging in the "wrong" behaviors. The modern division of labor, as reflected in differences in women's and men's domestic and occupational roles (see Chapter 2), leads to the formation of gender roles that dictate the behaviors appropriate for each sex. Children are expected to behave in accordance with these gender roles, with boys socialized to behave in a masculine manner and girls in a feminine manner. Parents play a large role in shaping their sons' and daughters' behavior, but other people and institutions have a considerable effect as well. Children's contacts with their peers are also important in the development of gender roles.[54]

In summary, arguments may be made for the influence of both biological forces (nature) and social-environmental forces (nurture) on the development of children and subsequent behavior of adults. No consensus has been reached among scholars as to whether nature or nurture is more important; indeed, the question seems misguided as their effects are so intertwined that it is difficult to separate them. Instead, nature and nurture are likely to intersect rather than operate alone to influence the presence of sex similarities and differences. The combined effects of nature and nurture may be best summarized as follows:

> People are hardwired to think and act in certain ways, some of which differ for males and females and others of which do not differ. Whether sex similarities or differences are learned or exhibited in a particular setting is influenced by the nature of the social-environmental forces operating in the setting.

Because biological forces are less amenable to change, we focus in the next section of the chapter on the influence of social-environmental forces.

GENDER SOCIALIZATION

Although the concept of androgyny offered a vision of a society free of the influence of gender roles and stereotypes, that society has not yet materialized—if it ever will. Boys grow up under the heavy influence of the male gender role and girls under the influence of the female gender role. To explain the effects of these influences, we need to examine how young males and females are socialized to live up to the expectations of the appropriate gender role. Although many social-environmental forces contribute to children's socialization into gender roles, we focus in this section on the influence of parents, schools, and media.

Parents

Parents are in a position to have a special effect on their child's development. They provide the opportunity for imitation of their own behavior and reinforcements for their children's behavior. Children imitate same-sex models more than different-sex models, although they could imitate any adult to whom they were exposed. Because parents are highly available and powerful, they are the role models whom children are most likely to copy, particularly during the preschool years. Boys spend more time with their fathers than girls do, and girls spend more time with their mothers than boys do. Parents who are absent, however, are unavailable to serve as role models.

Parents signal their likely influence on their children's development even before childbirth. The **gender-reveal party**, an event at which expectant parents reveal the sex of their child-to-be by the surprise display of something pink (think "girl") or something blue (think "boy") such as confetti, balloons, or a cake with a pink or blue color inside, has become a 21st century phenomenon.[55] After childbirth, children sleep in rooms decorated by their parents, play with toys chosen by their parents, dress in Halloween costumes procured by their parents, and so on.

Individuals' beliefs about gender stereotypes and roles and their resulting behavior are influenced by the transition to parenthood. Parents tend to become more traditional in their attitudes and behavior (including in their household division of labor) following the birth of their first child. In turn, parents' beliefs about gender stereotypes and roles influence how they raise their children. For example, children of parents who endorse gender stereotypes and roles tend to display attitudes and aspirations that are consistent with the sex segregation of occupations (see Chapter 2). In contrast, the children of parents with egalitarian attitudes and behavior tend to display egalitarian attitudes and aspirations that are inconsistent with the sex segregation of occupations.[56]

The effects of **maternal employment** on children's development have received considerable scholarly attention. (In comparison, perhaps because paternal employment is expected according to gender roles, its effects on children's development have received little attention.) Myths about maternal employment include that working mothers work only for the money, care only about their own needs, and neglect their children, thereby contributing to antisocial behavior. However, all children benefit from the income that their mothers as well as fathers earn, as increased family income has a positive effect on children's academic performance and reduces behavioral problems. Daughters of employed mothers score higher on measures of achievement such as grades and test scores than daughters of mothers who are not employed outside of the home. Also, husbands of employed mothers devote more time to household labor and childcare than do husbands of stay-at-home mothers, giving their daughters as well as sons another example of deviation from traditional gender roles.[57]

In addition, parents' workplace experiences influence their moods and parenting behaviors, which in turn influence how their children behave. Mothers and fathers whose jobs put them in a bad mood are more likely to punish their children, which negatively influences their children's motivation and academic performance and increases their behavioral problems at school. However, stay-at-home mothers whose family roles put them in a bad mood also are more likely to engage in punishing behavior, thereby contributing to their children's behavioral problems. Happier parents, no matter what roles they play in the household and workplace, tend to raise happier, better-adjusted sons and daughters.[58]

In conclusion, when present, parents are in a position to influence their children's interests and aspirations in ways that are carried out as the children become adults. In so doing, parents may reinforce or contradict the messages sent by gender stereotypes and roles.

Schools

Once they enter school systems, children are subject to the influence of additional authority figures besides their parents. They have more adult role models from which to choose, and they have more occasion to be rewarded or punished for their behavior. One of the first messages that children receive at school is the sex segregation of positions in the school system itself. The proportion of female teachers decreases from preschool and kindergarten teaching (97%, a female-intensive occupation) to elementary and middle school teaching (79%, a female-intensive occupation) to high school teaching (59%, a sex-neutral occupation). The proportion of female administrators also decreases from the position of school principal (55%, a sex-neutral occupation) to school superintendent (27%, a male-intensive occupation). The older the child and the higher the grade, the fewer female teachers; also, the higher the administrative level, the fewer female administrators. Overall, men oversee the school systems in which women teach, which does not escape students' attention.[59]

Sex differences in educational attainment and academic performance favoring female students are striking. Girls are more likely to graduate from high school than boys. As Table 2.2 indicates, women are more likely than men to earn college degrees at both the bachelor's and master's levels. Further, girls get better grades than boys across all ethnic groups, ages, subject areas, and levels of education beginning with early school years and extending through college.[60]

These sex differences do not necessarily mean that girls are innately smarter than boys, although advocates of biology-based sex differences might claim otherwise. Better grades are earned by students with better study habits and skills. Female students tend to be more organized, orderly, disciplined in their approach to schoolwork, and respectful of rules and regulations than male students, all of which contribute to their getting good grades and attaining higher educational levels. In contrast, boys are more likely to exhibit dysfunctional school behaviors, including cutting classes, disobeying rules, and being suspended or transferred to other schools for disciplinary reasons, all of which interfere with their getting good grades and being able to attain higher educational levels.[61]

Teachers' beliefs in gender stereotypes and roles influence their teaching practices, which in turn influence their students' learning in ways that lie outside the lesson plan. For example, a study of prekindergarten and elementary school teachers found that those with traditional beliefs were likely to promote same-sex over different-sex interactions among students and set up competitions between same-sex groups of girls and boys in the classroom. A separate study found that preschool teachers expected boys to be naturally physically aggressive and were lax in disciplining them for such behaviors, whereas they expected girls to behave passively and disciplined them more severely than boys when they were physically aggressive. As a result, boys and girls were disciplined differently for engaging in the exact same behavior. Thus, teachers may reinforce and perpetuate gender stereotypes and roles through their treatment of girls and boys in the classroom.[62]

They may also influence their students' self-esteem. Self-esteem may come from two sources: others' beliefs and perceptions and one's own accomplishments. According to the **reflected appraisals model of self-esteem**, sex differences occur in areas where societal expectations differ for men and women; people base their self-esteem on what others think of them. According to the **competencies model of self-esteem**, sex differences occur in areas where actual performance differs for men and women; people base their self-esteem on competency tests or other objective measures. A meta-analysis found no sex differences in self-esteem regarding academic performance across all educational levels. Given that females demonstrate higher academic performance in the form of better grades across all levels, the results of this meta-analysis support the reflected appraisals model over the competencies model. Females may discount their own academic abilities, even in areas where they excel, resulting in their academic self-esteem being lower than their performance warrants. In contrast, males may inflate their own academic abilities, even in areas where they trail, resulting in their academic self-esteem being higher than their performance warrants.[63]

Girls' self-esteem influences their choice of courses, fields of study, and eventual employment. For example, in high school, girls tend to avoid advanced mathematics and science courses, although girls who take such courses tend to earn higher grades than do boys. Even when girls are personally identified as being highly gifted in math and science, they have lower academic self-esteem and show less interest in pursuing careers in **science, technology, engineering, and mathematics (STEM)** fields than do their male peers. As a result, female undergraduates are less likely than male undergraduates to major in STEM fields. After their undergraduate schooling, women are less likely to pursue graduate degrees and seek employment in STEM fields as well.[64]

In summary, despite getting better grades, girls emerge from their school years with no greater academic self-esteem than boys: in this case, a sex similarity with lasting consequences. Girls may be both rewarded with good grades in the short run and held back in the workplace in the long run by their experiences in schools.[65]

Media

Children are exposed to many types of media, including television programs, movies, the internet, social media, and print media. They also are exposed to considerable advertising in almost all the media they consume. They access these media on multiple devices, including televisions, mobile devices, and laptop and desktop computers. Watching television and movies, using social media, and accessing the internet frequently are prominent activities in children's lives. Media influence children's development by providing a view, whether real or distorted, of the outside world.

Television, whether watched live or streaming, remains the media of choice among young children. Television is very accessible and easy to use. Unlike reading text-based content such as in magazines, books, or internet articles, watching television does not require literacy. It is always running and available, coming directly into the home, with most homes having multiple televisions. Children begin to watch television before they can walk or talk, and when not watching, they are exposed to considerable background television watched by others.[66]

Television has been described as the "great socializer." It teaches children what is important and how to behave. It also teaches gender stereotypes and roles. Stereotypical portrayals of females and males remain the norm in television programming aimed at children starting at ages 0–5. After watching these stereotypical portrayals, girls feel more pressure to be feminine and boys feel more pressure to be masculine. In television directed at children, gender stereotypes and roles remain prevalent.[67]

Animated movies aimed at children also convey messages about gender stereotypes and roles. For example, Walt Disney's classic—and first (1937)—animated movie of *Snow White and the Seven Dwarfs*, based on a Brothers Grimm fairy tale, is popular and streaming to this day. The movie depicts Snow White as cheerfully doing housework, first for the wicked queen and then for the dwarfs, while singing blissfully about the handsome prince she hopes to marry and keep house for. The dwarfs are depicted as both personal slobs and as a cohesive group epitomizing teamwork, good humor, and masculine protectiveness. They protect Snow White, and she picks up after them. According to an analysis of Disney's animated movies, early animations suggest that females are weak and avoid paid work, whereas more recent animations suggest that females are strong and may be engaged in paid work. Also, recent Disney animations have been more likely to involve women in the production process as producers, directors, and writers, which has led to more nuanced and less stereotypical character portrayals. However, the earlier animated movies are still available along with the recent ones, giving children a confusing set of messages about what traits they possess and how they should behave.[68]

In **movies aimed at adults** to which children may be exposed, either by seeing the movie or ads for it at home, the message is clear: White men are the most important players. In a study of the 100 top-grossing fictional films in each year over a 16-year period, less than one-third had a female lead or co-lead, and less than 20% had a person of color as lead or co-lead; women of color as leads or co-leads were few and far between. Characters with disabilities and LGBTQ+ characters were left out of movie roles in a manner disproportionate to their presence in the U.S. population. However, movies with female writers and directors had a more balanced sex composition of roles than those with male writers and directors. Overall, gender stereotypes and roles tend to be reinforced in movies aimed at adults, particularly when men are in charge of making the movies.[69]

Portrayals of **female managers and professionals in movies** are often unflattering. For example, in Hollywood movies, managerial and professional women have been portrayed as mean, scheming, promiscuous but distracted lovers, isolated, and unable to balance work and family. Such images may suppress women's career ambitions as adults and contribute to maintaining glass ceilings. They may also affect children's career aspirations and expectations directly if exposed to the movies or indirectly through the movies' influence on their parents.[70]

Television programs and movies do occasionally flout stereotypes and celebrate diversity. For a good example, we need only turn to the world of *Star Trek*, depicted in the original television series and several successors (e.g., *The Next Generation, Deep Space Nine, Voyager, Enterprise, Picard, Discovery, Strange New Worlds*) as well as several movies. *Star Trek* is set in a universe full of races of different kinds of beings. It assumes not only the existence of other life in this universe but the existence of compatible life; other kinds of beings are never viewed as completely alien. The challenge then becomes to understand, communicate, and get along with other races. The original crew of the *U.S.S. Enterprise* was all-inclusive. Although the crew had a White male captain, it had Black, Asian, Russian, Scottish, Anglo-Saxon, and Vulcan members. *Star Trek*'s portrayal of both females and males as well as members of different races in key positions of responsibility was rare in television at the time (the 1960s). Nichelle Nichols, who played Lieutenant Uhura in the original *Star Trek* series, was one of the first Black women in a leading role in a television series and later helped the U.S. National Aeronautics and Space Administration (NASA) to recruit women and members of minority groups as astronauts. According to George Takei, the Japanese American actor who played Mr. Sulu in the original series, "True Trekkies embrace diversity."[71]

Social media, including internet sites to which people post photos, stories, and comments and respond to others' postings, may influence children's self-esteem and body image. Being exposed to a multitude of images of friends' bodies on social media, as well as ads that show idealized bodies, may raise body image concerns for girls and boys who do not see themselves as fitting (or who are being told they do not fit) the prototypes of emphatic femininity or emphatic masculinity respectively. Girls are especially affected by what have been called **thinspiration** images—visual and textual images intended to motivate weight loss. If they post selfies (photos of themselves taken with mobile devices), girls who are highly invested in the likes and comments their selfies receive are more likely to have body image concerns and strive to meet the thinspiration ideal. In the worst-case scenario, thinspiration images may be associated with the eating disorders and cyberbullying of girls who do not fit the thinness norms that the images convey.[72] Although social media usage may foster adolescents' sense of social connectedness (a positive outcome), it also facilitates cyberbullying, with males more likely to be cyberbullies than females.[73]

In summary, although television and other media now portray women and men in roles that are somewhat less stereotypical than in the past, all forms of media generally do not represent women in the most positive ways except when they are emphatically feminine or adhere to gender roles. Why is this the case? It may be because women are underrepresented in the creation of all types of media. When women are involved in the creative process, the result tends to be women being the subject of more stories and actresses with greater centrality to the plot in more television and movie roles. Overall, media depictions of men and women in and outside the workplace largely convey and reinforce gender stereotypes and roles, which has enormous potential to influence children's perceptions of reality.[74]

BEYOND GENDER STEREOTYPES AND ROLES

With the assistance of parents, schools, and media, children learn about gender stereotypes and roles. However, children eventually face hazards as adults if they learn these lessons too well. In this section, we consider the limitations associated with strict belief in gender stereotypes and strict adherence to gender roles.

Limitations of Gender Stereotypes

Stereotyping, or the cognitive activity of sorting people into different groups based on some personal characteristic or characteristics and then assigning traits to members of each group, is a pervasive human phenomenon that may seem harmless at first glance. Several types of problems may result from an overreliance on stereotypes (in this case, gender stereotypes). First, without stereotyping, prejudice and discrimination would be less likely to take place.[75]

Second, although a given stereotype may accurately describe the average member of a group, it rarely applies to all group members. For example, when the Short BSRI is administered to undergraduate college students, males as a group score higher in masculinity and lower in femininity than females as a group.[76] Thus, gender stereotypes of men as predominantly masculine and women as predominantly feminine in traits hold for the *average* male and female undergraduate, respectively. However, this does not mean that *every* male undergraduate is predominantly masculine and *every* female undergraduate is predominantly feminine; there are individual differences within each group. When people are stereotyped on the basis of sex (or any other dimension of diversity), who they are as individuals may be overlooked.

Third, stereotypes imply that differences between members of different groups are a result of their group membership. This is virtually impossible to prove. When we examine whether females and males differ in any type of interest, ability, attitude, or behavior, we need to distinguish between two questions: "Is there a difference *between* females and males?" and "Is there a difference *on account of* their being female or male?"[77] Answering the first question is relatively simple; it involves only testing and comparing female and male populations. Answering the second question is much more difficult. It requires demonstrating that a difference is innate and due to biological sex alone (i.e., due to nature), which involves testing and comparing female and male populations who have been living under identical environmental conditions. Due to differences in the gender socialization of girls and boys (i.e., differences in nurture), these conditions are not present in any culture. Thus, people need to be cautious in what they conclude about the causes of sex differences in individuals' interests, abilities, attitudes, and behavior.

Limitations of Gender Roles

Different types of problems result from strict adherence to gender roles. Neither the female nor the male gender role offers an ideal prescription for an emotionally satisfying and rewarding life. A rigid adherence to either role may be hazardous to one's mental and physical health.[78]

The female gender role encourages dependence and surrender of control over many aspects of one's life to others. Reactions to this lack of control may be manifested in depression and other forms of illness. However, the female gender role places an emphasis on self-awareness, which could lead women to be more aware than men of symptoms of ill health, even if they were no less healthy. This role also encourages expression of feelings, including admission of difficulties, which can lead people to seek help from others.[79]

In contrast, the male gender role encourages aggressiveness and competitiveness, which can lead men to put themselves in risky situations. This role is also associated with emotional inexpressiveness, which may cause psychosomatic and other health problems. Lack of self-awareness keeps men from being sensitive to signals that all is not well with them. Adherence to the male gender role means suppressing one's feelings and always striving (or pretending) to be in control of one's own life. The effects of this unbridled push for dominance may take a toll on men, even though it may seem better to dominate than to be dominated.[80]

One way to shed light on the effects of the toll of gender roles is to examine sex differences in indicators of mental and physical health. We need to proceed with caution in using this approach because pressure to conform to gender roles is only one of many factors that could influence behavior and health.

Mortality statistics are striking. In 1900, life expectancy at birth for the U.S. population was 48 years for women and 46 years for men. Since then, these expectations have risen to 81 years for women and 76 years for men. The sex difference in mortality favoring women is present for U.S. individuals of all races and ethnic groups. Males die at a higher rate than females at all ages, ranging from one year or less to 85 years and older. Although life expectancy has increased substantially for women and men, the sex difference favoring women has also increased.[81]

Health statistics vary considerably for women and men. Overall, women experience more frequent illnesses and short-term disability than men. For example, women report higher rates of mood disorders such as depression and anxiety, eating disorders such as anorexia and bulimia, and minor physical ailments such as headaches and stomach upsets. However, women's health problems typically do not endanger their lives, and they take more actions to address their problems than men. They report more visits to physicians, use more prescription medicines and over-the-counter drugs, and restrict their activities due to health problems more.

In contrast, men suffer from more life-threatening diseases that cause permanent disability and earlier death than women. They suffer more from substance abuse involving alcohol or drugs and antisocial disorders such as aggression. They are more likely to be murdered, commit suicide, or to die in an accident while driving or participating in a dangerous sport. Men are also less likely to take health promotion messages seriously, to consult a doctor when physical health problems arise, or to seek therapy when mental health problems arise (hence, the need for Bogotá's Calm Line).[82]

Sex differences in health-related behaviors and outcomes carried over into the COVID-19 pandemic. Men were less likely than women to see the coronavirus as representing a serious health problem and take recommended precautions. For example, men were less likely than women to wash their hands, wear a mask, or comply with social distancing guidelines, all of which increased their likelihood of contracting the coronavirus. Perhaps not coincidentally, men were also more likely than women to die from COVID-19.[83]

In summary, mortality and health statistics suggest that women are sicker in the short run and men are sicker in the long run. At least part of the reason for these sex differences may be the strict adherence of women and men to gender roles.

WHAT'S NEXT?

This chapter began by posing several examples of issues of sex and gender that have played out in society in recent years and asking your reactions. Although there are both similarities and differences between females and males, most people believe that there are substantial differences. These beliefs are reflected in gender stereotypes (although stereotypes of women may be more dynamic than those of men) and sometimes in sexist attitudes. Women and men are expected to adopt roles that are consistent with gender stereotypes. However, individuals develop their own gender role identities (beliefs about themselves in relation to traditional definitions of masculinity and femininity). Individual behavior is influenced by a combination of biological and social-environmental forces. Parents, schools, and media shape children's behavior in a manner consistent with traditional notions of masculinity and femininity. Strict belief in gender stereotypes by adults may enhance sex-based prejudice and discrimination, and strict adherence to gender roles can be hazardous to the mental and physical health of adults.

Given the persistence of gender stereotypes and roles, is it possible to create settings in which expectations for behavior are not linked to sex or gender? I believe that change is possible and existing influences do not have to be taken for granted. Parents, teachers, and media may change the way they view gender-related issues. Parents and teachers may be made aware of the powerful effect of their expectations on children's learning. Institutions that train teachers can ensure that teachers are made aware of how their own expectations and interactions with students affect student performance. The media can do a better job of informing members of the public about gender-related issues and the health consequences of their behavior.

What societal changes would it take to reduce adherence to gender roles that is only for the sake of conforming to others' expectations—children's shoes that are not labeled as being for dolly babes or leaders? Unisex children's clothing departments in retail stores? More Calm Lines made available to males, females, and LGBTQ+ individuals? Videogames in which males are less emphatically masculine and females less emphatically feminine or in which women are warriors who rescue men in peril? Greater societal emphasis on the merits of androgyny compared with emphatic masculinity or emphatic femininity? Parents disconfirming gender roles in how they raise their children and distribute household responsibilities? Teachers treating students similarly for engaging in the same behavior, regardless of their sex? Television programs and movies that embrace diversity more and gender stereotypes and roles less? Realistic rather than idealized body images on social media? I hope to get the chance to find out.

4 MAKING EMPLOYMENT DECISIONS

by Laura M. Graves and Gary N. Powell

LEARNING OBJECTIVES

After reading this chapter, you should be able to do the following:

4.1 Understand the interdependence of self-selection and organizational selection decisions.

4.2 Describe sex differences that influence self-selection decisions, including reactions to jobs, reactions to organizations, and job search behavior.

4.3 Describe factors that influence the presence of sex discrimination in organizational selection decisions.

4.4 Identify ways in which self-selection and organizational selection decisions may be improved.

INTERDEPENDENCE OF SELF-SELECTION AND ORGANIZATIONAL SELECTION DECISIONS

Many of today's organizations utilize hiring practices designed to prevent sex discrimination as well as other types of discrimination. Although some organizations embrace nondiscriminatory practices to hire the best talent available, others are simply motivated by legal requirements. Because employers have substantial incentive to avoid sex discrimination in their employment practices, one might assume that sex and gender have little effect on employment decisions. Unfortunately, this assumption is incorrect.

The decisions of individual job seekers during the job search process are called **self-selection decisions**. In self-selection decisions, individuals actively choose which opportunities to pursue and which job offers to accept. Sex differences in self-selection decisions may result from differences in reactions to jobs and organizations. They may also result from differences in the job search behaviors that men and women use to find employment.[1]

The decisions of organizations and their representatives at various stages of the hiring process are called **organizational selection decisions**. In these decisions, organizations choose which applicants pass an initial screen to receive further consideration (e.g., by being invited to a formal interview or site visit) and ultimately receive job offers. Although the selection decisions of organizations are based primarily on applicants' qualifications, sex discrimination may occur. We need to consider how and when sex discrimination occurs and who and what discriminates against whom.[2]

Self-selection decisions and organizational selection decisions are interdependent in complex ways. Self-selection decisions affect the nature of the jobs that job seekers obtain, and they affect which applicants are available for organizations to make selection decisions about. If applicants are turned down for jobs, they need to initiate new self-selection decisions focusing on other potential employers. If highly qualified applicants turn down job offers for whatever reason (e.g., they are turned off by the hiring process or don't like the salary offer), organizations need to make new selection decisions about other applicants, and they may experience shortages of talented workers. Worker shortages were a particular problem during and following the COVID-19 pandemic, which made it more challenging for organizations to attract and retain highly qualified employees.[3]

In this chapter, we consider employment decisions by applicants (both potential and actual) and organizations. As we will see, sex and gender influence the decisions of both applicants and organizations.

SELF-SELECTION DECISIONS

Reactions to Jobs

As individuals seek job opportunities that fit their own characteristics, they may pursue different kinds of jobs. Differences in women's and men's desired jobs could occur if the gender socialization processes described in Chapter 3 lead individuals to prefer jobs that are consistent with the appropriate gender stereotype and role. The sex segregation of occupations further reinforces individuals' preference for jobs that mirror the appropriate gender stereotype and role. In this section, we explore sex similarities and differences in preferences for job attributes, work activities, and occupations.

Job attribute preferences refer to the extent to which an individual views different qualities and outcomes of paid work as desirable. Job attributes represent general characteristics of jobs such as working hours, geographical location, advancement opportunities, salary, benefits, relationships with coworkers, and opportunities for using skills and abilities. Preferences for job attributes are most important to job seekers at the beginning of the job search process and play a lesser role in actual job choice decisions, when organizational factors such as recruitment practices and reputation are more important.[4]

Sex differences in job attribute preferences have been prevalent but are diminishing, at least among college students. In past research on students, many of the sex differences that were present aligned with gender roles and stereotypes. For example, women were more concerned with job attributes that allow them to meet demands of the homemaker role (e.g., good hours and a short commute) than men. The opportunity for positive interpersonal relations (e.g., working with people, opportunity to help others, and opportunity to make friends) was especially important to women. In contrast, men considered salary, autonomy, the opportunity to exercise leadership and power, challenging work, and promotion opportunities as more important than women. However, in more recent research, sex similarities have outweighed sex differences in job attribute preferences among college students. Among employed individuals, the availability of flexible work schedules continues to be more important to women than men.[5]

Job attribute preferences may be influenced by the nature of one's family structure. For example, women who are mothers value flexibility more than childless women. Married men who are fathers value income and advancement more than single, childless men. The influence of family structure on individuals' careers and workplace experiences is discussed further in Chapter 8.[6]

Men and women differ in their **work activity preferences**. Generally, these differences are consistent with gender stereotypes and roles. For example, women tend to be more interested in work activities that involve people (e.g., taking care of people, performing community service), whereas men tend to be more interested in work activities that involve things (e.g., working with computers, machines, or tools). Further, sex differences in preferences are substantial and are likely to persist for years to come. It is worth noting that activity preferences may vary across sex and race subgroups. For instance, compared to White men, Black men are more likely to be interested in activities that involve people, perhaps because socialization experiences have exposed them to Black men in these roles or because of limited opportunities in the labor market.[7]

Sex differences in **occupational preferences** are also of interest. As the labor force participation of women increased in the second half of the 20th century, young women became more interested in pursuing male-intensive occupations. However, young men did not show a corresponding increased interest in pursuing female-intensive occupations. As a result, sex differences in occupational preferences have diminished somewhat but still remain.[8]

Why might individuals prefer occupations that are regarded as appropriate for members of their sex? Gender socialization processes certainly contribute to sex differences in occupational preferences. The sex segregation of occupations, described in Chapter 2, may also lead job seekers to restrict their occupational choices. Unless they have information to the contrary, most people assume that the individuals who work in a particular occupation possess the personal characteristics needed for success in that occupation. Thus, women are assumed to possess the attributes needed in female-intensive jobs, whereas men are assumed to possess attributes appropriate for male-intensive jobs. People also believe that success in female-intensive jobs requires feminine traits, whereas success in male-intensive jobs requires masculine traits.[9] The notion that success in an occupation dominated by one sex requires the personal characteristics associated with that sex is likely to have a chilling effect on job seekers of a different sex. Job seekers may believe that they cannot succeed in occupations in which they are outnumbered and consequently look elsewhere for employment. Both women and men suffer in some way when they restrict their occupational choices to those that seem suitable for members of their sex. However, women are more likely to suffer financially because female-intensive occupations pay less than male-intensive occupations.[10]

Of course, occupations are segregated by race, not only sex. Job seekers may have little exposure to occupations where members of their sex and race subgroups are underrepresented and may view them as inaccessible. For instance, as shown in Table 2.5, Asian men are overrepresented in lucrative STEM (science, technology, engineering, and mathematics) occupations compared to their representation in the United States (U.S.) labor force and should see these occupations as highly suitable choices. Other sex and race subgroups are underrepresented in these occupations and are less likely to see these occupations as suited to them.[11]

In summary, sex differences in preferences for job attributes, work activities, and occupations persist. As individuals make choices about the kind of work they would like to do, they are influenced by their own socialization experiences and by the distribution of male and female workers across occupations. Overall, individuals tend to seek jobs that are viewed as appropriate for members of their sex, thereby reinforcing the sex segregation of the workforce.

Reactions to Organizations

Sex differences in self-selection decisions may also be due to differences in women's and men's reactions to organizations. Human resource management programs and practices serve as signals for underlying organizational values. Job seekers use these signals to assess the fit between their own values and those of the organization. For women and people of color, initiatives such as diversity and work–family programs may be important signals concerning the value that the organization places on maintaining a diverse workforce and the likelihood of their own fit within the organization. Recruiter demographics and recruitment practices serve as further signals about working conditions in the organization.[12]

Inclusive diversity cultures make it easier for organizations to attract applicants. Although organizations that declare their commitment to diversity in recruitment advertisements increase their attractiveness to all job seekers, women and people of color pay particularly close attention to a prospective employer's diversity management practices. For instance, policies concerning affirmative action and the promotion of women and people of color into the managerial and executive ranks are more important to women and people of color. Female and Black college students are especially likely to express a desire to work for a company that has a balance of female and male managers and is racially diverse. However, if prospective applicants learn that a company is displaying counterfeit gender diversity—exaggerated images of gender diversity in its recruitment materials compared with its actual gender diversity—they are likely to perceive the company as insincere and view it as a less attractive employer; women are particularly sensitive to displays of counterfeit gender diversity. Further, if applicants who accept job offers eventually find that the organizational culture is not as diverse or inclusive as advertised, stated diversity policies may backfire. Inclusive diversity cultures are discussed at greater length in Chapter 9.[13]

The presence of **family-friendly programs** such as flextime, reduced hours, and on-site day care also seems to increase organizational attractiveness for all employees. Even individuals who pursue traditional career paths prefer flexible organizations that allow all workers to balance work and family. Flexible organizations may be favored because they are seen as more humane and modern. Also, as individuals devote more time to child rearing and household activities, they seek jobs with organizations that provide more flexibility. Because gender socialization may lead women to emphasize family roles to a greater extent than men, family-friendly programs may be especially attractive to women. The wide variety of family-friendly programs that organizations may offer are discussed in detail in Chapter 8.[14]

The **recruiter's sex** may differentially affect men's and women's evaluations of the organization's attractiveness. For instance, applicants may see job opportunities as less attractive when they are interviewed by female rather than male recruiters because women typically have less power than men in organizations. In addition, **sex similarity** between the job seeker and the recruiter may affect the job seeker's attraction to the organization. Sex similarity may lead to perceived similarity in attitudes and values, which in turn leads to interpersonal attraction or liking and more positive evaluations of the other party. Sex similarity may also enhance communication between the applicant and the recruiter. Because individuals are more open to influence from similar others, applicants may be more easily sold on a job by same-sex than by opposite-sex recruiters. The presence of a same-sex recruiter may also serve as a signal that individuals similar to the job seeker are valued at the organization.[15]

Recruitment practices may also influence reactions to organizations. A classic study obtained rich evidence on this issue from intensive interviews with undergraduate and graduate students throughout their job searches. In the interviews, the researchers tried to understand why students pursued or rejected job opportunities. Despite the fact that the researchers asked no questions about sex discrimination, half of the women in their sample mentioned a negative experience that might be a sign of such discrimination. For instance, in face-to-face interviews, corporate representatives commented on women's personal appearance or told them that they would not advance as fast as men. In addition, when students described why they became more negative or positive about particular organizations during their job searches, women were much more likely than men to cite their interactions with recruiters and other organizational representatives. Given the negative experiences of women in this study, it was not surprising that their evaluations of job opportunities were more affected by their interactions with organizational representatives.[16]

Recruitment practices can be demeaning to women in other ways. For example, use of so-called terms of endearment such as *honey, sweetie,* or *dear* by organizational representatives in interviews can turn off female applicants, as can reliance on gender-exclusive language such as *he* and *him* in describing the job and work environment. Experiencing hostile or benevolent sexism during the job search process also prompts negative reactions among female applicants. Women, including women of color who interview for jobs in high-tech companies, may base their decisions on whether to remain in the hiring process with a particular organization on their interactions with its representatives. If these interactions are negative, they may have long-lasting effects such that the women never consider another job in the organization again, even at the executive level.[17]

The use of **e-recruitment practices**, or recruitment practices conducted online, has expanded greatly in recent years. E-recruitment practices range from the simple posting of job opportunities online to live video interviews between applicants and organizational representatives to automated job interviews in which applicants are fed questions by an artificial intelligence (AI) system in a recorded interview and given a fixed time to respond to each question. In highly automated job interviews, applicants' responses, both verbal and nonverbal, may then be evaluated by AI. In general, the more highly automated and AI-based the recruitment practices, the more dehumanizing and exhausting they are for applicants, such that they feel they need to behave like robots to be understood by AI. As a result, applicants may give up on applying for jobs that require them to pass an automated job interview. Moreover, applicants are concerned about issues of fairness and equal opportunity in AI-based hiring. We would expect women and people of color to be especially concerned about these issues given the importance of organizational diversity practices to them.[18]

At the beginning of the e-recruitment process, when a job opportunity is posted online, the posting may include a short video or written information about the job. The language used in online job postings may be gendered and influence who applies for the job. For example, a study found that when a male recruiter in a video used stereotypically masculine terminology (e.g., determined) compared to stereotypically feminine terminology (e.g., sociable) in describing the job requirements, female college students were less likely to apply for the job; sex differences in intentions to apply for the job disappeared when the recruiter in the video was female. However, if a posting specifies job requirements (e.g., emotional stability) that female applicants believe will prompt recruiters' negative stereotypes of women (e.g., highly emotional), prospective female applicants may be turned off, especially if they are highly qualified and have other job opportunities that seem more attractive. Thus, the wording of job advertisements as well as the sex of the recruiter who is describing the job online may influence the sex composition and quality of the applicant pool.[19]

In summary, human resource management programs and practices differentially affect men's and women's attraction to job opportunities. Although most job seekers view organizations with inclusive diversity cultures and family-friendly programs in a positive light, these characteristics are especially important to women and people of color. Women are more likely to experience offensive behavior in their interactions with organizational representatives in person, and they are more likely to be negatively influenced in their reactions to organizations by online job descriptions that use terminology associated with gender stereotypes. As a result, interpersonal interactions and the wording of job advertisements are more important in women's than in men's job choice decisions. Overall, these findings suggest that organizations that want to attract the best available talent need to consider the signals conveyed by their diversity and work–family initiatives and their recruitment practices, whether conducted in person or online.

Job Search Behavior

Sex differences in **job search behavior** also influence the kinds of jobs that men and women obtain. According to traditional gender roles, men, as the primary wage earners in heterosexual households, should work harder at finding employment than women. Because men tend to have fewer household responsibilities, they have more time available to devote to their job searches. Indeed, a meta-analysis of the job search efforts of job seekers found that women spend less time searching for jobs than do men. Individuals who put more effort into their job search behavior are likely to receive more job offers and higher-status jobs.[20]

Men and women also differ in the methods they use to find jobs. Job search methods may be formal or informal. **Formal job search methods** include obtaining referrals from employment agencies, labor unions, and school placement officers, responding to "help wanted" ads on the internet and in social and print media, and sending résumés to employers. **Informal job search methods** consist of referrals from networks of friends, family members, professors, and business associates. Regarding formal methods, men are more likely to obtain jobs by sending résumés, whereas women are more likely to obtain jobs by scanning "help wanted" ads. Women and men do not differ in their use of informal job search methods. However, many individuals who find new jobs are not even actively engaged in job searches. Instead, they fall into jobs that they hear about informally from their social networks.[21]

Men's and women's **networks** differ substantially, and these differences may impact the success of their job searches. Traditionally, women have had networks that are more concentrated in the local community and comprising friends and relatives than are men's, perhaps because of women's greater domestic responsibilities and lower-status positions. In contrast, men have had more geographically dispersed networks containing a greater number of business contacts and high-status individuals. When men and women have used their networks to identify desirable jobs, they tend to rely on same-sex contacts; women find out about jobs from other women, and men find out about jobs from other men, with White men benefiting the most. Same-sex contacts restrict the jobs known to women compared to those known to men, funneling them to female-intensive jobs in their local communities with less status and lower pay than male-intensive jobs. Moreover, even when female job seekers' networks include higher-status male contacts, the benefits they receive from these contacts is less than the benefits received by male job seekers with similar contacts. White men are most likely to benefit from high-status contacts compared with members of other sex and race subgroups. As a result, women may benefit less from their social networks during the job search process.[22]

However, the increased use of **e-networks** has changed the nature of the networking process. E-networking reduces barriers to making contacts by eliminating the constraint of geographical proximity; there is no need to be introduced formally and physically meet to launch interactions with an e-network contact. As a result, women, who have been traditionally excluded from "good old boy" networks that meet in person, have more different-sex contacts in their e-networks than men do, which facilitates their having shorter job searches and attaining higher initial salaries.[23]

Also, women and men exhibit both similarity and differences in how they make use of networks during their job searches. For example, a study of job-seeking MBA students who reached out to school alumni found that both male and female MBAs engaged in *schmoozing* (socializing to build relationships with key others that will contribute to professional success) to learn about industries, identify job leads, obtain referrals, and the like. In addition, female MBAs engaged in *scouting* (gathering information about employers and career options to have the best chance for professional success) with other women to learn about gender dynamics in firms, organizational support for parenting, and the like; these women wanted to make sure that potential employers would give them a fair chance at succeeding professionally before applying for a job.[24]

Once they decide to apply for jobs, women and men differ in how they manage their **self-presentation** in application materials. For example, a study found that women used less feminine language to describe themselves and their interests in cover letters and résumés when applying for male-intensive jobs than when applying for female-intensive jobs, with the goal of heading off potential sex discrimination in male-intensive work settings. However, this strategy appeared to backfire for women, as they were less likely to receive a job offer for a male-dominated job when they used it. In contrast, men's use of language in application materials was consistent across male-intensive and female-intensive jobs. As a result, women (but not men) were managing whether they were seen in gender-stereotypical terms depending on the sex segregation of the job, but their self-presentation strategy yielded negative rather than positive results.[25]

Once they hold jobs, men and women differ in the strategies they use to obtain new jobs and the benefits derived from their chosen strategy. Women often adopt an **internal labor market strategy**, seeking promotions and earnings growth within a single organization. In contrast, men tend to use an **external labor market strategy**, seeking advancement by searching for jobs with new employers while continuing to work for their present employers. Because using an external labor market strategy increases individuals' compensation more than using an internal labor market strategy, sex differences in the strategy used contribute to the pay differential between men and women. Moreover, even when women seek external employment, it yields them little benefit. White men are the primary beneficiaries of an external labor market strategy. Women and people of color who change companies do not increase their pay compared to those who stay with their companies, perhaps because of discrimination in employment systems.[26]

When negotiating with potential employers about job opportunities, sex differences in job seekers' **salary expectations** may lead to sex differences in actual wages. Because women expect and accept less pay than men, they request and receive less pay in their salary negotiations than men in equivalent positions. For almost all occupations, young women have lower expectations regarding both their entry-level salary and their salary at the peaks of their careers than do young men. The sex difference in salary expectations is especially striking for male-intensive occupations. It occurs even when individuals estimate a fair salary for a particular job. Compared to men, women actually see lower pay as "fair pay."[27]

Several factors account for sex differences in salary expectations. First, women's lower salary expectations may be realistic. As victims of past discrimination in salary decisions, women simply may have lower standards. Second, as noted in our discussion of sex differences in job attribute preferences, salary is more important to men than to women. Women appear to be less concerned about salary and more concerned about other aspects of work, such as interpersonal relations. Third, men and women use different reference groups in determining salary expectations. Women typically base their salary expectations on the salaries of other women, whereas men base their salary expectations on the salaries of other men. Because men are likely to be more highly paid, this tendency may lead to sex differences in salary expectations favoring men, which in turn become a self-fulfilling prophecy. Further, women have been consistently found in studies to fare worse than men in salary negotiations, which contributes to their receiving lower salaries when they begin new jobs.[28]

Thus, differences in women's and men's job search methods contribute to differences in the jobs available to them and the salaries they receive. Men devote more time to their searches. As a result, men identify more and better job opportunities, although this sex difference may be reduced by the increased use of e-networking. Further, even when men and women find equivalent jobs, women's salaries may be lower. Compared to men, women are less likely to obtain wage increases by changing employers. Women appear to have lower pay expectations than men in the same occupation, putting them at a disadvantage when negotiating salaries.

In summary, male and female job seekers make different self-selection decisions regarding employment. They differ in their preferences for job attributes, work activities, and occupations in ways that contribute to the continued sex segregation of the workplace. Women and people of color are more influenced by the organization's human resource management programs and practices; policies that emphasize managing diversity and balancing work–family are especially attractive to women. Also, women are more attracted to organizations when they view selection practices as fair and have positive, nondiscriminatory interactions with organizational representatives. Finally, sex differences in job search behavior contribute to the employment of women in jobs that are lower paid than those of men.

ORGANIZATIONAL SELECTION DECISIONS

How and When Does Sex Discrimination Occur?

To understand how and when sex discrimination occurs in organizational selection decisions, it is helpful to examine how these decisions are made. Organizational decision makers use a matching process to assess applicants. Decision makers form **mental prototypes** (images of the ideal applicant). These prototypes define the traits and behaviors that are required for success in a particular job. As decision makers evaluate applicants, they favor the applicant whose attributes come closest to matching this prototype, especially if they expect to work collaboratively with the individual who is hired.[29]

Sex discrimination may arise from decision makers' prototypes of the ideal applicant. These prototypes may include traits that are specifically linked to a specific sex. When the tasks required for job performance are mostly masculine, men will be seen as more likely to succeed. For example, if the requirements for a managerial position emphasize stereotypically masculine behaviors such as making tough decisions or competing for scarce resources, decision makers' prototypes for the position will tend to emphasize masculine traits, with male applicants assumed to be better suited for the job and female applicants needing to work harder at demonstrating masculine traits to be seen as suitable. On the other hand, if the prototype for a job emphasizes feminine traits (e.g., childcare worker), female applicants will be assumed to be more suitable.[30]

In some cases, decision makers' prototypes explicitly specify the sex of the jobholder. When job incumbents or job applicants are predominantly from one sex, organizational decision makers' prototypes may specify the sex of the ideal applicant; applicants whose sex matches the prototype will be seen as more qualified and will be favored in the selection process. Among applicants for female-intensive jobs, female applicants are likely to be rated as more qualified, offered higher starting salaries and more challenging job assignments, and hired more often than males. In contrast, male applicants are likely to be preferred over females for male-intensive jobs. Decision makers do not hire blatantly unqualified applicants of the "correct" sex over highly qualified applicants of the "wrong" sex. However, they may hire moderately qualified applicants of the correct sex over slightly more qualified applicants of a different sex.[31]

An example from the restaurant industry demonstrates the use of sex as an explicit element of decision makers' ideal applicant prototypes. Imagine going to the most elegant restaurant in a large city to celebrate your birthday. This particular birthday is a significant milestone, and you are sparing no expense to enjoy an incredible dining experience. Look around the restaurant. What sex are the servers? They are probably mostly or entirely male. Now, imagine going to a less expensive restaurant such as the nearest sandwich shop. What sex are the servers? They are probably mostly female. A possible explanation for this phenomenon is that women prefer the limited tips earned in inexpensive restaurants and men prefer the more generous tips in expensive restaurants. Another is that men are more qualified to serve expensive food and women more qualified to serve inexpensive food. A more likely explanation is that managers of expensive restaurants possess ideal applicant prototypes that specify that servers should be male, whereas managers of inexpensive restaurants have prototypes that specify that servers should be female.

One study suggested that this is indeed the case. In the study, two male and two female students in an undergraduate economics course applied for jobs as servers at selected high-priced and low-priced restaurants in Philadelphia. One male and one female student would drop off an equivalent résumé at each restaurant. When a job offer was made to one of the two students, male students received the majority of offers from high-priced restaurants and female students received the majority of offers from low-priced restaurants. Thus, male applicants were preferred at expensive restaurants and female applicants were preferred at inexpensive restaurants. The preference for male servers at high-priced restaurants seemed to be due to the managers' beliefs about the preferences of patrons in these restaurants, who were more likely to be male than patrons in low-priced restaurants. Restaurant managers, regardless of their own sex, prefer servers whose sex matches patrons' expectations. Thus, their ideal applicant prototypes specify the sex of the jobholder.[32]

Sex discrimination based on mental prototypes may smolder inside the restaurant kitchen as well. As noted in Chapter 2, chefs and head cooks work in a male-intensive occupation (22.8% female). Prominent female chefs have reported that their industry is not comfortable with a woman in charge of food preparation. Female chefs are often insulted or ignored by male chefs in the main kitchen. As a result, they often gravitate toward being in charge of pastries, a more traditionally female area of expertise. Sex discrimination even affects who owns restaurants. Female restaurant owners have a harder time attracting investors and securing funding for their businesses than their male counterparts.[33]

Although our examples from the restaurant industry focus solely on the role of sex in prototypes of the ideal applicant, decision makers' prototypes sometimes include both the sex and race of the job holder. White and Asian males, for instance, may be favored in prototypes for high-tech occupations because of their overrepresentation in these roles. Similarly, because Black women historically have been overrepresented in low-status food service and cleaning roles, decision makers' prototypes may link Black women to these roles, thereby limiting their employment opportunities. Discrimination across sex and race subgroups may also occur when interviewers apply their prototypes of job holders to applicants of different races. Applicant race may affect decision makers' evaluations of applicants' masculinity and femininity, leading to differences in whether decision makers view applicants as suited for male-intensive and female-intensive jobs. A study of the effects of sex and race on perceptions of the masculinity, femininity, and hirability of applicants for male-intensive (i.e., security guard) and female-intensive (i.e., librarian) positions support this idea. Compared to Asian and White women, Black women were seen as higher in masculinity and lower in femininity. As a result, Black women tended to be seen as a better fit for the male-intensive security guard position than other women; they were also seen as slightly less suited for the female-intensive librarian position. Compared to Black and White men, Asian men tended to be seen as more feminine and less masculine. As a result, they were seen less suited for the security guard position and more suited for the librarian position than the other men.[34]

Sex discrimination also arises in the selection process because decision makers have a general tendency to devalue the qualifications of female applicants. In society, individuals are assigned status or esteem based on the demographic groups to which they belong. White people and men are typically ascribed higher status than people of color and women, with sex and race intersecting with other dimensions of diversity such as socioeconomic class to influence status assignments. Judgments of individuals' task competence are based, in part, on the status assigned to members of their demographic group. Individuals who belong to high-status groups are viewed as more competent than those of low-status groups. Because females are typically ascribed less status or esteem in society, they are generally seen as less competent than men. Although the exact level of competence assigned to women differs by race, decision makers typically believe that women are less qualified than men. As a result, male applicants are valued more than identically qualified female applicants. Moreover, to be seen as qualified, female applicants must provide more evidence of their ability than similarly qualified male applicants.[35]

Further, decision makers may hold stereotypical assumptions about women's lack of commitment to their careers. Women must be overqualified to counter the assumption that they are not committed to their work. One recent experimental study found that women were viewed as more hirable when they were overqualified rather than sufficiently qualified. In contrast, men were viewed as more hirable when they were sufficiently qualified rather than overqualified. Raters interpreted women's and men's qualifications differently. Women's overqualifications were viewed as a signal of commitment to careers and firms, while men's overqualifications were seen as a signal that they might leave the firm for other opportunities.[36]

Finally, sex discrimination may occur when the situation calls attention to the sex of the applicant. When applicant sex is highly conspicuous, decision makers are likely to access their gender stereotypes and status judgments, thereby increasing the chance of sex discrimination. Numerous factors increase the conspicuousness of applicants' sex. Applicants' sex is likely to be conspicuous when decision makers encounter applicants whose sex is atypical among applicants or job incumbents. A striking demonstration of the importance of the conspicuousness of applicant sex comes from a classic study on the effect of screens on sex discrimination in the selection decisions made by major symphony orchestras. Elite symphonies historically have discriminated against female musicians. Not so long ago, women's dressing rooms in symphony halls were rare because there were few women (if any) in the orchestra. When female musicians are underrepresented in major symphonies, sex is likely to be an explicit aspect of decision makers' prototypes of the ideal applicant, and applicant sex is likely to be conspicuous. The use of screens in orchestra auditions reduced the conspicuousness of applicant sex; in fact, it made applicant sex invisible. As a result, using screens considerably increased the likelihood of a female musician being selected for the orchestra. This study reinforces the notion that the conspicuousness of applicant sex is an important factor in determining whether sex discrimination occurs.[37]

Even if selection strategies such as use of screens in orchestra auditions are adopted, sex discrimination may still arise if applicant sex is conspicuous in the initial phase of the selection process. A different study of selection decisions by professional orchestras in Germany is illustrative. Applicants for orchestra positions first submitted a written application, and then selected applicants were invited to audition behind screens. Women composed less than 30% of all musicians in German orchestras. Also, women were more likely to play string instruments and less likely to play brass instruments. (Next time you attend a symphony concert, notice who is playing the harp compared with the trumpet or clarinet.) Women were discriminated against in decisions about which applicants to invite for auditions, but they had an equal chance for men to get a job once they were granted the opportunity to perform in a blind audition. Even though the use of screens accomplished its intended purpose of reducing discrimination at the final hiring stage of the selection process, sex discrimination was still present in decisions at the invitation stage because women's low proportions in German orchestras made applicant sex conspicuous.[38]

In most cases, the processes described here operate at an unconscious level. Most decision makers do not say to themselves, "Women simply aren't qualified for this job" or "I will act on my belief in gender stereotypes in evaluating applicants" or "I must hire a man for this position because this job is usually filled by men." However, some decision makers may consciously use what they believe are other peoples' biases as the basis for their decisions about applicants. If they think, for example, that employees or customers will feel uncomfortable with a female engineer or a male nurse, they may defer to that attitude in their hiring decisions even if they do not share it. Thus, elegant restaurants may hire primarily male servers because they believe that their patrons prefer to be waited on by male servers. Discrimination on the basis of customer preferences is illegal, as we discuss further in Chapter 9, but it does occur.

Our attention in this section has been on the how and when of sex discrimination in organizational selection decisions. Mental prototypes of decision makers play a large role in such decisions. These prototypes are most likely to lead to sex discrimination in decisions when job applicants or current jobholders are predominantly from one sex, the traits seen as required for the job are either stereotypically masculine or feminine, and applicant sex is highly conspicuous. Also, there is a general tendency to devalue the qualifications of female applicants.

Who and What Discriminates Against Whom?

Whether sex discrimination occurs in organizational selection decisions may be influenced by personal characteristics of decision makers as well as personal characteristics of applicants. It may also be influenced by whether decisions are made by real, live people or an AI system. Thus, it is important to examine who and what discriminates against whom.

Decision makers' **endorsement of gender stereotypes** is especially important in determining whether they discriminate against women in the hiring process. Individuals who endorse gender stereotypes are most likely to engage in sex discrimination. However, even individuals who refrain from gender stereotyping may engage in discrimination because of the deep-rooted tendency to evaluate male applicants more favorably than female applicants.[39]

Decision makers' sex may influence the nature of the criteria used to make organizational selection decisions. For example, a study of selection decisions in STEM occupations found that male decision makers regarded working long hours (a criterion that tends to favor males) as more important, whereas female decision makers placed greater importance on problem-solving ability (a more sex-neutral criterion). As a result, the male decision makers were more likely to hire male applicants, a trend that perpetuates STEM occupations as male intensive.[40]

Decision makers' sex may also affect the demographic composition of the applicant pool. A study of data from job applicants for faculty positions at a large U.S. university found that search committees chaired by men and composed of greater proportions of men yielded applicant pools that had lower proportion of females than search committees chaired by women and composed of greater proportions of women. Compared to female decision makers, male decision makers failed to take active steps (e.g., disseminating job advertisements to inclusive networks) to reach out to a more diverse set of applicants.[41]

Sex similarity between the interviewer and applicant may affect the likelihood of discrimination. As noted earlier, sex similarity may enhance their mutual liking and facilitate communication in the interview. As a result, applicants in same-sex interviews may share more information about themselves, thereby providing interviewers with a better understanding of what they have to offer. In addition, increased liking may lead interviewers to conduct more positive interviews and focus on positive information when forming their judgments of applicants. These effects of sex similarity may even apply to situations in which organizational representatives are simply evaluating résumés or applications. However, sex similarity or race similarity effects may diminish when structured employment interviews are used to evaluate applicants. Structured interviews are based on a comprehensive analysis of the job requirements, ask similar questions of all applicants, and use predetermined scales to evaluate applicants' responses. Such interviews reduce discrimination by increasing the amount of information about applicants' qualifications.[42]

Sex discrimination as well as race discrimination may enter into organizational selection decisions if the decision maker is an AI system used in an **e-selection** process. Although we might hope that the use of AI systems rather than human decision makers would eradicate bias in organizational selection decisions, a study of AI systems used by organizations found that 44% of the systems engaged in sex discrimination and 34% engaged in both sex and race discrimination. Why do these kinds of discrimination occur in AI systems? Consider who is designing the systems: White males in high-tech companies. The occupations of software developer (81% male, 55% White) and computer programmer (80% male, 68% White), comprising the people most likely to be specifying and coding AI systems, are both male intensive and the occupation of computer programmer is White intensive. Because the AI system designers are human, their design decisions may reflect their conscious or unconscious biases.[43]

Sex-based and race-based biases, as well as the intersection of the two, may enter into design decisions about AI systems used as part of an e-selection process in several ways. For example, at the first stage of the e-selection process, AI systems influence what ads are delivered to potential applicants about job opportunities on social networking sites, online job posting sites, and elsewhere. Designing AI systems that deliver job ads in a gender-neutral manner is likely to be difficult. In one recent study, an AI system that was explicitly designed to be gender-neutral in delivering ads for STEM careers did not achieve that goal. The system, which was also focused on minimizing costs, delivered fewer ads to women than men because women, especially young women, are a highly attractive demographic for advertisers and are more expensive to reach.[44]

At later stages, AI systems influence what data are collected about actual applicants, how AI-collected data are analyzed to determine evaluations of applicants, and how AI-generated evaluations are used to make organizational selection decisions. As a result, built-in biases of AI systems may influence which applicants advance through the e-selection process at various stages and ultimately receive job offers. For instance, Amazon developed an AI system for evaluating applicants' résumés that was based on a decade of résumés from applicants for technology jobs at the company. Because most of the résumés that were used to train the system came from men, the resulting system gave lower evaluations to women's résumés. It downgraded résumés that contained the word *women*, resulting in lower scores for graduates of women's colleges. The system also attached higher values to words such as *executed* and *captured*, which appeared more often in men's résumés. Although system designers tried to correct these flaws, the algorithm found other ways to devalue women's résumés.[45]

Sex discrimination may also be the result of decision makers' reactions to applicants' **physical attractiveness**. Even though assessments of attractiveness are highly subjective, people generally agree across cultures on who is attractive and who is not. They also agree that "what is beautiful is good." Attractive children and adults are judged and treated more positively than unattractive children and adults, even by people who know them. The preference for attractive applicants applies when digital avatars are used to represent applicants in computer-mediated interviews; applicants with more attractive avatars receive more favorable interview ratings. Further, attractive adults, especially men, are judged as being more competent—even when they are not actually more competent—than unattractive adults. In job interviews, physically attractive applicants are seen as more likable and ultimately as more suitable for hiring. However, the benefits of attractiveness may be limited for women. Although attractive women are more likely than unattractive women to get a job in which job incumbents are predominantly male, attractive men still have the advantage in getting the job.[46]

Applicants' attractiveness may be judged in many ways. First, their **facial attractiveness** may be judged in general, with more facially attractive applicants, especially men, receiving higher interview ratings. It may also be judged on whether they display an **older facial appearance**. One study found that applicants with older-appearing faces in photographs on résumés, regardless of how old they actually were, were judged as worse fits for the job and were less likely to be hired than applicants with younger-appearing faces. This may be because older-appearing applicants were judged to be less healthy and physically fit. It may also be because of ageism (prejudice directed toward older workers). In this case, the prejudice is directed toward older-*appearing* applicants, not necessarily older applicants.[47]

Further, age-related facial appearance may intersect with sex in judgments of facial attractiveness, such that women with older-appearing faces are judged as less attractive and worthy of being hired for a job than men with older-appearing faces. Recall the quote from the study of Hollywood movie stars described in Chapter 2: "Men's well-worn faces are thought to convey maturity, character, and experience. A woman's face, on the other hand, is valued for appearing young." Any disadvantage in hiring decisions for having an older-appearing face, whether outside or inside Hollywood, is likely to be experienced more by women than men.[48]

Obesity, a highly visible characteristic that affects judgments of attractiveness, also intersects with sex in organizational selection decisions. Although people have little control over their general level of attractiveness, they are expected to exert control over their body weight. Obese or simply overweight individuals are stereotyped as being lazier, less conscientious, less attentive to their personal hygiene, and less emotionally stable than their "normal weight" counterparts, even though there is little supporting evidence. Biases against hiring overweight applicants are particularly strong for women. In other words, a "thinness is good" standard is applied more to female applicants than to male applicants.[49]

Female applicants with a **visible pregnancy** also experience discrimination in selection decisions. An intriguing experimental study was conducted in which women played the role of either an applicant who is visibly pregnant, simulated by wearing a prosthesis to make her appear to be seven or eight months pregnant, or an applicant who is not visibly pregnant (called "nonpregnant"). The study found that visibly pregnant applicants received lower hiring recommendations than nonpregnant applicants who were equally qualified. Biases in selection decisions on the basis of pregnancy violate the U.S. Pregnancy Discrimination Act as well as laws in many other countries. They provide evidence of sex discrimination when women's appearance indicates that they are about to become mothers. They place applicants whose appearance is less indicative of their pregnancy in the uncomfortable position of having to decide whether to disclose it or not in the hiring process. Further, perceived pregnancy discrimination has a negative impact on mother and baby health. Of course, because men cannot get pregnant, anti-pregnancy biases contribute to sex discrimination on the basis of pregnancy only against women.[50]

In summary, sex discrimination in organizational selection decisions is highly complex and varies as a function of characteristics of the decision makers (e.g., endorsement of gender stereotypes, decision makers' sex), situation (e.g., sex similarity of applicant and interviewer and conspicuousness of applicant sex), and applicants (e.g., physical appearance, weight, and visible pregnancy). Also, sex discrimination in organizational selection decisions is not restricted to decisions made by people; AI systems also discriminate. We do not fully understand how and when such discrimination occurs and who or what is discriminating against whom. However, we certainly know enough to conclude that organizations need to guard against it.

IMPROVING EMPLOYMENT DECISIONS

We have painted a picture of how job seekers make self-selection decisions that often exhibit sex differences and how organizations make selection decisions that often discriminate on the basis of sex. In this section, we consider (1) what individual job seekers can do to improve their prospects for attaining a satisfying and rewarding job and (2) what organizations can do to improve their recruitment activities and selection decisions. Table 4.1 and Table 4.2 summarize recommended actions for individuals and organizations respectively.

TABLE 4.1 ■ Recommended Actions for Individuals

1. Engage in self-exploration activities to identify your preferred occupations and job attributes.
2. Use a broad range of job search methods, both formal and informal.
3. Be prepared to make good impressions in your job interviews.
4. Engage in practice interviews of all types.
5. Do research on potential employers before you contact them.
6. Select the job that best matches your preferred job attributes.
7. Be ready to negotiate your starting salary when you take a job.

TABLE 4.2 ■ Recommended Actions for Organizations

1. Send a message in promotional materials to school systems that members of all groups belong in all occupations.
2. Publicize employees who hold jobs that are atypical for their sex.
3. Develop job descriptions that include the full range of activities associated with the job.
4. Seek applicants from multiple sources.
5. Screen decision makers to determine whether they endorse gender and racial stereotypes.
6. Train decision makers to avoid biased decisions and discriminatory behavior in selection practices.
7. Formalize and standardize practices used in selection decisions.
8. Assess the effectiveness of all selection practices.
9. Reward recruiter effectiveness based on long-term results.
10. Promote an inclusive diversity culture and offer family-friendly programs to enhance organizational attractiveness.

Improving Self-Selection Decisions

Although organizational selection practices have a great impact on the jobs that individuals obtain, individuals can increase the likelihood of obtaining a satisfying and rewarding job by devoting substantial attention to identifying their own interests and to conducting job searches. First, job seekers should engage in self-exploration exercises to identify preferred occupations and job attributes. Career counselors, often available at universities and high schools, may be helpful in this process. Individuals should identify preferred activities and then determine the occupations that will allow them to pursue these activities. Given the influence of sex segregation of work on occupational preferences, job seekers need to ensure that they do not unnecessarily limit their options to occupations that are dominated by members of their own sex. For instance, females with an interest in medicine might consider becoming surgeons, and males with an interest in medicine might explore careers in nursing. Job seekers also should rank their own preferences for specific job attributes. Making such a list clarifies the specific kinds of positions within an occupation that may be suitable for the individual.

Second, job seekers need to devote considerable time and effort to their job searches and use a broad range of job search methods, both formal and informal. This will allow them to identify more and better alternatives from which to choose. Informal referrals are especially important in the job search process. Women may have fewer business contacts than do men and thereby may need to make special efforts to establish a broader range of social contacts. For instance, women as well as men should consider joining professional associations and e-networks of professionals to increase the diversity and breadth of their contacts.

Third, applicants should be prepared to make good impressions in their interviews, however the interviews may be conducted. Applicants who make greater use of **impression management tactics** such as expressed fit with the organization (e.g., stating interest in the position and enthusiasm for working for this organization) and self-promotion (e.g., making positive statements about oneself, one's past accomplishments, or one's future plans) are more likely to receive positive recruiter evaluations in job interviews and invitations for follow-up site visits. To reduce the chances of stereotyping, job seekers should provide as much information as possible to potential employers about their qualifications. Applicants need to make known their positive qualities, both in their submitted credentials (e.g., résumé, job application) and in their interactions with organizational representatives.[51]

Fourth, applicants benefit from attending job interview training classes and engaging in practice interviews. In-person interviews for a simulated job opportunity can be conducted with another class member playing the role of an organizational recruiter as part of a structured exercise that gives applicants an opportunity to receive feedback on the effectiveness of their impression management tactics.[52] Live video interviews can be conducted in the same manner over Zoom or another online tool, with the additional benefit that interviews can be recorded and played back so applicants can see their own behavior. Highly automated interviews can be simulated by having a class member feed the applicant interview questions on a screen and enforce a time limit on responses; such interviews can also be recorded and give applicants the opportunity to practice *not* acting like a robot while still being understood by an AI system.

Fifth, applicants should carefully assess the merits of each potential employer. During the initial employment interview, applicants should not expect to get much information other than whether there might be a potential match. If job seekers proceed to further discussions with an employer, they need additional information to make a good decision. Such information can be difficult to obtain, but it is available if the right questions are asked at the right time of the right people in a sensitive manner. It may be worthwhile for female applicants to consider the signals provided by recruiter behavior, as well as the presence of an inclusive diversity culture and availability of family-friendly programs, in evaluating the extent to which women are valued by the organization.

Finally, applicants should select the job that best matches their preferred job attributes and be ready to negotiate a starting salary. All job seekers should become informed about actual salary levels for the jobs that they are seeking. This is particularly important for women, who tend to have lower salary expectations that become self-fulfilling prophecies, as discussed earlier.

Improving Organizational Selection Decisions

One key source of sex segregation in today's organizations is the sex difference in occupational preferences. Individuals' occupational preferences are formed at a very young age. If organizations want to lower the level of sex segregation in the workplace, they need to influence the formation of children's occupational preferences. For example, many organizations distribute materials about careers to high school guidance counselors. These materials portray women and men in a greater variety of occupations than ever before. However, high school is not the place to start. If organizations expect to have an appreciable effect on the development of occupational preferences, they need to provide information about opportunities in their industries to young children, such as by sending speakers to elementary schools, youth groups, and other places where young children congregate. The best speakers may be members of the sex least represented in the occupations being discussed or mixed-sex teams that demonstrate that both women and men belong in the occupations; a female engineer and a male nurse would be ideal speakers on opportunities in the engineering and nursing professions, respectively. Organizations also need to ensure that their websites, which may be accessed by children as well as adults, convey the message both in pictures and text that members of all groups are welcome.

Organizations also need to reduce the sex segregation of jobs in their midst and devote more attention to their procedures for attracting and selecting applicants. First, they need to reduce the perception that particular jobs are appropriate for members of one sex. Many jobs require tasks associated with both women's and men's traditional roles. The full range of activities associated with particular jobs should be included in job descriptions in ads. One study found that wording associated with gender stereotypes in online job advertisements influenced perceptions and attractiveness of the jobs. Ads for male-intensive jobs tended to make greater use of "masculine" terms (e.g., *leader, competitive*, and *dominant*) than ads for female-intensive jobs, whereas the use of "feminine" terms (e.g., *support, understand*, and *interpersonal*) did not differ across male-intensive and female-intensive jobs. When ads for jobs included greater masculine than feminine terms, women found these jobs less attractive. Thus, gendered wording in job advertisements can contribute to sustaining the sex segregation of jobs.[53]

Second, organizations need to examine how they solicit applications. Most job seekers obtain jobs through informal contacts of the same sex, and most organizations rely heavily on referrals from employees to make new hires. Organizations must ensure that reliance on referrals does not promote the sex segregation of work. They need to consider alternative sources of applicants (e.g., online advertisements, employment agencies, campus placement centers, and professional groups) if reliance on referrals is limiting the diversity of new hires. They should ensure that techniques used to solicit applicants, including e-recruitment ads, do not restrict the sex composition of the applicant pool.

Third, organizations need to screen and train recruiters and other decision makers as well as designers of AI systems used in the e-selection process. Screening should include assessments of individuals' endorsement of gender and racial stereotypes and exclude those who are likely to be biased. Training of all those involved in the selection process is critical. Given the negative experiences of female applicants in the selection process, which may be accentuated for women of color, employers need to do a better job of training the people who attract and select applicants. Organizations should train individuals to avoid discriminatory behaviors and to be aware of the potential influences of gender stereotypes and the sex segregation of work. Designers of AI-based hiring systems need to understand the potential for bias in these systems and must develop expertise that allows them to maximize the advantages of such systems while minimizing the risks.[54]

Fourth, organizations need to reduce the likelihood of sex discrimination by formalizing and standardizing selection practices. Many organizations rely primarily on employment interviews to make hiring decisions. In the traditional in-person interview, interviewers ask vague questions about applicants' opinions and attitudes, goals and aspirations, and self-evaluations. Interview judgments based on such questions are highly subjective and, as a result, are susceptible to bias from gender and racial stereotypes. Unlike symphony orchestras, most organizations cannot solve the problem by putting screens between applicants and decision makers.

However, as noted earlier, organizations can implement structured interviews that are less susceptible to bias than traditional interviews. In structured interviews, the content of the interview and the evaluation process are standardized. Specific, job-related interview questions are asked of all applicants. Further, interviewers evaluate applicants on multiple scales with well-defined descriptions anchoring each level of each scale. These structured procedures force interviewers to obtain and to process information about the applicants' qualifications in a systematic and detailed manner, thereby reducing their reliance on stereotypes. In addition, the use of multiple interviewers with different viewpoints may reduce sex discrimination by offsetting the idiosyncratic biases of a single interviewer. Even highly automated interviews can be structured by asking all applicants the same questions for the same job. A review of court cases found that organizations are more likely to win discrimination suits when they use structured interviews.[55]

Fifth, organizations need to monitor selection practices to enhance their effectiveness and ensure that sex discrimination does not occur. Many organizations do poor jobs of assessing the effectiveness of their selection decisions. Recruiter performance is seldom tied to rewards, especially for recruiters who are line managers. To assess the effectiveness of selection practices, organizations should track the performance, satisfaction, turnover rate, and subsequent success of new hires. Assessment should also include measurement of the demographic composition of the applicant pool, the demographic composition of new hires, and differences in starting salaries and initial assignments as a function of sex and race. Attention to these measures helps organizations identify potentially discriminatory selection practices. Moreover, organizations should make performance appraisals and rewards contingent on the extent to which selection practices are effective and free from bias.

The need for monitoring the effectiveness of selection practices also applies to AI systems, not only human decision makers. At each stage of the selection process, organizations need to assess whether their AI systems lead to bias based on sex and other demographic factors. Although organization's AI systems are often proprietary and nontransparent, organizations should demonstrate—perhaps through audits by third-party experts—what they are doing to mitigate bias in those systems.[56]

Finally, organizations that are serious about attracting a diverse workforce should ensure that their policies and practices are consistent with this goal. An inclusive diversity culture and family-friendly programs enhance organizational attractiveness and may keep some individuals from self-selecting out of the selection process. In particular, policies that signal the organization's commitment to diversity will help attract women and people of color.

In summary, organizations need to take actions to reduce the perception that certain jobs are appropriate for members of a particular sex, both among young people and in their own midst. They need to ensure that their hiring processes allow them to attract and select the most qualified applicants regardless of sex, race, or any other irrelevant personal characteristics.

We have described how sex and its intersection with race, age, and other dimensions of diversity may affect the decision processes of both applicants and organizations and ultimately exacerbate sex-based status differences in organizations. Some organizations and job seekers have made substantial changes in how they explore employment relationships with each other, as indicated by past improvements in the hiring practices of symphony orchestras. Unless self-selection and organizational selection practices are improved along the guidelines suggested, fundamental issues such as the sex segregation of occupations and the gendered nature of prototypes of the ideal applicant will continue to negatively impact employment decisions.

5 WORKING IN DIVERSE TEAMS

by Laura M. Graves and Gary N. Powell

LEARNING OBJECTIVES

After reading this chapter, you should be able to do the following:

5.1 Understand the distinction between the effects of sex, sex similarity, and sex diversity in mixed-sex teams.

5.2 Discuss the nature of sex effects in mixed-sex teams.

5.3 Describe the effects of sex similarity on token members' experiences in mixed-sex teams.

5.4 Summarize the optimistic and pessimistic views of sex diversity effects in teams.

5.5 Recognize the role of situational factors in emphasizing or de-emphasizing the importance of members' sex in mixed-sex teams.

5.6 Describe when technologies used in virtual teams work to women's advantage or disadvantage.

5.7 Identify actions that may be taken by organizations, team leaders, and team members to build effective mixed-sex teams.

PREVALENCE AND IMPORTANCE OF TEAMS

Today's organizations extensively use work teams to achieve their strategic objectives. Teams produce goods and provide services, design new products, solve organizational problems, lead change efforts, and even lead entire organizations. As such, teams are central to organizational success. In addition, virtual teams have become increasingly popular, with their proliferation spurred on by the COVID-19 pandemic. Due to the prevalence and importance of teams in conducting work, we have reason to consider what happens in diverse teams under different conditions, what makes diverse teams productive or unproductive, and what contributes to satisfying or dissatisfying experiences for their members.[1]

As a result of women's increased participation in the labor force, teams are more likely to include members of a different sex and have sex-related issues arise than ever before. For example, Tim Hunt, a biochemist who won the Nobel Prize in physiology or medicine, became notorious for his comments about the effects of having women as well as men in laboratory teams. In a speech at the World Conference of Science Journalists, Hunt said, "Let me tell you about my trouble with girls. Three things happen when they are in the lab: You fall in love with them, they fall in love with you, and when you criticize them, they cry." Hunt resigned his position as honorary professor at University College London after his comments unleashed a torrent of fury and sarcasm on social media. A female professor tweeted that she was unable to do her science work as she had seen a photo of Hunt and was now hopelessly in love. Another said she would be unable to chair her department's morning meeting because she was swooning and crying. Other women responded by posting photos of themselves engaged in their work as scientists with the hashtag #distractinglysexy. A male professor tweeted that Hunt had won the Nobel Prize in being a "clueless, sexist jerk—probably not his last."[2]

Tim Hunt's comments called attention to a sex difference in crying in response to negative feedback that might occur in teams. Crying is a more socially acceptable behavior for females than males, which contributes to a sex difference in actual crying behavior. So, in a sense, Hunt's comments reflected the prospect that women in laboratory teams may be more likely to cry in response to negative feedback than men. Although any professional who cries in a work setting risks being taken less seriously, an experimental study found that men received lower performance evaluations when they cried in response to criticism, whereas women's performance evaluations were unaffected by whether they cried in response to the same level of criticism. This research finding suggests that because crying violates social norms more for men than women, crying in work settings is likely to cost men more than women. If Hunt was troubled by "girls" crying in lab teams, imagine how freaked out he would be if (or when) "boys" cried in lab teams.[3]

All of which goes to show that sex-related effects in teams, like much of what we discuss in this book, are hot (i.e., inflammatory) topics. In this chapter, we review the effects of sex, sex similarity, and sex diversity in mixed-sex teams. **Sex effects** arise when men's and women's behaviors or experiences as team members differ. **Sex similarity effects** occur when team members' behavior or experiences differ as a function of the extent to which they are similar to their teammates on the basis of sex. **Sex diversity effects** arise when team cohesion and performance vary as a function of the extent to which the team is heterogeneous with respect to sex.[4] We then consider how the nature of the situations in which mixed-sex teams operate influences whether these effects appear. Finally, we consider what actions team members and organizations may take to ensure that mixed-sex teams are effective.

SEX EFFECTS

Although behavior in all-male teams may differ from that in all-female teams, we focus in this section on behavior in mixed-sex teams. When women and men serve on the same team, sex serves as a basis for distinguishing between team members and influences members' interactions. Women's and men's behaviors may differ. Moreover, team members are likely to evaluate the behaviors of males and females differently.

Sex differences in **task behaviors** and **social behaviors** are likely in teams. Task behaviors contribute directly to the group's task, whereas social behaviors help maintain morale and interpersonal relations among team members. In groups with assigned tasks, both women and men devote most of their interactions to task-related communications. However, men devote a higher percentage of their communications to task behavior, and women display a higher percentage of positive social behaviors. These differences may occur because women engage more in socially oriented behavior than men in general. Women's emphasis on positive social behaviors in teams is consistent with their desire for positive interpersonal relationships in their jobs (see Chapter 4). It also contributes to their being more cooperative than men in mixed-sex interactions.[5]

Sex differences in communication styles are also likely among team members. Male team members are more likely to engage in behaviors intended to establish dominance than female team members. For example, men talk more, speak more assertively, interrupt other team members more often, and display more visual dominance by making more eye contact while talking and less eye contact while listening. In contrast, women talk less, smile more, are interrupted more, and display less visual dominance. Further, some men adopt communications styles that question women's competence, such as **mansplaining**—forcefully reversing the role of speaker and listener when women are speaking and discounting them as providers of useful knowledge—whereas women are less likely to engage in "womansplaining" when men are speaking.[6]

Consistent with sex differences in communication styles as well as societal status and roles, there is a sex difference in **attributions of competence** and credit for task contributions favoring men. Both team members and outside evaluators appear to devalue the contributions of women. Female team members may even devalue their own performance and not give themselves enough credit. Overall, women must provide greater evidence than men of their abilities to be judged as competent team members, which is a double standard driven by gender stereotypes. In turn, the sex difference in attributions of competence contributes to men exhibiting more dominance-oriented behaviors in teams and outperforming team members who are attributed less competence (i.e., women), which is a self-fulfilling prophecy.[7]

A telling sex difference in credit for task contributions was exhibited in a study of faculty teams who publish scholarly articles and the effects of their publications on their later receiving tenure. Scholarly disciplines differ in whether the norm is to have coauthors of a publication listed alphabetically, which offers no indication of their relative contribution, or listed in order of contribution; for sole-authored articles, there is no question as to who made the contribution. In economics, a discipline in which coauthors are listed alphabetically, men received more credit toward tenure for their coauthored articles than women did. Men were tenured at about the same rate regardless of whether they had coauthored or sole-authored publications; in other words, men were not penalized for coauthoring articles. However, women were less likely to receive tenure the more they coauthored. In contrast, in sociology, a discipline in which coauthors are listed in order of contribution, women and men received equal credit toward tenure for coauthored articles. In academia, depending on the discipline, women must provide more evidence than men of their abilities to be seen as competent team members.[8]

A study of architects, who work in a male-intensive occupation, offered further evidence of the devaluing of women's competence. Female architects reported more "prove it again" bias (i.e., the feeling that they had to repeatedly prove their competence) in work teams than male architects. White architects tended to experience less "prove it again" bias than architects from other racial and ethnic groups (e.g., Black, Asian, Hispanic).[9]

Even when women receive credit for their performance in teams, they may receive less **social support** from other team members. According to a study of ongoing teams of students in management courses, female members were recognized by their peers as making greater contributions to the completion of group assignments than male members. However, they also participated in fewer social interactions with other team members than their male counterparts. Even when women do more or better work in their teams than men, they still may be excluded from social networks.[10]

Men tend to have more **influence** in mixed-sex teams than women. This is not surprising, given men's greater dominance, higher proportion of task behavior, and greater perceived competence. In contrast, women's influence attempts are often ignored. One study of simulated jury decision-making found that unique information (i.e., that possessed by a single group member) influenced the group 72% of the time when it was introduced by a man but only 13% of the time when introduced by a woman. Further, women in mixed-sex teams tend to be more easily influenced than men, perhaps because their lower status and less favorable self-evaluations lessen their confidence in their own views.[11] Men are also more likely than women to emerge as **informal leaders** in mixed-sex teams that have no assigned leaders.[12]

Women cannot increase evaluations of their competence, influence, and leadership in mixed-sex teams simply by behaving like men. Confident, assertive women tend to be less influential and seen as less likable than confident, assertive men. In fact, confident, assertive women may be even less influential than nonassertive women, especially among male team members. Nonetheless, women can attain influence and acceptance if they combine assertive behaviors with social behaviors such as expressions of interpersonal warmth and a desire to cooperate with the team. Women must be "friendly and nice" in their influence attempts and demonstrate that they care for the good of the team. Such behavior is not required of men.[13]

There is also a sex difference in who performs (and gains from performing) **office housework tasks** in mixed-sex teams. Imagine a menial kind of task that every team member hopes will be completed by someone else, such as organizing an office party, writing the final report for a low-visibility project that no one is ever likely to read, serving on a low-status committee, and so on. The task will be time-consuming, not especially challenging or requiring special skills, and not recognized in the performance evaluation of the team member who completes it. In a team meeting, the manager asks for a volunteer to complete the task. Who volunteers?

Female team members are more likely than male team members to volunteer, to be asked to volunteer, and to accept requests to volunteer for office housework tasks. This sex difference is not driven by a sex difference in task preferences. Instead, it appears to be driven by a shared expectation that women (perhaps because of their lower societal status) will volunteer for office housework tasks in teams more than men. Women who live up to this expectation are left with less time to work on high-priority team tasks that would increase their likelihood of being promoted. However, when male team members perform office housework tasks, they are more likely to be promoted, perhaps because they are less expected to perform such tasks and more appreciated for doing so.[14]

In summary, sex effects in mixed-sex teams are consistent with differences in the status and social roles assigned to women and men. Compared with men, women tend to engage in fewer task behaviors and more social behaviors, have their competence questioned more, receive less credit for equivalent task contributions, exercise less influence and informal leadership, and perform more menial, office housework tasks but receive less benefit from doing so. Women who attempt to increase their influence by behaving like men encounter unique roadblocks that men do not face.

SEX SIMILARITY EFFECTS

An individual's experience in a team is not simply a function of sex but is also determined by the sex composition of the team. This section explores how team composition affects women's and men's experiences as team members. Do individuals in teams have more negative experiences when members of their sex are in the minority? Are women who are in the minority (e.g., the only female in a team of engineers) more likely to have negative experiences than men who are in the minority (e.g., the only male in a team of nurses)?[15]

In one of the first major studies of male–female work relationships, Rosabeth Moss Kanter examined the effects of the team's sex composition on individual team members. Based on her observations in a large corporation, she identified four types of work groups. **Uniform groups** of all males or all females represent one extreme. By definition, there are no male–female issues in uniform groups. **Balanced groups** of approximately equal numbers of women and men represent the other extreme. Kanter suggested that attributes other than sex influence how individuals interact in groups that are balanced on the basis of sex.[16]

Between these two extremes are skewed and tilted groups. **Skewed groups** have a ratio of one sex to another ranging from about 85:15 to almost 100:0. Members of the sex in abundance in skewed groups are called *dominants* because they control the group and its culture. Members of the other sex are called *tokens* because they are viewed as representatives of their sex rather than as individuals. **Tilted groups** have less abundance of one sex with the ratio ranging from about 65:35 to about 85:15. In tilted groups, dominants become a majority and tokens become a minority. Minority members may become allies and have more effect on group culture in tilted than in skewed groups. They are distinguishable from each other as well as from the majority type.

Kanter's primary interest was in the experiences of **tokens in skewed groups**. Because tokens are present only in small numbers, the rest of the group sees them as representing their sex, whether or not they want to do so. A token rarely becomes "just another member of the group." Tokens receive special treatment that is detrimental to their performance in and attachment to the group in several ways. First, tokens face performance pressures. Because they are highly visible, they get attention that dominants do not. This does not necessarily lead to recognition of their competence; tokens may have to work harder to get their accomplishments recognized. Second, differences between tokens and dominants tend to be exaggerated. Dominants emphasize what they have in common and exclude tokens from social activities. Third, the characteristics of tokens are often distorted or misperceived because of the dominants' tendency to stereotype them. Tokens are expected to behave in a manner consistent with the stereotype of their sex or risk rejection by the team.[17]

However, Kanter based her conclusions on an analysis of an environment in which men vastly outnumbered women in positions of authority. She assumed that her notions would apply equally to women in male-intensive groups and to men in female-intensive groups. Subsequent research has generally failed to support her assumption. Token women experience increased visibility, social isolation, and stereotyping, especially in male-intensive settings such as the military, law enforcement, and medicine. However, token men in female-intensive settings such as nursing, teaching, and social work may not experience the same negative consequences of numerical imbalance as token women. Instead, the visibility that token men receive may work to their advantage. For example, a study of police patrol teams and hospital nursing units found that token female police officers were annoyed by or resigned to their heightened visibility, whereas token male nurses enjoyed the extra attention. Most token male nurses felt that patients attributed a higher status to them than to female nurses, even when they identified themselves as nurses and not physicians. Most also thought that physicians took them more seriously and gave more responsibility to them than to female nurses.[18]

The intersection of sex and race may also affect the experience of being a token in a skewed group. For example, a study found that White male nurses were often mistaken by patients for physicians rather than nurses (see above), whereas Black male nurses were often mistaken by patients for housekeepers rather than nurses. Further, Black women who are tokens in skewed groups on the basis of both sex and race are likely to have more negative experiences than team members who are tokens on the basis of either sex or race.[19]

The effects of sex similarity cannot be predicted solely by looking at the proportions of women and men on a team. To fully understand the effects of the sex composition of teams on team members, we need to consider the situation in which the team operates. For example, sex similarity effects are less likely to occur when the organizational culture stresses the value of teamwork, perhaps because a greater emphasis on cooperative behavior reduces the bias against women in mixed-sex interactions. In contrast, when the organizational culture stresses the importance of acting independently, sex similarity effects are more likely to occur because women and men are freer to choose the behaviors they adopt in teams.[20]

SEX DIVERSITY EFFECTS

Early research on sex diversity effects focused extensively on the question of whether all-male or all-female teams perform better. All-male teams tended to be better at activities that require a high amount of task behavior, such as brainstorming and generating solutions to a problem. In contrast, all-female teams tended to be better at activities that call for a high amount of social behavior, such as reaching a consensus on the best solution.[21]

However, these findings are of limited value today. Creating all-female or all-male teams is not feasible given the diversity of today's workforce, and managers who attempt to do so will be vulnerable to charges of sex discrimination. Moreover, assigning all-female and all-male teams to different types of activities is not likely to be effective. The work requirements of teams (e.g., developing a global business strategy or a new product) cannot be easily divided into those demanding task-related activity and those demanding interpersonal savvy. In addition, teams are likely to interact over extended periods of time, increasing the importance of interpersonal relationships among members. Poor relationships decrease members' attraction to the team and increase the likelihood that they will choose to leave the team.

Understanding the effects of sex diversity on the effectiveness of mixed-sex teams is of practical importance in today's increasingly diverse organizations. There are two opposing views of the general effect of diversity on team effectiveness—an optimistic view and a pessimistic view.[22]

According to the **optimistic view of sex diversity effects**, members of diverse teams have different experiences, values, attitudes, and cognitive approaches. They bring varied knowledge and perspectives to the team's task, which enhance its creativity in generating novel ideas and solving problems; task deliberations are more thorough and wide-ranging in balanced teams on the basis of sex.[23] These positive effects of diversity are especially likely to occur on complex tasks such as new product design and innovation, which require multiple perspectives and varied knowledge. Greater sex diversity increases the amount of interaction between team members of a different sex over time and decreases prejudice and discrimination based on sex. This process improves relations among team members and increases member attachment to the team.

According to the **pessimistic view of sex diversity effects**, the effects of perceived similarity and identification with similar others cause team members to reject those who they view as different from themselves. This leads to the creation of factions (e.g., men vs. women, Asians vs. Whites vs. Blacks, older vs. younger members), conflict, and communication problems. Ultimately, poor social relations between subgroups of team members impair the performance of the group as a whole, and members' satisfaction with and commitment to the group is reduced.

Which of these two views better represents the effects of sex diversity in mixed-sex teams? The research evidence regarding the direction and magnitude of sex diversity effects is mixed. Some studies have found that sex diversity has a positive effect on team performance; other studies have found a negative effect; and still other studies have found no effect, thereby suggesting that neither the optimistic view nor the pessimistic view of sex diversity is warranted.[24] These results provide little guidance. Instead, a better answer, which takes into account evidence supporting each view, is that sex diversity in teams has both potential advantages in the form of increased creativity and enhanced social relations over time that contribute to team performance and potential disadvantages in the form of troubled relationships between subgroups and disaffection of team members that detract from team performance.

Thus, the appropriate goal for mixed-sex teams is to maximize the advantages of sex diversity while minimizing the disadvantages. Sex diversity in teams represents a **double-edged sword**, offering both an opportunity and a challenge for organizations. The trick is in knowing exactly how to handle the sword.[25]

THE ROLE OF SITUATIONAL FACTORS

As we have seen, mixed-sex teams have potential advantages but are susceptible to serious problems. Women's competence and task contributions may be devalued, and token women in skewed teams suffer additional negative effects from heightened visibility, social isolation, and stereotyping. Also, the effectiveness of the team may decline as its diversity increases if subgroups clash and team members drop out. However, these negative consequences are not inevitable. If the conditions under which mixed-sex teams operate de-emphasize the importance of sex, negative outcomes may be averted. Several situational factors appear to be important, including characteristics of the team, the nature of the task, the demographic composition of the organization and its senior officials, and the organizational culture.

The demographic characteristics of team members may lead to **team faultlines**, or divisions between members, which affect interactions among members. Team faultlines can be weak or strong, depending on the exact alignment of members' demographic characteristics. When there are many subgroups (e.g., young Black males, young White males, young Asian females, middle-aged White females, middle-aged White males) in a mixed-sex team, team faultlines are weak, and the effects of sex, sex similarity, and sex diversity on team members' experiences and team effectiveness are minimized. For example, a team comprising a 40-year-old White male engineer, a 65-year-old Black female engineer, a 45-year-old Asian male sales representative, and a 20-year-old White female sales representative theoretically could form subgroups based on age, race, occupation, or sex. This team has a weak faultline on the basis of sex because forming subgroups based on sex would lead to differences within each subgroup on other categories; in this case, subgroup formation is unlikely. In contrast, in a team composed of two middle-aged White male engineers and two young Black female sales representatives, sex aligns perfectly with three other dimensions of diversity—age, race, and occupation. This team has a strong faultline on the basis of sex as well as other personal characteristics; because it has only two possible subgroups, the likelihood of negative effects is enhanced. However, these negative effects are minimized when team members and leaders hold strong pro-diversity beliefs.[26]

Team longevity is another critical factor. As team members interact over extended periods of time, they gain additional information about one another, and stereotyping should be reduced. Relationships between members are formed based on similarity of underlying attitudes, values, and beliefs rather than sex similarity. The greater the team's longevity, the less important its sex composition. However, a great deal of time is needed to eliminate the effects of sex composition. According to a study of teams in hospitals and grocery stores, the negative effects of sex diversity disappear only when the average longevity of team members is three or more years. Moreover, longevity may not always eliminate the negative impact of sex dissimilarity. Individuals who are dissimilar from their teammates may be able to cope with incidents of discrimination and social exclusion when they first join the team. If these negative incidents continue over time, however, their coping ability may deteriorate, and they may psychologically withdraw from their teams by exhibiting greater absenteeism. Such an effect was demonstrated in a seven-year study of Swiss blue-collar employees; individuals who were dissimilar from their teammates with respect to sex were more likely to be absent from work as their longevity on the team increased.[27]

Tasks that are sex-neutral and require cooperation among team members reduce the negative consequences of diversity in mixed-sex teams. Tasks that are not associated exclusively with women or men minimize attention to sex differences, whereas tasks that are typically performed by members of one sex foster sex-based categorization (a focus on attention to sex differences). In addition, tasks that require cooperation among team members promote a sense of teamwork. When team members must work jointly to achieve collective goals and rewards, they are motivated to form accurate (rather than stereotypical) impressions of one another. Moreover, when cooperation leads the team to form a "team identity" (i.e., view themselves as a team), members categorize themselves as a single group rather than as subgroups on the basis of sex.[28]

The **demographic composition of the larger organization** also affects relationships between men and women in teams. Sex differences are less important in organizations where there is a great deal of sex diversity than in organizations where there is little. Negative outcomes also may be less likely to occur in female-intensive than male-intensive organizations. In female-intensive organizations, increasing sex diversity means that males are added to female teams. In male-intensive organizations, the reverse is true. Because females are more likely to welcome the addition of males to their teams than males are to welcome the addition of females to their teams, increasing diversity may be less problematic in female-intensive organizations.[29]

Further, the **sex composition of the organization's top management team** affects team members' interactions by influencing the relative status of women and men. When women work in organizations with few women in key roles, they are more likely to invoke gender stereotypes, devalue their own abilities, demonstrate less interest in participating in organizational activities, and compete with their female peers. In contrast, when there is more of a balance of power at the top of the organization between women and men, sex-based status differences in teams are eliminated or reduced.[30]

The organization's culture, especially its values regarding cooperation and diversity, has an important influence on what happens in mixed-sex teams. Organizations that foster a **cooperative culture** by encouraging individuals to focus on their common goals rather than on their own self-interests reduce the negative effects of sex diversity. For instance, the United States (U.S.) Army's strong culture, which emphasizes group cohesion and working toward shared mission and goals over individual characteristics, may reduce the impact of being a token woman. A study of over 4,000 women who were tokens in their units in the U.S. Army found that they did not experience more signs of stress (e.g., poor coping, sleep problems, alcohol abuse, lack of organizational trust) than men or than women who were not tokens. Moreover, the experiences of the small number of Black women who were tokens with respect to both sex and race did not differ from the experiences of non-tokens. A study in a very different environment, the MBA (master of business administration) classroom, also suggests that a cooperative culture has benefits. The study assigned diverse teams of MBA students to organizations that had either individualistic values (i.e., individual performance valued and rewarded) or cooperative values (i.e., teamwork valued and rewarded). The students who were the most different from their teammates with respect to sex, race, and nationality combined had fewer interactions with others, regardless of the culture of the organization. They did, however, experience more positive conflict (i.e., conflict over ideas) and more creativity in the cooperative organization than the individualistic organization. Thus, an organizational culture that emphasizes cooperation may lessen some of the negative effects of diversity and increase the likelihood that diversity will enhance performance.[31]

Organizations with diversity cultures that foster inclusion also reduce the likelihood of negative consequences in mixed-sex teams. In an **inclusive diversity culture**, organizational members value efforts to increase the representation of women, people of color, and individuals with disabilities and view members of these groups as qualified. Equal, unbiased treatment for equally qualified individuals is stressed, and differences in status based on sex and other visible demographic characteristics that might arise in skewed groups are reduced. Further, in an inclusive diversity culture, employees acknowledge differences among women and among men as well as between women and men. Recognition that individual differences are present within each sex allows team members to view each other as distinct persons, not merely as representatives of the two sexes. Moreover, organizations that regard the insights, skills, and experiences of individuals from different backgrounds as valuable business resources create a particularly productive environment for diverse teams. In such settings, the input of each individual is valued and respected because of—rather than in spite of—his or her background. We discuss how organizations can create an inclusive culture in Chapter 9.[32]

In summary, mixed-sex teams experience fewer disadvantages and more advantages when characteristics of the team, task, and organization de-emphasize sex differences. The negative effects of sex diversity are minimized in teams with weaker faultlines and greater longevity. Tasks that require the cooperation of team members reduce the extent to which sex is an important social category in teams. Finally, mixed-sex teams are likely to encounter fewer problems in organizations with cooperative, egalitarian values and high levels of sex integration in the workplace.

VIRTUAL TEAMS

There has been explosive growth in organizations' use of virtual teams in recent decades, a trend that accelerated during the COVID-19 pandemic.[33] Traditionally, team members worked in close physical proximity and could have face-to-face meetings and interactions when needed. Over time, teamwork became more virtual. The advent of email within organizations allowed team members to converse by sending messages to each other and using the "reply all" function to respond. Team-specific electronic workspaces with features such as chat rooms, discussion forums, and shared files also became available on organizational intranets. Organizations devoted resources to setting up meeting rooms with then-elaborate technology in which videoconferences with team members located elsewhere in similar rooms could take place. Now, the use of online virtual platforms with video calling capabilities (e.g., Zoom, Microsoft Teams, WebEx, Skype) allows team members who may be working from home or elsewhere to call in from their laptops to hold "live" meetings that are almost (but not quite) like face-to-face meetings.[34]

Virtual teams differ in the nature of the technologies used and the extent to which they are used. Some technologies are solely text-based (e.g., email, chat room, discussion forum), whereas other technologies incorporate video and audio capabilities (e.g., videoconference, meeting on an online virtual platform).[35] The type of communications technology used and the prevalence of its usage affects women's satisfaction with and inclusion in virtual teams.

When **text-based communications technologies** are used to facilitate virtual team interactions, they reduce the extent to which sex-based categorization occurs compared to face-to-face meetings. Sex differences in evaluations and influence tend to disappear when group members interact using these technologies. The benefits of text-based technologies occur even when individuals are aware of the sex of each group member. A key feature is that team members cannot see one another, thereby preventing any effects of perceived attractiveness on their reactions to each other. Although team members' names may still be perceived as male or female, text-based technologies allow team members to focus more on the content of the arguments than the characteristics of the individuals who make them. That is, the focus is more on the written word and less on who is writing it. Like the screens used in blind auditions for orchestra positions (see Chapter 4), they reduce the attention paid to the sex of the participant. They also benefit women more than men. Women tend to experience stronger feelings of inclusion and support in mixed-sex virtual teams using text-based technologies than do men. In addition, women in all-female virtual teams using such technologies are more satisfied than are men in all-male virtual teams. Women's virtual teams engage in higher levels of self-disclosure and agreement, and men's virtual teams display more conflict and less willingness to change their minds. Women's greater focus on positive social behaviors enhances their experiences in teams that interact primarily via text-based technologies.[36]

When virtual team interactions are shifted to **online virtual platforms** that incorporate video and audio capabilities, the sex differences described above for text-based communications technologies are reversed. Because team members are visible, women are more likely to be interrupted, have their competence questioned and comments ignored, have less influence on team decisions, and emerge less as team leaders than men, much as in face-to-face meetings. However, women face additional disadvantages in virtual teams from reliance on such technologies.[37]

First, as researchers discovered in a study conducted during the COVID-19 pandemic, a steady, day-long agenda of virtual meetings may cause team members to feel what has been called **Zoom fatigue**—the fatiguing effects of camera use during virtual meetings on online platforms. Women were found to suffer from Zoom fatigue more than men. Women are already under pressure to maintain perceptions of their attractiveness in the eyes of others, and the heightened emphasis on their grooming, attire, and gaze over a full day of virtual meetings on which they are on constant video display can be especially exhausting.[38]

Second, team meetings held over online virtual platforms restrict the opportunity for informal schmoozing that exists in face-to-face teams. Virtual team members who are physically dispersed cannot take a break from work and socialize with each other over a trip to the proverbial water cooler; they also cannot chat on their way into the meeting room. Instead, every interaction between team members that is not text-based and includes their image and voice needs to be scheduled in advance on an online platform, and it may be subject to monitoring if a company account on the platform is used to hold it, all of which discourages the frequency and openness of informal interactions. As a result, virtual team members may feel isolated from other members because the technology is limiting their ability to get to know each other as people.[39] Because having positive social interactions in teams is particularly important for women, they are more likely to feel the negative effects of this constraint of online virtual platforms.

Third, women (especially mothers) are more likely than men to experience family-related interruptions during team meetings held on online virtual platforms when working from home. Due to the sex segregation of unpaid domestic labor in dual-career, heterosexual households and women assuming the bulk of family responsibilities (including childcare; see Chapter 2), women face a greater risk of having a child wander into their virtual team meetings. Such family-related intrusions can raise concerns about women's professionalism and commitment to the team and organization that are less likely to be raised when men experience the same kind of intrusion. This sex difference in the possibility and potential consequences of family-related interruptions may contribute to women's increased fatigue from team meetings held on virtual online platforms.[40]

In summary, the nature of the communication technologies used influences sex effects in virtual teams. In some cases, the technologies used in virtual teams work to women's advantage, as in text-based communications among team members. Technologies may also work to their disadvantage, as in team meetings held over online virtual platforms. The challenge for organizations in making use of virtual teams is to create conditions under which all members feel satisfied with and included in teams to which they belong, regardless of their sex.

BUILDING EFFECTIVE MIXED-SEX TEAMS

Mixed-sex teams have both potential advantages and potential disadvantages and are affected by the characteristics of the situation in which they operate. How can organizations ensure that mixed-sex teams are effective other than by requiring that teams remain intact over a long period of time (which is seldom possible)? Organizations must create a working environment in which all individuals thrive, regardless of sex, race, and other demographic characteristics. However, team leaders and members also need to take action to ensure that mixed-sex teams are effective, whatever the working environment outside of the team. Tables 5.1 and 5.2 summarize recommended actions for organizations, team leaders, and team members.

TABLE 5.1 ■ Recommended Actions for Organizations and Team Leaders

1. Strive to have diverse work teams, but do not select team members or leaders solely on the basis of sex or other demographic characteristics.
2. Select team members with values and skills conducive to teamwork.
3. Structure work assignments to require cooperation among team members.
4. Make a wide array of communications technologies available to the team.
5. Do not assign tasks to team members on the basis of sex.
6. Encourage rotation of roles and tasks to develop team members for future roles.
7. Rotate office housework tasks among team members.
8. Reward team performance in addition to individual performance.
9. Train team members on how to manage team processes and how to deal with the difficulties created by stereotyping and dissimilarity.
10. Publicize qualifications of all individuals assigned to teams as leaders or members.
11. Provide opportunities for informal interactions in both face-to-face and virtual teams.
12. Encourage expression of diverse points of view and discourage dysfunctional team processes.

TABLE 5.2 ■ Recommended Actions for Team Members

1. Understand how your sense of self-identity influences your interactions with other team members.
2. Guard against your own stereotypes and prejudices as you evaluate others' behavior.
3. Build good relationships with other members of your team.
4. Perform your fair share of office housework tasks, but no more than your fair share.
5. If you are a member of the majority group, do not subject minority team members to performance pressures or exaggerate differences between you and them simply because they are in the minority. Reach out to minority team members to ensure they are included in informal social activities.
6. If you are a member of the minority group, take actions to enhance your own power and guard against stereotypes that limit your behavior.

Proactive Organizations and Team Leaders

Teamwork is never easy, whether the team consists of an organization's top management team, its board of directors, a lower-level cross-functional team, or some other combination of members. To ensure team effectiveness, organizations must pay attention to the design and development of teams. Throwing a collection of employees together and then calling them a team is insufficient to create a sense of teamwork, even when its members are homogeneous in demographic characteristics. Given the challenges associated with mixed-sex teams, the need to be proactive in designing and developing such teams is intensified. Team leaders must carefully design mixed-sex teams, train team members, help them get to know one another, and provide ongoing support.[41]

With respect to the design of the team, team leaders should address three questions: (1) Who will be on the team? (2) How will the task be structured? (3) How will performance be measured and rewarded? In choosing team members, they should strive for teams that are diverse on a number of demographic characteristics. It is best if demographic characteristics result in numerous subgroups with overlapping memberships. Individuals will belong to and identify with many different subgroups, thereby reducing the likelihood of divisions along sex or any other single dimension. Moreover, differences in the organizational status of team members should be minimized, especially if organizational rank is related to sex or some other demographic characteristic. Women's task contributions are likely to be impaired if they have lower organizational status than men. However, team leaders must refrain from choosing team members for their demographic characteristics rather than their skills and expertise. The ability to be effective team members must not be subordinate to demographic characteristics in team formation.[42]

What expertise should leaders look for in choosing team members? They must consider whether potential team members have the necessary technical knowledge, skills, and abilities to accomplish the task. They should select individuals with a high level of emotional intelligence, including self-awareness, self-regulation, motivation, empathy, and social skills. Collectively, team members should be capable of performing a range of task behaviors and social behaviors effectively and exhibit a minimum of individually oriented, disruptive behaviors. They should also select individuals with values and skills that are conducive to teamwork. Individuals who value collaboration over competition and gain pleasure from others' achievements will be better team players than those who value only competition and personal achievement.[43]

Team leaders need to consider the team's task structure, task assignments, and performance measurement and reward system. When possible, tasks should be structured to require high levels of cooperation among team members. When team members are dependent on each other and have to make mutual adjustments, they gain valuable experience working together and are less likely to engage in stereotyping. Teams should be given access to a full array of communications technologies. Leaders should also ensure that task assignments are not based on the sex of team members. If women and men are assigned tasks consistent with gender stereotypes and roles, sex differences in members' experiences will be accentuated. Rotation of tasks among team members will ensure that tasks are not linked exclusively to one sex and will develop team members for future roles. In particular, rotating office housework tasks among team members rather than asking for volunteers keeps women from feeling pressured to prove that they are team players by volunteering for tasks that men bypass. Finally, performance measurements and rewards should be implemented for the entire team. When only individual accomplishment is rewarded, team members have little incentive to cooperate with one another.[44]

Team members should receive training on how to deal with behavioral issues that arise in teams. Because teamwork does not come naturally to many individuals, team members must learn to cooperate with one another. Training in the areas of communication, conflict management, and decision making is valuable. Teams benefit from learning structured decision rules that bring order to team discussions and give all team members a chance to participate. In addition, team members should be trained to observe and evaluate their own processes. This is particularly important in diverse groups because the lack of interpersonal attraction may make interaction more difficult. Being skilled in process observation will help teams correct problems before there are major breakdowns in team functioning.[45]

In addition, diversity and anti-bias training should make team members aware of gender stereotypes and the potential negative effects of these stereotypes and sexist behavior on members' interactions. All team members should receive training, not only women or only men. Women can be coached to increase their task contributions and men to elicit and consider women's contributions. Moreover, all team members should be made aware of the possible negative effects of sex dissimilarity on interpersonal liking and performance. Team members can be taught techniques for reducing the biases associated with dissimilarity on the basis of demographic characteristics. Diversity training is discussed further in Chapter 9.[46]

Once the team has been designed and members have been trained, the leader should ensure that interactions are based on what individuals bring to the team, not their sex. When the team is initially formed, the qualifications and achievements of all team members should be publicized. Identifying the expertise of new team members in formal written communications as they are added will prevent team members from making erroneous assumptions about others' qualifications based on sex.

Leaders should also provide informal opportunities for team members to interact and get to know each other as people. In person, these opportunities may be provided by lunches and other social events. In the case of virtual teams that are geographically dispersed, actions may still be taken to promote their familiarity with each other. For example, virtual coffee hours or water cooler chats can be scheduled. The team leader may open each meeting on an online platform by taking a few minutes to give team members a chance to share something personal about themselves such as their nonwork interests or hobbies. Any steps to boost a sense of social connectedness among virtual team members will be to the advantage of all members and the team as a whole.[47]

As the team tackles its task, the leader must provide ongoing support to the team to ensure that it is functioning effectively. The leader should regularly assess the team's performance, including its short-term and long-term accomplishments. The leader should encourage expression of diverse perspectives on problems. The leader should also monitor how well the team is managing its interpersonal processes, including the extent to which it is being inclusive or excluding members on the basis of personal characteristics, failing to take advantage of differences in perspective, and experiencing miscommunication. Team members need to feel comfortable that they can speak up and be heard. For example, a no-interruption rule to ensure that diverse perspectives are fully heard may help offset the disadvantage of "speaking while female." Finally, the leader should be ready to identify problems in mixed-sex teams when they occur and then work with team members to develop and implement solutions to these problems.[48]

Responsible Team Members

Building effective mixed-sex teams is not only an organizational responsibility. Each team member must take responsibility for making the team work. Other than by seeking appropriate training, what can team members do? As a first step, each individual must develop an understanding of their own social identity. Each team member might ask themself the following questions: (1) What social categories do I use to describe myself and others? (2) How important is each of these categories to my identity? (3) How do I behave toward individuals who are of a different sex (race, sexual orientation, age, etc.)? (4) How do I feel about myself when I am in the presence of members of a different sex (race, sexual orientation, age, etc.)? (5) How are others' behaviors toward me influenced by my sex (race, sexual orientation, age, etc.)? Answering such questions will give individuals some idea of which social categories are most important to them and how these social categories affect their interactions with other team members.[49]

Second, team members must hone their ability to evaluate the behaviors of their teammates. Most people are not good at understanding the causes of others' behaviors and are even worse when they evaluate those who are different from them. To address this problem, team members' evaluations of other members' behaviors ideally will be based on careful, repeated observations. Quick judgments, which are likely to be based on gender stereotypes, are to be avoided. Team members also may check the accuracy of their evaluations by comparing them with those of others.[50]

Third, team members should establish and maintain good working relationships with other members. People sometimes feel awkward and uncomfortable working with people whom they view as unlike themselves. To overcome this discomfort, team members may identify common interests that provide a basis for relating. Such interests can be identified through informal conversation about nonwork topics. Identifying common interests eases future interactions, contributes to the development of relationships, and ultimately reduces stereotyping. Team members also may benefit by sharing appropriate personal information with other team members. Self-disclosure by one team member is likely to lead to self-disclosure by other members and create an environment of openness and trust.

Fourth, team members, especially women, need to monitor whether they are performing their fair share of office housework tasks—but no more than their fair share. They should refrain from volunteering for such tasks simply to be seen in favorable terms from other members, who will always appreciate not having to perform menial tasks themselves. By volunteering for more than their fair share of office housework tasks to try to be nice, women risk setting back their own career advancement.[51]

Fifth, members of skewed or tilted teams need to ensure that all members are fully integrated into the team. Members of the numerical majority should be especially careful to avoid the exclusion of those in the minority. A team member can be assigned to monitor member participation and ensure that all team members have an equal opportunity to contribute. Moreover, members of the majority should include those in the minority in informal social activities and make them feel welcome.[52]

Those who are in the minority need to take responsibility for their own roles in the team. There are several strategies that tokens or others in the numerical minority can adopt to build their power and influence in a team. Tokens can make themselves indispensable to the team by developing special areas of expertise. Other team members then will pay attention to them because of their expertise, not their sex. Tokens should also learn to diagnose power dynamics in teams so that they can maximize their own influence. In a particular situation, they might determine whether they should attempt to influence the assumptions on which decisions are based, the alternatives to be considered, or the information available about alternatives. Tokens also need to ensure that their own gender stereotypes do not dictate the nature of their participation in the team. Individuals sometimes limit their own behaviors to reflect gender stereotypes, even if these stereotypes do not reflect their true selves. Tokens may be especially likely to engage in stereotypical behavior because their numerical status makes gender stereotypes so prominent. Thus, tokens may find it valuable to consider whether their behaviors reflect their true selves or gender stereotypes.[53]

In conclusion, mixed-sex teams face challenges in reaching their full potential. Women's task contributions are often ignored or devalued by other team members. Individuals who are members of teams comprised primarily of different-sex individuals have more negative experiences than do individuals who are members of teams comprised primarily of same-sex individuals. Although the effects of being in the minority are not identical for women and men, both men and women are vulnerable to negative experiences when their sex is underrepresented. Moreover, as the level of sex diversity in a team increases, the effectiveness of the team may decline. These effects are not inevitable but depend on a host of factors, such as the team's characteristics and tasks as well as the organization's demographic composition and values. Mixed-sex teams are likely to experience problems in organizations with cultures that do not value collaboration and inclusion.

Although organizations, team leaders, and team members cannot address all of these problems, there is much that they can do to improve the functioning of a mixed-sex team. Team leaders must carefully design the team, provide proper training, help team members get acquainted, and provide continual support to the team. Team members need to understand their own social identities, improve the accuracy of their perceptions, develop relationships with one another, and avoid the dynamics created by a disproportionate representation of one sex. Above all, team leaders and their members must be patient. Mixed-sex teams may take more time to come together than same-sex teams because of their diversity. There may be frustrating moments for team leaders and members along the way. To Tim Hunt's dismay, some team members might even cry. However, with appropriate nurturing, mixed-sex teams can be more effective than either all-male or all-female teams.

6 LEADING PEOPLE

LEARNING OBJECTIVES

After reading this chapter, you should be able to do the following:

6.1 Describe alternative positions taken in the gender and leadership wars.

6.2 Summarize trends in preferences for male versus female leaders.

6.3 Discuss trends in leader stereotypes in relation to leader sex and other personal characteristics.

6.4 Understand the linkages of major leadership theories to gender stereotypes.

6.5 Describe sex differences in leader behavior and effectiveness.

6.6 Provide examples of person-centered and decision-maker–centered explanations for the existence of glass ceilings.

6.7 Identify actions that may be taken by organizations and individuals to promote effective leadership.

THE GENDER AND LEADERSHIP WARS (OR MY 15 MINUTES OF FAME)

Ever since the proportion of women in management positions began to increase significantly in the second half of the 20th century, considerable media and scholarly attention have been devoted to the question of whether women or men, if either, make better bosses. Although most topics related to sex and gender in the workplace elicit strong reactions, this topic stimulates especially heated debate. This is because corporate leaders or managers (terms I will use interchangeably) receive an enormous amount of attention, especially in societies that place a high value on individualism rather than collectivism, such as the United States (U. S.) and the United Kingdom.[1] In highly individualistic societies, the success of organizations is attributed to the wisdom, values, and practices of their founders or current leaders. When organizations fail to achieve expected results, their leaders are the first to be blamed. Consider the issues of sex, gender, and leadership together, and it is clear why so many people from all walks of life have strong opinions about what constitutes effective leadership and who is more likely to exhibit it.

I would like to describe my own 15 minutes of fame (or notoriety, depending on your perspective) in discussing this topic publicly. I was invited to participate in an online *New York Times* debate over the question, "Do women make better bosses?" I was one of six participants in the debate; the other five participants (all women) included researchers, consultants, and executives. In my contribution to the debate, I briefly summarized some of the research described later in this chapter—nothing controversial, or so I thought.[2]

After readers were invited to post comments on the online debate, more than 500 responses were received. Several themes emerged in the responses.

One theme was criticism of the composition of the debate panel itself. The panel was disparaged in various responses as "five females and one guy who wants to make his wife happy" (*NC*, response #85, not knowing that my wife, Laura Graves, is also my coauthor on two chapters in this book as well as other publications), "five women and one man who was formerly the Chair of the Women in Management Division of the Academy of Management" (*Disillusioned*, #289, implying that this credential provided a good basis to discredit anything I had to say), and "five women and one boomer man" (*Becky*, #66, presumably judging my age from my web page photo).

Many respondents took strong positions on the question that was posed, writing passionately about their own experiences pro and con with female bosses, male bosses, or both. They also tended to draw conclusions about what *all* male bosses and *all* female bosses are like, a tendency that was encouraged by the nature of the question being debated.

Some respondents answered "yes" to the question and argued that women are better bosses:

> In my experience, women make better bosses. Generally, they do not have that asinine alpha male schoolyard crap baggage. (*Paulie*, #84)

> As far as I can tell, women are better than men at just about anything. (*daldoc*, #444)

> Women make better leaders when given the chance and not only lately. (*John*, #439)

Other respondents answered "no" to the question and argued that men are better bosses:

> No! As a female, I'll take the male egos any day. At least you know what to expect from a guy. Men are more level tempered. They lay it on the line. Women are egotistical BIT_ES. (*smitel*, #344)

> From my humble experience and that of virtually all of my business associates, women managers are more ruthless, more arbitrary, less compassionate, more sociopathic, and tend to be less knowledgeable and less involved in whatever they are doing. It seems to be all about climbing the ladder. (*BJ*, #426)

> I can't understand them (women), so how can I work for them? (*katman*, #4)

A few respondents argued that neither women nor men make better bosses:

> Women are no better or worse than men in general. There are only good managers and bad managers. (*Nancy*, #3)

> I have had good and bad experiences with both sexes. It completely depends upon the individual and not the sex. (*Joel*, #223)

Still other respondents argued that both male and female bosses leave a lot to be desired:

> I have had two female bosses. Both were dishonest and manipulative. The male bosses I had were merely incompetent. (*hb*, #125)

Here is my favorite response of all:

> All bosses suck. This is a trick question. (*Jonathan*, #346)

As the online debate continued among readers, it turned on itself as some women criticized what they perceived as a sexist or clueless tone exhibited in many of the previous comments from men:

> This is one of the challenges women have faced in working for/with men. We deal with it. I suggest you do the same. (*Brenda*, #179, responding to *katman*, #4)

> The vitriol with which so many male commentators have greeted this debate demonstrates well the obstacles that women still face in the workplace. (*Rachel*, #244)

> The outpouring of "women make the most inferior, back-stabbing, emotional, menopausal, passive-aggressive, ineffectual, lazy bosses" or "have a family" sentiment in these comments is a pretty stark picture of how overt sexism is still alive and acceptable today. (*Caroline*, #302)

Although the online debate in which I played a role occurred more than a decade ago, the question of whether women or men (if either) make better bosses has never gone away—at least in the popular media—and still generates the same level of strong opinions and vitriol. If you doubt this point, try searching Google for the question, "Do women make better bosses?" At the time of writing, I found almost one billion entries in my own Google search, including the original online debate that gave me my 15 minutes of fame.

The purpose of this chapter is to offer an update on what may be called the **gender and leadership wars**. Its approach is analogous to the poem, "The Blind Men and the Elephant,"[3] based on a parable that originated in India in which six blind men of learning take a journey to see an elephant. The first man touches the elephant's side and concludes it is like a wall. The second holds the elephant's tusk and concludes it is like a spear. The third grips the elephant's trunk and concludes it is like a snake. The fourth feels the elephant's knee and concludes it is like a tree. The fifth grasps the elephant's ear and concludes it is like a fan. Finally, the sixth man seizes the elephant's tail and concludes it is like a rope. As the poem wraps up, the six men are heatedly debating the nature of the elephant and none understands what the others have "seen." They obviously have different ways of seeing the elephant. Each perspective provides some information about what the elephant is like, but none of the perspectives conveys a full sense of what the elephant is like. All of these perspectives need to be taken into account when considering the nature of the elephant.

In this spirit, the chapter examines the intersection of sex, gender, and leadership (i.e., "the elephant") from six different perspectives. First, it reviews individuals' preferences for male versus female leaders in general. Second, it compares stereotypes of leaders with gender stereotypes and examines whether leader stereotypes have changed over time. Third, it explores the linkages of major leadership theories to gender stereotypes. Fourth, it examines sex differences in leader behavior and effectiveness. Fifth, it considers glass ceilings (barriers to the attainment of top management positions by women). Finally, it considers what can be done to promote effective leadership by managers regardless of their sex.[4]

LEADER PREFERENCES

Individuals' preferences for male versus female leaders in general may reflect their personal biases or experiences and influence their responses to actual leaders. Ever since the 1950s, the Gallup Organization has regularly asked random samples of adults in various countries, "If you were taking a new job and had your choice of a boss, would you prefer to work for a man or a woman?" Respondents could also state that the sex of their new boss would make no difference to them. Historically, people have tended to express a preference for a male boss over a female boss.[5]

However, according to the most recent Gallup poll results, this tendency has disappeared among American adults. A majority (55%) stated that the sex of their boss would make no difference to them, and roughly equal percentages stated that they would prefer a male boss (23%) or a female boss (21%).[6]

In the Gallup results, leader preferences differed according to the age of the person being asked. In particular, American adults younger than 35 preferred a female boss over a male boss by 14% when they expressed a preference. Younger respondents may have been more likely to prefer a female boss than older respondents because they had greater experience in working with women as peers in educational programs and jobs. These results suggest that a generational shift may be taking place in leader preferences toward a greater preference for female leaders. If leader preferences for younger respondents in the Gallup results are mirrored in future generations, a bias favoring female leaders could replace the bias that once favored male leaders as new entrants to the labor force progress in their careers.

Leader preferences also differed according to the intersection of respondents' sex and age. Women under age 50 preferred a female boss over a male boss, whereas women 50 and older were more divided. In contrast, men 50 and older preferred a male boss over a female boss, whereas men under age 50 were more divided. The finding that younger women and older men had more clear-cut leader preferences than older women and younger men, respectively, is interesting. It suggests the potential for a clash between individuals over the linkage between sex and leadership on the basis of the combination of their own sex and age.

Further, leader preferences differed according to the intersection of employed respondents' sex and the sex of their current boss. About one-third of employed respondents stated that they had a female boss. Those with a female boss preferred a female boss over a male boss when they expressed a preference, whereas those with a male boss preferred a male boss over a female boss. Due to the increased representation of women in management over time, more employees than ever before have had a female boss, a trend that may have contributed to a shift in leader preferences.

Individuals' leader preferences may be influenced by their gender role identity—the beliefs about the extent to which they possess psychological traits associated with gender stereotypes (see Chapter 3). In a study, respondents answered the Gallup poll question and described themselves on the masculinity and femininity scales of the Short Bem Sex-Role Inventory (Short BSRI). When they expressed a preference, respondents who described themselves as highly masculine were more likely to prefer a male boss, whereas those who described themselves as highly feminine were more likely to prefer a female boss. In contrast, respondents who described themselves as possessing similar levels of masculine and feminine traits (as androgynous) were less likely to express any preference for a male or female boss. These results suggest that the preference to work for a male or female leader is a matter of gender as well as sex.[7]

In summary, although there has been a historical tendency for people to prefer a male boss over a female boss, recent evidence suggests that this tendency may be diminishing or disappearing. Poll and research results suggest that the preference to work for a male or female leader may be influenced by respondents' sex, age, gender role identity, and the sex of their current boss.

LEADER STEREOTYPES

Studies of the relationships among sex, gender stereotypes, and leader stereotypes were first conducted in the 1970s. Virginia Schein compiled a list of 92 characteristics that people commonly believe distinguish between men and women—the basis for gender stereotypes. She then asked a sample of U.S. middle managers to describe how well each of the characteristics fits women in general, men in general, or successful middle managers in general. Schein hypothesized that because the vast majority of managers were men, the managerial job would be regarded as requiring personal attributes thought to be more characteristic of men than women. In support of her hypothesis, she found that both male and female middle managers believed that a successful middle manager possessed personal characteristics that more closely matched beliefs about the characteristics of men in general than those of women in general.[8]

In more recent studies, U.S. women are less inclined to view management as the domain of men. They now associate the characteristics of successful managers more equally with those of women in general and men in general. A similar pattern of results is exhibited in countries with a range of national cultures, including the United Kingdom, Germany, Japan, China, Turkey, and Sweden: Both men and women believe that men are more similar to successful managers than women are, but men endorse such beliefs to a greater extent than women do. These results support the **think manager—think male** paradigm of leader stereotypes, especially among men.[9] Interestingly, a separate study found support for a "think follower—think female" perspective of followership, with the follower role characterized by more feminine or communal traits associated with women than the manager role.[10]

Tony Butterfield (my former dissertation adviser who became my lifelong collaborator, colleague, mentor, and friend) and I have taken a different approach to the analysis of leader stereotypes in a research program that also began in the 1970s. Over time, we have periodically asked part-time MBA (master of business administration) students in the United States—nearly all of whom work full time—and undergraduate business students to describe a "good manager" on the Short BSRI. We assess individuals' "good manager" descriptions on both masculinity and femininity.

When we first collected data, the proportion of women in management positions in the United States was just beginning to rise. Based on this trend, we hypothesized that a good manager would be seen as possessing similarly high levels of masculine and feminine traits (an androgynous profile). In doing so, we were influenced by the work of Sandra Bem, who had recently proposed androgyny as a new and improved standard for psychological health (see Chapter 3).[11] As Tony and I suggested in our study, "If the more effective person is androgynous, the more effective *manager* may be androgynous as well." However, our hypothesis was resoundingly rejected. A good manager was seen as possessing predominantly masculine characteristics by a majority of respondents in all groups, including undergraduate and part-time graduate males and females. Without intending it, our study launched what may be called the **think manager—think masculine** paradigm of leader stereotypes.[12]

As we continued to collect data on individuals' "good manager" descriptions, our new results were similar to our earlier results, with some change. Individuals still described a good manager in predominantly masculine terms. However, the proportion of respondents that described a manager as possessing predominantly masculine characteristics declined somewhat over time.[13]

Meta-analyses of research conducted through 2009 on the relationship between gender and leader stereotypes supported the same two trends that Tony and I had seen in our own research up to that time. First, stereotypes of individuals designated as managers or leaders emphasized masculine traits over feminine traits over about a four-decade period. Second, this emphasis decreased over the same period of time. As a result, managerial stereotypes had shifted toward becoming more androgynous, exhibiting more of a balance of masculine and feminine traits.[14]

Considered together, these two trends had long-term implications. If the trend of decline in emphasis on masculinity over femininity represented by the second trend were to continue unabated, one would expect an eventual convergence of emphasis on masculinity and femininity in managerial stereotypes. That is, there would eventually come a time when the first trend—that managerial stereotypes emphasize masculinity over femininity—would be nullified such that these stereotypes now emphasized an androgynous profile.

A decade later, using the exact same methodology as before, Tony and I with Xueting Jiang collected new data on individuals' "good manager" descriptions and combined it with data collected during each of the previous four decades to examine whether that time had arrived. Indeed, it had. In a research program that now spanned five decades, individuals' "good manager" descriptions exhibited a decreasing emphasis on masculinity and increasing emphasis on femininity over time, culminating in endorsement of an androgynous profile of the good manager by both undergraduate business students and part-time MBA students in the newly collected data. For the first time, respondents now described the good manager as possessing similar levels of masculine and feminine traits.[15]

I am not about to proclaim the advent of a new "think manager—think androgynous" paradigm of leader stereotypes based on the results of this one study. More research is needed to investigate whether these results, based on analysis of data from U.S. undergraduate business students and part-time MBA students, are also found in studies of other types of respondents in other cultures.[16]

Nonetheless, the new results are provocative, and their implications for workplace dynamics are considerable. If decision makers were to believe that effective leaders possess the balance of masculine and feminine traits that androgyny represents, they may be more likely to make selection and promotion decisions for managerial positions that are based on candidates' human capital—knowledge, skills, abilities, education, relevant work experience, and so on—rather than their sex. Such a shift in decision makers' cognitive processes from sex-based prototypes to sex-neutral prototypes would work toward leveling the playing field for women vis-à-vis men in the managerial ranks. Although other barriers to women's representation and advancement in the managerial ranks (to be discussed later in this chapter) are likely to remain, a change in leader stereotypes to an androgynous rather than masculine profile would represent one less barrier for women to overcome.[17]

Leader stereotypes may be influenced by the intersection of leader sex and race. Studies have found that leaders tend to be associated with *Whiteness*, defined as being categorized on the basis of race as White or being seen as possessing stereotypically White traits.[18] Combining these results with earlier results suggests a "think manager—think White male" paradigm of leader stereotypes.

Leader stereotypes may also be affected by the intersection of leader sex and sexual orientation. A study that followed Schein's procedure asked respondents to describe how well each of a list of characteristics fit successful managers, heterosexual male managers, heterosexual female managers, gay male managers, or lesbian female managers. Comparisons of these profiles indicated that heterosexual male managers were seen as more similar to the successful manager profile than gay male or lesbian female managers. Gay male managers were seen as similar to heterosexual female managers but not heterosexual male managers, reflecting a profile consistent with the female gender stereotype; in contrast, lesbian female managers were seen as similar to both heterosexual male and heterosexual female managers, reflecting more of a balance of masculine and feminine traits or an androgynous profile. Thus, a "think manager—think heterosexual male" paradigm may characterize leader stereotypes.[19]

Finally, the intersection of leader sex and parental status may affect leader stereotypes. Another study that followed Schein's procedure asked respondents to describe how well each of a list of characteristics fit successful middle managers, women, men, mothers, or fathers. Mothers were seen as more similar to successful middle managers than women in general, and fathers were seen as more similar to successful middle managers than men in general. However, fathers were seen as more similar to successful middle managers than mothers were. Thus, there seemed to be a parental advantage in leader stereotypes and a larger advantage for men than women. These results suggest the existence of a "think manager—think parent" paradigm of leader stereotypes.[20]

In summary, research on leader stereotypes has historically provided support for the think manager—think male paradigm focusing on leader sex and the think manager—think masculine paradigm focusing on the fit between gender stereotypes and leader stereotypes. Recent evidence suggests the possible emergence of a think manager—think androgynous paradigm to supplant the think manager—think masculine paradigm. In addition, leader stereotypes may be influenced by the intersection of leader sex with other personal characteristics such as race, sexual orientation, and parental status. Overall, leader stereotypes, which are subject to the influence of many factors in conjunction with leader sex, may determine whether and how the playing field for attaining and advancing in the managerial ranks is tilted in favor of some candidates over others.

LINKAGES OF LEADERSHIP THEORIES TO GENDER STEREOTYPES

Theories of leadership go back at least as far as Machiavelli, who in *The Prince*, offered leaders the following advice:

> [The question arises,] Is it better to be loved more than feared, or feared more than loved? The reply is that one ought to be both feared and loved, but as it is difficult for the two to go together, it is much safer to be feared than loved.[21]

Note the masculine imagery in Machiavelli's advice. Using terms with which we are by now familiar, he advises leaders to focus on agentic, dominance-oriented behaviors (associated with the masculine gender stereotype) to evoke fear rather than communal, warmth-oriented behaviors (associated with the feminine gender stereotype) to evoke love if there is a choice to be made. Of course, he was writing for princes, not princesses.

In this vein, early scholarly theories of what leaders do and what does and does not work well were based almost entirely on studies of male managers. A classic review of research on leadership published five decades ago discovered few studies that examined female leaders exclusively or even included female leaders in their samples.[22] When female managers were present in organizations being studied, they were usually excluded from the analysis because researchers thought that their few numbers might distort the results. It was as if female managers, even though their numbers were small, were less legitimate or less worthy of observation than male managers. Although researchers no longer exclude female managers from their samples, many of the existing theories of leadership were developed with male managers in mind.

There are two distinct types of behavior that managers may use to influence the actions of their subordinates. The first type, **task style** or task accomplishment, refers to the extent to which the manager initiates and organizes work activity and defines the way work is to be done. For example, a manager who reorganizes a department, develops a description of the function of each department member, formulates department and individual goals, assigns projects, and gives details on how projects should be conducted may be considered high in task style. The second type, **interpersonal style** or maintenance of interpersonal relationships, refers to the extent to which the manager engages in activities that tend to the morale and welfare of people. For example, a manager who expresses appreciation to subordinates for work performed well, demonstrates concern about their job and work satisfaction, and tries to build their self-esteem may be considered high in interpersonal style. A manager may be high in both task and interpersonal styles, low in both, or high in one but not the other.[23]

Managers may also exhibit different decision-making styles. A leader who exhibits a **democratic style of decision making** allows subordinates to participate in decision making, whereas a leader who exhibits an **autocratic style of decision making** discourages such participation. These are generally considered to be opposite decision-making styles.[24]

In recent decades, transformational and transactional leadership have received the most attention in leadership theories and research.[25] **Transformational leadership** motivates subordinates to transcend their own self-interests for the good of the group or organization by setting exceptionally high standards for performance and then developing subordinates to achieve these standards. In this way, they turn followers into leaders. Transformational leaders exhibit four types of behavior: (1) *charisma*, by displaying attributes that induce subordinates to view them as role models and behaviors that communicate a sense of values, purpose, and the importance of the mission; (2) *inspirational motivation,* by exuding optimism and excitement about the mission and its attainability; (3) *intellectual stimulation*, by encouraging subordinates to question basic assumptions and consider problems and tasks from new perspectives; and (4) *individualized consideration*, by focusing on the development and mentoring of subordinates as individuals and attending to their specific needs.[26]

In contrast, **transactional leadership** focuses on clarifying the responsibilities of subordinates and then responding to how well subordinates execute their responsibilities. Transactional leaders exhibit two kinds of behavior: (1) *contingent reward*, by promising and providing suitable rewards if subordinates achieve their assigned objectives and (2) *management by exception*, by intervening to correct subordinate performance either in anticipation of a problem or after a problem has occurred. Leaders who engage in active management by exception systematically monitor subordinate performance for mistakes, whereas those who engage in passive management by exception wait for subordinate difficulties to be brought to their attention before intervening. Transformational leaders may be transactional when it is necessary to achieve their goals. However, transactional leaders are seldom transformational.

Distinct from both transformational and transactional leadership is **laissez-faire leadership.** Laissez-faire leaders avoid taking responsibility for leadership altogether. Such leaders refrain from giving direction or making decisions and do not involve themselves in the development of their subordinates.

Several linkages may be made between gender stereotypes and leadership theories. A high propensity to exhibit task-oriented behaviors such as setting goals and initiating work activity is associated with the masculine gender stereotype. A high propensity to exhibit interpersonally oriented behaviors such as showing consideration toward subordinates and demonstrating concern for their satisfaction is associated with the feminine gender stereotype. When individuals exhibit a balance of task-oriented and interpersonally oriented behaviors, they adopt the profile of an androgynous leader.

Further, the autocratic style of decision making is more associated with the masculine stereotype, reflecting a greater emphasis on dominance and control over others. In contrast, the democratic style of decision making is more associated with the feminine stereotype, reflecting a greater emphasis on the involvement of others.[27]

Transformational leadership is positively associated with nurturance and agreeableness (feminine traits) and negatively associated with aggression (a masculine trait). Individualized consideration is congruent with the feminine gender stereotype because its developmental focus reflects a high concern with relationships and the needs of others. However, both active and passive management by exception are congruent with the masculine gender stereotype in their focus on correcting subordinates' mistakes because they stress immediate task accomplishment over long-term building of relationships and favor use of the leadership position to dominate others. In addition, contingent reward is congruent with the masculine gender stereotype because it is primarily task oriented. Laissez-faire leadership is not associated with either the masculine or feminine gender stereotype. Overall, transformational leadership appears to be more congruent with the feminine than the masculine gender stereotype, whereas transactional leadership appears to be more congruent with the masculine than the feminine gender stereotype.[28]

Recall that leader stereotypes have historically placed a high value on masculine characteristics. Even though early leadership theories were developed when there were far fewer women in leadership roles, a review of major theories does not support gender stereotypes. Instead, leadership theories do not suggest that either feminine or masculine behaviors are the key to leader effectiveness. Leadership theories in general have devoted little attention to androgynous leadership.

SEX DIFFERENCES IN LEADER BEHAVIOR AND EFFECTIVENESS

Researchers have devoted a great deal of attention to sex differences in leader behavior and effectiveness.[29] In fact, so many research studies have been conducted that several meta-analyses, which synthesize evidence across research studies, have been reported.

Sex differences have been examined in several types of leader behaviors. A meta-analysis of sex differences in task style, interpersonal style, and democratic versus autocratic decision-making style examined organizational studies that compare the actual behavior of men and women in equivalent leadership roles. Contrary to gender stereotypes, men and women did not differ in task style or interpersonal style. However, in support of gender stereotypes, women tended to be more democratic and less autocratic leaders than men.[30]

A meta-analysis of sex differences in transformational, transactional, and laissez-faire leadership found that female leaders are more transformational than their male counterparts. Women were rated higher than men on all dimensions of transformational leadership: charisma (especially attributes that motivate pride and respect), inspirational motivation, intellectual stimulation, and individualized consideration. Women also were rated higher than men on the contingent reward dimension of transactional leadership. In contrast, men were rated higher than women on the active and passive dimensions of transactional leadership and in laissez-faire leadership.[31]

Meta-analyses also have been conducted of the linkages of transformational, transactional, and laissez-faire leadership to leader effectiveness. Overall, these meta-analyses suggest that all of the dimensions of transformational leadership and the contingent reward dimension of transactional leadership are positively associated with leader effectiveness as reflected in individual, group, and organizational performance. In contrast, the passive management by exception dimension of transactional leadership and laissez-faire leadership are negatively associated with leader effectiveness.[32]

Cumulatively, what do these various meta-analyses tell us? If we combine meta-analytic results of the linkages of leader sex to transformational, transactional, and laissez-faire leadership with meta-analytic results of the linkages of these leadership styles to leader effectiveness, we find that (1) women are rated higher than men in behaviors that contribute to their effectiveness as leaders and (2) women are rated lower than men in behaviors that detract from their effectiveness as leaders.

However, situational factors may influence the linkage between sex and leader effectiveness. For example, male leaders may be more effective than female leaders in male-intensive settings such as the military, whereas female leaders may be more effective than male leaders in female-intensive settings such as education and social services. Male leaders may be more effective than female leaders when the particular leader role examined is more congruent with the male gender role, whereas female leaders may be more effective than male leaders when the particular leader role examined is more congruent with the female gender role. Further, male leaders may be more effective than female leaders in lower-level management positions, whereas female leaders may be more effective than male leaders in middle-level management positions. The position of middle manager is often regarded as requiring heavy use of interpersonal skills to wield influence, which would favor women according to gender stereotypes.[33]

An intriguing meta-analysis focused on perceptions of leader effectiveness. When self-ratings of leader effectiveness were examined, men rated themselves as more effective leaders than women rated themselves. In contrast, when ratings of leader effectiveness by others (e.g., bosses, peers, or subordinates) were examined, women were rated as more effective leaders than men. These results suggest that men overestimate and women underestimate their own leader effectiveness compared with how others perceive them as leaders. That is, in men's views, there is a male advantage in leader effectiveness that is not supported by observers' perceptions. Here is an example of what overconfidence in your own leadership abilities—which men have been found to possess as a group in abundance—may get you: glory in your own eyes ("What a great leader I am!") but not in the eyes of others.[34]

In summary, results of meta-analyses suggest a female leadership advantage. However, situational factors are likely to influence whether this advantage is displayed in a given organizational context. Also, as the media debate over whether women make better bosses as well as trends in leader preferences suggest, who possesses an advantage in the managerial ranks (if anyone) may depend on whom you ask.

It should be noted that evidence regarding the linkage between androgynous leadership and leader effectiveness is limited and is certainly insufficient to conduct a meta-analysis of research results.[35] However, recent evidence collected during a crisis situation may be instructive. During the early stages of the COVID-19 pandemic, U.S. states with female governors reported fewer deaths than states with male governors, a rough measure of leader effectiveness at the time. Analysis of press briefings suggested that female governors expressed both greater confidence (a masculine trait) and greater empathy (a feminine trait) than male governors, which resulted in their displaying an androgynous profile. Also, female heads of state during the same period of time led by exhibiting a combination of traits associated with femininity such as humanity (e.g., kindness, care, nurturance, compassion) and traits associated with masculinity such as courage (e.g., fortitude, bravery, valor, daring), thereby also exhibiting an androgynous profile. This evidence suggests that there is an androgynous leadership advantage.[36]

GLASS CEILINGS

The **glass ceiling** is defined as "a transparent barrier that [keeps] women from rising above a certain level in corporations."[37] The term is primarily used to refer to women's restricted access to top management levels, although glass ceilings can exist at any managerial level. According to the glass ceiling metaphor, success consists of climbing to the peak of a mountain and impediments to success consist of transparent, invisible ceilings that block or limit access to the peak for women; as a result, women can see the mountain peak, but they face greater obstacles than men in attaining it. Similar metaphors include labyrinth, sticky floor, glass chain, glass slipper, glass escalator, concrete ceiling (for women of color), celluloid ceiling (for women in Hollywood), and marble ceiling (for women in government).[38] I use the term *glass ceiling* because it has been the most popular metaphor to refer to barriers to women's attaining top management positions.

Many explanations have been proposed for the existence of glass ceilings—examples of which are reviewed in this section of the chapter.[39] To provide a simple example, consider where the concept of *organizational hierarchy*—a familiar organizational structure—came from. Might it possibly have come from men's greater display of dominance in patriarchal social systems, including in work teams (as discussed in Chapter 5) and in organizational settings overall? Hierarchies enable employees in higher-level positions (whomever they may be) to dominate employees in lower-level positions. Hierarchies may have become the prevalent organizational form because they were designed by men to meet the needs of men. Thus, organizational structures may be gendered because they originate in gendered social systems.[40]

Person-centered explanations for glass ceilings suggest that women's traits and behaviors are less suitable than those of men for top management positions. Early person-centered explanations for why there are so few women in top management positions included that (1) women exhibit a fear of success as an underlying personality characteristic, (2) women have less motivation to manage then men, (3) women believe stereotypes about themselves as unfit to manage and act accordingly, and (4) women's inclusion in the top management ranks causes societal harm because their children, husbands, and homes inevitably suffer. Overall, person-centered explanations have been largely discredited by scholars.[41] Nonetheless, they retain an enduring appeal for some people.

For example, the **opt-out revolution** has been offered as a person-centered explanation for glass ceilings in the popular media. According to media reports, educated women are increasingly choosing to opt out of careers that place them on the fast track to top management because of parenthood or other personal reasons.[42] A meta-analysis of sex differences in leadership aspirations found that women exhibited lower aspirations than men. However, rather than opting out, some scholars have argued that women are pushed out of managerial career tracks because of managers' biased evaluations of them as less career-motivated than men, which hinders their being developed for top management positions and suppresses their leadership aspirations.[43]

Tony Butterfield and I explored this person-centered explanation for glass ceilings further by examining the linkages of sex and gender role identity to aspirations to top management over a period of time spanning five decades in the same two early-career populations as for our "good manager" studies: undergraduate business students and part-time (evening) MBA students. Overall, respondents' gender role identity, especially the masculinity dimension, predicted aspirations to top management for each population. Respondent sex predicted aspirations to top management for undergraduate business students, with women's aspirations lower than those of men (but not for part-time MBAs). However, undergraduate women's aspirations to top management declined during the 21st century, whereas undergraduate men's aspirations to top management did not, suggesting a shift in the linkage of sex to these students' aspirations over time.[44]

Why did the relationship between respondent gender and aspirations to top management differ between these two early-career populations? Although all respondents were pursuing a business degree, part-time MBAs had more full-time work experience and were enrolled in a higher-level degree program than undergraduate business students. The MBA degree, which is viewed as explicitly preparing students for managerial careers, may have been more likely to attract students, regardless of their sex, who aspired to top management. Further, part-time MBAs may have been subjected to organizational norms that the appropriate level of aspiration for them to display (regardless of their sex) was to top management if they wanted to advance in managerial hierarchies. Displaying high aspirations to top management may have been one of the norms to which part-time MBA students needed to adhere to play the promotion game in their organizations. In contrast, undergraduate business students, prior to beginning their full-time careers, had not been subjected to such norms yet.[45]

Why might undergraduate women's aspirations to top management—but not those of undergraduate men—have declined during the 21st century? Perhaps undergraduate women had been influenced by media reports of women's presumed *lack* of aspirations to top management and inclinations to opt out of fast-track managerial careers. Self-help books with career advice from celebrity female executives ("female heroes") such as Sheryl Sandberg, who suggests that women need to **lean in** to overcome a "leadership ambition gap," have become a popular genre in this century. Such books are appealing to some women because they focus on what women can do to break through glass ceilings on their own.[46] However, Sandberg's critics have accused her of perpetuating a "fix the woman" focus by calling on women to change themselves to succeed and of being naïve by advocating—as a White, highly educated billionaire—that women should lean in to be successful in their careers; such advice may be insufficient for women of color or lower-income women to succeed. Also, it might be beneficial for women's success in life if men were to "lean out" a little.[47]

Nonetheless, in response to messages such as that offered by Sandberg, undergraduate women may have been increasingly opting out of aspiring to top management even before "opting in" to their full-time work careers. They may also have been influenced by their mothers' experiences in the workplace, which involve gender inequities that were hoped to eventually disappear in the optimistic days of the women's liberation movement but still remain five decades later. Further, undergraduate women may have lowered their aspirations to top management during this century in light of the fact that there are still so few women in top management. As women's college-age career aspirations predict whether they eventually achieve top management positions or not, this may be an example of a self-fulfilling prophecy.[48]

Decision-maker–centered explanations for glass ceilings focus on the cognitive processes, perceptions, and top manager prototypes held by the people who make the decisions about who gets promoted to the executive suite. These decisions are more likely to be influenced by decision makers' cognitive processes than decisions about lower-level managerial positions. The higher the position within the managerial ranks, the less the importance of "objective" credentials such as education and training.[49] As a result, women's increased educational attainment over the last five decades (see Chapter 2) has a greater effect on hiring and promotion into entry-level management positions than on promotions to top management. The effect of decision makers' biases and stereotypes is likely to be greater when there is less reliance on objective credentials and more reliance on subjective factors such as perceived fit.

In her classic study, Rosabeth Moss Kanter characterized the results of such decision-making processes as **homosocial reproduction.** She argued that the primary motivation in organizational bureaucracies is to minimize uncertainty and risk in decision making. Uncertainty is present whenever individuals are relied upon, and the effects of such uncertainty are greatest when these individuals hold significant responsibility for the direction of the organization, such as top executives. One way to minimize uncertainty in the executive suite is to close top management positions to people who are regarded as different. Women have a difficult time in entering top management positions because they are seen as posing too much uncertainty by male decision makers. As a result, male decision makers tend to overwhelmingly choose male candidates for top management positions.[50]

Decision makers' perceptions of the effects of senior-level women's hormones versus those of senior-level men offer an explanation for glass ceilings that focuses on biological forces (discussed in Chapter 3). Decision makers for promotions to top management, who are predominantly male, may perceive senior-level women as governed by fluctuating hormones throughout and beyond their reproductive years, indicating their lack of competence to make the rational decisions required of a top executive. In contrast, senior-level men's hormones are assumed to be less problematic; in fact, a combination of high testosterone and low cortisol levels is associated with men attaining high status in managerial hierarchies. The **perceived linkage between "reproductivity and productivity"** represents a barrier to women attaining top management positions that contributes to sex discrimination. The negative effects of this perceived linkage for women were also seen in research regarding sex discrimination on the basis of pregnancy, discussed in Chapter 4. They reflect a general discomfort with female bodies in the workplace—in this case, in top management positions.[51]

Decision makers' inclinations for hiring women for top management positions may be shaped by or reflected in the nature of their leisure activities. In particular, many top executives play golf, a male-dominated sport that has been especially exclusionary; elite country clubs have historically been segregated on the basis of sex as well as race, religion, and class. A study found that chief executive officers (CEOs) who golf were less likely to have a female member of their top management team (TMT) than non-golfing CEOs. The negative effect of a golfing CEO on female TMT representation was accentuated when the CEO had graduated from an elite university. Further, the sex gap in TMT earnings, if the TMT had a female member at all, was greater in organizations in which the CEO played golf. These results suggest that although golf has been described as an ideal opportunity for networking, it may limit female advancement to top management levels by imposing what may be called a **grass ceiling.**[52]

Decision makers also take into account the organizational context in which they are filling top management positions. Research suggests that when women do break glass ceilings, they are likely to find themselves on a **glass cliff**, such that their leadership positions are precarious or risky compared with those of their male counterparts. That is, during times of poor organizational performance, decision makers tend to adopt a "think crisis—think female" prototype. As a result, female CEOs experience greater pressures than their male counterparts from the onset of their terms. They come under greater threat from activist investors, have shorter tenure in the position, and are more likely to be fired even when their firm is performing well. Glass cliffs represent a second wave of sex discrimination that occurs as (some) women break through glass ceilings.[53]

Consistent with the notion of the glass cliff, women of color, men of color, and White women tend to be promoted to more precarious CEO positions than White men. Further, when firm performance declines during their tenure as CEOs, they tend to be replaced by White men, which has been dubbed the "savior effect." Thus, the intersection of the sex and race of candidates for CEO positions influences who faces a glass cliff if they assume the position.[54]

Female decision makers who have broken through glass ceilings may influence the advancement of lower-level women who might be future candidates for top management positions. The **consequences of women's breaking through glass ceilings for other women** have been depicted in both negative and positive terms. On the *negative* side, there is evidence of psychological "micro-violence" in women's work relations with other women. Women in top management have been found to exhibit micro-violence across organizational levels by manipulating relationships with, distancing themselves from, and hindering the advancement of lower-level women. Whereas early usage of the "queen bee" metaphor blamed top-level women themselves for having negative relations with lower-level women, others have blamed gendered social systems in which women in top management feel compelled to "ventriloquize patriarchal attitudes." This body of research suggests that individual women's rising above a glass ceiling may contribute to keeping other women below it, which also represents a second wave of sex discrimination[55]

On the *positive* side, there is evidence of senior women helping other women. For example, women are more likely to be promoted to top management positions when boards of directors have a greater proportion of female members as well as a female chair; in turn, female CEOs are more likely than male CEOs to seek female board directors. Also, higher proportions of women in top management positions have been found to contribute to lower-level women feeling less competitive with each other, which would minimize the kinds of micro-violence in women's work relations that were described above. Further, increases of women in top management have been associated with increases of women in lower-level managerial positions. This body of research suggests that individual women rising above a glass ceiling is aided by other women who have already risen above the same ceiling and who foster positive work environments for lower-level women. Given this mixed evidence, further research is needed to identify the conditions under which the presence of women in top management hinders or helps other women.[56]

If women in general experience barriers to attaining top management positions, women of color experience even greater barriers. Because of the predominance of White men in these positions, women of color are two degrees removed from what may be regarded as the "White male" top management prototype; in contrast, White women and men of color are one degree removed from this prototype. As a result, women of color are the most underrepresented group in the top management ranks. The intersection of sex and race influences the extent to which women of color experience barriers to their attaining top management positions and their experiences once they attain such positions.[57]

For example, Black female executives who have broken through glass ceilings experience what may be called **intersectional invisibility**. That is, because of their belonging to intersecting groups on the basis of sex and race, they are both invisible (few in number, likely to be overlooked) and hypervisible (standing out among their executive peers, likely to be highly scrutinized). The combination of invisibility and hypervisibility confers "outsider within" status to Black female executives. This status contributes to their experiencing either benign intersectional invisibility (the effects of their sex and race cancel each other) or hostile intersectional invisibility (the negative effects of their sex and race strengthen each other). Thus, the intersection of Black female executives' sex and race may yield no overall effect or a double disadvantage, depending on the direction of the intersectional effect.[58]

Although decision-maker–centered explanations for glass ceilings disagree on the underlying rationale, they agree that women tend to be discriminated against when decisions are made for promotions to top management. However, sex discrimination is not necessarily intentional; decision makers may be unaware of how their biases affect their decisions about top management positions. Unconscious cognitive processes, including decision makers' leader stereotypes, preferences for similar others, beliefs about hormonal influences, assessments of the fit of candidates for top management positions depending on the precariousness of the position, and other factors may lead to their making biased judgments that result in sex discrimination favoring men. Further, due to the influence of the intersection of sex and race, White men may possess a special advantage and women of color a special disadvantage in their attainment of and experiences in top management positions. Overall, these considerations suggest that any organizational processes that neutralize or eliminate the effects of biases on the basis of leader sex will contribute to the shattering of glass ceilings, which leads us to the implications of our viewing the "elephant" of the intersection of sex, gender, and leadership from different perspectives.

PROMOTING EFFECTIVE LEADERSHIP

In Chapter 3, Sandra Bem was quoted as saying that "*behavior* should have no gender."[59] Ideally, to amend Bem's statement, *leader behavior* should have no gender. As some of the comments on the *New York Times* online debate stated, the sex of individuals who hold leader roles should be of little concern. What should matter is how well individuals respond to the demands of the particular leader role that they occupy regardless of their sex.

What is required to create a working environment in which individuals with equal leadership abilities have an equal chance to be effective in the leader role? Table 6.1 summarizes recommended actions. To achieve this objective, prejudices against women as leaders must be confronted. Such prejudices are most likely to be exhibited in masculinized work settings in which the majority of leaders and followers are men and the leader role is associated with the male gender role. In such settings, the playing field is tilted in favor of men.[60]

To give women a greater chance of being effective in highly masculinized settings, organizations need to consider the ways in which leaders are evaluated. When leaders in masculinized settings are evaluated on the basis of whether they promote group cohesiveness and develop subordinates for future roles as well as accomplish tasks, female leaders—who rank higher in individualized consideration than male leaders—have more of an opportunity to be seen as effective. To take advantage of this opportunity, they need to have resources to promote subordinate development.

Organizations need to take steps to increase the legitimacy of female leaders. As for the selection of team members (see Chapter 5), the appointment of individuals to leadership roles should be accompanied by publicity about their special

TABLE 6.1 ■ Recommended Actions
1. Confront prejudices against leaders on the basis of their sex.
2. Evaluate leaders on the basis of group cohesiveness and development of subordinates for future roles as well as task accomplishment.
3. Publicize qualifications of individuals assigned to leader positions.
4. Develop the capabilities of all individuals to play leader roles.
5. Create conditions that give female and male leaders with equivalent credentials equal chances to succeed.
6. Confront beliefs that you do not have what it takes to be a great leader and prove them wrong.
7. If you are the first woman to hold a particular leadership position, take advantage of being seen as a symbol of change.
8. If you are a CEO, engage in gender-inclusive gatekeeping by pre-succession mentoring of and post-succession partnering with your successor.
9. Increase accountability of decision makers and promote uniformity on the decision-making process for all managerial positions.
10. Make promotion procedures for managerial positions well-known to all potential applicants.
11. Incorporate the concept of androgynous leadership into leadership training and development programs

skills, expertise, and accomplishments. This information should be provided for all individuals who assume leader roles (not only women) to avoid drawing attention to female leaders as a group. Such an action will reduce the potential for stereotyping of leaders according to their sex because of insufficient or inaccurate information.[61]

Male leaders in settings that are more congenial to women face somewhat different issues. Because men have more societal status than women, they are likely to be granted higher status in a feminized work setting than female leaders are granted in a masculinized work setting. However, male leaders may still be subjected to sexist attitudes. As discussed in Chapter 3, negative attitudes toward men may range from hostile sexism to benevolent sexism. Male leaders do not deserve to be the target of sexist attitudes any more than female leaders do. When sexist attitudes are directed toward male as well as female leaders, they have to be addressed.

No matter what the setting, organizations need to be ready to act when their members embrace stereotypical views or display prejudices toward members of a particular sex as leaders. Although beliefs (e.g., leader stereotypes) and attitudes (e.g., biases against women or men as leaders) are difficult to change, organizations must take steps to counteract problematic beliefs and attitudes. Leadership training programs should make individuals aware of the ways in which biases related to sex (as well as race, ethnicity, age, sexual orientation, etc.) can affect their decisions and teach them how to move beyond their own biases.[62]

When stereotyping of leaders occurs in an organizational setting, the risk is that potential or actual leaders will fall for the stereotypes and see themselves as others see them, whether or not their personal traits actually fit the stereotypes. No matter how they may be stereotyped, leaders of both sexes need to be ready to demonstrate their capabilities as leaders and to disprove anyone who thinks otherwise. Asking their superiors to back them up when others second-guess them may also be helpful in establishing their leadership credentials.[63]

Women who enter managerial levels numerically dominated by men are often seen as powerful symbols of changing organizational realities. The appointment of women to top management positions may mean that the organization now values the attributes associated with women. These women should be ready to take advantage of their potential status as symbols of change.[64]

However, for newly appointed female CEOs to overcome the glass cliff phenomenon and successfully enact organizational change, gender-inclusive gatekeeping by their (mostly male) predecessors is helpful. A study of CEO successions that involved female successors identified actions by CEO predecessors that were beneficial to their successors. The predecessor's handpicking an insider female successor with similar experience and career path and mentoring her to take challenging roles to increase the breadth of her experience and raise her visibility in the company was critical. Also, the predecessor's working with the successor in a post-succession partnership, often as chair of the corporate board of directors, promoted her success. Overall, the combination of pre-succession mentoring and post-succession partnering contributed to the predecessor turning over the legacy to the female successor and enhanced the likelihood that high organizational performance would follow.[65]

Conditions that contribute to the existence of glass ceilings need to be recognized and changed. The U.S. government provides a good example of conditions that discourage the existence of glass ceilings. It places a high degree of emphasis on procedural fairness in making promotion decisions for its nonmilitary top management positions (except those reserved for political appointees) known as the Senior Executive Service (SES). First, it requires that all open SES positions be made known through a public announcement. Second, it requires that all promotion decisions be made using the same basic procedure. Third, it requires that records be kept of the entire decision-making process. By providing structure to the decision-making process and enabling identification of decisions that are not properly made, these requirements make decision makers accountable for how their SES promotion decisions are made.[66]

The U.S. government's experience suggests that when decision making is open and a systematic procedure is used, conditions that contribute to the existence of glass ceilings may be averted. When procedures for promotion decisions are standardized and criteria for decisions are well established, qualified women may fare at least as well as qualified men. When procedures are not standardized or when criteria for promotion decisions are unspecified or vague, there may be more occasion for leader stereotypes and prejudices favoring men to affect the outcomes of the promotion process. The promotion procedures used for top management positions in the federal government may also be beneficially applied to promotion decisions about open management positions at lower levels.

Research evidence suggests that women tend to exhibit leader behaviors that contribute to leader effectiveness more than men do. However, this is *not* to say that organizations should choose women for leader roles on the basis of their sex. The challenge for organizations is to take advantage of and develop the capabilities of all individuals who have the potential to be effective leaders and then create opportunities and conditions that give all leaders a chance to succeed. The proper goal for leadership training and development programs is not to teach men how to behave more like women or to teach women how to behave more like men. No matter what the intersection of sex, gender, and leadership may be, the goal should be to enhance the likelihood that all leaders are effective.

Has the time of androgynous leadership arrived? Recent evidence suggests a shift toward both an androgynous leader prototype and an androgynous leadership advantage. While further evidence is being gathered about the merits of androgynous leadership, it may be useful for the concept to be incorporated into leadership training and development programs.[67]

In conclusion, as for the six blind men who journey to see the elephant, it may be beyond our grasp to gain a full sense of what the intersection of sex, gender, and leadership is like. However, unlike the six blind men, we don't need to engage in heated debate over whose view is superior. None of the ways of seeing that are presented in this chapter as different perspectives of this intersection is inherently superior to the other ways of seeing.[68]

The last word in this update from the gender and leadership wars appropriately comes from another of the more than 500 responses to the *New York Times* online debate:[69]

> Rather than looking backward, I hope that we will look toward the potential of men and women to be great managers and remove obstacles in their way. (*Julie*, #387)

7 DEALING WITH SOCIAL SEXUAL BEHAVIOR IN THE WORKPLACE

LEARNING OBJECTIVES

After reading this chapter, you should be able to do the following:

7.1 Appreciate the pervasiveness of different types of social sexual behavior in the workplace.

7.2 Discuss definitions of, explanations for, and individuals' experiences with sexual harassment.

7.3 Appraise the legacy of the #MeToo movement.

7.4 Discuss the causes, dynamics, and consequences of workplace romances.

7.5 Identify actions that may be taken by organizations and individuals to address social sexual behavior in the workplace when needed.

WHETHER WELCOME OR UNWELCOME, IT'S PERVASIVE

Social sexual behavior is a term that refers to a wide range of workplace behaviors that have a sexual component but no task-related component.[1] Some social sexual behaviors may be welcome by the parties involved, and other behaviors may be unwelcome. In this chapter, we discuss **sexual harassment**, the directing of unwelcome sexual attention by one member of an organization toward another, and **workplace romance**, the sharing of welcome sexual attention by two members of an organization, as distinct types of social sexual behavior. Sexual harassment is a matter of public concern with potential legal ramifications. Workplace romances are a frequent subject of public debate: How should participants and their organizations handle them? Even when organizational employees do not participate in romances, they frequently have to deal with the intermingling of work roles and sexual roles by other employees.

Sexual harassment is a pervasive phenomenon. Although the proportions of women and men who report having experienced sexually harassing behavior at work depend somewhat on the research method used to assess the prevalence of sexual harassment, over 50% of working women and over 30% of working men have reported experiencing it. A survey found that about 25% of LGBTQ+ (lesbian, gay, bisexual, transgender, and self-described queer) employees reported having experienced sexual harassment based on their sexual orientation or gender identity. Further, female-to-male transgender employees have reported experiencing *less* sexual harassment after their transition than before, whereas male-to-female transgender employees have reported experiencing *more* sexual harassment after their transition than before; these results parallel those for cisgender employees, with cisgender women having experienced more sexual harassment than cisgender men.[2]

Sexual harassment as a workplace phenomenon exploded into the public consciousness after allegations that Harvey Weinstein, co-founder and then chief executive officer (CEO) of Miramax (a prominent movie studio), had engaged in truly despicable behavior toward women—sexual harassment, assault, and rape over a period of almost three decades—became public knowledge. This pattern of behavior had persisted despite prior internal circulation of a memo detailing misconduct by Weinstein; many board members and company executives were already aware of his behavior toward women. On many occasions, he had reached financial settlements with women he had harassed that included nondisclosure agreements, which legally prevented them from speaking out about his behavior. It took public exposure of his appalling behavior to force the company's all-male board of directors to act. Three days after the initial allegations were published, Weinstein was fired by the remaining board members, one-third of whom had already resigned upon learning of the allegations or seeing the allegations go public. At the time of this writing, Weinstein is a convicted sex offender for multiple crimes and is serving prison time.[3]

After the initial allegations against Weinstein were published, a flood of further allegations against him from over 90 women as well as allegations against other powerful men soon followed. A hashtag movement called **#MeToo**, based on the original Me Too movement that was founded before hashtags even existed, was launched by victims of sexual harassment in support of other victims, with hundreds of thousands of women worldwide sharing their experiences. How sexual harassment was viewed by the public seemed qualitatively different than in the past, with deeper and more sustained outrage triggered than in earlier allegations of sexual harassment by powerful men. However, if the Weinstein allegations were unique, it was only in the level of depravity at top management levels that they portrayed. Numerous reports of rampant sexual harassment by other powerful men came to light in the wake of the #MeToo movement. In the year after the Weinstein allegations became public knowledge, the movement was reported to have brought down 201 powerful men and three powerful women, including the heads of Amazon Studios, Barnes and Noble, Wynn Resorts, and the CBS Corporation. Sexual harassment was now affecting the careers of CEOs as well as their company's bottom line. The legacy of the #MeToo movement is discussed later in the chapter.[4]

Workplace romance is also a pervasive phenomenon, with an estimated one-third of employees who are currently involved or have been romantically involved with a coworker and an estimated one-third to one-half of romantic relationships having commenced on the job. This proportion rose during the COVID-19 pandemic, even as much work was being conducted virtually.[5]

Similar to sexual harassment, workplace romance may affect the careers of CEOs and their companies' financial livelihoods. For example, the CEOs of companies such as McDonald's, Intel, REI, Lululemon, Best Buy, Highmark, Priceline, Starwood Hotels, Hewlett-Packard, and Boeing were forced to resign their jobs after affairs they had with employees became public knowledge. Negative publicity from the public disclosure of social sexual behavior by top executives, whether sexual harassment or workplace romance, tends to be frowned upon by investors and is reflected in decreased market valuations.[6]

Sexual harassment is illegal, but there are no laws against workplace romance. Also, sexual harassment typically victimizes and offends the target person and may promote a hostile work environment for others. There is not necessarily a "victim" of a workplace romance, although one or both parties may pay a price in their emotional health, task assignments, or career advancement if others see it as inappropriate. In such cases, the participants are seen as having brought on their own troubles rather than having been victimized by others.

Before we proceed, it should be noted that sometimes people strategically use their sexuality at work simply as a way to influence others and achieve desired goals. For example, a waitress at a comedy club who was interviewed for a study reported that she tried different looks such as wearing a miniskirt, short shorts, and a low-cut blouse to increase the size of tips she received from male customers. Her way of using her sexuality in such a work environment does not constitute either sexual harassment or workplace romance.[7]

In this chapter, we examine explanations for and experiences with both sexual harassment and workplace romance. In addition, we discuss what organizations and individuals can do in response to sexual harassment and workplace romance. As we shall see, social sexual behavior in the workplace poses a challenge for managers. They cannot ban social sexual behavior at work, but they also cannot ignore it.

SEXUAL HARASSMENT

In this section, we address the following questions: (1) How may sexual harassment be defined? (2) How may sexual harassment be explained? (3) What are peoples' experiences with sexual harassment?[8]

Definitions

Definitions of sexual harassment have been incorporated into laws and guidelines around the world. In the United States, the Equal Employment Opportunity Commission (EEOC) defines sexual harassment as an unlawful employment practice under Title VII of the 1964 Civil Rights Act. Its guidelines on sexual harassment state

> Unwelcome sexual advances, requests for sexual favors, and other verbal or physical conduct of a sexual nature constitute sexual harassment when (1) submission to such conduct is made either explicitly or implicitly a term or condition of an individual's employment, (2) submission to or rejection of such conduct by an individual is used as the basis for employment decisions affecting such individual, or (3) such conduct has the purpose or effect of unreasonably interfering with an individual's work performance or creating an intimidating, hostile, or offensive working environment.

An employer is held responsible for acts of sexual harassment when it knew or should have known of the conduct and failed to take immediate and appropriate corrective action.[9]

The European Union (EU) established standards for what constitutes illegal sexual harassment within its member nations. It defines *sexual harassment* as "any form of unwanted verbal, nonverbal or physical conduct of a sexual nature that occurs with the purpose or effect of violating the dignity of a person, in particular when creating an intimidating, hostile, degrading, humiliating or offensive environment." Although the directive allows latitude among EU members in deciding what specific behaviors constitute illegal sexual harassment, it has shaped the nature of members' legal approaches to sexual harassment.[10]

There is no universal legal definition of sexual harassment, and nation-specific definitions are subject to interpretation by courts. Nonetheless, common themes that the behavior is unwanted and negatively impacts targets' work experiences and environments have emerged in legal definitions across nations. Two types of sexual harassment have been generally recognized by courts as illegal: quid pro quo harassment and hostile environment harassment. In **quid pro quo sexual harassment**, the harasser asks the victim to participate in sexual activity in return for gaining a job, promotion, raise, or other reward. In **hostile environment sexual harassment**, the harasser directs unwanted social sexual behavior toward the target and, in doing so, creates a hostile work environment.[11]

In United States (U.S.) court cases involving sexual harassment below the Supreme Court level, plaintiffs have been more likely to win their cases when (1) the harassment was more severe, (2) supporting witnesses were present, (3) supporting documents were available, (4) they had complained to superiors or management prior to filing charges, and (5) management took no action upon being notified of the alleged harassment. If plaintiffs have none of these factors in their favor, their odds of winning the case are less than 1%. If all five factors are in their favor, their odds of winning are almost 100%. In addition, plaintiffs are less likely to win a case if they were involved in a prior workplace romance with the alleged harasser.[12]

Personal definitions as well as legal definitions of sexual harassment matter. Most people agree that some line needs to be drawn between acceptable and unacceptable social sexual behavior in the workplace. However, it is impossible to draw a firm line that will be acceptable to all. For example, some types of social sexual behavior at work (e.g., complimenting a coworker's appearance or attire) are welcomed by some people and considered sexual harassment by others, which presents courts with a challenge in enforcing sexual harassment laws when identical behavior may prompt such different reactions. Thus, from both a legal and an individual perspective, we need to consider which types of social sexual behavior people find most and least offensive while recognizing that their judgments of exactly what behaviors constitute sexual harassment may vary.

Social sexual behaviors that individuals may consider sexual harassment include verbal requests, verbal comments, and nonverbal displays. Specific behaviors of each type may be classified from more severe (presented first) to less severe. **Verbal requests** include sexual bribery (pressure for sexual favors with threat or promise of reward), sexual advances (pressure for sexual favors with no threat or promise), relationship advances (repeated requests for an intimate relationship that is unwanted by the target), and more subtle advances (questions about one's sex life). **Verbal comments** include personally directed remarks (insulting jokes or remarks made directly to the target), other-directed remarks (insulting jokes or remarks about the target to others), and general sexual references. **Nonverbal displays** include sexual assault, sexual touching, sexual looks or gestures, and sexual materials (display of pornography or other materials). Also, harassing behaviors are considered more severe when (1) the harasser is at a higher hierarchical level than the target, (2) the harasser has behaved similarly toward the target and others over time, and (3) there are job consequences for the target.[13]

Sexual harassment may occur both face-to-face and virtually. What may be called **textual harassment**—the sending of offensive or inappropriate digital messages to coworkers via social media or other communication technologies—has emerged as a matter of concern as such technologies have become more prevalent. Textual harassment also varies from more severe to less severe. Both face-to-face and textual harassment raise questions of workplace boundaries. For example, sexual harassment that occurs during work-related travel may be considered "in the workplace" for legal purposes. However, if one employee sends a digital message to another employee that is construed as sexual harassment (e.g., a sexually suggestive comment about an innocent vacation photo in beach attire that was intended for family and friends) from a personal social media account and not a work account, has the sexually oriented behavior taken place "in the workplace" or not?[14]

Individuals' definitions of sexual harassment may differ according to their personal characteristics. The sex difference in definitions is robust: Men perceive a narrower range of behaviors as constituting sexual harassment and are more tolerant of sexual harassment than women. Further, individuals who rate higher in hostile sexism are less likely to perceive sexual harassment.[15]

Individuals' definitions of sexual harassment may also differ according to characteristics of their organizational situations. For example, a survey of perceptions of sexual harassment across managerial levels found that lower-level managers were more likely to see sexual harassment as a problem than middle-level managers. Top executives were the least likely to acknowledge the existence of sexual harassment and most likely to believe that the amount of sexual harassment at work is greatly exaggerated. Also, employees are less likely to define behavior as sexual harassment when they work in highly sexualized industries or have prior work experience in such industries. However, employees are more likely to define behavior as sexual harassment when their employer has formal policies against it.[16]

In summary, legal definitions of sexual harassment dictate legally acceptable standards of behavior in the workplace in various nations. However, individuals' personal definitions of sexual harassment influence the kinds of social sexual behaviors they feel entitled to initiate and their responses to behaviors initiated by others. Individuals' definitions are in turn influenced by personal characteristics (e.g., sex, hostile sexism) and situational characteristics (e.g., managerial level, experience in highly sexualized industries, organizational policies). Thus, drawing a line between acceptable and unacceptable social sexual behavior in the workplace is not simple. Opinions differ over where the line should be drawn, making it difficult for organizations to fulfill their obligation to take corrective action against sexual harassment and to prevent it.

Explanations

Different types of explanations have been offered for why sexual harassment occurs: person-centered, situation-centered, and social-system–centered.[17] In this section of the chapter, examples of each type of explanation are reviewed.

The **natural/biological model** of sexual harassment, a person-centered explanation, suggests that the phenomenon arises from individuals' basically sexual nature and represents a type of behavior to be accepted rather than a problem to be solved. People with strong sex drives are sexually aggressive toward others due to their natural and inevitable biological urges. Note that the natural/biological model is not necessarily limited to female–male work relations; people may act on both different-sex and same-sex attraction by exhibiting sexually aggressive behavior at work.[18]

The **individual differences model** of sexual harassment, another person-centered explanation, recognizes that some people engage in sexual harassment and others do not, even when they live and work under the same conditions. Even though most harassers are men, most men (and most women) are not harassers. Individuals vary widely in their propensity to harass others. The individual differences model suggests that personal characteristics influence who is most likely to engage in sexual harassment.[19]

For example, individuals' tendencies to embrace benevolent or hostile sexism predict whether they will engage in sexual harassment. Male employees who are higher in benevolent sexism direct milder forms of social sexual behavior toward female employees in the belief that they are flattering the targets. However, male employees who are higher in hostile sexism direct more severe types of social sexual behavior toward female employees, thereby creating a hostile work environment for all employees.[20]

Sexual harassment represents a type of aggressive behavior, and individuals differ in their inclinations to be sexual aggressors. The confluence model of sexual aggression describes sexually aggressive men as high on two dimensions: hostile masculinity (being insecure and defensive around women, gaining gratification from controlling or dominating them) and impersonal sex (having a noncommittal or game-playing orientation to sexual relations, which is different from having a strong sex drive). Men who are high on these two dimensions of sexual aggression seem more likely to engage in sexual harassment than men who are low on one or both dimensions.[21]

The individual differences model also suggests that some people are more likely to be targeted by sexual harassers than others. As noted earlier, most targets of sexual harassment are women. However, there are individual differences among women in who is targeted by harassers. For example, a study found that women who described themselves as high in masculinity on the Short Bem Sex-Role Inventory, regardless of their level of femininity, experienced more sexual harassment than those who described themselves as low in masculinity. That is, sexual harassment was being used as a way to punish "uppity women" who exhibited an abundance of masculine traits, thereby failing to conform to the female gender stereotype.[22] These results were contrary to what the natural/biological model would predict, because sexual harassment was being directed toward women who were violating rather than meeting feminine ideals.

The **organizational model** of sexual harassment, a situation-centered explanation, suggests that certain organizational characteristics set the stage for its occurrence. Sexual harassment represents a significant problem in all types of organizations, including academic, military, government, and nonprofit as well as private-sector organizations.[23] However, organizations differ in the nature of the situations (including structures and environments) in which their employees work.[24]

For example, organizational hierarchies grant higher-level employees power over lower-level employees, which gives them the opportunity to engage in quid pro quo sexual harassment by using the promise of rewards or the threat of punishments to obtain sexual gratification from others. The organizational model suggests that sexual harassment is most prevalent in organizations with large power differentials; when power differentials are smaller, employees are less likely to report being harassed. In support of this perspective, a meta-analysis of studies on sexual harassment in different types of organizations found that women in the military, a type of organization that emphasizes hierarchy-based power differentials, reported having experienced sexual harassment to a greater extent than women in universities, a type of organization that is characterized by smaller power differentials.[25]

Organizations differ in the extent to which their cultures tolerate sexual harassment. They may (or may not) have policies and procedures in place that define sexual harassment and declare it as unacceptable behavior, policies may be strong (or weak) and enforced (or not), and managers at different levels may be intolerant (or tolerant) of sexual harassment; this set of actions or inactions collectively determines the organizational culture's tolerance for sexual harassment. Quid pro quo and hostile environment sexual harassment are most likely to occur in organizational cultures that display a high tolerance for sexual harassment.[26]

Organizational situations also differ in whether observers are present who witness an incident of sexual harassment as it occurs but are not directly involved in it. Quid pro quo sexual harassment is most likely to occur without observers present. However, in the case of hostile environment sexual harassment that directly affects the work environment, observers are more likely to be present. Observers of potential incidents of sexual harassment might prevent it from occurring by their very presence on the assumption that most potential harassers would not like their behavior to be witnessed for fear of it coming back to haunt them. However, when they witness sexual harassment, observers are faced with a choice of whether to intervene to try to stop it or not. Whether they actually intervene is likely to be influenced by the organizational culture's tolerance for sexual harassment.[27]

The gendered nature of social systems influences the prevalence of sexual harassment in workplaces. The **sociocultural model** of sexual harassment, a social-system–centered explanation, depicts the phenomenon as a manifestation of patriarchal societies that expect men to be dominant and women to be compliant. In such societies, sexual harassment has little to do with sexuality; instead, its purpose is to preserve men's social status by keeping women economically dependent and subordinate. Thus, individuals with the least amount of power in society are the most likely to be harassed.[28]

In support of the sociocultural model, male harassers are less likely to target White women than Black women, who generally have less power in society. In the same vein, reflecting the effect of the intersection of the victim's sex and race, women of color are more likely to be victims of sexual harassment than men of color or White women. White men, who generally have the most power in society, are least likely to be victims of sexual harassment.[29]

It should be noted that power granted by societal processes is different from that granted by organizational hierarchies. Organizations vary in their emphasis on hierarchy and the magnitude of their power differentials. However, organizations operate within societal contexts (even multinational corporations with facilities located around the world) that are likely to influence their internal processes, including the level of sexual harassment exhibited within their boundaries.

The **gender role spillover model**, another social-system–centered explanation, emphasizes the effects of gender role expectations that are shaped by gendered societal processes. The term *gender role spillover* refers to the carryover into the workplace of gender role expectations that are irrelevant to the conduct of work (e.g., expectations regarding social sexual behaviors). Gender role spillover is most likely to occur when the sex ratio of a group is skewed, making minority members more noticeable and subject to special attention (see Chapter 5). Women in male-intensive groups and men in female-intensive groups experience gender role spillover because they are assumed to be basically different from members of the dominant sex and therefore are treated differently. As part of their differential treatment, they are likely to experience more sexual harassment than individuals who stand out less in their work environments.[30]

In summary, the natural/biological model views sexual harassment as inevitably arising from individuals' basically sexual nature. The individual differences model suggests that individuals vary in their likelihood to harass and be harassed by others. The organizational model suggests that characteristics of organizational situations such as power differentials in hierarchies, organizational cultures that tolerate sexual harassment, and the presence of observers influence the occurrence of sexual harassment. The sociocultural model suggests that patriarchal systems and power differences in society contribute to the occurrence of sexual harassment. The gender role spillover model suggests that gender role expectations foster sexual harassment, especially when groups have a skewed sex ratio. Each of these explanatory models provides a partial explanation of why sexual harassment occurs. In addition, many of the factors described may operate simultaneously. To understand the relative merits of these models, we need to examine experiences with sexual harassment in a variety of work situations.

Experiences

Experiences of sexual harassment tend to vary according to characteristics of the victim, perpetrator, and work environment.[31] Most victims experience the less severe forms of sexual harassment identified earlier rather than the more severe forms. As noted earlier, more women are sexually harassed at work than men, and more women of color are harassed than members of other groups on the basis of sex and race. The majority of female victims are harassed by men, and the majority of male victims are harassed by women, supporting the natural/biological model for heterosexual employees; same-sex sexual harassment may also be explained by the natural/biological model. Sexual harassment of LGBTQ+ employees may be explained by the sociocultural model if such employees are regarded to have less power in society than heterosexual employees.[32]

Female victims are harassed more by their immediate or higher-level supervisors than by their subordinates. This difference supports the organizational model of sexual harassment as applied to organizational hierarchies. The power differential resulting from the relative positions in the hierarchy of the harasser and victim appears to contribute to the experiences of female victims. In contrast, male victims are harassed by their superiors and subordinates in approximately equal proportions. However, coworkers and other employees without supervisory authority over victims are the most common workplace harassers.

Female and male victims of sexual harassment are more likely than nonvictims to work exclusively or mostly with members of the other sex, supporting the gender role spillover model. They are also more likely than nonvictims to be under the age of 35 and unmarried, which supports the natural/biological model if younger and unmarried employees are assumed to be more sexually attractive and available.

In response to unwelcome social sexual behavior, almost half of female and male employees ignore the behavior or do nothing. Very few female and male victims go along with the behavior directed toward them, refuting the natural/biological model from the victim's perspective. Contrary to the sociocultural model, which assumes a power differential in society favoring men, female victims are more likely to ask harassers to stop than male victims. However, female victims are also more likely to avoid the harassers altogether than male victims. Few female or male victims report the behavior to a supervisor or human resources department.

Why don't more victims report the sexual harassment they have experienced? For female victims, they have to deal with the anticipated doubts of others if they were to speak up. There are several common misconceptions for doubting victims' accounts of sexual harassment: (1) she doesn't act like a victim; (2) she stayed friendly with her perpetrator; (3) she did not come forward right away; and (4) she did not fight back. This combination of anticipated reactions, although insufficient as grounds for denying a victim's account, may contribute to explaining why so many female victims of sexual harassment remain silent afterward. The fear may be that "they won't believe you anyway."[33]

However, victims may also fear retaliation if they were to report the sexual harassment they have experienced. Reporting it may make things worse for the victim if the organization does nothing in response. The organizational culture regarding sexual harassment is likely to influence whether victims come forward to report and whether they suffer harmful consequences if they do.[34]

Contrary to the natural/biological model's depiction of sexual harassment as not posing a problem to be solved, overwhelming research evidence indicates that the costs of sexual harassment are high. It has negative effects on employees' physical health (e.g., headaches, sleep disturbance, fatigue) and mental health (e.g., loss of self-esteem and self-confidence, anxiety, depression). Even at low frequencies or low severity, sexual harassment exerts a significant negative impact on employees' job-related attitudes, such as their sense of job satisfaction, organizational commitment, and feeling of involvement in their work. Further, it interferes with the functioning and performance of work teams and the organization as a whole. Thus, even if sexual harassment is regarded as natural and inevitable as the natural/biological model suggests, this does not mean that it represents harmless behavior.[35]

We have focused on the effects of sexual harassment on the immediate victim. However, sexual harassment may create a hostile work environment for employees not personally targeted by offensive behavior. The perspective of observers of sexual harassment is important. Observers' responses to unwanted sexual attention directed toward others range from ignoring the behavior to intervening personally in an incident to reporting it to authorities. Observers generally are more likely to take action when the behavior has more serious consequences for the victim, when they believe that most people would consider the behavior sexual harassment, and when they believe that the behavior poses a moral issue.[36]

We have also focused on sexual harassment within organizations directed by employees toward other employees. However, employees may be sexually harassed by customers as well; the customer should not always be "king" (a male metaphor). Customer sexual harassment is especially prevalent and costly to employees in service industries that require close contact with customers. In most service industries, deference to customers ("service with a smile") is the norm and employees are financially dependent on customers (e.g., for tips). These working conditions increase customer power over employees and make sexual harassment by customers more likely.[37]

In conclusion, individuals' experiences with sexual harassment are considerably different. Although both men and women may be the targets of unwanted sexual attention, women are more likely to be harassed. It is not surprising that women see more sexual harassment in the workplace than men do: They are more conscious of sexual harassment than men because they experience it more. Harassment of LGBTQ+ employees is also prevalent. The personal costs of being harassed for all victims, regardless of their sex or sexual orientation, are high. Their employers also face the prospect of diminished individual productivity, increased employee health care expenses, and costly litigation. The natural/biological model suggests that sexual harassment will never be completely eliminated in the workplace. However, all parties benefit when its occurrence is minimized.

LEGACY OF THE #METOO MOVEMENT

The #MeToo hashtag movement was inspired by allegations of rampant sexual harassment by Harvey Weinstein, a media company CEO, to give victims a voice and ultimately to try to prevent sexual harassment and provide support to victims when it does occur. What is the movement's legacy likely to be? It may have both positive and negative effects in the long run.

On the one hand, the #MeToo movement's long-term effects will be positive if men in power inclined to engage in sexual harassment become less likely to do so because of fear of having their behavior damage their careers and, in prominent cases, their being publicly shamed. Such fears would be legitimate. As noted earlier, in the year after the Weinstein allegations, more than 200 powerful men lost their jobs after public allegations of sexual harassment; in contrast, in the year before the allegations, less than 30 powerful men were reported to have resigned or been fired after public allegations of sexual harassment. Also, despite having to process difficult emotions, the support women receive after tweeting about their experiences of sexual harassment may be beneficial as a demonstration of solidarity; it may also help to increase their feelings of self-esteem and decrease their feelings of self-doubt. In response to the #MeToo movement, many companies have introduced more stringent sexual harassment policies and less tolerant organizational cultures, and many corporate boards of directors have had to rethink how to respond to sexual harassment allegations against top executives and what constitutes a fireable offense.[38] Catherine MacKinnon, the legal scholar whose pioneering work contributed to sexual harassment being defined as an unlawful employment practice, said, "#MeToo has done what the law could not."[39]

Further, lower-level employees may feel more empowered to speak out against misbehavior at high levels as a result of the #MeToo movement. For example, after Google asked for the resignation of a top executive due to a sexual harassment complaint that it judged to be credible, it softened the blow by giving him a $90 million exit package on the way out. Once this series of events—the harassment complaint, the forced resignation, the lavish exit package—was publicly disclosed four years later, thousands of Google employees staged an orchestrated wave of walkouts from its worldwide offices one week later. Not coincidentally, one week after the walkouts, Google announced that it would be overhauling its sexual misconduct policy.[40]

As another example of employee empowerment following the #MeToo movement: After complaints of sexual harassment by female employees against higher-level male executives at Nike were being routinely ignored, a group of female employees took the matter into their own hands. They covertly surveyed other female Nike employees and discovered a litany of complaints. Somehow, a packet of the completed surveys landed on the Nike CEO's desk. Within weeks, at least six top male executives had either left Nike or announced that they would be leaving the company. The group of departing executives included the head of diversity and inclusion, which makes me wonder exactly what he thought he was doing to make female employees feel more "included" at Nike. Also not coincidentally, one week after public reports of these events, the Nike CEO promised changes in how women would be treated in the company.[41]

On the other hand, the #MeToo movement's long-term effects will be negative if well-meaning men in power become reluctant to mentor lower-level women, which would help the women to advance in their careers, because of fear that their good intentions may be misinterpreted. One male executive said when interviewed at a conference, "I now think twice about spending one-on-one time with a young female colleague;" he spoke only under the condition of anonymity because he regarded the topic as "just too sensitive." An anonymous male colleague said in response, somewhat ironically, "Me, too." Men may also be more reluctant to hire attractive women, especially for jobs that require close interpersonal interactions with men.[42]

Just as the intersection of sex and race influences which individuals are more likely to be targeted by sexual harassers, it may influence who feels included in the #MeToo movement. The movement was launched by a Black woman, Tarana Burke, before hashtags even existed. However, the hashtag movement of the same name that was launched by a White actress, Alyssa Milano, has received far greater attention. One criticism of the #MeToo movement has been that it represents another example of the "whitewashing" of a feminist movement when brought into mainstream conversation. Women of color may ask, "What about #UsToo?"[43] All women's experiences of sexual harassment by powerful men deserve attention, not only the experiences of women of a particular race.

Finally, the #MeToo movement has been said to put a "nail in the coffin" of workplace romance for many young employees. Sexual harassment at work has been under a larger and more intense microscope since the advent of the movement. As a result, Millennial and Gen Z employees have increasingly regarded being romantically involved with a colleague as a bad idea.[44] Is it? Let's talk about that.

WORKPLACE ROMANCE

Sexual interest in a coworker is not always unwelcome.[45] In some cases, it is reciprocated and serves as the basis for a relationship between two employees that goes beyond their work roles. Workplace romances (mutually desired relationships between two people at work in which some element of sexuality or physical intimacy exists) have become more prevalent in recent years due to fundamental changes in the workplace. Individuals have greater opportunity to become involved in a heterosexual workplace romance as the proportion of women in the labor force has increased, especially in managerial and professional jobs. Also, employees are expected to work longer hours, facilitated by technology that fosters their spending more time digitally tethered to their work and less time with family members.[46] As a result, the work environment, whether offline or online, has become increasingly conducive to the formation of romantic relationships. In this section, we examine the causes, dynamics, and consequences of workplace romances.

Causes

Robert Sternberg's triangular theory of love provides a perspective on loving relationships in general that may be applied to the formation of romantic relationships in the workplace. Love may be explained in terms of three components: **intimacy**—feelings of closeness and connectedness in a relationship, **passion**—feelings of romance and sexual attraction and the desire for sexual consummation, and **decision/commitment**—the decision that one loves someone else and the commitment to maintain that love. Intimacy is at the core of many kinds of loving relationships, such as love of a parent, sibling, child, or close friend. Passion is linked to certain kinds of loving relationships, especially romantic ones involving sexual activity. Decision/commitment is highly variable over different kinds of loving relationships. The importance of these components depends in part on whether the relationship is short term or long term, with passion being prominent in a short-term romance.[47]

Sternberg's theory may be used to distinguish among factors that contribute to interpersonal attraction (i.e., feelings of intimacy) and factors that contribute to romantic attraction (i.e., feelings of passion and, in some cases, decision/commitment as well as feelings of intimacy). Workplace romance takes place in three stages. First, feelings of interpersonal attraction arise toward another organizational member. Second, feelings of romantic attraction toward the same person follow. Third, the decision is made to engage in a workplace romance.[48]

Interpersonal attraction is influenced by physical and functional proximity. **Physical proximity** refers to closeness that results from the location of employees' areas of work. **Functional proximity** refers to closeness that results from the actual conduct of work, whether face-to-face or via communication technologies. Employees who are closer in rank and status are likely to be higher in functional proximity. Employees who interact with each other more frequently or more intensely because of ongoing work relationships tend to be higher in both physical and functional proximity. Generally, employees with higher physical and functional proximity are more likely to be attracted to each other. Interpersonal attraction is also influenced by attitude similarity; individuals who are more similar in attitudes like each other more.[49]

Whether interpersonal attraction leads to romantic attraction is influenced by the perceived physical attractiveness of the other person. In turn, whether romantic attraction leads to a workplace romance is influenced by several factors. Individuals' general attitudes toward workplace romance influence whether they act on feelings of romantic attraction. In addition, individuals may engage in a workplace romance if they believe that doing so will fulfill **job motives** (e.g., desire for advancement, job security, or financial rewards), **ego motives** (e.g., desire for excitement, adventure, or ego satisfaction), or **love motives** (e.g., desire for intimacy, passion, and decision/commitment).[50]

As for sexual harassment, there is a sex difference in attitudes toward workplace romance: Women have more negative reactions than men do. Women are more likely to worry that a workplace romance would hurt them on the job, are more reluctant to get involved in one, and are more discreet about it when they do. In contrast, men have more favorable attitudes toward workplace romance and are more welcoming of positive social sexual behavior at work.[51]

The nature of individuals' jobs influences whether they get involved in a workplace romance. Individuals whose jobs are more autonomous, allowing them to make more decisions about their own work and to move more freely inside and outside the organization, are less subject to the constraining presence of others and more likely to participate in workplace romances. Business trips, which entail high levels of both physical and functional proximity away from coworkers and supervisors, are particularly conducive to romance.[52]

The organizational culture regarding the acceptability of workplace romance, which varies by industry, influences whether coworkers act on their feelings of mutual attraction; workplace romances are more likely in highly sexualized cultures. As for sexual harassment, the culture regarding workplace romance may be influenced by the sex ratio of the work unit. Recall that gender role spillover—the carryover into the workplace of individuals' expectations based on gender roles—is more likely to occur when a group's sex ratio is skewed in favor of a particular sex. Employees may be more inclined to become romantically involved when the work setting is numerically dominated by members of one sex. In this kind of environment, employees may be more likely to see each other as sex objects and thereby prospective romantic partners.[53]

Technology both within and outside the workplace plays an important role in facilitating and supporting workplace romances. Partners in romantic relationships may communicate using a wide variety of communication technologies, including work phones, personal calls or texts, work or personal email accounts, and personal social media accounts. These technologies may be used both inside and outside of work. They also may play different roles at different stages of workplace romances, including the initiation, maintenance, and (in some cases) dissolution stage.[54]

In summary, interpersonal attraction created by functional or physical proximity at work sets the stage for workplace romance. As employees interact, interpersonal attraction may evolve into romantic attraction and, ultimately, a workplace romance. Romantic attraction is most likely to lead to an actual romance when employees have positive attitudes toward workplace romance and work autonomously in environments that are more accepting of it.

Dynamics

Once two people enter into a workplace romance, what kinds of dynamics occur and how do they evolve over time? Workplace romances differ according to the match between the motives (job, ego, or love) of the two participants. Nine different combinations of these three motives are possible. However, four combinations of partners' motives tend to be more prevalent than other combinations: (1) ego for both partners—a **fling**, (2) love for both partners—**true love**, (3) job for both partners—a **mutual user relationship**, and (4) ego for one partner and job for the other partner—a **utilitarian relationship**. Flings are characterized by high excitement for both participants and tend to be short-lived. True love relationships are characterized by the sincerity of both participants and may result in marriage or cohabitation, an increasingly common family structure (see Chapter 8). Mutual user relationships are primarily job motivated. Utilitarian relationships involve a trade-off between different motives of the two participants, with the less powerful partner seeking to further job-related goals through involvement with a more powerful partner in pursuit of ego gratification.[55]

Power and dependency are key variables in understanding the dynamics of workplace romances. Three types of dependency may be present in a work relationship. **Task dependency** occurs when employees depend on others to perform tasks effectively. **Career dependency** occurs when employees desire advancement that is dependent on the consent of others. In normal manager–subordinate relationships, managers depend on subordinates to perform tasks whereas subordinates rely on managers for career advancement. In a workplace romance, a **personal/sexual dependency** is introduced. The addition of this third dependency threatens the normal exchange of task and career dependencies.[56]

Whenever there is an imbalance of power in a romantic relationship, there is a high potential for exploitation of the participant with the higher level of dependency. The potential for exploitation is especially high in a **hierarchical romance** in which participants are at different organizational levels with high task and career dependency. For example, the higher-level participant in a hierarchical relationship can use the lower-level participant's personal/sexual dependency to force an increase in task performance. In addition, the lower-level participant can use the higher-level participant's personal/sexual dependency to argue for favorable task assignments or work conditions. When either of these instances occurs, the relationship becomes utilitarian. Exploitation, however, is not limited to hierarchical romance but also may appear in a **lateral romance** in which participants are at the same organizational level with less task and career dependency. A power imbalance may occur in a lateral romance simply because one participant is more dependent on the personal/sexual exchange than the other.[57]

Most couples try to keep their workplace romances hidden from coworkers but fail in the attempt. Because coworkers disapprove of hierarchical romances more than lateral romances, participants in hierarchical romances are more likely to try to hide the relationship. Workplace romances in which one or both partners are married also create greater incentives for secrecy.

The components of love, dependency, and motive in workplace romances are seldom static and may evolve over time. The levels of intimacy, passion, and decision/commitment felt by participants in a loving relationship seldom remain constant. Changes in task and career dependencies may alter the dynamics of their work relationship and romance. In addition, participants' motives for engaging in the romance may change. Growing satisfaction with the relationship may lead to increasing mutual commitment or declining satisfaction may lead to terminating the relationship. Both partners have to deal with the other partner's changing feelings about the relationship, even if their own feelings remain the same.[58]

There are great difficulties associated with the end of a romance and the return to being only coworkers, including the rejected lover's lower self-image and self-esteem. In addition, what was once workplace romance may become sexual harassment if one participant desires to continue the relationship but the other does not. Dissolved hierarchical romances between a supervisor and an immediate subordinate are the relationships most likely to become sexual harassment; when they do, they raise legal issues that often lead to court cases.[59]

We have not distinguished between the dynamics of different-sex and same-sex workplace romances. We would expect the dynamics of both types of relationships to be similar. However, same-sex romance is particularly hazardous for participants due to heterosexism in the workplace. Because of this, individuals interested in a same-sex romance face greater risks than other individuals when they look for a partner at work. Participants in a same-sex workplace romance, whether or not their sexual orientation is known to coworkers, have more reasons for secrecy: They may experience more serious repercussions.[60]

Consequences

There may be both positive and negative consequences of workplace romances for participants, their partners outside of work, coworkers, and the organization as a whole. Participants in workplace romances face a variety of outcomes. For example, their productivity, motivation, and involvement may decrease during the early stages of the romance (when they are more distracted) and increase in later stages of the romance (when it has become a normal part of their lives). They may also feel more socially connected and physically attractive as a result of the relationship. The romance may lead to their marrying or living with each other. However, it may also lead to their divorcing or breaking up with their current partners, with economic as well as social consequences. For example, an interesting study found that CEO divorce contributed to lower organizational performance when the CEO was more distracted by the divorce.[61]

Participants who are more satisfied with the romance tend to be more satisfied with other aspects of their jobs. In particular, workplace romance has a positive impact on the performance, motivation, and involvement of participants who enter the romance with a love motive. Love-motivated individuals may feel the need to impress their partners through higher productivity and to alleviate their supervisors' fears that the romance will negatively affect their work. In addition, they may simply be happier because they have filled their need for companionship and now have more time and energy for work.

Romance within mentoring relationships, however, may lead to negative consequences for the protégé. Successful mentoring relationships, judged by the development of the protégé, are characterized by a productive level of intimacy between the mentor and protégé that does not result in workplace romance. Less-successful mentoring relationships are characterized by either unproductive intimacy (leading to a romantic relationship and poor development of the protégé) or unproductive distance (which also leads to insufficient development of the protégé).[62]

Depending on the circumstances, coworkers' reactions to workplace romances range from approval to tolerance to outright objection. At a minimum, workplace romance stimulates gossip among coworkers. Whether the gossip is positive or negative depends on the type of romance. A true love relationship stimulates the most positive gossip. Most people root for lovers in principle because they want to believe that romances can have happy endings. However, a utilitarian relationship stimulates more negative gossip, especially if it represents a hierarchical romance between a superior and subordinate. When coworkers strongly disapprove of a workplace romance, they may adopt extreme strategies such as ostracism of participants in informal interactions, quitting the organization to remove themselves from what they see as an intolerable situation, or informing the spouse of one or both participants with whom they may have socialized at corporate functions. If a coworker adopts the latter strategy, the romance may lead to divorce.[63]

In general, people do not care what their fellow employees do as long as it does not affect the conduct of work. However, if coworkers perceive the lower-level participant in a hierarchical romance to be motivated by job concerns such as advancement or job security, their reactions may turn sharply negative. For example, when a lower-level woman becomes involved with a senior-level male executive, coworkers are likely to see the woman as motivated more by job concerns and the man more by ego concerns. That is, coworkers perceive a utilitarian relationship, even if the romantic relationship is better characterized as true love or a fling. In general, coworkers react most negatively to the traditional workplace romance in which a lower-level female participant is involved with a higher-level male participant.[64]

The managerial response to a workplace romance also influences coworkers' reactions. Possible managerial actions, to be discussed at greater length in the last section of the chapter, range from ignoring the romance to positive action (e.g., counseling) to punitive action (e.g., warning, reprimand, transfer, or termination). Coworkers prefer that punitive action be taken when the romance is hierarchical rather than lateral, when one or both participants is motivated by job concerns, and when there is a greater conflict of interest and disruption of the conduct of work. When managerial action is to be taken at all, coworkers prefer that equivalent actions be directed toward both participants. Thus, coworkers' reactions are influenced by the ramifications of a workplace romance, not the existence of the romance itself.[65]

In conclusion, as with sexual harassment, individuals' experiences with workplace romance differ greatly. Women are more likely to be judged negatively if they are involved with a higher-level man than vice versa. Thus, it is not surprising that women have more negative attitudes toward workplace romance than men do. The overall effects of workplace romance on organizations vary widely. The effects for participants may be positive (e.g., increased individual productivity, motivation, and involvement), neutral (e.g., increased levels of gossip with no other impact), or negative (e.g., decreased productivity, motivation, and involvement). The effects for coworkers may also be positive, neutral, or negative. When a workplace romance has negative effects on the conduct of work, organizations need to be ready to act.

ADDRESSING SOCIAL SEXUAL BEHAVIOR AT WORK

Table 7.1 summarizes recommended actions for organizations and individuals in dealing with both sexual harassment and workplace romance to make the work environment a comfortable place for all.

TABLE 7.1 ■ Recommended Actions
1. Adopt a zero-tolerance policy against sexual harassment.
2. Train employees to recognize sexual harassment and how to respond to it.
3. Designate a party to whom employees may bring complaints of sexual harassment and other offensive behavior without fear of reprisal.
4. Investigate employee allegations of sexual harassment and take appropriate action.
5. If you are on a corporate board of directors, be proactive in addressing sexual harassment by top executives and encouraging an organizational culture that does not tolerate such behavior.
6. Do not ignore sexual harassment directed toward you or others in the belief that it will eventually cease. Let others know about the behavior, and if you feel safe in doing so, use your organization's procedure to file a complaint.
7. If you hear about sexual harassment, provide emotional support to the victim.
8. If you witness sexual harassment, intervene.
9. Offer counseling to employees who need help in handling sexual harassment or workplace romances.
10. Take organizational action when workplace romance affects the conduct of work—especially when it is a hierarchical or utilitarian romance—but ignore it otherwise.
11. Weigh the potential costs of a workplace romance against the potential benefits before getting involved.

Sexual Harassment at Work

Unless organizations address sexual harassment, they may be held in violation of the law and risk loss of productivity and alienation of a large portion of their workforce. Many cases of sexual harassment (although not all) require managerial action. In addition, organizations and their employees benefit from managerial actions that discourage harassment from ever occurring.

The U.S. EEOC guidelines state,

> Prevention is the best tool for the elimination of sexual harassment. An employer should take all steps necessary to prevent sexual harassment from occurring, such as affirmatively raising the subject, expressing strong disapproval, developing appropriate sanctions, informing employees of their right to raise and how to raise the issue of harassment under Title VII, and developing methods to sensitize all concerned.[66]

To comply with this directive, organizations need to adopt a zero-tolerance policy against sexual harassment, educate employees about the issue, and establish formal grievance procedures to deal with allegations of harassment. **Sexual harassment policies** should clearly specify the types of behaviors that are forbidden and their penalties; managers and nonsupervisory employees should be made aware that sexual harassment could cost them their careers. New employees should be informed of the policy on sexual harassment during their initial orientation, and all employees should be reminded of the policy periodically.

Sexual harassment training programs should detail the reasons for policies, the variety of forms of sexual harassment, and proper responses to allegations of harassment. They should make it clear that unacceptable behaviors include textual harassment both inside and outside the workplace as well as face-to-face sexual harassment. Separate bystander intervention training and manager training programs may also be effective in presenting sexual harassment as a challenge that all employees and managers must be prepared to deal with.[67]

In dealing with cases of alleged sexual harassment, organizations should follow this general principle: *The severity of the action taken should be based on the severity of the alleged offense and the certainty that an offense was committed.*

After a complaint of sexual harassment has been directed to a designated party, organizational policy can be effectively implemented by a **formal grievance procedure:**[68]

1. Interview the complainant, the accused, and possible witnesses.
2. Check personnel files for evidence that documents prior animosities between the parties, previous complaints against the accused or by the complainant, and recent discrepancies in the work record of the complainant or the accused.
3. Assess the severity of the alleged offense, considering the type of behavior, intent, power position of the accused relative to the complainant, and frequency of occurrence. Actions by complainants' supervisors should be considered more serious offenses than the same actions by coworkers.

Repeated incidents should be considered more serious offenses than isolated cases. The severity of both quid pro quo and hostile environment sexual harassment should be considered.

4. Assess the certainty that an offense was committed. Solid evidence in the form of either witnesses or documents to support the complaint provides assurance that there actually was an offense. Matters are less certain when there is less than overwhelming evidence to support the complaint. Whether an offense was committed is in greatest doubt when the only evidence to support the complaint is the complainant's word.

5. Determine appropriate actions to be taken. Severe actions (e.g., dismissal, demotion, suspension, or transfer of accused) are to be taken when the alleged offense is severe and the certainty that it was committed is high. In such cases, the work record of the complainant should be restored if unjustly blemished. Mild actions (e.g., no record of complaint in file of the accused or a record with annotation that the accusation was not proven, letter to the accused stressing organizational policy against sexual harassment, or announcement reminding employees of organizational policy) are to be taken when the alleged offense is mild and the certainty that it was committed is low. Moderate actions (e.g., a warning or disciplinary notice in the file of the accused with removal of the notice if no subsequent offense occurs within a specified period of time or required counseling for the accused) are to be considered in cases that fall between these two extremes. A combination of actions of different levels of severity may be appropriate.

Such a procedure demonstrates that an organization is willing to take action to minimize the incidence of sexual harassment. It also acknowledges individual differences in definitions of sexual harassment by matching the action taken with the severity of the offense and the certainty of its occurrence. Clear and objective administration of such procedures protects organizations from liability and increases the probability that their work environment is free of sexual harassment. To make the procedure work, organizations need to create a justice-oriented culture that does not stigmatize the reporting of cases of alleged sexual harassment by victims or witnesses and counters fears of a #MeToo backlash from reporting.[69]

That said, can you imagine a top-level executive who already engages in rampant sexual harassment going to a sexual harassment training program and being convinced by it to refrain from all future harassing behaviors? And can you imagine the same top-level executive's harassing behaviors, if a target of those behaviors filed a formal complaint, being thoroughly investigated and appropriately penalized by the human resources department whose manager is likely to report directly or indirectly to the harasser? No, neither can I. In major corporations, virtually all men at lower levels have learned that even if they are inclined to harass women, they risk their employment and livelihood if caught. Men at the top, if they are so inclined, play by different rules, and sexual harassment policies and training programs are unlikely to curb their behavior.[70]

However, corporate CEOs answer to boards of directors, which have the power to fire them at will. In the wake of the #MeToo movement, boards of directors of many publicly traded firms have learned that sexual harassment scandals may cause trouble for them, too. For example, stockholders may sue the board for breaching its fiduciary duties by failing to avoid or address sexual harassment scandals. Board concerns should go beyond trying to avoid lawsuits. Instead, boards of directors should act proactively by (1) addressing sexual harassment by the CEO and other top executives promptly and decisively if it occurs and (2) encouraging organizational cultures that show zero tolerance for such behavior. Both types of actions by boards of directors will benefit employees as well as stockholders.[71]

Further, no matter how well intentioned a formal grievance procedure is, it will have little effect unless employees who feel that they have been harassed or have witnessed harassment are willing to take action. Many victims are reluctant to use formal procedures. If they take any action at all, most victims choose to deal with the situation themselves. However, going along with the offensive behavior, making a joke of it, or pretending to ignore it typically does not resolve the issue.[72]

I recommend that targets and witnesses of unwelcome social sexual behavior *not* ignore the behavior. After the Harvey Weinstein allegations became public, I was asked, "What advice do you give young women (and men) as they enter the workforce? What can they do to protect themselves from workplace predators?"[73] Here is my advice:

1. If you are subjected to unwelcome social sexual behavior, you need to let someone know about it. You can't keep it to yourself and suffer in silence. If you stay silent, you will not find out how many supporters and how much support you have. Most people find such behavior as despicable as I do. Also, if you stay silent, you might find yourself wondering what you did to provoke the behavior, which is not a productive line of thought. You do not deserve to be treated the way Weinstein treated women.

2. If someone tells you that they have been a target of unwelcome social sexual behavior, offer all the emotional support you can. This is part of what makes you a decent human being.

3. If you witness an incident of unwelcome social sexual behavior, intervene or interrupt it, even if it places your career at risk. This is also part of what makes you a decent human being.

4. If you work in an organization that has a human resources department and sexual harassment policy (and most large organizations do), report the behavior. If the organization is smart, it will have an established policy that

will protect your anonymity and confidentiality while investigating such an incident if at all possible.

5. Speaking as an apprentice black belt holder in the Tang Soo Do style of martial arts (at the Quest Martial Arts school in Thompson, Connecticut[74]), I recommend self-defense training for everyone. One hopes you will never need to use it outside of the martial arts school you attend, but you never know.

Victims' reluctance to take such actions does not relieve organizations of their obligations to create an environment free of sexual harassment and to provide support for employees who have been harassed. Even if no formal complaint has been filed, the organization should be prepared to initiate action if it uncovers significant evidence of wrongdoing. In investigating and redressing the wrongdoing, it should respect the wishes of victims who wish to remain anonymous. The organization should also provide support for employees who have been harassed, including off-the-record counseling to help them understand the available options for resolving the problem and to assist them in coping with the emotional consequences of harassment.[75]

In summary, organizations may deal with sexual harassment in several ways. They should (1) establish a firm policy against sexual harassment; (2) provide training to employees about sexual harassment, including workplace norms and regulations in cultures with which they have contact; (3) set up and administer a formal grievance procedure; (4) ensure that employees are aware of both policies and procedures; and (5) provide counseling to help employees cope psychologically with harassment and decide what to do about it. Victims should not bear the burden of having to solve or deal with problems created by their harassers. Organizations and their boards of directors have a responsibility to monitor the work environment and make it as harassment free as possible.

Romance in the Workplace

There are sharp differences of opinion over whether workplace romance can and should be banned. Catharine MacKinnon, one of the first scholars of sexual harassment who was quoted earlier in the chapter about the #MeToo movement, argued that most of what passes for workplace romance is actually sexual harassment in disguise, resulting from a patriarchal system in which women are powerless to avoid being exploited sexually, and should be treated accordingly. Margaret Mead, a famed anthropologist, argued that much like taboos against sexual expression in the family that are necessary for children to grow up safely, taboos against sexual involvement at work are necessary for men and women to work together effectively.[76] However, most people agree that it is foolish to try to ban welcome sexual attention from the workplace.

In practice, most organizations are realistic and do not try to outlaw workplace romance. According to a survey of human resource management professionals, less than half of organizations have a written or verbal policy about workplace romance.

Among organizations that have a policy, almost all ban hierarchical romances between supervisors and direct reports. The reasons most frequently cited for having a policy include concerns about real or perceived favoritism, the potential for claims of sexual harassment, and the potential for retaliation if the romance ends. The most frequent managerial responses to violations of the policy, if one exists, include transfer within the organization, counseling, formal reprimand, and termination.[77]

Having a written policy helps organizations in dealing with workplace romances and their consequences. The policy should explain the types of romantic relationships that are acceptable and unacceptable in the work environment and the potential ramifications for the participants of having an inappropriate relationship. It should also specify the point at which participants are responsible for revealing their relationship to the organization. Participants who only have eyes for each other may not be aware of the complexities of workplace romances, such as the risks associated with being involved in a hierarchical relationship with a direct report or the effect of their relationship on coworkers.[78]

Assuming that such a policy exists, how should organizations respond when two employees become romantically involved? The general principle to follow in dealing with workplace romance is the same as that for dealing with sexual harassment: The severity of the action taken should be based on the severity of the alleged offense and the certainty that an offense was committed. However, unlike sexual harassment, the existence of a workplace romance does not necessarily represent an offense. *The primary concern of management ought not to be who is involved with whom but whether the necessary work is getting done and done well.*

If there is no disruption to the accomplishment of work goals, then there is little need to take any action. However, a relationship in which there is the potential for task-related or career-related decisions to be influenced by romantic considerations presents some threat. Coworkers may fear that the relationship will influence the conduct of work or suspect that it is already having an effect, causing their morale and productivity to suffer. When the romantic partners have committed no actual offense but there is the potential for offense, management should step in. The couple should be told that if they continue the relationship, work assignments and/or reporting responsibilities will be changed to reduce the potential for disruption of the conduct of work. In this case, punitive action is not in order, but the situation does need to be addressed by management.

When it is certain that task-related or career-related decisions have been influenced by romantic considerations, there is greater cause for concern. This situation calls for punitive action against *both* participants. The hierarchical level of the participants should not be allowed to affect the actions taken. This recommendation runs counter to the common practice that the lower-status person bears the brunt of punitive action. However, when both individuals are punished (rather than only the person at the lower level) the appearance of an equitable decision will have the most positive effect on morale and productivity.[79]

Management can also contribute to a satisfactory resolution of romance-related issues by offering counseling to all individuals involved—the couple, the managers of work areas that are disrupted by the relationship, and the coworkers in those areas. Coworkers need to have a designated neutral party with whom they can consult about a troublesome romantic relationship. As their manager may be one of the participants, they need the freedom to report their concerns without fear of reprisal.

Individuals need to weigh the potential costs against the potential benefits when deciding whether to begin a workplace romance. The potential costs include negative effects of a workplace romance on their careers (e.g., loss of coworkers' respect or lack of advancement due to violations of workplace norms), self-esteem (e.g., questioning of basis for their work-related rewards), and family (e.g., marital strife or divorce). The potential benefits include meeting their personal needs at work and being happier as a result. When caught up in the passion of the moment, individuals may not be thinking clearly of the consequences. Nonetheless, they may gain from considering these consequences before they act on their feelings.[80]

In conclusion, although workplace romance seldom poses a legal threat unless a dissolved romance leads to sexual harassment, it poses potential problems for organizations. Two types of romance have the most damaging effects on individual, group, and organizational effectiveness: (1) a hierarchical romance in which one participant directly reports to the other and (2) a utilitarian romance in which one participant satisfies personal and sexual needs in exchange for satisfying the other participant's task-related or career-related needs. Negative effects of workplace romance on the conduct of work need to be addressed by organizations in some manner. However, workplace romance often has only positive effects, such as when both participants are single and committed to each other. In such cases, coworkers will be happy for the couple, and organizations need not respond.

Although social sexual behavior in the workplace cannot be fully managed, we have outlined steps that organizations can take to respond to the negative effects of both sexual harassment and workplace romance. In taking such steps, organizations create a more comfortable (if not entirely asexual) work environment for their employees. We also have suggested actions that employees may take to influence their own destinies. As a convenient site for people to meet their personal needs, the workplace may be more exotic than ever. However, it need not be a battlefield over the intersection of sexuality and work.

8 MANAGING THE WORK–FAMILY INTERFACE

LEARNING OBJECTIVES

After reading this chapter, you should be able to do the following:

8.1 Understand employees' increasing desires for work–family balance.

8.2 Distinguish between objective and subjective career success.

8.3 Describe trends in family structures.

8.4 Recognize ways in which work and family roles may be enemies, allies, and segmented or integrated as employees juggle these roles.

8.5 Define and provide examples of work–family decisions by individuals.

8.6 Describe different approaches dual-career couples may take in making work–family decisions.

8.7 Identify ways in which organizations may be family friendly through their programs and culture.

8.8 Identify ways in which employees may promote their own work–family balance.

INCREASING DESIRES FOR WORK–FAMILY BALANCE

Most people would like to have some degree of control over how they allocate time and energy to the roles in their lives. Although they may be engaged in many different roles (worker, spouse or partner, parent, child, part-time student, community service volunteer, etc.), this chapter focuses on work and family roles because these are the two roles in which many people are most involved and with which they identify the most. To gain more control over their lives, employees need to work for an employer that at least acknowledges that they have a life outside of work. If this is not the case, they may quit working for others to start their own business for the purpose of gaining control. Whether people work for themselves or others, they need to devote attention to managing their **work–family interface**—how their work role influences their family role and vice versa—to "make work and family work."[1]

In managing their work–family interface, most people seek a sense of **work–family balance**. Balancing work and family does not mean devoting equal time to one's work and family roles. Two people might distribute their time between work and family roles identically but differ in the sense of balance they experience. It also does not mean being equally involved in the two roles; one person may achieve a strong sense of balance from being primarily involved in family, whereas another person may achieve the same sense of balance from being primarily involved in work. Instead, the notion of work–family balance represents satisfaction with how things are going in one's work role in relation to how things are going in one's family role.[2]

The importance of work–family balance has become particularly acute in the millennial generation. As discussed in Chapter 2, many women in prior generations rejected the female gender role that specified their proper place as in the home, or primarily focused on home, by enhancing their educational attainment and entering the labor force in managerial and professional jobs in large numbers. In the same vein, the generation of fathers currently raising children is increasingly rejecting the male gender role that specifies their proper place as at work, or primarily focused on work. As the global diversity and inclusiveness officer for Ernst & Young put it, "Men are doubling down on their daddy duties. They want to have impact at home as well as work."[3]

Desires for work–family balance were also accentuated by the COVID-19 pandemic. Work–family lockdowns imposed during the pandemic prompted many employees to reassess how much they want to dedicate themselves to their work life vis-à-vis their family life and to better align their work and family identities with their internal beliefs rather than societal expectations. As a result, employees have been increasingly quitting all-consuming jobs for the purpose of improving their work–family balance. In response, companies in industries that rely on a regular infusion of fresh talent are being forced to compete more than ever to offer the most generous parental leave and other family-friendly benefits to attract and retain employees.[4]

Despite these trends, employees from all generations, especially managers and professionals, are increasingly being pressured by their employers to devote as much time to work as possible. Organizational cultures that stress long work hours decrease the amount of time (or at least "quality time") that employees have available to devote to their families. Enhanced communication technologies aid such organizations by facilitating the encroachment of work on employees' family lives. Many people find it difficult or impossible to turn off work when they are technically at home but digitally tethered to work. For example, they may feel compelled to log in to their email accounts late at night to scroll through and respond to messages received to maintain the impression that they are on call at all times. Because work communications that require a quick response can arrive any time, recipients face a challenge in establishing satisfactory boundaries between their work and family roles.[5]

This chapter is about how to manage the work–family interface to achieve a sense of balance and success in life and what employers as well as societies can do to help employees to achieve this goal. First, we consider what constitutes "success" for individuals in their work and family lives and how their definitions of success in each realm influence their sense of work–family balance. Second, we review the ways in which family structures have become more diverse over time. Third, we consider challenges involved in juggling work and family roles and how individuals' experiences in one role may influence their experiences in the other role, both positively and negatively. Fourth, we review important decisions individuals may make that influence the nature of their work–family interface. Fifth, we consider how couples may differ in the kinds of work–family decisions they face. Sixth, we consider ways employers may contribute to shaping their employees' work–family interface, both in the family-friendly programs they offer and the family-friendly culture they provide. Finally, we offer suggestions for how working people, whether self-employed or working for others, may enhance their own sense of balance and manage their work–family interface successfully.

Throughout the chapter, we consider sex differences in aspects of how people manage the work–family interface. The intersection of sex, gender, and the work–family interface is not as simple as gender roles would suggest.[6] Indeed, the most recent entrants to the labor force are the least likely to endorse gender roles. In times like these, sex differences in how individuals manage the interface between their work and family roles are no longer straightforward.

WHAT DOES IT MEAN TO BE SUCCESSFUL?

Individuals may experience success in both their work life and family life. In addition, they may be successful in achieving a satisfactory level of work–family balance. However, as we shall see, the term *success* needs to be used with caution.

Career or work success is the more familiar concept. Both objective and subjective measures may be used to assess career success. In most research studies, **objective career success** is measured by variables such as earnings, level of position in the organizational hierarchy, and rate of advancement or promotion. When objective variables are used to measure career success, people's careers are deemed more successful when they receive more pay, hold positions at higher levels, advance at a faster rate, and so on.[7]

In contrast, **subjective career success** is measured by variables that reflect individuals' satisfaction with their attainment of personally meaningful career outcomes, including the nature of their current job, potential for advancement, job security, pay, relationships with coworkers, and so on. When subjective variables are used to measure career success, people's careers may be considered successful at any level in the organizational hierarchy, no matter how much they are paid and how rapid their advancement. What counts is that they are satisfied with where they are and with their future prospects. Interestingly, a cross-cultural study conducted in 36 nations found that androgynous employees reported the highest subjective career success.[8]

Objective and subjective career success are positively related; people who achieve greater objective career success tend to be more satisfied with their careers. However, career success in objective terms does not necessarily lead to career satisfaction. The factors that lead to objective career success may be very different from those that lead to subjective career success.[9]

Women and men tend to focus on different types of measures in assessing their career success, with men focusing more on objective measures and women focusing more on subjective measures. Men tend to regard **status-based satisfiers** such as earning a high salary, getting promoted faster than their peers, and rapidly advancing to higher organizational levels as more important than women. In contrast, women tend to regard **socioemotional satisfiers** such as having supportive coworkers, working as part of a team, and helping others at work as more important than men. Men's greater reliance on objective measures of success that emphasize getting ahead in organizations is consistent with the male gender role. When men achieve greater objective success, they are better able to fulfill their traditional responsibilities as breadwinners for their families. In contrast, women's reliance on subjective measures of success is consistent with the female gender role. Women's focus on their feelings about their careers corresponds with the stereotype of women as expressive. In addition, the high value that women place on positive interpersonal relationships necessitates the use of subjective measures. The quality of relationships is best captured by subjective, not objective, measures.[10]

The notion of "family success" is analogous to career success. I can envision objective measures that could serve as indicators of this type of success, such as marital status (married or not married) or relationship status (significant other or no significant other), number of children, number of sports in which children play (and their success in goals or points scored), prestige of children's colleges, number of family members, number of photos posted by family members on social media in which one is tagged, and so on. Obviously, measuring family success using objective variables such as these would be absurd. Family success *has* to be measured subjectively. Satisfaction with family, which focuses on the perceived quality of family life, is more telling than objective measures of family status.

The term *success* has been used in considering family life to make a point about what constitutes success for individuals. The traditional "male model" of career success emphasizes objective measures and focuses on work life. In contrast, what may be called a "female model" of career success emphasizes subjective measures and includes consideration of family life as well as work life. This is not to say that all men define success solely by objective measures or that all women define success solely by subjective measures. Instead, traditional notions of career success need to be expanded to include concepts that have been associated with how women as well as men view success.[11]

When we examine the actual levels of career success achieved by men and women, we find evidence of both sex similarities and sex differences. For example, several studies have tracked the career success of male compared to female MBA (master of business administration) graduates who earned their degrees from the same institutions during the same period of time. These studies have found no sex difference in the level of subjective career success achieved. Over time, as their common educational experience recedes, female MBA graduates are no more or less satisfied with their careers than their male counterparts. However, the same studies have found a sex difference in the level of objective career success achieved as time passes. Eventually, female MBA graduates lag behind their male counterparts in indicators of objective career success such as income and managerial level.[12]

Further, family factors have opposite effects on objective career success for men and women. Men's objective career success is positively associated with and enhanced by being married, having a spouse who does not work, and having children. In contrast, these family factors are negatively associated with and pose obstacles to women's objective career success. These results support the existence of a motherhood penalty and fatherhood bonus, already discussed in Chapter 2, in objective career success.[13]

The phenomenon that women express no more dissatisfaction with their careers than men despite the fact that they hold jobs with less pay and authority has been called the **paradox of the contented female worker**. What would account for this paradox? Working men and women may experience similar levels of subjective career success because they perceive little discrepancy between what they obtain from their jobs in objective terms and what they expect to obtain. If women *expect* less objective career success than men, perhaps they will be as satisfied as men are when their expectations are met. In addition, if women *value* objective career success less than men, they will place less emphasis on it when subjectively evaluating their own success. The paradox of the contented female worker is most likely to be seen in female-intensive occupations, in which women are more likely to compare themselves with lower-paid women than in male-intensive or sex-neutral occupations.[14]

The same paradox has been observed among business owners. Women-owned firms tend to rank lower than men-owned firms on measures of objective success such as sales, income, rate of growth, and business performance compared with competitors. However, there is no sex difference in business owners' subjective success. Despite differences in objective success, male and female business owners are similarly satisfied with the success of their businesses, supporting the **paradox of the contented female business owner**. Overall, female business owners place less value on achieving business success in traditional terms and more value on the quality of their relationships with employees and contributions to society than male business owners.[15]

It is not for us to say what being successful should mean for individuals in their work or family lives or the balance they strike between the two. Similar to family success, satisfaction with work–family balance seems more indicative of achieving success in work–family balance for organizationally employed and self-employed workers than any objective measure could assess.[16] However, it is important to recognize that personal definitions of what constitutes success tend to differ. Sex differences in the meaning of success are likely to be reflected in the experiences people have and the decisions they make in managing the work–family interface.

WE ARE FAMILY

The nature of family structures has changed considerably over time as a result of declining adherence to gender roles such as women's increased labor force participation and men's increased desire for work–family balance. Other societal trends such as increased life expectancy, reduced fertility rates, delays in childbearing, high rates of movement in and out of couple relationships, and increased exposure to stepfamilies have also contributed to family change.[17]

According to United States (U.S.) statistics for families with children, the most prevalent (i.e., the "new normal") family structure is now the dual-career heterosexual married couple in which both parents are employed; 44% of families with children fall into this category. There is a two-way tie for the second most prevalent family structure between the married couple in which only the father is employed, the once-traditional family structure in which the father serves as breadwinner and the mother as homemaker (18% of families with children), and the female-headed family in which the mother is employed (also 18% of families with children). Male-headed families in which the father is employed comprise 7% of families with children, whereas married couples in which only the mother is employed comprise 3% of families. The other 10% of families with children have no employed parent.[18]

These statistics depict the dramatic change in what is considered normal for a family structure. As they show, the family structures of women and men differ considerably. Mothers are more than twice as likely to be employed single parents as fathers are. However, in married couples, fathers are about six times more likely to be their family's sole breadwinner than mothers are. Even at top management levels, the sex difference in family structures is pronounced. As women assume managerial positions at increasingly higher levels, they are less likely to be married or to have children than are men in equivalent positions. As noted earlier, the more successful the man's career in objective terms, the more likely he is to be married, have an unemployed spouse, and have children, whereas the opposite holds true for women.

Such statistics do not include unmarried couples who are cohabitating (i.e., living together in an intimate relationship). The number of cohabitating couples has increased considerably over time, and many couples form their "first union" (i.e., a shared domestic life and address) as a transition to eventually getting married. Almost half of U.S. women live with a partner as a first union, with about 40% of their premarital unions transitioning to marriage within three years, about 30% remaining intact beyond three years, and about 30% dissolving during that time. Overall, cohabitating couples represent what has become a common family structure as either an alternative to or step toward marriage.[19]

Such statistics also do not include same-sex households, which are increasing in number, as is the number of such households raising children. In the U.S., same-sex marriage became legally recognized first by many states and then by the federal government, thereby increasing the options for family structure available to LGBTQ+ (lesbian, gay, bisexual, transgender, and self-described queer) individuals. Compared with heterosexual couples living together, same-sex couples living together are less likely to be married rather than cohabitating, less likely to have children in the household, more likely to be interracial, and more highly educated (i.e., more likely to have both partners with at least a bachelor's degree).[20]

Additional changes in family structures have coincided with societal trends, such as trends toward delayed childbearing and fewer children per family. Further, as a result of the trend toward increased life expectancy discussed in Chapter 3, many people are delaying retirement and working longer because they are healthier at the traditional retirement age, want to keep working, or need the income. Employees who otherwise might have retired keep working for the income to subsidize eldercare for their parents as well as childcare.[21]

As we see, family structures have become increasingly differentiated as the traditional pattern of male breadwinner and female homemaker has given way to dual-career couples, single-parent households, same-sex households, and other alternatives. Even the institution of marriage, traditionally the cornerstone of family life, is in flux as an increasing proportion of children are raised outside of marriage and the opportunity to marry has been increasingly extended to same-sex as well as different-sex couples. This is clearly an era of increasing family diversity.

A JUGGLING ACT

There are different schools of thought about the linkage between work and family roles. According to an optimistic view, people benefit from juggling their work and family roles. When people participate heavily in multiple life roles (e.g., engaged in employment outside the home while caring for those within), they are able to avoid the worst aspects of any one role. Their involvement in one role enhances their functioning in the other. As a result, they have a heightened sense of well-being and subjective career success. According to a pessimistic view, people suffer from trying to juggle their work and family roles. When people attempt to participate in both work and family roles to any significant extent, they face an inevitable time crunch. Either they flee home in response to the pressures or appeals of work or they sacrifice career success to devote themselves primarily to their families. The reality for many people lies somewhere between these optimistic and pessimistic views. A "trade-offs" view suggests that there are both costs and benefits to juggling work and family roles. The challenge for people in achieving a satisfactory level of work–family balance then becomes to minimize the costs of role juggling while maximizing the benefits.[22]

Women may be better at juggling work and family roles than men. A study of heterosexual dual-career couples found that when faced with high work demands, women were more likely to provide emotional support of their partner's needs at home than men were under the same conditions. In the same vein, when faced with high family demands, women were more likely to provide emotional support to their coworkers than men were. These results may be due to women's being higher in feminine or communal behaviors in showing high concern for the needs of others, even when faced with high role demands themselves, which would be consistent with traditional gender roles. Also, working women in heterosexual couples may simply have more experience at being role jugglers than their partners due to their handling the bulk of family responsibilities.[23]

Work and Family as Enemies

A pessimistic view of the work–family interface suggests that individuals' work and family roles are inevitable enemies and continually interfere with each other. Individuals who attempt to juggle work and family roles are likely to experience some degree of **work–family conflict** as a result of simultaneous pressures from work and family roles that are mutually incompatible. Such conflict may come about because work interferes with family (work-to-family conflict), such as when long hours at work are required, or because family interferes with work (family-to-work conflict), such as when a child is sick and needs to stay home from school with adult care. Work–family conflict has considerable negative consequences for employees, their partners, their children, and their employers. High levels of work–family conflict produce feelings of dissatisfaction and distress within both roles that detract from well-being and life satisfaction.[24]

Three types of work–family conflict may occur for individuals: time-based, strain-based, and behavior-based.[25] **Time-based conflict** results from the finite amount of time that is available to handle both work and family roles. Time spent working generally cannot be devoted to family activities and vice versa. This type of conflict is influenced by the nature of individuals' family structures. For example, parents experience more time-based family-to-work conflict than nonparents, parents of younger children more than parents of older children, and parents of large families more than parents of small families.[26]

Strain-based conflict results when strain in one role spills over into the other role. Strain at home may decrease performance at work and negatively affect objective career success, and strain at work may affect one's behavior as a parent or spouse. Negative emotions created by tensions and exhaustion in one role may spill over into and interfere with performance in the other role.[27]

Behavior-based conflict occurs when incompatible behaviors are required for work and family roles, such as aggressiveness and objectivity at work and warmth and nurturance at home. For example, managers who adhere to the think manager—think masculine stereotype may feel caught between the sense of dominance and emotional detachment exhibited at work and the emotional expressiveness expected at home. Shifting gears between work and home is required to avoid this type of conflict.[28]

These three types of work–family conflict may be experienced by all employees. LGBTQ+ employees, however, may also experience a unique type of conflict. **Stigma-based conflict** may be prompted by heterosexist pressures from coworkers that lead LGBTQ+ employees to suppress the sharing of family information at work (e.g., family photos). It may also be prompted by organizational policies such as the lack of same-sex partner benefits, and organizational cultures that fail to be family friendly toward all employees regardless of their family structure. When present, stigma-based conflict leads to additional strain-based work-to-family conflict for LGBTQ+ employees beyond that experienced by heterosexual employees.[29]

Overall, sex differences in work–family conflict appear to be minimal. However, sex differences in how people spend their time influence their level of time-based conflict in both directions. For example, men devote more hours to work than women, leading to higher levels of time-based work-to-family conflict. In contrast, women devote more hours to family than men, leading to higher levels of time-based family-to-work conflict. During the COVID-19 pandemic, these sex differences were exacerbated for heterosexual parents, when school and childcare closures led mothers to reduce their work hours and increase their family hours; in contrast, fathers' work and family hours were relatively unaffected. Compared with heterosexual parents, gay and lesbian parents distribute their work and family responsibilities more equally, which reduces their overall level of time-based work–family conflict. These results demonstrate the importance of time allocation decisions in determining the amount and direction of conflict people experience.[30]

Work–family conflict increases for individuals when the demands placed on them in either the work or family role increase. The greatest potential for conflict occurs when individuals face simultaneous demands to participate in both a work and a family activity and neither activity can be rescheduled. In general, when faced with conflicting demands, individuals are likely to choose the activity about which others (e.g., boss or spouse) are pressuring them most. They are also likely to choose the activity in the role with which they most identify.[31]

Providing a vivid example of how work and family can be enemies, one of my evening MBA students who was working full time told the following story in a class I taught on managing diversity: A couple of months before, Jennifer (not her real name) was forced to choose between an important work activity (demand on a Saturday morning for emergency overtime work that day) and an important family activity (her mother's 50th birthday party, which she had arranged for the same Saturday). She had worked for several months in arranging the party and in getting her family to agree to the arrangements. She lined up the restaurant at which the party would be held. She arranged the group gifts, prepared for the follow-up party to be held at her house afterwards—the whole works. This was going to be a special day for Jennifer, her mother, and everyone else involved. Early on that Saturday morning, Jennifer received a call from her boss and was told that she had to come to work that day. When she began to describe her plans for the day, she was cut off and told, "The board doesn't want excuses. The board wants work." The 50th birthday party was held on that Saturday at Jennifer's house . . . but without Jennifer present. Instead, she spent the whole Saturday at work. According to Jennifer, it wasn't even an emergency that led her to be called to work. She was forced to make the heart-wrenching choice of going to work instead of the party. As a result of her choice, Jennifer experienced high time-based work-to-family conflict that day; in fact, she quit the job and company soon afterward. If she had chosen to go to the party instead, she would have experienced high time-based family-to-work conflict.[32]

Work–family conflict may be alleviated by informal **social support** that people receive in both their work and family roles. Receiving support at both work and home has been shown to enhance individuals' overall sense of well-being as well as their mental and physical health. Social support may be both tangible (e.g., information, advice, or assistance) and intangible (e.g., affirmation, affection, or trust). In addition, it may be expressed as a willingness to reschedule activities so one can avoid potential work–family conflict. For example, if Jennifer's boss had been willing to reschedule or reassign weekend work so she could have attended her mother's 50th birthday party, this would have indicated that the organization supported her participation in an important family activity and would have resolved the conflict, and she might not have quit her job.[33]

Employees' experiences with work–family conflict and the social support that may alleviate it differ across national cultures. For example, Chinese employees are more likely to have their parents as live-ins or dependents than U.S. employees. In addition, most adult children who do not reside with their parents live close to them. This high proximity facilitates the exchange of care between elderly parents and their married children. Elderly parents in China not only are more dependent economically and emotionally on their adult children than their U.S. counterparts but also are more important providers of childcare and household assistance. Although the net amounts of work–family conflict experienced by Chinese compared to U.S. employees may be similar, dual-career couples in China experience both greater stress from having to provide for their parents and greater support from their parents than dual-career couples in the United States.[34]

Work and Family as Allies

An optimistic view of the work–family interface suggests that individuals' work and family roles may be allies that continually enrich or enhance each other. **Work–family enrichment** is experienced by individuals who benefit from juggling work and family roles. It has considerable positive consequences for employees, their families, and their employers, including high job satisfaction and organizational commitment as well as high family satisfaction and good mental and physical health. As for conflict, enrichment may be present in either direction: work-to-family or family-to-work. For example, family life may help to make one a better leader and work life may help to increase one's social networks outside of work.[35]

Work–family enrichment is defined as the extent to which individuals' experiences in one role—work or family—improve their quality of life in the other role by improving either their performance in the other role or their positive affect (i.e., feelings) about it. It takes place when resources generated in one role are applied in a way that promotes high performance or positive affect in the other role. Several types of resources may serve this purpose. **Skills** acquired in one's family or work role, such as interpersonal skills and the ability to multitask, may enhance one's effectiveness in the other role. **Perspectives** obtained in one role, such as the importance of self-direction for personal development or respect for individual differences, may also be applied in the other role. **Psychological and physical resources** developed or nurtured in one role can increase performance in the other role; for example, self-esteem, confidence, and good mental and physical health that are generated from positive experiences and attention to physical fitness in one's personal life may promote work performance and positive work-related attitudes.[36]

Individuals may also generate **social-capital resources**—tangible support in the form of information, advice, or assistance in one role that benefits the other role. For example, information provided by an employee's spouse may be useful to the employee's career, and a colleague may help one's child gain admission to the colleague's alma mater. **Flexibility** in the work or family role may also enrich performance in the other role. For example, flexibility in the work role as a result of flexibility supports (to be discussed later in the chapter) may help an individual to meet family responsibilities better, and flexibility in the family role as a result of a partner's handling childcare may help an individual to perform more effectively on the job. Finally, **material resources** gathered in one role, such as bonus income from employment and inheritance or gifts from family members, may be used to enrich the other role.

Women experience greater work-to-family enrichment resulting from the application of nonmaterial resources than men. As discussed in Chapter 3, consistent with gender stereotypes, women tend to be higher than men in femininity, a psychological trait that places a high emphasis on interpersonal relationships. As a result, women may be especially committed to and knowledgeable about meeting their family's needs. Because they feel greater responsibility than men for the emotional well-being of their family, women may be more motivated to transfer nonmaterial resources acquired at work to enhance their family's well-being. However, because men earn higher pay than women to bring to their families, they are higher in work-to-family enrichment resulting from the application of material resources. Also, as for work–family conflict, individuals' experiences with work–family enrichment may differ across national cultures.[37]

Work and Family as Segmented or Integrated

To influence the degree of interdependence between their work and family roles, individuals may establish boundaries or borders around each role. Work and family roles vary in their **boundary permeability**—the degree to which they allow aspects of other roles to be addressed in the given role. Some people prefer to keep work matters at work, which requires an impermeable family role boundary, whereas others prefer to be able to respond to work matters while at home, which requires a permeable family role boundary. In the same vein, some people prefer to keep family matters at home, which calls for an impermeable work role boundary, whereas others prefer to be able to respond to family matters while at work, which requires a permeable work role boundary.[38]

Individuals vary in their preferences for segmenting or integrating their work and family roles. **Segmenters** prefer to keep these roles disconnected from each other by maintaining impermeable boundaries. In contrast, **integrators** prefer to have these roles interwoven in their lives by maintaining permeable boundaries that allow them to merge or blend aspects of work and family. The extent to which people prefer to segment work from family (e.g., by not bringing work home or responding to work-related communications at home) may differ from the extent to which they prefer to segment family from work (e.g., by not initiating or responding to family texts or calls at work). However, individuals' **preferred segmentation** of one role (work or family) from the other may differ from the level of **actual segmentation** of one role from the other that they experience. Not surprisingly, segmenters had greater difficulty in coping with work–family lockdowns during the COVID-19 pandemic than integrators because they could no longer maintain impermeable boundaries, resulting in a greater mismatch between their preferred and actual segmentation.[39]

Advances in communication technologies have contributed to the increased blurring of boundaries between work and family roles, which presents a greater challenge for segmenters than ever before. Employees can be more connected with coworkers while at home, and family members can be more connected with each other while one or more of them is at work. Further, technology has made it easier for employees in jobs that do not require their physical presence to work from home, if that is what they and their employers prefer, and for employees to be on call from work at home, which employers (but not employees) may prefer. When work demands can be made remotely, employees may feel the need to respond to the demands, no matter when such demands arrive or what they are doing or planning to do with their families, to maintain the appearance of being fully committed to their jobs. Work demands made remotely contribute to the unpredictability of work, which may add stress to family life.[40]

Segmenting work and family roles may have both advantages and disadvantages. Individuals who are successful in segmenting work from family are able to keep work demands from interrupting the time they devote to family, turn off work stressors when in their family role, and leave behaviors at the office that would be dysfunctional at home. As a result, they experience less work-to-family conflict than individuals who are less successful at segmenting work from family or less inclined to do so. However, they are also less likely to transfer positive emotions from work to family or see the relevance of applying skills or perspectives developed at work to their family role, resulting in them experiencing less work-to-family enrichment. In the same vein, individuals who successfully segment family from work restrict the amount of both family-to-work conflict and family-to-work enrichment they experience. Thus, there are trade-offs involved in the segmentation or integration of work and family roles.[41]

According to gender roles, men should emphasize the primacy of work in their lives by segmenting their family role from their work role but not their work role from their family role. In contrast, women should emphasize the primacy of family in their lives by segmenting their work role from their family role but not their family role from their work role. A meta-analysis offered mixed support for the applicability of gender roles to individuals' levels of actual segmentation. As gender roles would predict, men were more likely than women to segment their family role from their work role, which reduced the level of family-to-work conflict they experienced. However, contrary to gender roles, men were more also likely than women to segment their work role from their family role, which reduced the level of work-to-family conflict they experienced. Overall, these results suggest the existence of a sex difference in actual segmentation, such that men are more likely to be segmenters and women are more likely to be integrators.[42]

In conclusion, individuals may have negative experiences from juggling their work and family roles that result in work–family conflict (work and family as enemies) or they may have positive experiences that result in work–family enrichment (work and family as allies). They may experience both conflict and enrichment in different situations and at different points in time, and they may experience each in the direction of work-to-family or family-to-work. If they disconnect their work and family roles from each other by maintaining impermeable role boundaries (work and family as segmented), they will experience less conflict or enrichment than if they maintain permeable role boundaries that allow merging or blending of some aspects of their work and family roles (work and family as integrated).

Ultimately, if people are able to minimize the level of work–family conflict and maximize the level of work–family enrichment, they will be closer to achieving a sense of balance between these two important roles in their lives. Whether they achieve this goal will be influenced by their own decisions as well as decisions made by other parties that affect them.

WORK–FAMILY DECISIONS BY INDIVIDUALS

Throughout their lives, individuals make a stream of decisions in their work and family roles. **Work–family decisions** consist of decisions in one role (work or family) that are informed by consideration of the other role.[43] Although they do not have full control over their lives and are subject to work and family pressures, people play active roles in shaping their lives. Thus far, we have examined phenomena such as conflict and enrichment that influence individuals' sense of balance as they manage the work–family interface. Next, we examine several work–family decisions that may influence the extent and direction of conflict and enrichment that individuals experience. Although we focus on how family factors inform decisions individuals make in their work role, work factors may also inform decisions individuals make in their family role (e.g., decisions to marry or divorce).[44]

In general, individuals may make three broad types of decisions regarding their work domain—role entry, participation, and exit decisions—that may be influenced by factors in their family domain. **Role entry decisions** involve choices about whether to enter a particular work role. **Role participation decisions** involve choices regarding how one engages in a particular work role. **Role exit decisions** involve choices regarding leaving a particular work role.[45]

Decision About Whether to Work Part Time or Full Time

The decision about whether to seek full-time or part-time employment represents a role entry decision. Part-time jobs are in the minority in the workplace, but their proportion is significant; the proportion of all U.S. jobs that are part time is about 15%.[46] In addition, many part-time workers hold multiple jobs. Part-time work offers people the opportunity for better work–family balance. It can help to lower work–family conflict and increase life satisfaction. It may also provide a transition to or from full-time employment. However, part-time work also has drawbacks. Part-time employees have lower status in organizations than full-time employees doing the same kind of work. Their hourly wages are lower, they are less likely to receive health insurance benefits, their jobs are less secure, and their career prospects are more limited.[47]

Women and men differ in the tendency to hold part-time rather than full-time jobs. Women hold about two-thirds of all part-time jobs, which may be influenced by their placing greater importance than men on work–family balance when seeking employment. About 25% of the U.S. female labor force and about 12% of the U.S. male labor force are employed part time.[48] Overall, although women's greater tendency than men to hold part-time jobs may offer them a greater sense of work–family balance and subjective career success, it restricts their objective career success.

Decision About Whether to Work at Home

The decision about whether to work at home represents a role participation decision. Employees may be able to choose their work location depending on the nature of their jobs (e.g., physical presence required to perform the job or not) and the preferences of their employer. This choice was taken away from all except essential workers during work–family lockdowns in response to the COVID-19 pandemic.[49] Working at home may have both positive and negative consequences.

On the positive side, working from home eliminates the need for commuting from home to work and back. Long commutes, while providing the opportunity to transition between roles and ruminate about work or family, are particularly risky for pregnant employees and endanger their infant's health at birth. Working from home may help to alleviate or reduce the need for paid childcare, which may make it especially attractive to mothers, given that they tend to handle the bulk of family responsibilities in dual-career heterosexual households. It increases the potential for family-to-work enrichment if other people are present at home while one is working. Working from home is likely to be the preferred work mode for integrators.[50]

On the negative side, working from home increases the potential for both work-to-family conflict and family-to-work conflict. It may particularly be a challenge for parents of young children, depending on the availability and affordability of paid childcare. If both partners of a heterosexual couple work from home, the woman is more likely to have to deal with this challenge. Also, if more women choose to work from home than men, offices may become more male-dominated physically, which may hinder women's objective career success by reducing their opportunities for mentoring. Working from home is likely to be unattractive to segmenters.[51]

Overall, the decision to work from home is more likely to be affected by family factors for women than men. It represents a double-edged sword that may be appealing to them in juggling their work and family roles in the short run but hazardous to their careers in the long run.

Decision About Whether to Have a Voluntary Employment Gap or Take a Parental Leave

Employment gaps (periods of time during which individuals leave and then rejoin the labor force) represent a combination of role exit and role entry decisions. They may be either voluntary or involuntary on the part of the employee. Women are more likely than men to have employment gaps early in their careers. In addition, their employment gaps are more likely to be voluntary for purposes of child-rearing.[52]

The voluntary employment gap violates the stereotype of a successful career, which is largely based on the experiences of men. An uninterrupted career pattern is assumed to demonstrate stability and commitment to work. Time away from work, unless for the purpose of enhancing educational credentials, is often assumed to lead to deterioration of skills and knowledge and to reflect less commitment to work. As a result, when people choose to take time out from their work careers for any reason, their subsequent advancement and earnings are likely to suffer. Thus, women's greater tendency to have voluntary employment gaps contributes to their achieving lower long-term objective career success.

Further, when companies offer paid parental leave for new parents, new fathers are more reluctant to take advantage of the opportunity than new mothers because they legitimately fear that they will be stigmatized for doing so. Even though men experience a fatherhood bonus in objective career success, their careers may suffer if they request paternity leave upon becoming fathers because they will not appear to be putting work first in their lives, thereby violating the male gender role. In contrast, even though women face a motherhood penalty in objective career success, they know that they will be likely to receive societal approval if they request maternity leave because such a request is consistent with the female gender role.[53]

In conclusion, evidence about how people make a wide range of role entry, participation, and exit decisions regarding their work domain, including the three examples of such decisions reviewed here, is clear: Women's decisions at work are more likely to be work–family decisions (i.e., decisions that are informed by consideration of family factors) than those of men. However, the decline in endorsement of gender roles over time, especially among men and recent entrants to the labor force, suggests that these sex differences may be diminishing.[54]

WORK–FAMILY DECISIONS BY COUPLES

Thus far, we have focused on decisions individuals make at work that, whether informed by consideration of their family role or not, may have considerable consequences for their families. This begs the question of how work decisions that affect families are to be made: by individuals acting alone or jointly with their families. In this section, we focus on work–family decisions made by dual-career couples (whether married or unmarried) because this has become the dominant family structure.[55]

When a couple makes a work–family decision, it is making a choice about one or both partners' involvement in work and family activities, with decisions about work activities informed by family considerations and decisions about family activities informed by work considerations. The goal of its work–family decisions is to enhance the family's well-being and to enable both partners to achieve a satisfactory level of work–family balance.

Not all work–family decisions need to be made by the couple, even if both partners are affected. Their decisions may involve minor matters that can be easily dealt with by one of the partners or recurring matters for which routines may be established. For example, a couple may decide to take turns in who will leave work early to pick up a sick child from school when the occasion arises. In contrast, **anchoring decisions**–major decisions that influence the couple's overall approach to managing the work–family interface–call for both partners' involvement in decision making. Further, a dual-career couple may experience a **shock event**—a disruptive, novel, and critical event in one partner's work domain (e.g., unexpected layoff, promotion opportunity) or family domain (e.g., unplanned pregnancy, diagnosis of a life-threatening illness). Both partners need to be involved in the anchoring decision about how to deal with a shock event.[56]

A **relocation decision** that involves the family's moving for one partner to take a new job while the other partner quits a job and seeks new employment is a particularly complex and difficult anchoring decision. It involves a combination of role entry and exit decisions for both members of the couple in their work roles (start new jobs or leave old jobs) and family roles (select a new home and move from the old home). Research suggests a sex difference in the willingness to relocate: Heterosexual couples are more likely to relocate for the husband's career than for the wife's career. Women are more likely than men to enter occupations in which they can work anywhere (e.g., nursing) and move easily in support of a spouse's career while maintaining employment opportunities for themselves. For women in such occupations, their philosophy about anticipated relocations may be "I will follow him," established long before a particular relocation decision needs to be made. In contrast, men's careers tend to be more geographically constrained and not as easily transportable to a different location.[57]

As they make anchoring decisions, partners in dual-career couples may vary in how they construe their family identity. One's family identity answers the question, "Who am I as a family member?" Some people construe their family identity primarily in terms of **career-oriented behaviors**; they see their primary role in the family as providing material resources that enhance the family's material well-being (i.e., "being a breadwinner"). Other people construe their family identity primarily in terms of **caregiving behaviors**; they see their primary role in the family as ensuring that family members are nurtured and supported, either directly (e.g., by feeding and bathing a child, by comforting and encouraging a partner) or indirectly (e.g., by arranging the provision of childcare or eldercare, by facilitating opportunities for a family member's development). Still other people construe their family identity in terms of both career-oriented and caregiving behaviors to enhance their family's well-being in multiple ways.[58]

Because each partner may have a career construal, caregiving construal, or career-and-caregiving construal of family identity, different combinations may emerge that influence the couple's approach to work–family decision making and the types of decisions it faces.[59] The **complementary couple**, in which one partner has a career construal and the other a caregiving construal, represents one combination of partners. In such couples, the partner with the caregiving construal is more likely to decide to work part time rather than full time and be the one who picks up sick children from school or arranges and monitors eldercare for one of their parents than the partner with the career construal. If the partner with the career construal is male and the partner with the caregiving construal is female, this type of couple represents the once-traditional family structure that adheres to gender roles in its work–family decision making.

The **career-first couple**, in which both partners construe their family identity primarily in terms of career-oriented behaviors, represents a second combination. Such couples are likely to face work–family decisions about how to outsource their caregiving responsibilities while ensuring that quality care is being provided by others. Their mutual career-oriented family identities may even influence the kind of family structure they choose for themselves—that is, one that is as free from caregiving responsibilities (e.g., child-free) as possible.

The **caregiving-first couple**, in which both partners construe their family identity primarily in terms of caregiving behaviors, represents a third combination. Members of such couples are likely to seek jobs with flexible work hours that enable them to meet their caregiving needs while still earning sufficient material resources to maintain their desired quality of life.

Finally, the **career-and-caregiving couple**, in which both partners construe their family identity in terms of both career-oriented and caregiving behaviors, represents a combination that seeks to have it all. Its work–family decisions are likely to focus on how both partners may find work that meets their needs for objective and subjective career success as well as provides sufficient flexibility to meet their caregiving needs. In doing so, the couple needs to make decisions that avoid or minimize work–family conflict that can arise from each partner trying to be a star in both roles.

As we see, the types of work–family decisions made by dual-career couples differ according to the family identities of the partners. Some couples adhere to traditional gender roles, but most do not. The challenge heterosexual couples face is not falling back on gender roles in work–family decision making when these roles do not fit their family identities. Dual-career couples also need to recognize that not all work–family decisions need to be made jointly. Otherwise, their life together may be something that happens while they are busy making other plans.

BEING FAMILY FRIENDLY

Individuals' success in managing the work–family interface is influenced by the work environments that their employers provide and the strategies they adopt. To understand the intersection of work and family more fully, we need to examine the roles of both employers and employees. In this section, we consider formal work–family programs that organizations may offer and the influence of the organizational culture.[60] Table 8.1 summarizes recommended actions for organizations to be family friendly.

TABLE 8.1 ■ Recommended Actions for Organizations

1. Offer a wide range of family-friendly programs to employees.
2. Offer paid maternity and paternity leave.
3. Offer assistance to employees in meeting childcare and eldercare needs.
4. Offer flexible work arrangements to employees when possible.
5. Make working remotely available to qualified employees when the job allows it.
6. Offer counseling when organizational decisions affect the family (e.g., relocation).
7. Offer employment assistance to spouses of relocated employees.
8. Offer training on how to deal with family issues (e.g., getting a child into college).
9. Provide incentives for managers to permit subordinates to take advantage of flexible work arrangements.
10. Offer a family-friendly culture that is singles-friendly and LGBTQ+-family-friendly as well as heterosexual-family-friendly.
11. Adopt a model of the successful career that does not penalize employees' having career interruptions or their not being available to meet work needs at all times.

Family-Friendly Programs

Organizations may make work–family decisions that are informed by consideration of their employees' desires for work–family balance. **Family-friendly programs** are intended to help employees meet their family needs while fulfilling their work responsibilities. Making such programs available for employee usage helps organizations to attract and retain talented employees, which has a positive impact on their long-term performance. However, male employees are less likely than female employees to take advantage of family-friendly programs or even be aware of their existence.[61]

Several types of work–family programs may be offered. **Maternity and paternity supports** may include paid or unpaid maternity and paternity leave, time off for prenatal health care, hygienic nursing facilities, and work accommodations for pregnant and nursing employees. Such supports help the mother's and newborn child's health, promote the father's and mother's bonding with the child, and help the family maintain its material well-being if time off for leave is paid. Offering paid maternity leave is especially critical for U.S. mothers and their families, as the United States is one of only two of 185 nations that are members of the International Labour Office (ILO) that does not mandate the availability of paid maternity leave. About half of ILO nations mandate the availability of paternity leave (as does the U.S.), with most of these nations also requiring a cash benefit (but not the U.S.). Overall, about one-quarter of U.S.

employees have access to a paid parental leave as a result of their organization's decision to offer such support.[62]

Dependent care supports that organizations may offer include onsite or nearby childcare centers, financial assistance for childcare or eldercare services, and information about or referrals to such services. These supports help employees ensure that they are aware of and can afford quality caregiving services. Employees' needs for dependent care vary greatly, and organizations need to consider their financial resources and the diversity of their employees' family lives when deciding how best to address these needs. Even when resources are scarce, there are many kinds of actions that can be taken to assist employees with meeting these needs. Dependent care supports are associated with positive work-related attitudes, employee well-being, and reduced turnover. They are likely to be especially valued by employees who are single parents or in career-first couples that are outsourcing their caregiving responsibilities.[63]

Flexibility supports may include flextime, telecommuting or working remotely, part-time work, personal leaves and sabbaticals, and job sharing. These supports are highly popular with many employees because flexibility in their work schedules enables them to gain greater control over their work and family lives, including when they work, where they work, and how much they work. For example, parents may find it easier to accommodate their children's regular schedules and predictable events, such as teacher conferences. In addition, they may be able to respond better to emergencies and unanticipated events such as sudden illnesses, weather-related school closings, and breakdowns in childcare arrangements. Flexibility in work arrangements appeals to all employees, not only parents, because it symbolizes a focus on getting the work done rather than how, when, or where it is done. Flexibility supports yield benefits for employers such as decreased absenteeism and turnover and increased productivity.[64]

Flextime, which allows planned variations from normal work hours, is a popular type of flexibility support. Managerial and professional employees make the greatest use of flextime programs. Flextime may consist of changes to the starting and ending times of the workday or compression of the workweek into fewer days (e.g., four 10-hour days instead of five 8-hour days). It may also allow variation in the work schedule from one workday to the next. Flextime has a positive impact on employees' productivity, absenteeism, and job satisfaction, which benefits their employers as well.[65]

Telecommuting—doing some or all of one's work remotely—is also a popular type of flexibility support, especially for integrators. As with flextime, telecommuting is most common for managerial and professional employees. It gives employees flexibility in the location and timing of work by allowing them to work out of a virtual office. Telecommuters report that working at home increases their productivity by reducing interruptions and distractions and enhancing their concentration. It also helps them balance work and family; their increased presence at home enables them to better fulfill caregiving and household responsibilities and strengthens family relationships. However, telecommuting can blur the distinction between work and family roles in unproductive ways as telecommuters face interruptions and distractions while working at home. As a result, telecommuting may both decrease work-to-family conflict and increase family-to-work conflict. The challenge for telecommuters then becomes how to integrate work and family in productive ways. When this challenge is met, telecommuting benefits both employees and employers.[66]

Informational and social supports offered by organizations may include employee assistance programs, counseling for employees and their families when organizational decisions affect the family (e.g., a promotion offer that requires relocation), employment assistance for spouses of relocated employees, and support groups for employees with similar family needs. Organizations may take a proactive role in helping their employees minimize conflict and maximize enrichment, thereby achieving a satisfactory level of work–family balance through such supports. They may offer training in how to enlist a spouse's support to alleviate work–family conflict. Further, they may alleviate employees' stress by providing useful information about matters that concern employees outside of work. For example, some firms offer educational programs about how to get one's child into and through college, including advice about the admissions process, testing, financial aid, and financial planning; this form of work-to-family enrichment is particularly appreciated by parents of college-bound children.[67]

A one-size-fits-all approach to designing family-friendly programs is unlikely to work. For example, most corporate work–family programs were designed for the family needs of married employees with children in mind although other employees have family needs as well. Further, not all married employees with children have the same family needs. The numbers and ages of children vary as well as their places of residence; blended families with stepchildren are increasingly common. Younger children require different care than older children, and the rearing of multiple children is more demanding than that of a sole child. The employment status of the spouse or significant other also varies. Spouses and significant others differ in income contributed to the household and time and energy devoted to their work and family roles. Other family members such as parents, siblings, and extended family may also play important roles in people's lives either as a source of support or in need of support themselves. Different types of family needs may intersect with each other. Further, individuals may have multiple intersecting identities (e.g., on the basis of their sex, LGBTQ+ status, and career and caregiving construals) that influence the nature of their family needs.[68]

In summary, there are many programs that employers may offer their employees in the interest of being family friendly. All of the programs described in this section have their costs, some greater than others depending on the nature of the program, number of employees covered, and utilization rates. All of these programs are likely to have benefits to organizations as well as at least some employees. The challenge for organizations is to recognize the unique family needs of groups of employees and then identify ways to meet these needs that benefit both employees and the organization.

However, work–family programs may prompt a **work–family backlash** among some employees. Work–family backlash is most likely to occur when programs are perceived as inequitable in their availability or intended beneficiaries, when potential users fear repercussions for their careers if they take advantage of the programs, or when the programs are seen as intended to "enclose" employees at work rather than enable them to achieve work–family balance. For example, an onsite childcare center or fitness center may be perceived as an attempt to lure employees into working longer hours rather than as a convenient way to help them meet their childcare needs or maintain their health. In such instances, the programs may prompt negative reactions that undermine organizational goals. To avoid work–family backlash, organizations need to consider the messages being sent by their organizational culture, which we discuss in the next section.[69]

Family-Friendly Culture

Being family friendly involves more than offering a variety of work–family programs. It also means providing a **family-friendly culture** in which *all* employees, not only heterosexual married employees, feel comfortable in taking advantage of programs that are intended to benefit them.

Family-supportive managers are a crucial link in creating a family-friendly culture. Employees are more likely to utilize work–family programs when they have a supportive manager who empathizes with their desire for work–family balance and actively facilitates their ability to manage their work–family interface. Having a family-supportive manager reduces employees' work–family conflict and increases their work–family enrichment, which gives them greater incentive to stay with the organization. It also improves their sense of well-being and the quality of their marital relationships. Evidence suggests that organizations can effectively train their managers on how to be family-supportive, which contributes to having a family-friendly culture.[70]

Despite the benefits of family-friendly programs for both employees and employers, managers may resist implementing them. According to a study of the factors that affect managerial decisions about whether to approve requests for flexible work arrangements, the most important factor was the criticality of the subordinate's job assignment. Subordinates whose work was more critical to the work unit were less likely to have their requests approved than noncritical subordinates; subordinate sex had no effect on managers' decisions. These are curious results. Employees who are trusted with more critical job tasks would seem to deserve special treatment. However, in this study, their managers viewed such employees as the *least* desirable candidates for flexible work arrangements. Critical employees should not have to transfer to less-critical jobs to qualify for these arrangements. To reap the benefits of family-friendly programs, organizations need to educate their managers on the corporate benefits of such programs and provide incentives to managers to implement them.[71]

Organizations need to establish a **singles-friendly culture** that combats "singlism," or the pervasive stereotype single people face in everyday life that they are workaholics with no family life. Most single, childless ("child-free") employees are part of a family that may include parents, grandparents, siblings, aunts and uncles, cousins, and other extended family members. Although single, childless employees may not need family-friendly programs targeted toward them in particular, they need to feel that their unique needs are being recognized and addressed. For example, they need to feel included in social events at work such as the annual company picnic for employees and their families, which should include both child-friendly and singles-friendly activities. They also need equal access to employee benefits and respect for their family lives. Single, childless employees need to know that there are similar work expectations for themselves and employees with children. They should not be expected to travel more for business, to work more hours when coworkers miss work for family reasons, or to work at times when coworkers are not expected to work.[72]

Organizations also need to establish a **LGBTQ+-family–friendly culture** that counteracts the unique barriers that LGBTQ+ employees often face in the work environment. They need to feel comfortable communicating about their family structure and feel that it is accepted in the first place if they are to gain access to relevant benefits. Once they know that their family structure is accepted, they need a safe environment in which to discuss their work–family needs.[73]

Finally, to be truly family friendly, organizations need to avoid having what may be called a **family sacrifice culture**. Women react more negatively and experience more work-to-family conflict than men in family sacrifice cultures. For example, an organizational culture that defines a successful career as an uninterrupted sequence of promotions to higher levels and assumes that requests to take time out from career for family reasons, which are made more by women than men, reflect a lack of career commitment may be regarded as a family sacrifice culture. Organizations that want to create family-friendly cultures need to expand their notions of what constitutes career success to include voluntary employment gaps and lateral moves. They should encourage, rather than discourage, employees to take advantage of work–family programs, recognizing that employees who do so are likely to be more committed—not less committed—to the organization.[74]

An organizational culture that expects key employees to work long hours and be available 24/7, which stalls women's career advancement more than that of men, may also be regarded as a family sacrifice culture; this is what Jennifer experienced in the work–family conflict incident described earlier in the chapter. While work still needs to get done, expectations of long work hours may counteract any positive effect that family-friendly programs might foster. Employees who prefer some degree of segmentation of their work role from their family role will feel stressed out from the pressure; they may quit their job and the organization because of heightened work-to-family conflict, burnout, and resentment by their partners. If an organization has a family sacrifice culture, it can offer all the family-friendly programs it wants and talk about how family friendly it is, but the real story is something different.[75]

In conclusion, many employees choose not to participate in programs intended to be family friendly because they fear they will be stigmatized as not committed to their work. Employees, especially those who construe their family identity in terms of career-oriented behaviors and seek to achieve objective career success, need to feel that they work in an organizational culture that allows them to participate in such programs without derailing their careers. When organizations recognize that they are employing whole individuals who have lives outside of work and not merely jobholders, they are more likely to be family friendly in their programs and cultures. They are also more likely to attract and retain productive employees.

BALANCING WORK AND FAMILY

The challenge for all individuals, whatever their family structure may be, is to manage the interface between their work and family lives to achieve a sense of work–family balance. Meeting this challenge is no simple matter. Negotiating a satisfactory balance between work and family interests may seem like a full-time job in itself. Social support from family members and employers may make the task more manageable, but employees can do much to help themselves. Table 8.2 summarizes recommended actions for individuals to balance their work and family roles.

TABLE 8.2 ■ Recommended Actions for Individuals

1. Be aware of what work–family balance means to you and your identities regarding the importance of work and family in your life.
2. Cultivate social support from all possible sources.
3. Get a mentor, if possible.
4. Use all of your paid vacation days.
5. Adopt coping strategies for dealing with stresses in your work and family roles.
6. Decide how much you wish to segment your work role from your family role and vice versa while recognizing the implications for the levels of work–family conflict and enrichment you experience.
7. Collaborate on anchoring work–family decisions with your partner if you are a dual-career couple.

First, people need to be aware of what exactly constitutes work–family balance to them. What is the relative importance of the roles in their life, which may include work and family as well as a host of other roles (volunteer, student, etc.)? With which role or roles do they identify the most? If individuals identify primarily with their work role or construe their family identity primarily in terms of career-oriented behaviors, their work decisions should seek to maximize their sense of career success, whether assessed objectively or subjectively. If they identify primarily with their family role or construe their family identity primarily in terms of caregiving behaviors, their work decisions should represent work–family decisions by placing high emphasis on family considerations. However, if individuals identify highly with both work and family, their work decisions need to be carefully calibrated to take into account the potential impact on their sense of work–family balance. Individuals' satisfaction with work–family balance comes from being satisfied and successful in the roles that are important to them.[76]

People need to cultivate social support in both work and family roles for their involvement in the other role—from their manager and coworkers at work and from their spouse or partner and other family members at home. If they face pressures to participate in conflicting activities in both their work and family roles, they will benefit by mobilizing support in the form of release from time demands that will alleviate the need to make a choice. Through the support mobilization process, they may avoid work–family conflict.[77]

Mentors—senior individuals with advanced experience and knowledge who provide guidance to their protégés—may be a valuable source of social support. Although some organizations have formal programs that assign mentors to protégés, informal mentoring relationships are the most common and the most helpful. Mentors typically help protégés in their career development by acting as coaches and sponsors. Mentors also enhance protégés' satisfaction with their careers by offering friendship, counseling, and acceptance. Thus, mentors contribute to their protégés' objective and subjective career success. In addition, mentors may contribute to their protégés' management of the work–family interface by being sensitive to and supportive of their goals for work–family balance. Although women face greater barriers to forming formal mentoring relationships than men, they are just as likely to develop informal mentoring relationships.[78]

People also need to develop coping strategies to deal with stress from the demands of their work and family roles. A simple coping strategy is making use of all of one's paid vacation days. This strategy is not available to all U.S. employees, as federal labor laws do not require payment for time not worked, even on federal holidays. As a result, compared to other advanced economies, the United States has been described as the **no-vacation nation.**[79]

Vacations have many health benefits. They provide a relatively long period of time for employees to get away from stresses at work and home in a more relaxing environment. They also allow employees to devote a more extended period of time than evenings or weekends off to family activities and personal interests. Women tend to use more of their paid vacation days than men, which is consistent with their engaging in more health-promoting behaviors, as discussed in Chapter 3. Employees who are married or cohabitating and have children at home also use more of their paid vacation days. However, perhaps due to the influence of family sacrifice cultures, employees who work longer hours tend to use less of their paid vacation days, which has a negative impact on their health.[80]

Other strategies may help individuals cope with stress in one role but not alleviate stress in the other role. For example, cognitive disengagement or detachment may be an effective strategy for coping with work-related stress but not with family-based stress. Reassurances of emotional attachment and commitment may be effective when directed toward family members but not when directed toward bosses, subordinates, and peers at work. Individuals need coping strategies for dealing effectively with stress in both of these domains. In addition to unilateral coping strategies, couples may reduce their overall amount of stress by providing mutual support.[81]

Whether they work for themselves or others, individuals face a challenge in managing the boundaries between their work and family roles. Segmenters take the risk of preventing work–family enrichment (the positive side of the work–family interface) in the interest of preventing work–family conflict (the negative side). Integrators, on the other hand, take the risk of increasing work–family conflict to an undesirable level while maximizing their opportunities for work–family enrichment. There is no simple solution to this dilemma.[82]

When dual-career couples make work–family decisions, especially anchoring decisions, they need to collaborate to ensure that they are meeting the needs of both partners and the family as a whole. This begins with their agreeing on exactly what constitutes family well-being and what their plan is for achieving it. Collaborative work–family decision making is beneficial in several ways. First, a work–family decision that is collaboratively made is likely to be higher in quality than a decision made by one partner alone. Second, it is more likely to be accepted by both partners, with mutual buy-in aiding in its implementation. Third, it may contribute to strengthening the relationship. In contrast, a work–family decision made unilaterally by one partner and imposed on the other is likely to be resented, even if it is in the other partner's best interest, because the way in which the decision is made may prompt negative emotions.[83]

In conclusion, as their careers unfold, individuals may set goals for work–family balance in accordance with their identities and adopt plans for action to achieve these goals. In doing so, they need to resist gender roles that do not reflect who they really are. With help from their employers and families, despite all of the challenges they face, individuals and couples may ultimately achieve their balance goals and contribute to shaping their own lives.

9 PROMOTING NONDISCRIMINATION, DIVERSITY, AND INCLUSION

LEARNING OBJECTIVES

After reading this chapter, you should be able to do the following:

9.1 Appreciate the similarity in how companies express their commitment to diversity.

9.2 Understand the rationale for promoting nondiscrimination, including complying with equal employment opportunity (EEO) laws, taking affirmative action while promoting equity, and avoiding or reducing the costs of discrimination.

9.3 Describe the rationale for promoting diversity, including the benefits of sex diversity in the top management and governance ranks.

9.4 Discuss the rationale for promoting inclusion, including the advantages of an inclusive diversity culture over a monolithic or pluralistic culture.

9.5 Identify actions that may be taken by organizations to promote nondiscrimination, diversity, and inclusion, including setting and communicating goals, identifying and rewarding the right behavior, stimulating employee involvement, educating employees, and implementing cultural change.

ORGANIZATIONAL COMMITMENT TO DIVERSITY

At XYZ Company, belonging begins with us; we believe that belonging is a catalyst to empower our diverse workforce to reach their potential every day. Our diverse perspectives come from many sources including gender, race, age, national origin, sexual orientation, culture, education, and professional and life experience. We're deeply committed to the work we're doing to develop a diverse workforce and provide an equitable workplace that empowers all employees. Diversity includes, inclusion empowers, and when we bring everybody in, we can do the best work of our lives together.

We celebrate our people, ideas, and experiences, creating a culture where all employees are appreciated, valued, and able to contribute to their full potential.[1]

Does XYZ Company sound like a great place to work or what? Actually, it doesn't exist, at least as a single company. The five statements in the opening passage are excerpts from the diversity policies posted on the web sites of the top five corporations in the *Fortune* 500, a list of the largest U.S. corporations.[2] (See Note 1 for the sources of the statements in order.) Can you tell the companies apart based on these excerpts? Neither can I.

Organizations tend to be positively rated by their employees if they make such statements and if they acknowledge diversity-related public issues as they arise. For example, many corporations responded to issues regarding police violence against Black Americans (which triggered the Black Lives Matter movement) by releasing public statements condemning racism and affirming their diversity policies.[3]

Indeed, if such statements represented what the workplace is really like, it would be reasonable to conclude that the merits of having a diverse workforce have been fully recognized and embraced. However, the reality is more complex. Organizations are quite diverse in how they deal with the notion of diversity. Although some firms live up to such statements, many firms establish diversity policies solely to reduce their liability, which sends a mixed message. Employees may question whether such statements represent "happy talk" intended to mask persistent discrimination or a real commitment to eradicate it.[4]

In general, organizations may take three types of actions:

1. **Promote nondiscrimination** in treatment of people and decisions about people. This means promoting compliance by all employers with federal, state, and local equal employment opportunity (EEO) laws. Such laws ban discrimination on the basis of sex, race, ethnicity, national origin, age, religion, and other personal characteristics. Taking affirmative action while promoting equity may be required to overcome the effects of past discrimination. Promoting nondiscrimination also means refraining from discrimination on the basis of job-irrelevant personal characteristics even if it is not illegal.

2. **Promote diversity** among employees in all jobs and at all levels. The focus of promoting diversity is on the *quantity* of employees from groups in different jobs and at different organizational levels. Organizations may attempt to increase the diversity of their labor force for business reasons.

3. **Promote inclusion** of employees from all groups in the organizational culture. The focus of promoting inclusion is on the nature or *quality* of work relationships among employees who belong to different groups. There are no laws that require organizations to provide a work environment in which

members of all groups feel comfortable and accepted. Organizations may engage in this kind of action if they see some advantage to doing so.

Organizations benefit from pursuing all three types of actions: promoting nondiscrimination, promoting diversity, and promoting inclusion. An organization successful in these actions is less likely to be the target of costly litigation. Its employees bring a wider range of perspectives to work issues, which result in more creative solutions to problems facing the organization. Such an organization is most likely to attract and retain highly qualified employees from all groups and to take full advantage of their talents.

In this chapter, we consider the case for promoting nondiscrimination, diversity, and inclusion. Next, we consider specific actions that organizations may take to promote a nondiscriminatory, diverse, and inclusive culture. We wrap up with conclusions for the book.

WHY PROMOTE NONDISCRIMINATION?

In this section, we first review the legal requirements regarding sex discrimination with which organizations must comply, both in complying with EEO laws and in taking affirmative action while promoting equity. Next, we review the costs of sex discrimination for employees, groups, and organizations.

Comply with Equal Employment Opportunity Laws

Federal, state, and local laws govern the actions of employers, with federal laws having the broadest impact. We focus our attention in this section on federal EEO laws pertaining to sex discrimination in the United States.[5]

Title VII of the Civil Rights Act and the Equal Pay Act are the most significant pieces of U.S. federal legislation that address sex discrimination. Title VII prohibits discrimination on the basis of sex (as well as race, color, religion, and national origin) in any employment condition, including hiring, firing, promotion, transfer, compensation, and admission to training programs. It has been extended to ban discrimination because of pregnancy, childbirth, or related medical conditions and to ban sexual harassment (see Chapter 7). Also, the ban on sex discrimination has been extended to ban discrimination on the basis of sexual orientation and transgender status.[6] Title VII is considered the most comprehensive EEO law and has served as a model for other EEO laws banning age discrimination in employment (against older, not younger people) and discrimination against qualified people with disabilities. The Equal Pay Act makes it illegal to pay members of a particular sex at a lower rate than members of a different sex if they hold jobs that require equal skill, effort, and responsibility under similar working conditions in the same firm. The Equal Employment Opportunity Commission (EEOC) is charged with administering Title VII and the Equal Pay Act. Individuals may also go to court, on their own behalf or on behalf of a class of employees or potential employees, to seek compliance with the laws.

According to **Title VII of the Civil Rights Act**, two basic types of organizational practices are considered discriminatory: those that involve disparate treatment and those that result in disparate impact. **Disparate treatment discrimination** occurs when sex is intentionally used as a basis for treating people unequally. For example, one employer violated Title VII by asking a female applicant whether she planned to get pregnant and quit and if her husband would mind when she had to "run around the country with men." Male applicants, obviously, were not asked such questions. Another employer violated Title VII by asking questions about pregnancy, childbearing, and childcare of only female applicants.[7]

Disparate impact discrimination occurs when an employment practice affects people of different sexes unequally, unless it is job related and justified by the needs of the business. For example, a company's minimum height requirement for a certain job was rejected as discriminatory when it was shown to rule out more women than men and was not essential to job performance. Under the disparate impact standard, whether the employer discriminates intentionally is irrelevant. All that matters is whether an employment practice has unequal results and, if so, whether it serves a legitimate need (such as apprenticeship training for skilled craft positions and licensing requirements for nurses and teachers) that cannot be met by an alternative practice with less disparate impact.

Employers are *not* required by EEO laws to meet employment quotas for specific groups of workers (e.g., since 45% of the area's labor force or population is female, 45% of employees should be female). Hiring quotas may be mandated by courts, however, to remedy imbalances caused by past discrimination. For example, if an employer's past hiring practices promoted sex discrimination, it may be expected to take action to rectify these inequalities. In such cases, employers may give temporary preference to qualified applicants from underrepresented groups to achieve a long-term balance in the representation of those groups among their employees.

Although the vast majority of court cases involving Title VII on the basis of sex have dealt with discrimination against women, discrimination against men is also covered. For example, a court ruled against Pan American World Airways in the 1970s for limiting its flight attendants to women. In court, Pan American cited survey results that passengers preferred female flight attendants. A psychologist testified that women are better than men at comforting and reassuring passengers simply because they are women; note the reliance on gender stereotypes in this testimony. Yet another psychologist testified that applicant sex was the most practical screening device to rule out obviously unfit applicants (i.e., men). Nonetheless, Pan American lost the case.[8]

The Title VII ban on sex discrimination makes an exception for discrimination based on a **seniority system**. For example, the U.S. Supreme Court ruled that an employer cannot be ordered to ignore a seniority system when making layoffs, even if the effect is to reduce the number of women hired under an affirmative action plan.

Another permissible exception to Title VII arises when an individual's sex represents a **bona fide occupational qualification (BFOQ)** or legitimate condition of employment. Employee sex may be specified as a BFOQ in situations involving hygiene (e.g., cleaning of washrooms during periods when they are in use), health care (such as counseling of rape victims), and safety. It may also be specified as a BFOQ for reasons of authenticity or genuineness. For example, it is legal for producers of movie and television programs and directors of theatrical plays to hire only women to act female parts and only men to act male parts; however, this is not a requirement. The refusal to hire an individual because of customer preferences or gender stereotypes, as in the Pan American case, is illegal.

In a classic case that was the subject of considerable media attention, the EEOC filed charges against Hooters, a restaurant chain that features waitresses in short shorts and form-fitting tank tops or T-shirts, for requiring its wait staff ("Hooters Girls") to be female. The issue was whether Hooters is in the restaurant business, as the EEOC saw it, or the sex business, as Hooters saw it. The EEOC claimed that no physical trait unique to women is required to serve food and drink to customers in a restaurant. In response, Hooters claimed that its requirements for wait staff represented a BFOQ. It argued that the primary job function of Hooters Girls is "providing vicarious sexual recreation" by wearing skimpy outfits that meet tight (pun intended) specifications. Hooters Girls also are expected to "enhance the titillation by their interaction with customers. They are to flirt, cajole, and tease the patrons." Hooters settled with the EEOC by paying compensation to men who were denied the opportunity to serve as Hooters Girls and by creating support jobs such as bartender and host that would be filled without regard to applicant sex. However, Hooters essentially won the case by being allowed to continue luring customers with an exclusively female wait staff that met its attractiveness and dress standards. As the company now states on its website,

> Being a Hooters Girl is an honor bestowed upon only the most entertaining, goal oriented, glamorous and charismatic women. Hooters girls have that special gift for making every guest feel welcome. She is an American icon the world over. *A waitress she is not.* [emphasis added][9]

The Equal Pay Act is based on the principle of equal pay for equal work. The equal work standard requires that jobs be only substantially equal, not identical. Equal work is defined by four factors: skill, effort, responsibility, and working conditions. *Skill* refers to the experience, training, education, and ability needed to perform the job; the skill level of the job (not the job holders) determines whether two jobs are equal. *Effort* refers to the amount or degree of effort—mental or physical—required for a job. *Responsibility* refers to the degree of accountability required in the performance of a job. For example, a wage differential may be justified for employees who are required to become acting supervisor in the absence of a regular supervisor. *Working conditions* refer to the physical surroundings and safety concerns of a job, such as inside versus outside work and adequate heat and ventilation. The fact that jobs are in different departments is not sufficient to demonstrate a difference in working conditions.

Pay differences are permitted between men and women engaged in equal work if they result from a seniority system, a merit system, a system that measures earnings by quality or quantity of production, or some job-related factor such as a shift differential or a difference in experience. For example, a court upheld higher pay for salespeople in the men's department of a clothing store over those in the women's department because the company demonstrated that the men's department was the more profitable. In another case, however, women received 10% less pay than their male counterparts who did the same basic job. The men occasionally did heavier work, but this was infrequent and not done by all men. The court, ruling that the employer's lower wage rate for women was based on an artificially created job classification and that the extra duties of some men did not justify paying all of them more, awarded back wages to the women.

Sex discrimination does not legally exist if pay differences are due to differences in skill, effort, responsibility, or working conditions or to differences in the value that the marketplace attaches to particular jobs. However, if an organization has identified pay inequities that cannot be accounted for by job-related or market-related factors, then corrective action may be required. This does not necessarily mean immediately rectifying all differences or lowering anyone's pay, but it does mean fostering a commitment over the long run to eliminate unjustifiable disparities.

Take Affirmative Action While Promoting Equity

Affirmative action represents an extension of the notion of nondiscrimination. Its purpose is to overcome the effects of past discrimination by allowing members of a victimized group to compete on equal terms with members of the favored group. Legally mandated practices for this purpose have been called *affirmative action, employment equity, positive action*, and other terms in various countries. They were introduced in the United States in the 1930s to compensate for past unfair labor practices against union organizers and members. They were later used to assist veterans' reentry to the workplace after World War II.[10]

U.S. organizations with 50 or more employees or federal contracts exceeding $50,000 per year are required to prepare and implement written affirmative action plans. An acceptable affirmative action plan must contain an analysis of the sex composition of all major job classes and an explanation for the underrepresentation of women in any job class. It must also contain goals and commitments to relieve any deficiencies revealed by the analysis. Finally, the plan must describe detailed steps that the organization will take to make a good-faith effort to meet its goals and to remedy all other EEO deficiencies. These steps should include a program for outreach to and recruitment of women for the job classes in which they are underrepresented.

Thus, the goal of an affirmative action plan is to promote diversity on the basis of sex in job classes in which women are underrepresented. If the plan has its intended result, the outcome is that male-intensive job classes become more balanced in their sex composition. Organizations are not under a legal requirement to take affirmative action for the purpose of making female-intensive job classes more balanced.

According to U.S. guidelines, unless sex is a BFOQ for a job, employers must actively recruit members of different sexes for the job. Advertisements for jobs cannot express a sex preference for jobholders. Employers must take affirmative action to encourage women to apply for jobs from which they previously have been excluded. This can be accomplished by various means. For example, recruitment at women's colleges may be regarded as evidence of a good-faith effort to meet affirmative action goals. In addition, if women are underrepresented in managerial jobs and specific training programs have been demonstrated to enhance employees' chances of attaining these jobs, a commitment to include women in such programs is an important element of an affirmative action plan. Organizations are required to file periodic reports on their affirmative action initiatives and to make their records available to federal administrators.

It should be noted that the whole notion of affirmative action—whether in business, government, or academia—tends to raise questions about equity and fairness as well as arouse strong emotions. Increasing the chances that members of one group will experience more favorable outcomes (e.g., hiring and promotion decisions or admission decisions) than members of another group is often objected to as "reverse discrimination." In fact, majority group members may misperceive win–win affirmative action policies as unfairly benefiting underrepresented groups even when they benefit from the policies themselves. The challenge for organizations in implementing and communicating about affirmative action policies is to maintain perceptions of equity among members of advantaged groups, who have historically *not* suffered the effects of various types of discrimination that have been documented throughout this book, while improving opportunities for historically disadvantaged groups (i.e., **to take affirmative action while promoting equity**).[11]

Many people mistakenly view U.S. affirmative action policies as mandating quotas for members of certain groups (e.g., women or people of color) in jobs or entering classes of colleges and universities. Using academia as an example, affirmative action often occurs in admission decisions in the form of preferential treatment for groups such as children of past or potential donors (i.e., "affirmative action for the rich"), children of alumni ("legacy" admits), military veterans, and athletes. Further, this preferential treatment may take many forms, including guaranteed admission, points added to an applicant's evaluation score, and a specified number of spaces in the entering class if minimum academic requirements are met, the latter being the case for athletes in sponsored sports at many colleges and universities. Only in the last case, spaces reserved for athletes who are academically qualified, can the treatment be considered as establishing a quota, and it is perfectly legal; there is no ban against affirmative action practices that favor athletes. However, if a similar quota was established on the basis of sex, color, religion, or national origin, it would generally be considered illegal as specified in Title VII unless intended to address past discrimination. Thus, a broad perspective should be taken on what the term *affirmative action* means and on what types of affirmative action are legally mandated, illegal, or not the subject of any U.S. law.[12]

It should also be noted that quotas for women on corporate boards of directors have been legally mandated in many countries (not including the United States). This is a rare instance in which quotas on the basis of sex have been institutionalized into law. The purpose of these legally mandated quotas is to increase female representation in specific corporate positions in which women have historically been underrepresented. Research so far indicates that they are having the intended effect, with higher quotas related to higher female representation on boards of directors—including the position of board chair—in countries with such laws.[13]

In summary, most U.S. organizations are expected to take affirmative action to remedy the effects of past sex discrimination if it has occurred. Although we have focused on U.S. legal requirements, the governments of many other countries make similar demands on organizations.

Avoid or Reduce Costs of Discrimination

The costs of workplace discrimination can be high for individuals, groups, and organizations. **Individual costs of discrimination** are not confined to costs incurred by employees; they also include costs for job applicants who never become employees due to discriminatory hiring practices. Physical health outcomes that may be negatively affected by discrimination include indicators of cardiovascular disease such as blood pressure and heart rate variability, substance abuse, food-related disorders, and other symptoms of physical illness. Psychological health outcomes that may be negatively affected by discrimination include psychological distress, indicators of general well-being such as self-esteem and life satisfaction, and indicators of mental illness such as symptoms of depression, anxiety, and posttraumatic stress disorder. For employees, discrimination may negatively affect their present and future objective success, job stress, turnover, performance, sense of belonging, and other work-related attitudes and behavior.[14]

Group costs of discrimination occur on the basis of sex, as we have documented throughout this book, as well as many other bases. Chapter 1 referred to racism, ageism, heterosexism, and ableism as examples of types of discrimination besides sexism that have costs for particular groups. As further examples, discrimination against groups may also take the form of color discrimination (against individuals with certain skin tones), weight discrimination (against the overweight or obese), religious discrimination (against individuals who subscribe to religious beliefs in the minority), and immigrant status discrimination (against documented or undocumented immigrants), all of which have costs for the groups discriminated against.[15]

Further, any two or more of these group bases for discrimination may intersect with each other to magnify the negative costs of discrimination for particular groups. For example, when Black women make claims of sex or race discrimination, their claims are less likely to be believed than those made by White women or Black men. This message that their claims of discrimination are less credible has costs for Black women on the basis of the intersection of their sex and race. They may feel more stigmatized than members of other groups if they speak up about their experiences of discrimination and feel that they cannot be authentic if they refrain from speaking up.[16]

Organizational costs of discrimination occur when organizations are found guilty of discrimination in court—and sometimes even when they aren't. In making decisions about whether corporations have engaged in illegal discrimination, courts tend to rely on two principles. First, **intentionality** must be demonstrated; if the alleged discriminatory treatment was unconscious or unintentional, a claim of sex discrimination is harder to prove. Second, **explicitness** must be demonstrated; if the alleged discriminatory treatment was ambiguous and there is no "smoking gun" evidence, a claim of sex discrimination is also harder to prove. Plaintiffs are most likely to win court cases of alleged sex discrimination if the behavior in question was high in intentionality and explicitness.[17]

Convicted firms of discrimination incur direct costs from fines, punitive damages, and legal fees and indirect costs from reputational damage. Firms also suffer long-term financial consequences when convicted. For example, a study found that the top 300 companies on the *Fortune* 500 list convicted of discrimination involving either disparate treatment or disparate impact had lower returns on assets and sales in the five years following the conviction compared to companies that were not convicted. Some of these costs were incurred even if the accused firm was not convicted or admitted no guilt. Damage to the reputation of the accused firm, whether or not it was found guilty in court, may lead current and prospective employees as well as potential customers to have less regard for it and act accordingly. Further, defending a firm against charges of illegal discrimination consumes top management attention that is better directed elsewhere. Overall, the organizational costs of discrimination provide a powerful business argument for promoting nondiscrimination.[18]

WHY PROMOTE DIVERSITY?

Several socioeconomic trends suggest that organizations may benefit from promoting diversity. Here are some examples:[19]

First, the U.S. labor force has become more diverse in recent decades. As in many other countries, it has become more heterogeneous on the basis of sex, race, ethnicity, national origin, religion, and many other dimensions of diversity. Organizations with management practices appropriate for a homogeneous group of employees need to rethink their human resource management strategies.

Second, the relative skills that members of different groups bring to the workplace have changed. In particular, the educational attainment of female entrants to the labor force has risen dramatically in recent decades to become comparable to and, in some disciplines, exceed that of male entrants. Within all racial and ethnic groups in the United States, women now constitute the majority of individuals who earn bachelor's and master's degrees across all disciplines (see Table 2.2). Organizations that promote diversity by attracting highly educated women to historically male-intensive jobs and occupations are at an advantage in competing with organizations that do not.

Third, there has been a worldwide shift in recent decades from a primarily manufacturing-based economy to an economy based more on the delivery of services. Service industries place greater importance on educational attainment and less on physical strength than do manufacturing industries. Because women and men compete for service jobs on more equal terms, service industries are more diverse on the basis of sex than are manufacturing industries and have a narrower sex gap in pay. Service firms need to implement management practices that are appropriate for their increasingly diverse workforces on the basis of sex.[20]

Fourth, the increasing globalization of business in recent decades, including multinational business operations and worldwide marketing of products and services, has created new opportunities and demands for organizations and their employees. Organizations need to be responsive to customers and to attract and retain employees, who are increasingly diverse in national origin. Organizations that want to take advantage of global business opportunities face greater challenges than do those that confine their business activities to the home market. They must learn to interact with and please customers from a variety of national cultures. At the same time, employees are increasingly having multicultural experiences from which they may benefit both individually and interpersonally. Overall, a globally diverse workforce, both within and among nations, may be better able to design, market, and sell products and services that meet the full range of consumer needs in the global marketplace.[21]

All of these trends suggest that organizations benefit from promoting diversity. In addition, meta-analyses and research studies have generally found a positive relationship between sex diversity at high ranks and organizational performance. Companies with higher numbers and proportions of women in their top management team (TMT) and board of directors (i.e., greater diversity in their top management and governance ranks on the basis of sex) tend to perform better on financial measures of return than other companies in their industries. Thus, greater sex diversity in the top management and governance ranks of organizations is associated with stronger financial performance.[22]

Nonfinancial measures of organizational performance may also be affected by sex diversity in the upper echelons. For example, U.S. National Football League team organizations with a critical mass of female TMT members (two or more) experienced fewer player arrests for off-the-job misconduct than teams with zero or one female TMT members; such arrests are associated negatively with team publicity, sponsorships, and merchandise sales. As another example, medical firms with a critical mass of female members on their board of directors were faster to recall dangerously defective products than firms with zero or one female board members. These results may be because women tend to exhibit higher ethical standards (including frowning on employee misconduct) and higher concern for corporate social responsibility (including removing highly dangerous products from the market). Having a critical mass of female leaders at high ranks, which means going beyond having a token female TMT or board member, may be necessary before they are able to influence organizational performance in these directions. Indeed, recalling Chapter 7, imagine how Miramax's critical mass of female board members may have influenced the board's reactions to the rampant misconduct toward women of Harvey Weinstein as chief executive officer (CEO).[23]

Correlation, of course, does not prove causality. Although a company's long-term record of having a critical mass of women at high ranks could lead to higher profitability, more profitable firms may do a better job of identifying, attracting, and advancing the best female talent to serve in their top ranks. Profitable firms typically attain their success by making smarter decisions than their competitors. One of these smart decisions may be promoting sex diversity in their upper echelons.

However, moving beyond a critical mass of female leaders to achieve greater sex diversity at high ranks may present a challenge. A study found that corporate boards of directors that added women tended to settle in on exactly two female directors. Decision makers were less likely to add a woman to a board once it included two women, the absolute minimum needed for a critical mass. This phenomenon was labeled **twokenism**, a variation of the term *tokenism*, which refers to a sole woman in a group (see Chapter 5). It suggests that majority group (i.e., male) decision makers have a limit on how much sex diversity in corporate boards they are willing to accept.[24]

WHY PROMOTE INCLUSION?

Taking steps to promote nondiscrimination and diversity but ignoring the need for inclusion may limit an organization's ability to reap the full benefits of a diverse workforce. Although increased employee diversity may enhance organizational performance, it also poses potential problems. It is easier to maintain a sense of cohesiveness in homogeneous organizations than in diverse organizations. People tend to be more attracted to and feel more comfortable in social settings in which they interact primarily with people like themselves. However, as noted in Chapter 5, diversity may be a double-edged sword. It may increase decision-making creativity and the congruence of the organization with the marketplace, but it may also decrease employees' attachment to the organization. Unless the potential problems associated with diversity are addressed, its potential benefits may not be fully realized.[25] The organization's **diversity culture** influences the extent to which these problems appear.

Taylor Cox distinguished among three types of diversity cultures—monolithic, pluralistic, and inclusive.[26] A **monolithic culture** focuses on minimum compliance with EEO laws. It is most likely to be manifested in organizations that are characterized by a large majority of employees from one group (e.g., White men), especially in the managerial ranks. Differences between majority and minority group members are resolved by the process of assimilation, whereby minority group employees are expected to adopt the norms and values of the majority group to survive. A monolithic culture is characterized by low levels of intergroup conflict because there are few members of minority groups and these members have outwardly adopted, if not inwardly embraced, the majority group's norms and values. It conveys a straightforward message to employees and potential job applicants: We do not particularly welcome or care about diversity.

A **pluralistic culture** focuses on the *quantity* of majority and minority group members in different jobs and levels. It is most likely to be seen in organizations that have a more heterogeneous workforce and have taken steps to promote diversity but have not gone beyond that. These steps may include managerial training on EEO issues and human resource management (HRM) policies that stress recruitment and advancement of members of minority groups. The primary approach to resolving cultural differences is assimilation, just as in a monolithic culture. A pluralistic culture is characterized by high levels of intergroup conflict if members of the majority group resent practices used to boost minority group membership; even though overt discrimination may have been banished, prejudice is still likely. It conveys a mixed message: We promote diversity, but we expect employees from minority groups to make efforts to fit in with the majority group.

An **inclusive culture** does more than promote diversity; it also focuses on the *quality* of work relationships among members of different groups. It responds to cultural differences by encouraging members of different groups to respect the norms and values of other groups in contrast to the assimilation required in monolithic and pluralistic cultures. Organizations with an inclusive culture attempt to bring about qualitative changes in their work environments through increased appreciation of the range of skills and values that dissimilar employees offer and increased use of teams that include members culturally distinct from the dominant group. The goal is to create a culture in which employees from all groups feel comfortable and appreciated and are given a chance to make meaningful contributions. In an inclusive culture, the knowledge, skills, insights, and experiences of employees from different groups are regarded as valuable resources that the organization may use to advance its mission. An inclusive culture is characterized by low levels of intergroup conflict due to the absence of prejudice and discrimination accompanied by the appreciation of individuals from different groups. It conveys a consistent message: We welcome members of all groups as full participants in our organizational culture, and we strive to take full advantage of what they have to offer. Employees who see themselves as multicultural by identifying with two or more groups are particularly likely to value this message.[27]

It is more difficult to assess the effects of promoting inclusion on organizational performance than the effects of promoting diversity. Researchers may obtain data on the sex composition and performance of public corporations from publicly filed reports. Researchers, however, do not have the opportunity to assess the diversity cultures of organizations unless they are granted permission to do so. Organizations that are doing little to promote inclusion may not want their business practices to be scrutinized and thereby may be reluctant to grant researchers such permission. In contrast, organizations that are doing a better job of promoting inclusion may be more eager to showcase their progress.[28]

Nonetheless, as discussed in Chapter 4, more inclusive cultures are more attractive to job seekers, particularly women and people of color, which makes it easier for organizations to have large applicant pools from which to select the best talent. In the same vein, having an inclusive culture makes it easier for organizations to retain valued employees. Such a culture promotes employees' growth, development, and psychological safety and encourages them to experiment with creative and innovative ideas. A meta-analysis found that employees' agreement that their employer's culture is indeed inclusive yields benefits in organizational performance.[29]

In conclusion, promoting inclusion is likely to contribute to full utilization and retention of valued employees from all groups and enhance the bottom line. Employees from different groups, especially minority groups, can tell whether their organizational culture is monolithic, pluralistic, or inclusive. They are well aware of the message that the organization's diversity culture is sending, including whether it is sending a mixed message or simply engaging in happy talk. They are most likely to be attracted to and commit themselves to an organization that promotes a culture in which members of all groups are valued and respected. Such organizations are likely to have a competitive advantage over firms in the same industry that are weaker in promoting inclusion or fail to make the attempt.

ORGANIZATIONAL ACTIONS

We have presented arguments for why organizations gain from promoting nondiscrimination, diversity, and inclusion. In this section, we consider these issues from a practical perspective—what organizations need to do.[30] First, appropriate goals should be adopted and communicated. Second, the representation of individuals of different sexes in different jobs and at different levels should be analyzed and a cultural audit performed to determine how well the company is achieving its diversity goals. Third, a management system should be adopted that sets concrete objectives for critical employees and provides incentives for them to meet these objectives. Fourth, employee resource groups should be sponsored to stimulate employee involvement as well as to identify obstacles to the achievement of diversity goals. Fifth, employees should receive education and training that enhance their abilities and readiness to meet assigned objectives. Finally, changes in the organizational culture should be implemented as needed to ensure that goal achievement is sustained. Table 9.1 summarizes recommended actions for organizations and their employees.

TABLE 9.1 ■ Recommended Actions

1. Set and communicate the organizational goals of promoting nondiscrimination, diversity, and inclusion.
2. Comply with all EEO laws.
3. Use contingent rhetoric rather than value-in-diversity rhetoric in corporate communications.
4. Encourage employees to be champions of diversity.
5. Provide incentives for managers to meet organizational goals.
6. Maintain integrity in procedures and equity in outcomes when personnel decisions are made.
7. Make sure that employees understand how affirmative action works in the organization.
8. Work with employee network groups formed out of employees' common interests in planning and implementing cultural change.
9. Provide diversity training that educates employees about organizational goals and gives them the knowledge and skills they need to work toward these goals.
10. Offer educational programs that meet employees' developmental needs.
11. Analyze the organization's composition and culture to determine what specific improvements are needed and then set objectives for attaining them.
12. Ensure that the achievement of organizational goals and objectives is rewarded by the management system and supported by the organizational culture.
13. Continually monitor the organization's progress relative to its goals and take appropriate actions to ensure that improvements are permanent.

Set and Communicate Goals

The first step to be taken is to set goals for the organization's diversity culture. The appropriate goals for *all* organizations—large or small, public or private, profit or nonprofit—are to be nondiscriminatory, diverse, and inclusive in their employment practices.

Assuming that an organization sets these goals, it then needs to communicate them to employees. How organizational goals are presented and sold to employees plays a large role in determining whether they are achieved. They may be presented to employees as legal, moral, or business issues. The **legal argument** does not fully work because it suggests that compliance with the law is most important; it promotes only a minimal effort to achieve goals of nondiscrimination and diversity (but not inclusion) and solely for legally protected groups. The **moral argument**, that achieving these goals is an end in itself, seldom works because people seldom agree on what the "right thing" is to do and then may do what they view as the right thing only when it is personally advantageous. The **business argument** is most effective in promoting nondiscrimination, diversity, and inclusion throughout the organization because it points to the impact on bottom-line profits, which most employees see as ultimately affecting their own livelihoods.[31]

Corporate communications should convey the message that promoting nondiscrimination, diversity, and inclusion are important organizational goals. These communications may include statements on web pages, speeches by top executives, newsletters, status reports, recognition events, special awards, and publicity for employees who have done good work toward these goals.

However, the nature of the rhetoric used in corporate communications is critical. One type of rhetoric, called **value-in-diversity rhetoric**, simply states that diversity is beneficial to the organization (it enhances creativity, etc.); the opening passage exemplifies value-in-diversity rhetoric. A second type of rhetoric, called **contingent rhetoric**, states that diversity is only beneficial if the challenges it poses are overcome, both stating the challenges themselves (it may create conflict, lead to moral debates, etc.) and processes for overcoming these challenges (it requires accountability, may involve feeling uncomfortable, etc.). Contingent rhetoric acknowledges the reality that diversity may be a double-edged sword that requires addressing potential problems; in contrast, value-in-diversity rhetoric is more disconnected from reality. A study of rhetoric on company websites found that contingent rhetoric was less common but more effective in stimulating employee commitment toward corporate goals than value-in-diversity rhetoric. Leaders were more hesitant to use contingent rhetoric than value-in-diversity rhetoric in their speeches, statements on company websites, and the like due to the fear of appearing prejudiced. However, this is the chance that leaders have to take in communicating about corporate goals if their communications are to have the most positive impact on employees' efforts to achieve these goals.[32]

Top management commitment is critical to achieving organizational goals. The chief executive of an organization plays an important role in setting its primary values. In organizations with strong track records in managing diversity, the CEO galvanizes employees to take diversity seriously by making them aware of diversity issues facing the firm and by personally stimulating needed changes. **Champions of diversity** are needed—people who take strong public and personal stands on the need for cultural change in the organization and behave as role models in creating change. Having a critical mass of diverse executives is also beneficial in implementing cultural change.[33]

Identify and Reward the Right Behavior

Making a good sales pitch for promoting nondiscrimination, diversity, and inclusion does not ensure that employees will act accordingly. An organization also needs a sound management system that encourages employees to engage in the right kinds of behavior on a regular basis.

First comes an analysis of what the organization needs to do to achieve its goals. For example, data may be collected on seven types of metrics that span the employee life cycle: (1) attrition, both voluntary and involuntary; (2) performance evaluations; (3) promotion rates; (4) leadership pipeline—top performers regarded as on the fast track to top management levels; (5) the employment pipeline as measured by applications, interviews, job offers, and acceptance rates; (6) pay equity; and (7) inclusion. Comparisons should be made on each metric between data for members of underrepresented groups versus members of the majority group within pay grades, organizational levels, and departments. Collecting data on how the organization is performing on such metrics allows it to assess its overall performance on achieving its diversity goals and to set specific goals for managers.[34]

In the case of inclusion, the organizational analysis will require a **cultural audit**, a snapshot of the current organizational culture. It assesses the nature of the organizational culture as experienced by employees, which is not necessarily what top management thinks the culture is or should be. It also assesses how the organizational culture influences the treatment of members of different groups. Surveys, interviews, focus groups, and meetings may be used to gather information for the audit. A successful audit uncovers obstacles to the full attainment of organizational goals. Obstacles may include stereotypes and prejudices that affect employees' interactions with one another and managers' decisions regarding recruitment, performance appraisals, promotions, compensation, and other employment practices.[35]

Next comes the specification of objectives. Managers will put more effort into promoting nondiscrimination, diversity, and inclusion if they are expected to meet concrete objectives in pursuit of each of these goals. For example, the PQ Corporation—a global provider of specialty catalysts, materials, chemicals, and services that "enable environmental improvements, enhance consumer products, and increase personal safety"—implemented a unique procedure to meet the objective of promoting nondiscrimination in employment decisions. The key to the procedure was the "selection checklist," a two-part document that a manager completed for each candidate interviewed for a position. The first part contained questions about each step in the selection process and the degree of possible discrimination (e.g., "Did you perform or do you have a current job analysis for this position?" "Was the position posted internally?" "Were reasons for rejection based on job-related deficiencies and not related to nonjob-related factors such as a handicap or religious beliefs?") Each question had to be answered *yes, no,* or *not applicable.* The questions answered with a *no* reflected possible incidents of discrimination by the manager. The second part documented the correlation between the job criteria (i.e., skills and knowledge required to perform major job functions) and the attributes of the candidate.[36]

PQ's selection checklist was intended to make managers aware of the process they used to make their decisions. Objectives for managers were stated in terms of percentages of discriminatory incidents. Managers' checklists were passed on to their superiors, who could then assess how well the corporate goal of nondiscrimination was being achieved. If managers faked the checklist to cover up discrimination, they did so with the knowledge that this behavior was contrary to organizational goals and could expose it to an EEO lawsuit.

In the same vein, some healthcare providers have implemented computerized checklists that minimize sex discrimination by encouraging practitioners such as doctors and nurses to follow appropriate procedures and make appropriate diagnoses for particular health conditions. These checklists have eliminated or reduced sex differences favoring men in treatment of identical conditions, including blood clots, heart attacks, and knee pain. Checklists are particularly effective when they are mandatory; in this case, healthcare practitioners can use their own judgment and override what is recommended, but they cannot opt out of learning the recommendation and knowing that they are not going along.[37]

Managers should be expected to meet concrete objectives for promoting diversity in their work units in accordance with organizational goals. For example, organizations may set the goal of achieving **full representation**, defined as having their workforce reflect the available labor force in the industry on the basis of sex, race, and other dimensions of diversity. Managers may then be evaluated on the extent to which they meet this corporate goal compared with the talent pool in their own occupations.[38]

As organizations seek to meet diversity goals, the importance of both procedural fairness and equitable outcomes in personnel decisions needs to be emphasized. Maintaining integrity in decision-making procedures works to prevent or reduce bias against marginalized groups. Maintaining equity in decision-making outcomes works to ensure that more competent applicants receive more favorable decisions. Managers should be clearly informed that taking affirmative action does *not* mandate setting quotas for members of certain groups. Instead, it calls for a good-faith effort to reach out to and recruit a diverse pool of potential applicants for open positions or assignments while still making final personnel decisions on the basis of equity.[39]

Once an organization develops and assigns specific objectives, these should become part of the manager's overall performance appraisal. Managers should be made aware that their success at promoting nondiscrimination, diversity, and inclusion will be evaluated by their supervisors. Good performance in these areas should be reinforced with tangible rewards such as promotions, salary increases, and favorable task assignments; failure to meet objectives should result in the withholding of such rewards. Actions speak much louder than words of approval or disapproval. By giving managers explicit knowledge of the organization's diversity goals and incentives to meet personal objectives consistent with these goals, an effective management system overcomes resistance from managers.

Stimulate Employee Involvement

Organizations benefit when employees from all groups feel personally involved in attaining the goals of nondiscrimination, diversity, and inclusion. For example, Microsoft supports a wide variety of employee resource groups (ERGs). Separate groups, some with overlapping interests, target female employees, Black employees, Asian employees, Hispanic employees, Native American employees, LGBTQ+ (lesbian, gay, bisexual, transgender, and self-described queer) employees, employees with disabilities, employees with families, and employees who are current or former military members and their families.[40]

These groups have engaged in many worthwhile activities both outside and inside Microsoft. For example, the Families at Microsoft ERG was instrumental in the development of leaves for employees who are caregivers during the COVID-19 pandemic. The Women at Microsoft ERG awards a scholarship for college to a graduating high school senior who identifies as a woman or nonbinary person and intends to pursue a career in science, technology, engineering, the arts, or math (STEAM). The Military at Microsoft ERG offers programs for veterans and military members transitioning to a post-military career to help them develop foundational tech skills. The GLEAM (Global LGBTQIA+ Employees and Allies at Microsoft) ERG helped shape an informational video series to educate employees about concepts related to gender identity, gender expression, and sexual orientation. The Blacks at Microsoft ERG provides ongoing feedback on Microsoft's Racial Equity Initiative and sponsors a Minority Student Day, an annual outreach event to educate students on careers in the tech industry. All of these activities support corporate goals for contributing to the community, encouraging careers at Microsoft as well as other high-tech companies, and fostering the connections among and the development of employees.

Organizations may also form groups on their own to involve employees in deciding how they deal with diversity issues. For example, one organization established an advisory council of a cross section of employees. The council met monthly to discuss issues related to a diverse workforce. Corporate activities that resulted from the council included a diversity booth at the annual family picnic, articles on diversity in the company newsletter, training on refraining from discrimination, guidelines for first-line supervisors on appraising employees, and a suggestion box called "Dr. Equality." The council also assisted in the design of employee opinion surveys.[41]

ERGs and advisory councils serve several purposes that benefit both the organization and its members. Such groups help the organization become aware of and address the concerns of employees. As a result, employees are more likely to feel that the organization indeed cares about their concerns, which fosters their commitment to the attainment of corporate goals. The outreach activities of such groups also help the organization be a good citizen in the community. Finally, they act as a vehicle for employee self-help by providing opportunities for networking, personal support, and career development.

In addition, given the preponderance of men in leadership positions, engaging men in the attainment of organizational goals is in an organization's best interest. It helps prevent a win–lose mentality that gains for women mean losses for men. In general, when men become more aware of sex bias in organizational practices, they are more likely to believe that it is important for the organization to set and achieve the goals of nondiscrimination, diversity, and inclusion. Men with a strong sense of fair play are more likely to be aware of sex bias and become champions for gender inclusiveness at work, which makes them powerful change agents. For example, they may champion the organization's offering of family-friendly programs from which men may benefit (such as paid paternity leaves) and act as role models for other men in taking advantage of such programs. They may also be attentive to sex differences in any kind of workplace treatment that entails sex discrimination and speak up when they see problems.[42]

Educate Employees

Educational initiatives such as training programs serve to promote the organizational goals of nondiscrimination, diversity, and inclusion as well as to develop employees.

Diversity training programs have been demonstrated by meta-analyses to have a wide range of positive effects on employees' knowledge, attitudes, skills, and on-the-job behaviors. These positive effects tend to be greater when the proportion of women in a training program is higher, which may be because women tend to have more favorable reactions to diversity training in general.[43]

Diversity training programs may be offered to employees at all levels to meet a range of objectives, depending on a needs assessment:[44]

1. Increase participants' knowledge about diversity issues, including EEO laws, changing societal demographics, and the business case for attention to these issues.

2. Increase participants' familiarity with organizational policies regarding inappropriate workplace behavior (e.g., sexual harassment) and what they should do if they experience or witness such behavior.

3. Increase participants' awareness of their own stereotypes and prejudices based on sex as well as race, ethnicity, age, national origin, sexual orientation, abilities and disabilities, and other primary and secondary dimensions of diversity.

4. Increase participants' skills in moving beyond their stereotypes and prejudices as they work with dissimilar customers and coworkers.

5. In multinational organizations, increase participants' fluency in other languages and knowledge of other national cultures.

6. Increase managers' skills in making bias-free decisions, such as decisions about selection, compensation, performance appraisal, promotion, and development.

7. Increase managers' skills in dealing with diversity-related incidents.

8. By addressing these objectives, change the organization's diversity culture itself.

Diversity training programs should have an expected outcome: As a result of the program, something should change. To determine whether the desired change has occurred, program outcomes should be measured on a long-term basis, not only at the end of the last session. For example, participants' assessment of what was most useful about a program and how it helped them may be solicited three, six, or twelve months afterward. If the program's objective is to modify the organization's diversity culture, periodic surveys of employees' attitudes toward diversity may provide information on whether this objective is being met.[45]

One issue that arises in the design of diversity training programs is whether they should rely on **voluntary or mandatory participation**. Voluntary training is associated with more positive outcomes for participants than mandatory training, which may be because volunteers are more supportive of the program's goals and aware of the need for cultural change. That is, voluntary diversity training programs may be "preaching to the choir." However, allowing employees to opt out of diversity training may send a signal that top management does not regard it as particularly important to the achievement of corporate objectives. Making participation mandatory sends the message that top management regards the training as critical to the achievement of corporate goals.[46]

When participation in diversity training is mandatory, the program facilitator needs to find a way of dealing with reluctant participants. Under these circumstances, the challenge is to get *all* participants, including White men, to believe that they have something to gain from the training. If participants believe that the purpose of the training is only to promote political correctness (self-censorship of language or behavior to avoid the risk of offending others), then achievement of the objectives may be thwarted. Diversity training programs should be designed to get everyone working toward the same corporate goals, not to embarrass or blame anyone.[47]

A further diversity issue that arises in educating employees is whether some training programs should be offered or sponsored that are intended solely for women or whether all company-supported programs should be mixed-sex in composition. Advocates for **women's leadership programs**, designed for women who aspire to top management positions, argue that such programs offer a safe space for women to network with female peers while working on their own leadership development. However, skeptics of women-only programs argue that such programs are counterproductive in creating an artificial environment in which mixed-sex interactions are eliminated by design. Also, women-only programs do not provide the same opportunity for women to add male peers to their networks that mixed-sex programs provide.[48]

The challenge for organizations in educating employees of different sexes is to help them diagnose their unique developmental needs rather than making any assumptions about sex differences in these needs and then offer or sponsor training programs that help meet these needs. Women-only programs seem to represent one way in which women may meet their personal developmental needs. If organizations meet this challenge, the educational experiences they offer will foster the achievement of corporate as well as individual goals.

Implement Cultural Change

An organization's diversity culture influences how group differences are taken into account. It consists of a general perception of the value the organization places on being nondiscriminatory, diverse, and inclusive. Organizational culture is an elusive concept. It lies beneath the surface of organizational life, yet it influences every aspect of how employees are treated and how work is conducted. Because organizational culture is deep-seated, often going back to the values of the founder, it cannot be changed overnight. If an organization sets goals of promoting nondiscrimination, diversity, and inclusion and its culture does not fully support achievement of these goals, some form of cultural change is needed.[49]

The first step in implementing cultural change is to decide, based on a cultural audit and corporate goals, how the culture needs to be improved. Cultural change will be especially critical if the diversity culture is monolithic. Organizations with a pluralistic culture, which promotes diversity but not inclusion, will also need to make some cultural changes. Even organizations that already have an inclusive culture may benefit from some modifications to their diversity cultures.

The second step is to develop a plan that charts the course for cultural change. The plan may include revisions to existing policies and practices, including the management system and new programs such as educational initiatives. Top management support of the plan for cultural change is crucial but not sufficient to bring about cultural change. The participation of first-line supervisors in development of the plan is also critical to its success. First-line supervisors are those most responsible for getting work done in organizations. If they are told by top management to implement a plan for cultural change but do not participate in its development, they will not be committed to the plan. Long-lasting cultural change can be brought about only when the change is accepted and owned by all of the employees who will be involved in making the change effective.[50]

The third step is to launch the change effort itself. For the launch to be effective, leaders of the change effort need to specify objectives, achieve early results to demonstrate the value of the effort, and assess progress along the way. The management system should reward behavior that contributes to the achievement of needed cultural change.

The final step, once the initial change effort is complete, is to ensure that cultural changes take hold and are not temporary. Long-term maintenance of the organizational culture is necessary. Maintenance involves monitoring the results of the change effort to guard against backsliding and motivating employees to confront and overcome obstacles to sustained cultural change. Cultural audits should be conducted on a regular basis to determine whether intended changes are in place and to identify further needs for change.

Multinational corporations face additional challenges in changing their diversity cultures. Change efforts are especially likely to fail if managers in the home office impose their notions of diversity on operations in other areas of the world. Such efforts may be viewed as cultural imperialism and resented by managers outside the home office. The challenge for a multinational organization that seeks to be inclusive is to engage in efforts to influence the *organizational* culture while taking differences in *national* culture into account.[51]

All organizations benefit from promoting nondiscrimination, diversity, and inclusion. Even organizations with a history of such actions need to continue to make special efforts to attract qualified applicants from all groups, offering satisfying jobs and a welcoming culture. When organizations take such actions, they are likely to attract the best talent available, stimulate employee involvement and commitment, and enhance the bottom line.

CONCLUSIONS FOR THE BOOK

In Chapter 1, the following question was posed: "Is it only a matter of time until the proportions of women and men in all managerial levels and all occupations become essentially equal, until women and men are paid equal wages for equal work, and until individuals' work experiences are unaffected by their biological sex?" As we have seen, the answer to this question at this point in time is "Not quite." How the question is ultimately answered will depend on actions that organizations and individuals take.

Throughout this book, we describe the effects of sex and gender in the workplace. We identify issues that arise as different-sex individuals seek employment, work together in teams, serve as leaders, exhibit social sexual behavior at work, and manage the interface between their work and family roles to attain a sense of balance in their lives. In previous chapters as well as this one, we offer numerous recommendations for improving interactions between employees and promoting the full utilization of members of all groups in the workplace.

Overall, more actions are recommended for organizations than for individuals. However, organizations consist of people who work together to provide products or services. Thus, *all* of the recommended actions are ones that people may take. Also, although this book's title stresses the managerial role, *all* of us—current and future members of the labor force, managers and non-managers—may contribute toward making a better workplace.

In all likelihood, some sex differences in workplace preferences, experiences, and behaviors will remain. We need to be clear on what the facts about sex differences are but not suggest what they should be. Instead, our overriding concern should be with gender differences, that is, beliefs about how males and females differ and should behave. When gender differences are guided more by stereotypes than by facts about sex differences, they have a corrosive impact on interactions at work.

The goal is to create a nondiscriminatory, diverse, and inclusive workplace—a world in which all members, regardless of their sex and other group memberships, are valued for what they bring to the workplace and are granted the opportunity to make full use of their talents. By taking actions such as the ones recommended, all of us can contribute to the establishment of such a world. What a wonderful world this would be!

NOTES

CHAPTER 1

1. Woolley, H. T. (1910). A review of the recent literature on the psychology of sex. *Psychological Bulletin, 7*, 335–342, quote on p. 340.
2. Fiske, S. T. (2010). Venus and Mars or down to Earth: Stereotypes and realities of gender differences. *Perspectives on Psychological Science, 5*, 688–692, quote on p. 688.
3. Milar, K. S. (2000). The first generation of women psychologists and the psychology of women. *American Psychologist, 55*, 616–619.
4. Goldin, C. (2021). *Career and family: Women's century-long journey toward equity*. Princeton University Press; Goldin, C. (2014). A grand gender convergence: Its last chapter. *American Economic Review, 104*, 1091–1119; Blau, F. D., Brinton, M. C., & Grusky, D. B. (Eds.). (2006). *The declining significance of gender?* (pp. 3–34). Russell Sage Foundation; Powell, G. N. (1989). Male/female work roles: What kind of future? *Personnel, 66*(7), 47–50.
5. Gill, R., Kelan, E. K., & Scharff, C. M. (2017). A postfeminist sensibility at work. *Gender, Work and Organization, 24*, 226–244; Broadbridge, A., & Simpson, R. (2011). 25 years on: Reflecting on the past and looking to the future in gender and management research. *British Journal of Management, 22*, 470–483, quote on p. 475.
6. Miller, C. C. (2018, December 3). Americans value equality at work more than equality at home. *New York Times*. Retrieved December 6, 2018, from https://www.nytimes.com/2018/12/03/upshot/americans-value-equality-at-work-more-than-equality-at-home.html
7. Pew Research Center. (2020). *Worldwide optimism about future of gender equality, even as many see advantages for men*. Pew Research Center. Retrieved September 13, 2022, from https://www.pewresearch.org/global/2020/04/30/worldwide-optimism-about-future-of-gender-equality-even-as-many-see-advantages-for-men/
8. Sipe, S. R., Larson, L., McKay, B. A., & Moss, J. (2016). Taking off the blinders: A comparative study of university students' changing perceptions of gender discrimination in the workplace from 2006 to 2013. *Academy of Management Learning & Education, 15*, 232–249; Sipe, S. R., Johnson, C. D., & Fisher, D. K. (2009). University students' perceptions of gender discrimination in the workplace: Reality versus fiction. *Journal of Education for Business, 84*, 339–349.
9. U.S. Department of Labor, Bureau of Labor Statistics. (2023). *Labor force statistics from the Current Population Survey*, Table 2. Retrieved May 4, 2023, from https://www.bls.gov/cps/cpsaat02.pdf; International Labour Organization (2018). *World employment social outlook: Trends for women 2018*. International Labour Office. Retrieved September 14, 2022, from https://www.ilo.org/wcmsp5/groups/public/---dgreports/---dcomm/---publ/documents/publication/wcms_619577.pdf

10. Catalyst. (2020, January 15). *Pyramid: Women in S&P 500 companies.* Catalyst. Retrieved July 23, 2020, from https://www.catalyst.org/research/women-in-sp-500-companies/; Powell, G. N., & Butterfield, D. A. (2015). The glass ceiling: What have we learned 20 years on? *Journal of Organizational Effectiveness: People and Performance, 2*, 306–326; International Labour Office. (1993). Unequal race to the top. *World of Work: The Magazine of the International Labour Office* (U.S. ed.), *2*, 6–7.

11. Hinchliffe, E. (2023, January 12). Women CEOs run more than 10% of *Fortune 500* companies for the first time in history. *Fortune.* Retrieved May 1, 2023, from https://www.shrm.org/executive/resources/pages/women-fortune-500-2023.aspx; Brooke-Marciniak, B. (2015, March 3). The real story: There are not enough women CEOs. *Forbes.* Retrieved March 10, 2015, from http://www.forbes.com; Catalyst. (2014). *Historical list: Fortune 500 CEO positions held by women.* Catalyst. Retrieved June 19, 2015, from https://www.catalyst.org/wp-content/uploads/2019/05/Catalyst_Women_Fortune_CEOs_1972-2019_Historical_List_5.16.2019.pdf; Parker, T. (2013, January 1). The dawn of the age of female CEOs. *Investopedia.* Retrieved September 17, 2015, from http://www.investopedia.com; Carter, N. M., & Silva, C. (2010). Women in management: Delusions of progress. *Harvard Business Review, 88*(3), 19–21.

12. World Economic Forum. (2022). *Global gender gap report 2022.* World Economic Forum. Retrieved September 15, 2022, from https://www3.weforum.org/docs/WEF_GGGR_2022.pdf

13. Charles, M. (2011). A world of difference: International trends in women's economic status. *Annual Review of Sociology, 37*, 355–371; England, P. (2010). The gender revolution: Uneven and stalled. *Gender and Society, 24*, 149–166.

14. World Economic Forum. (2022). *Global gender gap report 2022.* World Economic Forum. Retrieved September 15, 2022, from https://www3.weforum.org/docs/WEF_GGGR_2022.pdf

15. For an excellent guide to key terms and concepts that is followed in this section of the chapter, see American Psychological Association. (2015). *Key terms and concepts in understanding gender diversity and sexual orientation among students*. American Psychological Association. Retrieved September 12, 2022, from https://www.apa.org/pi/lgbt/programs/safe-supportive/lgbt/key-terms.pdf

16. Guenther, E. A., Humbert, A. L., & Kelan, E. K. (2018). Gender versus sex. *Oxford Research Encyclopedia of Business and Management* (pp. 1–30). Oxford University Press; Caplan, P. J., & Caplan, J. B. (2009). *Thinking critically about research on sex and gender* (3rd ed.). Pearson; Lippa, R. A. (2005). *Gender, nature, and nurture* (2nd ed.). Erlbaum; Archer, J., & Lloyd, B. (2002). *Sex and gender* (2nd ed.). Cambridge University Press; Korabik, K. (1999). Sex and gender in the new millennium. In G. N. Powell (Ed.), *Handbook of gender and work* (pp. 3–16). SAGE; Unger, R. K. (1979). Toward a redefinition of sex and gender. *American Psychologist, 34*, 1085–1094.

17. Ellemers, N. (2018). Gender stereotypes. *Annual Review of Psychology, 69*, 275–298; Wood, W., & Eagly, A. H. (2010). Gender. In S. T. Fiske, D. T. Gilbert, & G. Lindzey (Eds.), *Handbook of social psychology* (5th ed., Vol. 1; pp. 629—667). Wiley; Martin, C. L., & Ruble, D. N. (2009). Patterns of gender development. *Annual Review of Psychology, 61*, 353–381.

18. Hyde, J. S., Bigler, R. S., Joel, D., Tate, C. C., & van Anders, S. M. (2019). The future of sex and gender in psychology: Five challenges to the gender binary. *American Psychologist, 74*, 171–193; Köllen, T. (2016). Intersexuality and trans-identities within

the diversity management discourse. In T. Köllen (Ed.), *Sexual orientation and transgender issues in organizations: Global perspectives on LGBT workforce diversity* (pp. 1–20). Springer Nature; American Psychological Association. (2015). *Key terms and concepts in understanding gender diversity and sexual orientation among students*. American Psychological Association. Retrieved September 12, 2022, from https://www.apa.org/pi/lgbt/programs/safe-supportive/lgbt/key-terms.pdf; Pichler, S., & Ruggs, E. N. (2015). LGBT workers. In A. J. Colella & E. B. King (Eds.), *The Oxford handbook of workplace discrimination* (pp. 177–195). Oxford University Press; Meier, S. C., & Labuski, C. M. (2013). The demographics of the transgender population. In A. K. Baumle (Ed.), *International handbook on the demography of sexuality* (pp. 289–327). Springer Science + Business Media.

19. Hyde, J. S., Bigler, R. S., Joel, D., Tate, C. C., & van Anders, S. M. (2019). The future of sex and gender in psychology: Five challenges to the gender binary. *American Psychologist, 74*, 171–193; Reilly, D. (2019). Gender can be a continuous variable, not just a categorical one: Comment on Hyde, Bigler, Joel, Tate, and van Anders (2019). *American Psychologist, 74*, 840–841.

20. Cherry, K. (2022). What does LGBTQ+ mean? *Very Well Mind*. Retrieved September 23, 2022, from https://www.verywellmind.com/what-does-lgbtq-mean-5069804; American Psychological Association. (2015). *Key terms and concepts in understanding gender diversity and sexual orientation among students*. American Psychological Association. Retrieved September 12, 2022, from https://www.apa.org/pi/lgbt/programs/safe-supportive/lgbt/key-terms.pdf

21. American Psychological Association. (2015). *Key terms and concepts in understanding gender diversity and sexual orientation among students*. American Psychological Association. Retrieved September 12, 2022, from https://www.apa.org/pi/lgbt/programs/safe-supportive/lgbt/key-terms.pdf, p. 21.

22. Dictionary.com. (2022). *LGBT+: Definition*. Retrieved September 15, 2022, from https://www.dictionary.com/browse/lgbtq; American Psychological Association. (2015). *Key terms and concepts in understanding gender diversity and sexual orientation among students*. American Psychological Association. Retrieved September 12, 2022, from https://www.apa.org/pi/lgbt/programs/safe-supportive/lgbt/key-terms.pdf

23. Gawronski, B., & Strack, F. (Eds). (2012). *Cognitive consistency: A fundamental principle in social cognition*. Guilford Press; Madon, S., Willard, J., Guyll, M., & Scherr, K. C. (2011). Self-fulfilling prophecies: Mechanisms, power, and links to social problems. *Social and Personality Psychology Compass, 8*, 578–590; Eden, D. (2003). Self-fulfilling prophecies in organizations. In J. Greenberg (Ed.), *Organizational behavior: The state of the science* (2nd ed., pp. 91–122). Erlbaum.

24. Loden, M., & Rosener, J. B. (1991). *Workforce America: Managing employee diversity as a vital resource*. Business One Irwin.

25. Cox, T., Jr. (1993). *Cultural diversity in organizations: Theory, research & practice*. Berrett-Koehler, pp. 48–51.

26. J. G. Smith, personal communication, July 5, 2017.

27. Cox, T., Jr. (1993). *Cultural diversity in organizations: Theory, research & practice*. Berrett-Koehler, pp. 48–51.

28. Lyons, B. J., Martinez, L. R., Ruggs, E. N., Hebl, M. R., Ryan, A. M., O'Brien, K. R., & Roebuck, A. (2018). To say or not to say: Different strategies for acknowledging a visible disability. *Journal of Management, 44*, 1980–2007; Santuzzi, A. M., & Waltz,

P. R. (2016). Disability in the workplace: A unique and variable identity. *Journal of Management, 42*, 1111–1135; Baldridge, D. C., & Veiga, J. F. (2001). Toward a greater understanding of the willingness to request an accommodation: Can requesters' beliefs derail the Americans with Disabilities Act? *Academy of Management Review, 26*, 85–99.

29. Hennekam, S., & Ladge, J. J. (in press). Free to be me? Evolving gender expression and the dynamic interplay between authenticity and the desire to be accepted at work. *Academy of Management Journal*; Fletcher, L., & Everly, B. A. (2021). Perceived lesbian, gay, bisexual, and transgender (LGBT) supportive practices and the life satisfaction of LGBT employees: The roles of disclosure, authenticity at work, and identity centrality. *Journal of Occupational and Organizational Psychology, 94*, 485–508; Mohr, J. J., Markell, H. M., King, E. B., Jones, K. P., Peddie, C. I., & Kendra, M. S. (2019). Affective antecedents and consequences of revealing and concealing a lesbian, gay, or bisexual identity. *Journal of Applied Psychology, 104*, 1266–1282; Capell, B., Tzafrir, S. S., Enosh, G., & Dolan, S. L. (2018). Explaining sexual minorities' disclosure: The role of trust embedded in organizational practices. *Organization Studies, 39*, 947–973; Ragins, B. R., Singh, R., & Cornwell, J. M. (2007). Making the invisible visible: Fear and disclosure of sexual orientation at work. *Journal of Applied Psychology, 92*, 1103–1118.

30. Follmer, K. B., Sabat, I. E., & Siuta, R. L. (2020). Disclosure of stigmatized identities at work: An interdisciplinary review and agenda for future research. *Journal of Organizational Behavior, 41*, 169–184; Lynch, J. W., & Rodell, J. B. (2018). Blend in or stand out? Interpersonal outcomes of managing concealable stigmas at work. *Journal of Applied Psychology, 103*, 1307–1323.

31. Martin, A. E., & Mason, M. F. (2022). What does it mean to be (seen as) human: The importance of gender in humanization. *Journal of Personality and Social Psychology, 123*, 292–315.

32. Hall, E. V., Hall, A. V., Galinsky, A. D., & Phillips, K. W. (2019). MOSAIC: A model of stereotyping through associated and intersectional categories. *Academy of Management Review, 44*, 643–672; Rodriguez, J. K., Holvino, E., Fletcher, J. K., & Nkomo, S. M. (2016). The theory and praxis of intersectionality in work and organisations: Where do we go from here? *Gender, Work and Organization, 23*, 201–222; Cole, E. R. (2009). Intersectionality and research in psychology. *American Psychologist, 64*, 170–180; Ferdman, B. M. (1999). The color and culture of gender in organizations: Attending to race and ethnicity. In G. N. Powell (Ed.), *Handbook of gender and work* (pp. 17–34). SAGE.

33. Arifeen, S. R., & Gatrell, G. (2020). Those glass chains that bind you: How British Muslim women professionals experience career, faith and family. *British Journal of Management, 31*, 221–236; Rosette, A. S., Ponce de Leon, R., Koval, C. Z., & Harrison, D. A. (2018). Intersectionality: Connecting experiences of gender with race at work. *Research in Organizational Behavior, 38*, 1–22; Ridgeway, C. L., & Kricheli-Katz, T. (2013). Intersecting cultural beliefs in social relations: Gender, race, and class binds and freedoms. *Gender & Society, 27*, 294–318; Bowleg, L. (2008). When Black + lesbian + woman ≠ Black lesbian woman: The methodological challenges of qualitative and quantitative intersectionality research. *Sex Roles, 59*, 312–325.

34. Kreiner, G., Mihelcic, C. A., & Mikolon, S. (2022). Stigmatized work and stigmatized workers. *Annual Review of Organizational Psychology and Organizational Behavior, 9*, 95–120; Zhang, K., Wang, M. S., Toubiana, M., & Greenwood, R. (2021). Stigma beyond

levels: Advancing research on stigmatization. *Academy of Management Annals, 15*, 188–222; Summers, J. K., Howe, M., McElroy, J. C., Buckley, M. R., Pahng, P., & Cortes-Mejia, S. (2018). A typology of stigma within organizations: Access and treatment effects. *Journal of Organizational Behavior, 39*, 853–868; Hebl, M. R., & King, E. B. (2013). The social and psychological experience of stigma. In Q. M. Roberson (Ed.), *Oxford handbook of diversity and work* (pp. 115–131). Oxford University Press.

35. Dixon, J., & Langdridge, D. (2022). Beyond prejudice as antipathy: Understanding kinder, gentler forms of discrimination. In C. Tileagă, M. Augoustinis, & K. Durrheim (Eds.), *The Routledge handbook of discrimination, prejudice, and stereotyping* (pp. 213–230). Routledge; Dhanani, L. Y., Beus, J. M., & Joseph, D. L. (2018). Workplace discrimination: A meta-analytic extension, critique, and future research agenda. *Personnel Psychology, 71*, 147–179; Jones, K. P., Peddie, C. I., Gilrane, V. L., King, E. B., & Gray, A. L. (2016). Not so subtle: A meta-analytic investigation of the correlates of subtle and overt discrimination. *Journal of Management, 42*, 1588–1613; King, E. B., & Jones, K. P. (2016, July 13). Why subtle bias is so often worse than blatant discrimination. *Harvard Business Review*. Retrieved September 26, 2022, from https://hbr.org/2016/07/why-subtle-bias-is-so-often-worse-than-blatant-discrimination; Dovidio, J. F., Hewstone, M., Glick, P., & Esses, V. M. (Eds.). (2010). *The SAGE handbook of prejudice, stereotyping, and discrimination*. SAGE; Fiske, S. T. (1998). Stereotyping, prejudice, and discrimination. In D. T. Gilbert, S. T. Fiske, & G. Lindzey (Eds.), *The handbook of social psychology* (4th ed., Vol. 2, pp. 357–411). McGraw-Hill.

36. Vigdor, N. (2019, November 10). Apple Card investigated after gender discrimination complaints. *New York Times*. Retrieved September 23, 2022, from https://www.nytimes.com/2019/11/10/business/Apple-credit-card-investigation.html#:~:text=The%20criteria%20used%20by%20the,a%20statement%20on%20Saturday%20night; Fisman, R., & Luca, M. (2016). Fixing discrimination in online marketplaces. *Harvard Business Review, 94*(12), 89–95; Datta, A., Tschantz, M. C., & Datta, A. (2015). Automated experiments on ad privacy settings: A tale of opacity, choice, and discrimination. *Proceedings on Privacy Enhancing Technologies, 1*, 92–112; Miller, C. C. (2015, July 9). When algorithms discriminate. *New York Times*. Retrieved July 18, 2017, from https://www.nytimes.com/2015/07/10/upshot/when-algorithms-discriminate.html; Sweeney, L. (2013). Discrimination in online ad delivery. *Communications of the ACM, 56*(5), 44–54.

37. Jones, K. P., Sabat, I. E., King, E. B., Ahmad, A., McCausland, T. C., & Chen, T. (2017). Isms and schisms: A meta-analysis of the prejudice-discrimination relationship across racism, sexism, and ageism. *Journal of Organizational Behavior*, 38, 1076–1110; Becker, J. C., & Sibley, C. G. (2016). Sexism. In T. D. Nelson (Ed.), *Handbook of prejudice, stereotyping, and discrimination* (2nd ed., pp. 315–336). Psychology Press.

38. Ruggs, E. N., Hebl, M. R., & Shockley, K. M. (2023). Fighting the 400-year pandemic: Racism against Black people in organizations. *Journal of Business and Psychology, 38*, 1–5; Roberts, S. O., & Rizzo, M. T. (2021). The psychology of American racism. *American Psychologist, 76*, 475–487; Jones, K. P., Sabat, I. E., King, E. B., Ahmad, A., McCausland, T. C., & Chen, T. (2017). Isms and schisms: A meta-analysis of the prejudice-discrimination relationship across racism, sexism, and ageism. *Journal of Organizational Behavior*, 38, 1076–1110; Richeson, J. A., & Sommers, S. R. (2016). Toward a social psychology of race and race relations for the twenty-first century. *Annual Review of Psychology, 67*, 439–463; Reskin, B. (2012). The race discrimination system. *Annual Review of Sociology, 38*, 17–35; Smedley, A., & Smedley, B. D. (2005).

Race as biology is fiction, racism as a social problem is real. *American Psychologist, 60*, 16–26, quote on p. 16.

39. Beier, M. E., Kanfer, R., Kooij, D. T. A. M., & Truxillo, D. M. (2022). What's age got to do with it? A primer and review of the workplace aging literature. *Personnel Psychology, 75*, 779–804; Dill, K. (2019, November 3). Younger workers report seeing more discrimination. *Wall Street Journal*. Retrieved November 7, 2019, from https://www.wsj.com/articles/younger-workers-report-seeing-more-discrimination-11572793201; Jones, K. P., Sabat, I. E., King, E. B., Ahmad, A., McCausland, T. C., & Chen, T. (2017). Isms and schisms: A meta-analysis of the prejudice-discrimination relationship across racism, sexism, and ageism. *Journal of Organizational Behavior*, 38, 1076–1110; Macdonald, J. L., & Levy, S. R. (2016). Ageism in the workplace: The role of psychosocial factors in predicting job satisfaction, commitment, and engagement. *Journal of Social Issues, 72*, 169–190; Posthuma, R. D., & Campion, M. A. (2009). Age stereotypes in the workplace: Common stereotypes, moderators, and future research directions. *Journal of Management, 35*, 158–188.

40. Peel, E., Ellis, S. J., & Riggs, D. W. (2022). Lesbian, gay, bisexual and transgender people: Prejudice, stereotyping, discrimination and social change. In C. Tileagă, M. Augoustinis, & K. Durrheim (Eds.), *The Routledge handbook of discrimination, prejudice, and stereotyping* (pp. 104–117). Routledge; Sears, B., Mallory, C., Flores, A. R., & Conron, K. J. (2021). *LGBT people's experiences of workplace discrimination and harassment*. Williams Institute, UCLA School of Law. Retrieved February 21, 2022, from https://williamsinstitute.law.ucla.edu/publications/lgbt-workplace-discrimination/; Priola, V., Lasio, D., De Simone, S., & Serri, F. (2014). The sound of silence: Lesbian, gay, bisexual and transgender discrimination in "inclusive organizations." *British Journal of Management, 25*, 488–502; Herek, G. M., & McLemore, K. A. (2013). Sexual prejudice. *Annual Review of Psychology, 64*, 309–333; Ragins, B. R., & Cornwell, J. M. (2001). Pink triangles: Antecedents and consequences of perceived workplace discrimination against gay and lesbian employees. *Journal of Applied Psychology, 86*, 1244–1261.

41. Rosado-Solomon, E. H., Koopmann, J., Lee, W., & Cronin, M. A. (2023). Mental health and mental illness in organizations: A review, comparison, and extension. *Academy of Management Annals, 17*, 751–797; Bogart, K. R., & Dunn, D. S. (2019). Ableism special issue introduction. *Journal of Social Issues, 75*, 650–664; Nario-Redmond, M. R., Kemerling, A. A., & Silverman, A. (2019). Hostile, benevolent, and ambivalent ableism: Contemporary manifestations. *Journal of Social Issues, 75*, 726–756; Olkin, R., Hayward, H., Abbene, M. S., & VanHeel, G. (2019). The experiences of microagressions against women with visible and invisible disabilities. *Journal of Social Issues, 75*, 757–785.

42. Hare-Mustin, R. T., & Marecek, J. (1988). The meaning of difference: Gender theory, postmodernism, and psychology. *American Psychologist, 43*, 455–464; Woolley, H. T. (1910). A review of the recent literature on the psychology of sex. *Psychological Bulletin, 7*, 335–342, quote on p. 340.

43. Eagly, A. H., & Revelle, W. (2022). Understanding the magnitude of psychological differences between women and men requires seeing the forest and the trees. *Perspectives on Psychological Science, 17*, 1339–1558; Eagly, A. H. (2018). The shaping of science by ideology: How feminism inspired, led, and constrained scientific understanding of sex and gender. *Journal of Social Issues, 74*, 871–888; Hyde, J. S. (2014). Gender similarities and differences. *Annual Review of Psychology, 65*, 373–398; Hyde, J. S. (2005). The gender similarities hypothesis. *American Psychologist, 60*, 581–592;

Eagly, A. H. (1995). The science and politics of comparing women and men. *American Psychologist, 50*, 145–158.

44. Bluhm, R. (2021). Neurosexism and our understanding of sex differences in the brain. In S. Crasnow & K. Intemann (Eds.), *Routledge handbook of feminist philosophy of science* (pp. 316–327). Routledge; Fine, C. (2013). Is there neurosexism in functional neuroimaging investigations of sex differences? *Neuroethics, 6*, 369–409.
45. Fiske, S. T. (2010). Venus and Mars or down to Earth: Stereotypes and realities of gender differences. *Perspectives on Psychological Science, 5*, 688–692; Belle, D. (1985). Ironies in the contemporary study of gender. *Journal of Personality, 53*, 400–405.
46. Hahn, A., & Gawronski, B. (2019). Facing one's implicit biases: From awareness to acknowledgement. *Journal of Personality and Social Psychology: Interpersonal Relations and Group Processes, 116*, 769–794; Soll, J. B., Milkman, K. L., & Payne, J. W. (2015). A user's guide to debiasing. In G. Keren & G. Wu (Eds.), *Wiley Blackwell handbook of judgment and decision making* (Vol. 1, pp. 924–951). Wiley Blackwell; Larrick, R. P. (2004). Debiasing. In D. J. Koehler & N. Harvey (Eds.), *Blackwell handbook of judgment and decision making* (pp. 316–337). Blackwell.
47. Caplan, P. J., & Caplan, J. B. (2009). *Thinking critically about research on sex and gender* (3rd ed.). Pearson, pp. 2–4; Lippa, R. A. (2006). The gender reality hypothesis. *American Psychologist, 61*, 639–640.

CHAPTER 2

1. Ferguson, C. (1966). *The male attitude*. Little, Brown.
2. Chafe, W. H. (1976). Looking backward in order to look forward: Women, work, and social values in America. In J. M. Kreps (Ed.), *Women and the American economy: A look to the 1980s* (pp. 6–30). Prentice Hall.
3. Smith, B. G. (2000). Industrial Revolution. In A. M. Howard & F. M. Kavenik (Eds.), *Handbook of American women's history* (pp. 269–270). SAGE; Tilly, L. A., & Scott, J. W. (1978). *Women, work, and family*. Holt, Rinehart & Winston.
4. Hansen, K. V. (1989). "Helped put in a quilt": Men's work and male intimacy in nineteenth-century New England. *Gender & Society, 3*, 334–354; Foner, P. (Ed.). (1977). *The factory girls*. University of Illinois Press; Welter, B. (1966). The cult of true womanhood: 1820–1860. *American Quarterly, 18*, 151–174, quote on p. 152.
5. Doyle, J. A. (1983). *The male experience*. Brown.
6. Seller, M. S. (2000). Shirtwaist makers' strike of 1909. In A. M. Howard & F. M. Kavenik (Eds.), *Handbook of American women's history* (pp. 515–516). SAGE.
7. Diner, H. R. (2000). Immigration. In A. M. Howard & F. M. Kavenik (Eds.), *Handbook of American women's history* (pp. 266–268). SAGE.
8. Griffith, E. (2022). *Formidable: American women and the fight for equality 1920–2020*. Pegasus; Buenker, J. D. (2000). Nineteenth Amendment to the Constitution (1920). In A. M. Howard & F. M. Kavenik (Eds.), *Handbook of American women's history* (p. 402). SAGE; Chafe, W. H. (1976). Looking backward in order to look forward: Women, work, and social values in America. In J. M. Kreps (Ed.), *Women and the American economy: A look to the 1980s* (pp. 6–30). Prentice Hall.

9. Anderson, S. (1935). *Puzzled America*. Appel, p. 46, quoted in Dubbert, J. L. (1979). *A man's place: Masculinity in transition*. Prentice-Hall, p. 210.

10. Howard, A. M. (2000). Depression era (1929–1941). In A. M. Howard & F. M. Kavenik (Eds.), *Handbook of American women's history* (p. 146). SAGE; Fox, M. F., & Hesse-Biber, S. (1984). *Women at work*. Mayfield; Dubbert, J. L. (1979). *A man's place: Masculinity in transition*. Prentice-Hall.

11. Griffith, E. (2022). *Formidable: American women and the fight for equality 1920–2020*. Pegasus; Greene, C. E. (2000). "Rosie the Riveter." In A. M. Howard & F. M. Kavenik (Eds.), *Handbook of American women's history* (pp. 484–485). SAGE. For greater insight into the economic roles women played in this era, I recommend visiting the Rosie the Riveter Museum in the Rosie the Riveter National Historical Park in Richmond, California, https://www.nps.gov/rori.

12. U.S. Department of Commerce, Bureau of the Census. (2000). *Current Population Survey*, computed from data for October 2000. Retrieved December 6, 2000, from https://www.census.gov/programs-surveys/cps/data.html; U.S. Department of Labor, Bureau of Labor Statistics. (1989). *Handbook of labor statistics* (pp. 235–239, Table 55). Government Printing Office; U.S. Department of Commerce, Bureau of the Census. (1975). *Historical statistics of the United States: Colonial times to 1970* (p. 133, Series D49–62). Government Printing Office.

13. U.S. Department of Commerce, Bureau of the Census. (2000). *Current Population Survey*, computed from data for October 2000. Retrieved December 6, 2000, from https://www.census.gov/programs-surveys/cps/data.html; Weiner, L. Y. (1985). *From working girl to working mother: The female labor force in the United States, 1820–1980*. University of North Carolina Press; U.S. Department of Commerce, Bureau of the Census. (1975). *Historical statistics of the United States: Colonial times to 1970* (pp. 131–132, Series D29–41, and p. 133, Series D49–62). Government Printing Office.

14. Griffith, E. (2022). *Formidable: American women and the fight for equality 1920–2020*. Pegasus; Goldin, C., & Katz, L. F. (2002). The power of the pill: Oral contraceptives and women's career and marriage decisions. *Journal of Political Economy, 110*, 730–770; *The Economist*. (1999, December 31). Oral contraceptives: The liberator, p. 102.

15. U.S. Department of Labor, Bureau of Labor Statistics. (2002). *Employment and Earnings*, computed from Table 9. Retrieved April 24, 2002, from https://www.bls.gov/cps; U.S. Department of Commerce, Bureau of the Census. (1975). *Historical statistics of the United States: Colonial times to 1970* (pp. 139–140, Series D182–232). Government Printing Office.

16. Friedan, B. (1974). *The feminine mystique* (10th anniversary ed.). Norton, quote on p. 18.

17. Chafe, W. H. (1976). Looking backward in order to look forward: Women, work, and social values in America. In J. M. Kreps (Ed.), *Women and the American economy: A look to the 1980s* (pp. 6–30). Prentice Hall, quote on p. 20.

18. Griffith, E. (2022). *Formidable: American women and the fight for equality 1920–2020*. Pegasus; Yelton-Stanley, S. K., & Howard, A. M. (2000). Women's liberation movement. In A. M. Howard & F. M. Kavenik (Eds.), *Handbook of American women's history* (pp. 640–641). SAGE.

19. Griffith, E. (2022). *Formidable: American women and the fight for equality 1920–2020*. Pegasus; Yelton-Stanley, S. K. (2000). National Organization for Women (NOW). In

A. M. Howard & F. M. Kavenik (Eds.), *Handbook of American women's history* (p. 382). SAGE; *Ms.* (1979, December). Special issue: The decade of women.

20. Sedmak, N. J., & Vidas, C. (1994). *Primer on equal employment opportunity* (6th ed.). Bureau of National Affairs.

21. Ledvinka, J., & Scarpello, V. G. (1991). *Federal regulation of personnel and human resource management* (2nd ed.). PWS-Kent, pp. 63–65.

22. Faludi, S. (1999). *Stiffed: The betrayal of the American man.* Perennial; Pleck, J. H., & Sawyer, J. (Eds.). (1974). *Men and masculinity.* Prentice-Hall.

23. Faludi, S. (1991). *Backlash: The undeclared war against American women.* Anchor; Ebeling, K. (1990, November 19). The failure of feminism. *Newsweek*, p. 9; Goodman, E. (1985, March 8). Feminists' mid-life shock. *Hartford Courant*, p. B9.

24. Nadal, K. L. (2013). *That's so gay! Microaggressions and the lesbian, gay, bisexual, and transgender community.* American Psychological Association; Carter, D. (2004). *Stonewall: The riots that sparked the gay revolution.* St. Martin's Press; Kane, M. D. (2003). Social movement policy success: Decriminalizing state sodomy laws, 1969–1998. *Mobilization: An International Journal, 8*, 313–334; Morin, S. F., & Rothblum, E. D. (1991). Removing the stigma: Fifteen years of progress. *American Psychologist, 46*, 947–949.

25. Turchik, J. A., & Wilson, S. M. (2010). Sexual assault in the U.S. military: A review of the literature and recommendations for the future. *Aggression and Violent Behavior, 15*, 267–277; Fitzgerald, L. F., Magley, V. J., Drasgow, F., & Waldo, C. R. (1999). Measuring sexual harassment in the military: The Sexual Experiences Questionnaire (SEQ-DoD). *Military Psychology, 11*, 243–263; Disch, L., & Kane, M. J. (1996). When a looker is really a bitch: Lisa Olson, sport, and the heterosexual matrix. *Signs, 21*, 278–308.

26. Jaschik-Herman, M. L., & Fisk, A. (1995). Women's perceptions and labeling of sexual harassment in academia before and after the Hill–Thomas hearings. *Sex Roles, 33*, 439–446.Abramson, J. (1992, October 5). Reversal of fortune: Image of Anita Hill, brighter in hindsight, galvanizes campaigns. *Wall Street Journal*, pp. A1, A6.

27. Fassin, E. (2002). Sexual events: From Clarence Thomas to Monica Lewinsky. *Differences, 13*, 127–158; Powell, G. N. (1998, September 30). How "the affair" would be handled in the private sector. *Hartford Courant*, A13.

28. Pollock, E. J. (2000, February 7). In today's workplace, women feel freer to be, well, women. *Wall Street Journal*, pp. A1, A20; Letters to the editor: So now we're sex kittens again? (2000, February 18). *Wall Street Journal*, p. A15.

29. Leopold, J., Lambert, J. R., Ogunyomi, I. O., & Bell, M. P. (2021). The hashtag heard round the world: How #MeToo did what laws did not. *Equality, Diversity and Inclusion: An International Journal, 40*, 461–476.; Bogen, K. W., Bleiweiss, K. K., Leach, N. R., & Orchowski, L. M. (2021). #MeToo: Disclosure and response to sexual victimization on Twitter. *Journal of Interpersonal Violence, 36*, 8257–8288; Kantor, J., & Twohey, M. (2019). *She said: Breaking the sexual harassment story that helped ignite a movement.* Penguin Press; Gill, R., & Orgad, S. (2018). The shifting terrain of sex and power: From the "sexualization of culture" to #MeToo. *Sexualities, 21*, 1313–1324.

30. Stannard, E. (2022, October 31). Transgender people in CT seeking medical care can face ignorance and stigma. Not at Hartford HealthCare's new gender health center. *Hartford Courant*. Retrieved October 31, 2022, from https://www.courant.

com/2022/10/31/transgender-people-in-ct-seeking-medical-care-can-face-ignorance-and-stigma-not-at-hartford-healthcares-new-gender-health-center/; Hewlett, S. A., & Yoshino, K. (2016, February 2). LGBT-inclusive companies are better at 3 big things. *Harvard Business Review*. Retrieved October 28, 2022, from hbsp.harvard.edu; Martins, J., Pombo, N., Tomiyoshi, M., Trein, M., Watson, M., Castro, M., Schmidt, C., Kersting, A., Miyuki, P., de Souza, D., Zatti, M., Blume, D., Nunes, L., Mastrangelo, J., & Bohn, H. (2016). Implementing LGBT-diversity management in a global company: The case of SAP. In T. Köllen (Ed.), *Sexual orientation and transgender issues in organizations: Global perspectives on LGBT workforce diversity* (pp. 553–560). Springer Nature; Pichler, S., & Ruggs, E. N. (2015). LGBT workers. In A. J. Colella & E. B. King (Eds.), *The Oxford handbook of workplace discrimination*. Oxford University Press.

31. Nguyen, T. T., Criss, S., Michaels, E. K., Cross, R. I., Michaels, J. S., Dwivedi, P., Huang, D., Hsu, E., Mukhija, K., Nguyen, L., Yardi, I., Allen, A., Nguyen, Q. C., & Gee, G. C. (2021). Progress and push-back: How the killings of Ahmaud Arbery, Breonna Taylor, and George Floyd impacted public discourse on race and racism on Twitter. *SSM—Population Health, 15*, 100922; Buchanon, L., Bui, Q., & Patel, J. K. (2020, July 3). Black Lives Matter may be the largest movement in U.S. history. *New York Times*. Retrieved October 28, 2022, from https://www.nytimes.com/interactive/2020/07/03/us/george-floyd-protests-crowd-size.html; Brown, M., Ray, R., Summers, E., & Fraistat, N. (2017). #SayHerName: A case study of intersectional social media activism. *Ethnic and Racial Studies, 40*, 1831–1846.

32. Moore, E., & Philip, A. (2022). Black Lives Matter: True commitment or tokenism? In E. B. King, Q. M. Roberson, & M. R. Hebl (Eds.), *The future of scholarship on race in organizations* (pp. 137–177). Information Age Publishing; Winfield, A. (2020, October 2). How #BLM has redefined D&I in the workplace. *Human Resource Executive*. Retrieved October 28, 2022, from https://hrexecutive.com/how-blm-has-redefined-di-in-the-workplace/; Smith, R. A. (2020, July 30). Black professionals say workplaces have changed since George Floyd—but not enough. *Wall Street Journal*. Retrieved July 30, 2022, from https://www.wsj.com/articles/black-professionals-workplaces-havent-change-george-floyd-11659127328

33. Bennett, J. (2022, June 16). "I feel proud, and I feel mad as hell": Gloria Steinem on *Ms.* Magazine and feminism today. *New York Times*. Retrieved June 16, 2022, from https://www.nytimes.com/2022/06/16/opinion/gloria-steinem-ms-magazine-feminism.html; World Economic Forum (2022). *Global gender gap report 2022*. Retrieved November 1, 2022, from https://www.weforum.org/reports/global-gender-gap-report-2022/; Griffith; Horowitz, J., & Igielnik, R. (2020). *A century after women gained the right to vote, majority of Americans see work to do on gender equality*. Pew Research Center. Retrieved September 13, 1922, from https://www.pewresearch.org/social-trends/2020/07/07/a-century-after-women-gained-the-right-to-vote-majority-of-americans-see-work-to-do-on-gender-equality/

34. This section of the chapter is primarily based on Powell, G. N. (2020). Work–family lockdown: Implications for a post-pandemic research agenda. *Gender in Management: An International Review, 35*, 639–646.

35. Sandford, A. (2020, March 4). Coronavirus: Half of humanity now on lockdown as 90 countries call for confinement. *Euronews*. Retrieved November 2, 2022, from https://www.euronews.com/2020/04/02/coronavirus-in-europe-spain-s-death-toll-hits-10-000-after-record-950-new-deaths-in-24-hou

36. Harter, J. (2020, April 7). How leaders are responding to COVID-19 workplace disruption. *Gallup*. Retrieved May 11, 2020, from https://www.gallup.com/workplace/307622/leaders-responding-covid-workplace-disruption.aspx#:~:text=In%20times%20of%20uncertainty%20and,they%20do%20best%20every%20day.

37. Griffith, E. (2022). *Formidable: American women and the fight for equality 1920–2020*. Pegasus; Milliken, F. J., Kneeland, M. K., & Flynn, E. (2020). Implications of the COVID-19 pandemic for gender equity issues at work. *Journal of Management Studies, 57*, 1767–1772.

38. Robertson, C., & Gebeloff, R. (2020, April 18). How millions of women became the most essential workers in America. *New York Times*. Retrieved May 7, 2020, from https://www.nytimes.com/2020/04/18/us/coronavirus-women-essential-workers.html#:~:text=208-,How%20Millions%20of%20Women%20Became%20the%20Most%20Essential%20Workers%20in,has%20been%20designated%20as%20essential.&text=Every%20day%2C%20Constance%20Warren%20stands,regular%20customers%20come%20and%20go; Powell, G. N. (2020). Work–family lockdown: Implications for a post-pandemic research agenda. *Gender in Management: An International Review, 35*, 639–646;.

39. Ashman, R., Radcliffe, R., Patterson, A., & Gatrell, C. (2022). Reordering motherhood and employment: Mobilizing "mums everywhere" during COVID-19. *British Journal of Management, 33*, 1125–1143; Shockley, K. M., Clark, M. A., Dodd, H., & King, E. B. (2021). Work–family strategies during COVID-19: Examining gender dynamics among dual-earner couples with young children. *Journal of Applied Psychology, 106*, 15–28; Miller, C. C. (2020, May 6). Nearly half of men say they do most of the home schooling. 3 percent of women agree. *New York Times*. Retrieved May 7, 2020, from https://www.nytimes.com/2020/05/06/upshot/pandemic-chores-homeschooling-gender.html; Lyonette, C., & Crompton, R. (2015). Sharing the load? Partners' relative earnings and the division of domestic labour. *Work, Employment and Society, 29*, 23–40.

40. Griffith, E. (2022). *Formidable: American women and the fight for equality 1920–2020*. Pegasus; Lewis, H. (2020, March 19). The coronavirus is a disaster for feminism. *The Atlantic*. Retrieved April 30, 2020, from https://www.theatlantic.com/international/archive/2020/03/feminism-womens-rights-coronavirus-covid19/608302/; Chung, H. (2020, March 30). Return of the 1950s housewife? How to stop coronavirus lockdown reinforcing sexist gender roles. *The Conversation*. Retrieved August 26, 2020, from https://theconversation.com/return-of-the-1950s-housewife-how-to-stop-coronavirus-lockdown-reinforcing-sexist-gender-roles-134851; Friedan, B. (1974). *The feminine mystique* (10th anniversary ed.). Norton.

41. U.S. Department of Labor, Bureau of Labor Statistics. (2022). *Labor force characteristics by race and ethnicity, 2020*. Retrieved November 3, 2022, from https://www.bls.gov/opub/reports/race-and-ethnicity/2020/home.htm

42. Atkin, A. L., Christophe, N. K., Stein, G. L., Gabriel, A. K., & Lee, R. M. (2022). Race terminology in the field of psychology: Acknowledging the growing multiracial population in the U.S. *American Psychologist, 77*, 381–393.

43. Roos, P. A., & Stevens, L. M. (2018). Integrating occupations: Changing occupational sex segregation in the United States from 2000 to 2014. *Demographic Research, 38*, 127–154; Levanon, A., & Grusky, D. B. (2016). The persistence of extreme gender segregation in the twenty-first century. *American Journal of Sociology, 122*, 573–619; Seron, C., Silbey, S. S., Cech, E., & Rubineau, B. (2016). Persistence is cultural:

Professional socialization and the reproduction of sex segregation. *Work and Occupations, 43*, 178–214; Jacobs, J. A. (1999). The sex segregation of occupations: Prospects for the 21st century. In G. N. Powell (Ed.), *Handbook of gender and work* (pp. 125–141). SAGE.

44. U.S. Department of Labor, Bureau of Labor Statistics. (2022). *Labor force statistics from the Current Population* Survey, computed from Table 9. Retrieved November 4, 2022, from https://www.bls.gov/cps.

45. U.S. Department of Labor, Bureau of Labor Statistics. (2022). *Labor force statistics from the Current Population Survey*, Table 11. Retrieved November 4, 2022, from https://www.bls.gov/cps.

46. Catalyst. (2020, January 15). *Pyramid: Women in S&P 500 companies.* Catalyst. Retrieved July 23, 2020, from https://www.researchgate.net/figure/Women-in-S-P-500-Companies_fig1_340225018

47. Rosette, A. S., Ponce de Leon, R., Koval, C. Z., & Harrison, D. A. (2018). Intersectionality: Connecting experiences of gender with race at work. *Research in Organizational Behavior, 38*, 1–22; Byars-Winston, A., Fouad, N., & Wen, Y. (2015). Race/ethnicity and sex in U.S. occupations, 1970–2010: Implications for research, practice, and policy. *Journal of Vocational Behavior, 87*, 54–70; Tomaskovic-Devey, D., Stainback, K., Taylor, T., Zimmer, C., Robinson, C., & McTague, T. (2006). Documenting desegregation: Segregation in American workplaces by race, ethnicity, and sex, 1966–2003. *American Sociological Review, 71*, 565–588.

48. U.S. Department of Labor, Bureau of Labor Statistics. (2022). *Labor force statistics from the Current Population Survey*, computed from Table 39. Retrieved November 7, 2022, from https://www.bls.gov/cps.

49. Goldin, C. (2021). *Career and family: Women's century-long journey toward equity.* Princeton University Press; Blau, F. D., & Kahn, L. M. (2017). The gender wage gap: Extent, trends, and explanations. *Journal of Economic Literature, 55*, 789–865; Roos, P. A., & Gatta, M. L. (1999). The gender gap in earnings: Trends, explanations, and prospects. In G. N. Powell (Ed.), *Handbook of gender and work* (pp. 95–123). SAGE.

50. U.S. Department of Labor, Bureau of Labor Statistics. (2022). *Labor force statistics from the Current Population Survey*, computed from Table 37. Retrieved November 7, 2022, from https://www.bls.gov/cps.

51. Torre, M. (2018). Stopgappers? The occupational trajectories of men in female-dominated occupations. *Work and Occupations, 45*, 283–312; Miller, C. C. (2016, March 18). As women take over a male-dominated field, the pay drops. *New York Times*. Retrieved October 30, 2017, from https://www.nytimes.com/2016/03/20/upshot/as-women-take-over-a-male-dominated-field-the-pay-drops.html; Mandel, H. (2013). Up the down staircase: Women's upward mobility and the wage penalty for occupational feminization, 1970–2007. *Social Forces*, 91, 1183–1207; England, P., Allison, P., & Wu, Y. (2007). Does bad pay cause occupations to feminize, does feminization reduce pay, and how can we tell with longitudinal data? *Social Science Research, 36*, 1237–1256.

52. Miller, C. C. (2017, May 13). The gender pay gap is largely because of motherhood. *New York Times*. Retrieved May 13, 2017, from https://www.nytimes.com/2017/05/13/upshot/the-gender-pay-gap-is-largely-because-of-motherhood.html?smid=url-share; England, P., Bearak, J., Budig, M. J., & Hodges, M. J. (2016). Do highly paid, highly skilled women experience the largest motherhood penalty? *American*

Sociological Review, 81, 1161–1189; Correll, S. J., Benard, S., & Paik, I. (2007). Getting a job: Is there a motherhood penalty? *American Journal of Sociology, 112*, 1297–1338; Anderson, D. J., Binder, M., & Krause, K. (2003). The motherhood wage penalty revisited: Experience, heterogeneity, work effort, and work-schedule flexibility. *Industrial and Labor Relations Review, 56*, 273–294.

53. Goldin, C. (2021). *Career and family: Women's century-long journey toward equity.* Princeton University Press; Goldin, C., Kerr, S. P., Olivetti, C., & Barth, E. (2017). The expanding gender earnings gap: Evidence from the LEHD-2000 census. *American Economic Review, 107*, 110–114; Bobbitt-Zeher, D. (2007). The gender income gap and the role of education. *Sociology of Education, 80*, 1–22; Roos, P. A., & Gatta, M. L. (1999). The gender gap in earnings: Trends, explanations, and prospects. In G. N. Powell (Ed.), *Handbook of gender and work* (pp. 95–123). SAGE.

54. De Pater, I. E., Judge, T. A., & Scott, B. A. (2014). Age, gender, and compensation: A study of Hollywood movie stars. *Journal of Management Inquiry, 23*, 407–420, quote on p. 410; Lee, J. (2014, January 31). Study: Hollywood female stars paid way less after 34. *USA Today*. Retrieved February 5, 2014, from https://www.usatoday.com/story/news/nation-now/2014/01/30/hollywood-women-pay-salary-men/5050433/

55. Judge, T. A., & Cable, D. M. (2011). When it comes to pay, do the thin win? The effect of weight on pay for men and women. *Journal of Applied Psychology, 96*, 95–112, quote on p. 96.

CHAPTER 3

1. Zillman, C. (2017, August 14). "Dolly Babe" vs. "Leader": Clarks is called sexist for girls' and boys' shoe names. *Fortune*. Retrieved August 22, 2017, from https://fortune.com/2017/08/14/clarks-shoes-sexist/; L. L. Gilson, personal communication, August 22, 2017.

2. Prang, A. (2021, October 24). Gender-neutral toys for children gain ground. *Wall Street Journal*. Retrieved October 25, 2021, from https://www.wsj.com/articles/gender-neutral-toys-for-children-gain-ground-but-opposition-persists-11635038039; State of California, Legislative Counsel Bureau. (2021, October 9). *Assembly Bill No. 1084, Gender neutral retail departments*. Retrieved November 22, 2022, from https://www.leginfo.legislation.ca.gov; Bilefsky, D. (2017, September 4). Gender war, aisle 3: Unisex kids' clothes stir British backlash. *New York Times*. Retrieved September 10, 2017, from https://www.nytimes.com/2017/09/04/world/europe/uk-britain-gender-children-john-lewis.html

3. Gross, J. (2021, July 20). Women's handball players are fined for rejecting bikini uniforms. *New York Times*. Retrieved July 22, 2021, from https://www.nytimes.com/2021/07/20/sports/norway-beach-handball-team.html?smid=url-share; Gross, J. (2021, November 1). Facing outrage over bikini rule, handball federation signals "likely" change. *New York Times*. Retrieved November 16, 2022, from https://www.nytimes.com/2021/08/12/sports/norway-beach-handball-team.html?smid=url-share; International Handball Federation (2021). *Rules of the game: Beach volleyball*. Retrieved November 11, 2022, from https://www.ihf.info

4. Way, N. (2019). Reimagining boys in the 21st century. *Men and Masculinities, 22*, 926–929; Komisar, E. (2019, January 16). Masculinity isn't a sickness. *Wall Street Journal*. Retrieved January 21, 2019, from https://www.wsj.com/articles/

masculinity-isnt-a-sickness-11547682809; American Psychological Association (2018). *APA guidelines for the psychological practice with boys and men*; Petter, O. (2018, November 20). Toxic masculinity leaves most young men feeling pressured to "man up." *Independent*. Retrieved August 16, 2019, from https://www.independent.co.uk/life-style/toxic-masculinity-international-mens-day-2018-gender-stereotypes-man-up-a8641136.html

5. Turkewitz, J. (2021, October 18). Hello? This is Colombia's antimachismo hotline. *New York Times*. Retrieved October 18, 2021, from https://www.nytimes.com/2021/10/18/world/americas/colombia-machismo-hotline-masculinity.html?smid=url-share; Sánchez, N. (2020, December 23). Now Bogotá has a listening line for men. *City of Bogotá, Colombia*. Retrieved November 11, 2022, from https://bogota.gov.co/en/international/now-bogota-has-listening-line-men

6. Turkewitz, J. (2021, October 18). Hello? This is Colombia's antimachismo hotline. *New York Times*. Retrieved October 18, 2021, from https://www.nytimes.com/2021/10/18/world/americas/colombia-machismo-hotline-masculinity.html?smid=url-share; Sánchez, N. (2020, December 23). Now Bogotá has a listening line for men. *City of Bogotá, Colombia*. Retrieved November 11, 2022, from https://bogota.gov.co/en/international/now-bogota-has-listening-line-men

7. Ellemers, N. (2018). Gender stereotypes. *Annual Review of Psychology, 69*, 275–298; Eagly, A. H., & Wood, W. (2012). Social role theory. In P. A. M. Van Lange, A. W. Kruglanski, & E. T. Higgins (Eds.), *Handbook of theories of social psychology* (Vol. 2, pp. 458–476). SAGE; Wood, W., & Eagly, A. H. (2010). Gender. In S. T. Fiske, D. T. Gilbert, & G. Lindzey (Eds.), *Handbook of social psychology* (5th ed., Vol. 1, pp. 629–667). Wiley; Martin, C. L., & Ruble, D. N. (2009). Patterns of gender development. *Annual Review of Psychology, 61*, 353–381.

8. Families and Work Institute. (2014). *Generation and gender in the workplace*. Retrieved August 23, 2017, from familiesandwork.org; Galinsky, E., Aumann, K., & Bond, J. T. (2011). *Times are changing: Gender and generation at work and at home.* Families and Work Institute. Retrieved December 18, 2017, https://www.familiesandwork.org/research/2009/times-are-changing-gender-and-generation-at-work-and-at-home/; Kite, M. E. (2001). Changing times, changing gender roles: Who do we want women and men to be? In R. K. Unger (Ed.), *Handbook of the psychology of women and gender* (pp. 215–227). Wiley.

9. PsycINFO. (2023, May 6). Search on "sex differences." *PsycINFO*. Retrieved May 6, 2023, from https://www.ebsco.com; Hare-Mustin, R. T., & Marecek, J. (1988). The meaning of difference: Gender theory, postmodernism, and psychology. *American Psychologist, 43*, 455–464.

10. Borenstein, M., Hedges, L. V., Higgins, J. P. T., & Rothstein, H. R. (2021). *Introduction to meta-analysis* (2nd ed.). Wiley; Maccoby, E. E., & Jacklin, C. N. (1974). *The psychology of sex differences.* Stanford University Press.

11. Halim, M. L. D. (2016). Princesses and superheroes: Social-cognitive influences on early gender rigidity. *Child Development Perspectives, 10*, 155–160; Halim, M. L., Ruble, D. N., Tamis-LeMonda, C. S., Zosuls, K. M., Lurye, L. E., & Greulich, F. K. (2014). Pink frilly dresses and the avoidance of all things "girly": Children's appearance rigidity and cognitive theories of gender development. *Developmental Psychology, 50*, 1091–1101.

12. Davis, J. T. M., & Hines, M. (2020). How large are gender differences in toy preferences? A systematic review and meta-analysis of toy preference research. *Archives*

of Sexual Behavior, 49, 373–394; Todd, B. K., Fischer, R. A., Di Costa, S., Roestorf, A., Harbour, K., Hardiman, P., & Barry, J. A. (2018). Sex differences in children's toy preferences: A systematic review, meta-regression, and meta-analysis. *Infant and Child Development, 27*, e2064; Dinella, L. M., & Weisgram, E. S. (2018). Gender-typing of children's toys: Causes, consequences, and correlates. *Sex Roles, 79*, 253–259; Weisgram, E. S., Fulcher, M., & Dinella, L. M. (2014). Pink gives girls permission: Exploring the roles of explicit gender labels and gender-typed colors on preschool children's toy preferences. *Journal of Applied Developmental Psychology, 35*, 401–409.

13. L. Bowes, personal communication, December 19, 2006.

14. Boyd, H., & Murnen, S. K. (2017). Thin and sexy vs. muscular and dominant: Prevalence of gendered body ideals in popular dolls and action figures. *Body Image, 21*, 90–96; Baghurst, T., Hollander, D. B., Nardella, B., & Haff, G. G. (2006). Change in sociocultural ideal male physique: An examination of past and present action figures. *Body Image, 3*, 87–91; Rogers, M. F. (1999). *Barbie culture.* SAGE.

15. Gerwig, G. (Director). (2023). *Barbie*. [Film]. Warner Brothers. Retrieved July 31, 2023, from https://www.barbie-themovie.com; Harriger, J. A., Schaefer, L. M., Thompson, K., & Cao, L. (2019). You can buy a child a curvy Barbie doll, but you can't make her like it: Young girls' beliefs about Barbie dolls with diverse shapes and sizes. *Body Image, 30*, 107–113; *Tiny shoulders: Rethinking Barbie*. (2018). Retrieved November 22, 2022, from https://www.hulu.com; Gilbert, S. (2018, May 1). Can Barbie really have it all? *The Atlantic*. Retrieved November 22, 2022, from https://www.theatlantic.com/entertainment/archive/2018/05/tiny-shoulders-review-hulu/559277/

16. Dion, J., Hains, J., Vachon, P., Plouffe, J., Laberge, L., Perron, M., McDuff, P., Kalinova, E., & Leone, M. (2016). Correlates of body dissatisfaction in children. *Journal of Pediatrics, 171*, 202–207; Rice, K., Prichard, I., Tiggemann, M., & Slater, A. (2016). Exposure to Barbie: Effects on thin-ideal internalization, body esteem, and body dissatisfaction among young girls. *Body Image, 19*, 142–149; Sherman, A. M., & Zurbriggen, E. L. (2014). "Boys can be anything": Effect of Barbie play on girls' career cognitions. *Sex Roles, 70*, 195–208; Dittmar, H., Halliwell, E., & Ive, S. (2006). Does Barbie make girls want to be thin? The effect of experimental exposure to images of dolls on the body image of 5- to 8-year-old girls. *Developmental Psychology, 42*, 283–292.

17. Coyne, S. M., Rogers, A., Shawcroft, J., & Hurst, J. L. (2021). Dressing up with Disney and make-believe with Marvel: The impact of gendered costumes on gender typing, prosocial behavior, and perseverance during childhood. *Sex Roles, 85*, 301–312; Dinella, L. M. (2017). Halloween costume choices: Reflections of gender development in early childhood. *Journal of Genetic Psychology, 178*, 165–178; Nelson, A. (2000). The pink dragon is female: Halloween costumes and gender markers. *Psychology of Women Quarterly, 24*, 137–144.

18. McCullough, K. M., Wong, Y. J., & Stevenson, N. J. (2020). Female video game players and the protective effect of feminist identity against internalized misogyny. *Sex Roles, 82*, 266–276; Near, C. E. (2013). Selling gender: Associations of box art representation of female characters with sales for teen- and mature-rated video games. *Sex Roles, 68*, 252–269; Martins, N., Williams, D. C., Harrison, K., & Ratan, R. A. (2009). A content analysis of female body imagery in video games. *Sex Roles, 61*, 824–836; Beasley, B., & Standley, T. C. (2002). Shirts vs. skins: Clothing as an indicator of gender role stereotyping in video games. *Mass Communication & Society, 5*, 279–293.

19. Lippa, R. A. (2005). *Gender, nature, and nurture* (2nd ed.). Erlbaum, pp. 158–159; Archer, J., & Lloyd, B. (2002). *Sex and gender* (2nd ed.). Cambridge University Press, pp. 73–74; Larson, R. W., & Verma, S. (1999). How children and adolescents spend time across the world: Work, play, and developmental opportunities. *Psychological Bulletin, 125*, 701–736; Ross, H., & Taylor, H. (1989). Do boys prefer Daddy or his physical style of play? *Sex Roles, 20*, 23–33.

20. Larson, R. W., & Verma, S. (1999). How children and adolescents spend time across the world: Work, play, and developmental opportunities. *Psychological Bulletin, 125*, 701–736.

21. Merriam-Webster. (2023). *Sissy*. Retrieved May 6, 2023, from https://www.merriam-webster.com/dictionary/sissy; Merriam-Webster. (2023). *Tomboy*. Retrieved May 6, 2023, from https://www.merriam-webster.com/dictionary/tomboy; Coyle, E. F., Fulcher, M., & Trübutschek, D. (2016). Sissies, mama's boys, and tomboys: Is children's gender nonconformity more acceptable when nonconformity traits are positive? *Archives of Sexual Behavior, 45*, 1827–1838; Archer, J., & Lloyd, B. (2002). *Sex and gender* (2nd ed.). Cambridge University Press, pp. 80–81.

22. Midgley, C., DeBues-Stafford, G., Lockwood, P., & Thai, S. (2021). She needs to see it to be it: The importance of same-sex athletic role models. *Sex Roles, 85*, 142–160; Ahlqvist, S., Halim, M. L., Greulich, F. K., Lurye, L. E., & Ruble, D. (2013). The potential benefits and risks of identifying as a tomboy: A social identity perspective. *Self and Identity, 12*, 563–581; Martin, C. L., & Dinella, L. M. (2012). Congruence between gender stereotypes and activity preference in self-identified tomboys and non-tomboys. *Archives of Sexual Behavior, 41*, 599–610; Giuliano, T. A., Popp, K. E., & Knight, J. L. (2000). Footballs versus Barbies: Childhood play activities as predictors of sport participation by women. *Sex Roles, 42*, 159–181.

23. Miller, C. C. (2018, September 14). Many ways to be a girl, but one way to be a boy: The new gender rules. *New York Times*. Retrieved January 28, 2019, from https://www.nytimes.com/2018/09/14/upshot/gender-stereotypes-survey-girls-boys.html

24. Bushman, B. J., & Huesmann L. R. (2010). Aggression. In S. T. Fiske, D. T. Gilbert, & G. Lindzey (Eds.), *Handbook of social psychology* (5th ed., Vol. 2, pp. 833–863). Wiley; Archer, J. (2004). Sex differences in aggression in real-world settings: A meta-analytic review. *Review of General Psychology, 8*, 291–322; Knight, G. P., Guthrie, I. K., Page, M. C., & Fabes, R. A. (2002). Emotional arousal and gender differences in aggression: A meta-analysis. *Aggressive Behavior, 28*, 366–393; Eagly, A. H., & Steffan, V. J. (1986). Gender and aggressive behavior: A meta-analytic review of the social psychological literature. *Psychological Bulletin, 100*, 309–330.

25. Kuschel, R. (1992). "Women are women and men are men": How Bellonese women get even. In K. Björkqvist & P. Niemelä (Eds.), *Of mice and women: Aspects of female aggression* (pp. 173–185). Academic Press.

26. Lee, Y. E., Simon, L. S., Koopman, J., Rosen, C. C., Gabriel, A. S., & Yoon, S. (2023). When, why, and for whom is receiving help actually helpful? Differential effects of receiving empowering and nonempowering help based on recipient gender. *Journal of Applied Psychology, 108*, 773–793; Ruiz, A. G. (2019). White knighting: How help reinforces gender differences between men and women. *Sex Roles, 81*, 529–547; Howard, J. A., & Hollander, J. (1997). Altruism and aggression: Gendered dynamics of helping and harming others. In *Gendered situations, gendered selves: A gender lens on social psychology* (pp. 117–148). SAGE; Eagly, A. H., & Crowley, M. (1986). Gender

and helping behavior: A meta-analytic review of the social psychological literature. *Psychological Bulletin, 100*, 283–308.

27. Hall, J. A., Horgan, T. G., & Murphy, N. A. (2019). Nonverbal communication. *Annual Review of Psychology, 70*, 271–294; Hall, J. A., & Gunnery, S. D. (2013). Gender differences in nonverbal communication. In J. A. Hall & M. L. Knapp (Eds.), *Nonverbal communication* (pp. 639–669). De Gruyter Mouton; LaFrance, M., Hecht, M. A., & Paluck, E. L. (2003). The contingent smile: A meta-analysis of sex differences in smiling. *Psychological Bulletin, 129*, 305–334.

28. Larwood, L., & Wood, M. M. (1977). *Women in management.* Lexington Books, p. 33.

29. Broverman, I. K., Vogel, S. R., Broverman, D. M., Clarkson, F. E., & Rosenkrantz, P. S. (1972). Sex role stereotypes: A current appraisal. *Journal of Social Issues, 28*(2), 59–78.

30. Cuddy, A. J. C., Fiske, S. T., & Glick, P. (2008). Warmth and competence as universal dimensions of social perception: The stereotype content model and the BIAS map. In M. P. Zanna (Ed.), *Advances in experimental social psychology* (Vol. 40, pp. 61–149). Elsevier; Fiske, S. T., Cuddy, A. J. C., & Glick, P. (2007). Universal dimensions of social cognition: Warmth and competence. *Trends in Cognitive Sciences, 11*, 77–83; Cuddy, A. J. C., Fiske, S. T., & Glick, P. (2004). When professionals become mothers, warmth doesn't cut the ice. *Journal of Social Issues, 60*, 701–718.

31. Operario, D., & Fiske, S. T. (2001). Stereotypes: Content, structures, processes, and context. In R. Brown & S. Gaertner (Eds.), *Blackwell handbook of social psychology: Intergroup processes* (pp. 22–44). Blackwell; Fiske, S. T. (1998). Stereotyping, prejudice, and discrimination. In D. T. Gilbert, S. T. Fiske, & G. Lindzey (Eds.), *The handbook of social psychology* (4th ed., Vol. 2, pp. 357–411). McGraw-Hill; Hilton, J. L., & von Hippel, W. (1996). Stereotypes. *Annual Review of Psychology, 47*, 237–271; Hamilton, D. L., & Sherman, J. W. (1994). Stereotypes. In R. S. Wyer Jr. & T. K. Srull (Eds.), *Handbook of social cognition* (2nd ed., Vol. 2, pp. 1–68). Erlbaum; Rothbart, M. (1981). Memory processes and social beliefs. In D. L. Hamilton (Ed.), *Cognitive processes in stereotyping and intergroup behavior* (pp. 145–181). Erlbaum.

32. Hsu, N., Badura, K. L., Newman, D. A., & Speach, M. E. P. (2021), Gender, "masculinity," and "femininity": A meta-analytic review of gender differences in agency and communion. *Psychological Bulletin, 147*, 987–1011; Eagly, A. H., Nater, C., Miller, D. I., Kaufmann, M., & Sczesny, S. (2020), Gender stereotypes have changed: A cross-temporal meta-analysis of U.S. public opinion polls from 1946 to 2018. *American Psychologist, 75*, 301–315; Haines, E. L., Deaux, K., & Lofaro, N. (2016). The times they are a-changing . . . or are they not? A comparison of gender stereotypes, 1983–2014. *Psychology of Women Quarterly, 40*, 353–363; Lueptow, L. B., Garovich-Szabo, L., & Lueptow, M. B. (2001). Social change and the persistence of sex typing: 1974–1997. *Social Forces, 80*, 1–35.

33. Eagly, A. H., & Diekman, A. B. (2003). The malleability of sex differences in response to changing social roles. In L. G. Aspinwall & U. M. Staudinger (Eds.), *The psychology of human strengths: Fundamental questions and future directions for a positive psychology* (pp. 103–115). American Psychological Association; Diekman, A. B., & Eagly, A. H. (2000). Stereotypes as dynamic constructs: Women and men of the past, present, and future. *Personality and Social Psychology Bulletin, 26*, 1171–1188.

34. Motro, D., Evans, J. B., Ellis, A. P. J., & Benson, L., III (2022). Race and reactions to women's expressions of anger at work: Examining the effects of the "angry Black woman" stereotype. *Journal of Applied Psychology, 107*, 142–152; Rosette, A. S., Ponce

de Leon, R., Koval, C. Z., & Harrison, D. A. (2018). Intersectionality: Connecting experiences of gender with race at work. *Research in Organizational Behavior, 38*, 1–22; Clarke, H. M., & Arnold, K. A. (2017). Diversity in gender stereotypes? A comparison of heterosexual, gay and lesbian perspectives. *Canadian Journal of Administrative Sciences, 34*, 149–158.

35. Gartzia, L., & Ryan, M. (2022). The subtlety of gender stereotypes in the workplace: Current and future directions for research on the glass cliff. In C. Tileagă, M. Augoustinos, & K. Durrheim (Eds.). *The Routledge international handbook of discrimination, prejudice, and stereotyping* (pp. 58–72). Routledge; Heilman, M. E. (2012). Gender stereotypes and workplace bias. *Research in Organizational Behavior, 32*, 113–135.

36. Bem, S. L. (1974). The measurement of psychological androgyny. *Journal of Consulting and Clinical Psychology, 42*, 155–162.

37. Wood, W., & Eagly, A. H. (2015). Two traditions of research on gender identity. *Sex Roles, 73*, 461–473; Wood, W., & Eagly, A. H. (2009). Gender identity. In M. R. Leary & R. H. Hoyle (Eds.), *Handbook of individual differences in social behavior* (pp. 109–125). Guilford Press.

38. Cross, S. E., & Madson, L. (1997). Models of the self: Self-construals and gender. *Psychological Bulletin, 122*, 5–37.

39. Lenney, E. (1979). Androgyny: Some audacious assertions toward its coming of age. *Sex Roles, 5*, 703–719.

40. Bem, S. L. (1978). Beyond androgyny: Some presumptuous prescriptions for a liberated sexual identity. In J. A. Sherman & F. L. Denmark (Ed.), *The psychology of women: Future directions in research* (pp. 1–23). Psychological Dimensions, quote on p. 19.

41. Choi, N., Fuqua, D. R., & Newman, J. L. (2009). Exploratory and confirmatory studies of the structure of the Bem Sex-Role Inventory short form with two divergent samples. *Educational and Psychological Measurement, 69*, 696–705; Choi, N., Fuqua, D. R., & Newman, J. L. (2008). The Bem Sex-Role Inventory: Continuing theoretical problems. *Educational and Psychological Measurement, 68*, 881–900; Hoffman, R. M., & Borders, L. D. (2001). Twenty-five years after the Bem Sex-Role Inventory: A reassessment and new issues regarding classification variability. *Measurement and Evaluation in Counseling and Development, 34*, 39–55; Bem, S. L. (1981). Gender schema theory: A cognitive account of sex typing. *Psychological Review, 88*, 354–364.

42. Choi, N., Fuqua, D. R., & Newman, J. L. (2009). Exploratory and confirmatory studies of the structure of the Bem Sex-Role Inventory short form with two divergent samples. *Educational and Psychological Measurement, 69*, 696–705; Campbell, T., Gillaspy, J. A. Jr., & Thompson, B. (1997). The factor structure of the Bem Sex-Role Inventory (BSRI): Confirmatory analysis of long and short forms. *Educational and Psychological Measurement, 57*, 118–124; Bem, S. L. (1981). *Bem Sex-Role Inventory: Professional manual.* Consulting Psychologists Press.

43. This section of the chapter is primarily based on portions of Graves, L. M., & Powell, G. N. (2008). Sex and race discrimination in personnel decisions. In S. Cartwright & Cary L. Cooper (Eds.), *The Oxford handbook of personnel psychology* (pp. 438–463). Oxford University Press.

44. Becker, J. C., & Sibley, C. G. (2016). Sexism. In T. D. Nelson (Ed.), *Handbook of prejudice, stereotyping, and discrimination* (2nd ed., pp. 315–336). Psychology Press; Glick, P., & Fiske, S. T. (2001). An ambivalent alliance: Hostile and benevolent sexism as complementary justifications for gender inequality. *American Psychologist, 56*,

109–118, quote on p. 109; Glick, P., Fiske, S. T., Mladinic, A., Saiz, J. L., Abrams, D., Masser, B., Adetoun. B., Osagie, J. E., Akande, A., Alao, A., Annetje, B., Willemsen, T. M., Chipeta, K., Dardenne, B., Dijksterhuis, A., Wigboldus, D., Eckes, T., Six-Materna, I., Exposito, F., Moya, M., & López, W. (2000). Beyond prejudice as simple antipathy: Hostile and benevolent sexism across cultures. *Journal of Personality and Social Psychology, 79*, 763–775; Glick, P., & Fiske, S. T. (1996). The Ambivalent Sexism Inventory: Differentiating hostile and benevolent sexism. *Journal of Personality and Social Psychology, 70*, 491–512.

45. Warren, C., Wax, A., Brush, O. T., Magalona, J., & Galvez, G. (2023). Development and validation of the benevolent sexism in the workplace scale. *Journal of Occupational and Organizational Psychology, 96*, 473–502; Hideg, I., & Ferris, D. L. (2016). The compassionate sexist? How benevolent sexism promotes and undermines gender equality in the workplace. *Journal of Personality and Social Psychology, 111*, 706–727; King, E. B., Botsford, W., Hebl, M. R., Kazama, S., Dawson, J. F., & Perkins, A. (2012). Benevolent sexism at work: Gender differences in the distribution of challenging developmental experiences. *Journal of Management, 38*, 1835–1866; Russell, B. L., & Trigg, K. Y. (2004). Tolerance of sexual harassment: An examination of gender differences, ambivalent sexism, social dominance, and gender roles. *Sex Roles, 50*, 565–573.

46. Glick, P., Lameiras, M., Fiske, S. T., Eckes, T., Masser, B., Volpato, C., Manganelli, A. M., Pek, J. C. X., Huang, L-L., Sakalli-Ugurlu, N., Castro, Y. R., Pereira, M. L. D., Willemsen, T. M., Brunner, A., Six-Materna, I., & Wells, R. (2004). Bad but bold: Ambivalent attitudes toward men predict gender inequality in 16 nations. *Journal of Personality and Social Psychology, 86*, 713–728; Glick, P., & Fiske, S. T. (1999). The Ambivalence toward Men Inventory: Differentiating hostile and benevolent beliefs about men. *Psychology of Women Quarterly, 23*, 519–536.

47. Watkins, M. B., Kaplan, S., Brief, A. P., Shull, A., Dietz, J., Mansfield, M., & Cohen, R. (2006). Does it pay to be a sexist? The relationship between modern sexism and career outcomes. *Journal of Vocational Behavior, 69*, 524–537.

48. Ruggs, E. N., Hebl, M. R., & Shockley, K. M. (2023). Fighting the 400-year pandemic: Racism against Black people in organizations. *Journal of Business and Psychology, 38*, 1–5; Roberts, S. O., & Rizzo, M. T. (2021). The psychology of American racism. *American Psychologist, 76*, 475–487; Jones, K. P., Sabat, I. E., King, E. B., Ahmad, A., McCausland, T. C., & Chen, T. (2017). Isms and schisms: A meta-analysis of the prejudice-discrimination relationship across racism, sexism, and ageism. *Journal of Organizational Behavior, 38*, 1076–1110; Richeson, J. A., & Sommers, S. R. (2016). Toward a social psychology of race and race relations for the twenty-first century. *Annual Review of Psychology, 67*, 439–463; Dovidio, J. F., Gaertner, S. L., & Kawakam, K. (2010). Racism. In J. F. Dovidio, M. Hewstone, P. Glick, & V. M. Esses (Eds.), *The SAGE handbook of prejudice, stereotyping, and discrimination* (pp. 312–327). SAGE.

49. Swim, J. K., Aikin, K. J., Hall, W. S., & Hunter, B. A. (1995). Sexism and racism: Old-fashioned and modern prejudices. *Journal of Personality and Social Psychology, 68*, 199–214; Reid, P. T. (1988). Racism and sexism: Comparisons and conflicts. In P. A. Katz and D. A. Taylor (Eds.), *Eliminating racism: Profiles in controversy* (pp. 203–221). Plenum.

50. Motro, D., Evans, J. B., Ellis, A. P. J., & Benson, L., III (2022). Race and reactions to women's expressions of anger at work: Examining the effects of the "angry Black woman" stereotype. *Journal of Applied Psychology, 107*, 142–152; Szymanski, D. M., & Lewis, J. A. (2016). Gendered racism, coping, identity centrality, and African

American college women's psychological distress. *Psychology of Women Quarterly, 40*, 229–243; Lewis, J. A., & Neville, H. A. (2015). Construction and initial validation of the Gendered Racial Microaggressions Scale for Black women. *Journal of Counseling Psychology, 62*, 289–302; Lewis, J. A., Mendenhall, R., Harwood, S. A., & Huntt, M. B. (2013). Coping with gendered racial microaggressions among Black women college students. *Journal of African American Studies, 17*, 51–73.

51. Eagly, A. H., & Wood, W. (2013). The nature-nurture debates: 25 years of challenges in understanding the psychology of gender. *Perspectives on Psychological Science, 8*, 340–357; Lippa, R. A. (2005). *Gender, nature, and nurture* (2nd ed.). Erlbaum, pp. 158–159; Archer, J., & Lloyd, B. (2002). *Sex and gender* (2nd ed.). Cambridge University Press.

52. Buss, D. M. (2020). Evolutionary psychology is a scientific revolution. *Evolutionary Behavioral Sciences, 14*, 316–323; Eagly, A. H., & Wood, W. (2013). The nature-nurture debates: 25 years of challenges in understanding the psychology of gender. *Perspectives on Psychological Science, 8*, 340–357; Lippa, R. A. (2005). *Gender, nature, and nurture* (2nd ed.). Erlbaum, pp. 158–159; Archer, J., & Lloyd, B. (2002). *Sex and gender* (2nd ed.). Cambridge University Press; Udry, J. R. (2000). Biological limits of gender construction. *American Sociological Review, 65*, 443–457.

53. Confer, J. C., Easton, J. A., Fleischman, D. S., Goetz, C. D., Lewis, D. M. G., Perrilloux, C., & Buss, D. M. (2010). Evolutionary psychology: Controversies, questions, prospects, and limitations. *American Psychologist, 65*, 110–126; Buss, D. M. (2009). The great struggles of life: Darwin and the emergence of evolutionary psychology. *American Psychologist, 64*, 140–148; Buss, D. M. (1995). Evolutionary psychology: A new paradigm for psychological science. *Psychological Inquiry, 6*, 1–30.

54. Eagly, A. H., & Wood, W. (2013). The nature-nurture debates: 25 years of challenges in understanding the psychology of gender. *Perspectives on Psychological Science, 8*, 340–357; Wood, W., & Eagly, A. H. (2010). Gender. In S. T. Fiske, D. T. Gilbert, & G. Lindzey (Eds.), *Handbook of social psychology* (5th ed., Vol. 1, pp. 629–667). Wiley; Martin, C. L., & Ruble, D. N. (2009). Patterns of gender development. *Annual Review of Psychology, 61*, 353–381; Lippa, R. A. (2005). *Gender, nature, and nurture* (2nd ed.). Erlbaum, pp. 158–159; Wood, W., & Eagly, A. H. (2002). A cross-cultural analysis of the behavior of women and men: Implications for the origins of sex differences. *Psychological Bulletin, 128*, 699–727; Eagly, A. H., & Wood, W. (1999). The origins of sex differences in human behavior: Evolved dispositions versus social roles. *American Psychologist, 54*, 408–423.

55. Toles-Patkin, T. (2021). Gender reveal parties and the construction of the prenatal gendered environment. *Explorations in Media Ecology, 20*, 175–193; MacPhee, D., & Prendergast, S. (2019). Room for improvement: Girls' and boys' home environments are still gendered. *Sex Roles, 80*, 332–346; Guignard, F. P. (2015). A gendered bun in the oven: The gender-reveal party as a new ritualization during pregnancy. *Studies in Religion/Sciences Religeuses, 44*, 479–500.

56. Lawson, K. M., Crouter, A. C., & McHale, S. M. (2015). Links between family gender socialization experiences in childhood and gendered occupational attainment in young adulthood. *Journal of Vocational Behavior, 90*, 26–35; Croft, A., Schmader, T., Block, K., & Baron, A. S. (2014). The second shift reflected in the second generation: Do parents' gender roles at home predict children's aspirations? *Psychological Science, 25*, 1418–1428; Katz-Wise, S. L., Priess, H. A., & Hyde, J. S. (2010). Gender-role attitudes and behavior across the transition to parenthood. *Developmental*

Psychology, 46, 18–28; Marks, J. L., Lam, C. B., & McHale, S. M. (2009). Family patterns of gender role attitudes. *Sex Roles, 61*, 221–234.

57. Pilkauskas, N. V., Brooks-Gunn, J., & Waldfogel, J. (2018). Maternal employment stability in early childhood: Links with child behavior and cognitive skills. *Developmental Psychology, 54*, 410–427; Lucas-Thompson, R. G., Goldberg, W. A., & Prause, J. (2010). Maternal work early in the lives of children and its distal associations with achievement and behavior problems: A meta-analysis. *Psychological Bulletin, 136*, 915–942; Goldberg, W. A., Prause, J., Lucas-Thompson, R., & Himsel, A. (2008). Maternal employment and children's achievement in context: A meta-analysis of four decades of research. *Psychological Bulletin, 134*, 77–108; Tan, S. J. (2008). The myths and realities of female employment. In A. Marcus-Newhall, D. F. Halpern, & S. J. Tan (Eds.), *The changing realities of work and family: A multidisciplinary approach* (pp. 9–24). Wiley-Blackwell.

58. Stewart, W., & Barling, J. (1996). Fathers' work experiences effect children's behaviors via job-related affect and parenting behaviors. *Journal of Organizational Behavior, 17*, 221–232; MacEwen, K. E., & Barling, J. (1991). Effects of maternal employment experiences on children's behavior via mood, cognitive difficulties, and parenting behavior. *Journal of Marriage and Family, 53*, 635–644; Barling, J., MacEwen, K. E., & Nolte, M-L. (1993). Homemaker role experiences affect toddler behaviors via maternal well-being and parenting behavior. *Journal of Abnormal Child Psychology, 21*, 213–229.

59. U.S. Department of Labor, Bureau of Labor Statistics (2022). *Labor force statistics from the Current Population Survey*, Table 11. Retrieved November 4, 2022, from https://www.bls.gov/cps/tables.htm; U.S. Department of Education, National Center for Education Statistics (2022). *Digest of education statistics*, computed from Tables 212.08. Retrieved December 13, 2022, from https://nces.ed.gov; Minichello, J. (2021, April 23). American Superintendent 2020 decennial study now available. *AASA, The School Superintendents Association*. Retrieved December 13, 2022, from https://www.aasa.org/publications/all-publications

60. Reilly, D., Neumann, D. L., & Andrews, G. (2019). Gender differences in reading and writing achievement: Evidence from the National Assessment of Educational Progress (NAEP). *American Psychologist, 74*, 445–458; Voyer, D., & Voyer, S. D. (2014). Gender differences in scholastic achievement: A meta-analysis. *Psychological Bulletin, 140*, 1174–1204; Buchmann, C., DiPrete, T. A., & McDaniel, A. (2008). Gender inequalities in education. *Annual Review of Sociology, 34*, 319–337.

61. Williams, J. A. (2016). Girls can be anything . . . but boys will be boys: Discourses of sex difference in education reform debates. *Nevada Law Journal*. Retrieved September 29, 2017, from https://law.unlv.edu/nevada-law-journal; Duckworth, A. L., & Seligman, M. E. P. (2006). Self-discipline gives girls the edge: Gender in self-discipline, grades, and achievement test scores. *Journal of Educational Psychology, 98*, 198–208.

62. Farago, F., Martin, C. L., Granger, K. L., Santos, C. E., & Miller, C. F. (2022). Teachers' gender-role attitudes and gendered classroom practices. *Sex Roles, 87*, 471–486; Gansen, H. M. (2019). Push-ups versus clean-up: Preschool teachers' gendered beliefs, expectations for behavior, and disciplinary practices. *Sex Roles, 80*, 393–408.

63. Chokshi, N. (2018, April 7). Do men think they're better at science than women do? Well, actually . . . *New York Times*. Retrieved April 7, 2018, from https://www.nytimes.com/2018/04/07/science/men-women-science.html; Cooper, K. M., Krieg, A., &

Brownell, S. E. (2018). Who perceives they are smarter? Exploring the influence of student characteristics on student academic self-concept in physiology. *Advances in Physiology Education, 42*, 200–208; Ahmad, R., Imran, H., Khanan, S. J., & Riaz, Z. (2013). Gender differences in domain specific self-esteem of adolescents. *Asian Journal of Social Sciences and Humanities, 2*, 432–440; Gentile, B., Grabe, S., Dolan-Pascoe, B., Twenge, J. M., Wells, B. E., & Maitano, A. (2009). Gender differences in domain-specific self-esteem: A meta-analysis. *Review of General Psychology, 13*, 34–45.

64. Schmader, T. (2023). Gender inclusion and fit in STEM. *Annual Review of Psychology, 74*, 219–243.

65. Damour, L. (2019, February 7). Why girls beat boys at school and lose to them at the office. *New York Times*. Retrieved December 13, 2022, from https://www.nytimes.com/2019/02/07/opinion/sunday/girls-school-confidence.html

66. Statistica Research Department. (2022, November 17). Children and media in the U.S.: Statistics and facts. *Statistica*. Retrieved December 16, 2022, from https://www.statista.com/topics/3980/children-and-media-in-the-us/; Lapierre, M. A., Piotrowski, J. T., & Linebarger, D. L. (2012). Background television in the homes of U.S. children. *Pediatrics, 130*, 839–846.

67. Lamer, S. A., Dvorak, P., Biddle, A. M., Pauker, K., & Weisbuch, M. (2022). The transmission of gender stereotypes through televised patterns of nonverbal bias. *Journal of Personality and Social Psychology, 123*, 1315–1335; Douglas, S., Tang, L., & Rice, C. (2022). Gender performativity and postfeminist parenting in children's television shows. *Sex Roles, 86*, 249–262; Kang, S., & Hust, S, J. T. (2022). Traditionally and narrowly defined: Gender portrayals in television programming targeting babies and toddlers. *Sex Roles, 86*, 576–586.

68. Shawcroft, J. E., Coyne, S. M., Zurcher, J. D., & Brubaker, P. J. (2022). Depictions of gender across eight decades of Disney animated film: The role of film producer, director, and writer gender. *Sex Roles, 86*, 346–365; Griffin, M., Harding, N., & Learmonth, M. (2017). Whistle while you work? Disney animation, organizational readiness and gendered subjugation. *Organization Studies, 38*, 869–894; Hand, D. (Director). (1937). *Snow white and the seven dwarfs*. [Film]. Walt Disney. Retrieved May 6, 2023, from https://movies.disney.com.

69. Neff, K. L., Smith, S. L., & Pieper, K. (2023). *Inequality in 1,600 popular films: Examining portrayals of gender, race/ethnicity, and age of leads/co-leads from 2007 to 2022*. USC Annenberg Inclusion Initiative. Retrieved May 6, 2023, from https://assets.uscannenberg.org/docs/aii-inequality-1600-films-20230216.pdf; USC Annenberg Inclusion Initiative. (2020). *Inequality in 1,300 popular films: Examining portrayals of gender, race/ethnicity, LGBTQ, and disability from 2007–2019*. Retrieved May 6, 2023, from https://assets.uscannenberg.org/docs/aii-inequality_1300_popular_films_09-08-2020.pdf; Ramakrishna, A., Martinez, V. R., Malandrakis, N., Singla, K., & Narayanan, S. (2017). Linguistic analysis of differences in portrayals of movie characters. *Proceedings of the 55th Annual Meeting of the Association for Computational Linguistics*, 1669–1678; Barr, J. (2017, August 4). Look who's still talking the most in movies: White men. *New York Times*. Retrieved August 8, 2017, from https://www.nytimes.com/2017/08/04/arts/diversity-films-women-race.html

70. Ezzedeen, S. R. (2015). Portrayals of career women in Hollywood films: Implications for the glass ceiling's persistence. *Gender in Management: An International Journal, 30*, 239–264; Ezzedeen, S. R. (2013). The portrayal of professional and managerial

women in North American films: Good news or bad news for your executive pipeline? *Organizational Dynamics, 42*, 248–256.

71. Weber, B. (2022, July 31). Nichelle Nichols, Lieutenant Uhura on "Star Trek," dies at 89. *New York Times*. Retrieved July 31, 2022, from https://www.nytimes.com/2022/07/31/obituaries/nichelle-nichols-dead.html; Grove, L. (1999, September 16). Captain's Log, Stardate 1999: Mr. Sulu pushes diversity on TV. *Washington Post*. Retrieved September 16, 1999, from http://www.washingtonpost.com; Richards, T. (1997). *The meaning of Star Trek*. Doubleday.

72. Butkowski, C. P., Dixon, T. L., & Weeks, K. (2019). Body surveillance on Instagram: Examining the role of selfie feedback investment in young women's body image concerns. *Sex Roles, 81*, 385–397; Ghaznavi, J., & Taylor, L. D. (2015). Bones, body parts, and sex appeal: An analysis of #thinspiration images on popular social media. *Body Image, 14*, 54–61; Perloff, R. M. (2014). Social media effects on young women's body image concerns: Theoretical perspectives and an agenda for research. *Sex Roles, 71*, 363–377.

73. Allen, K. A., Ryan, T., Gray, D. L., McInerney, D. M., & Waters, L. (2014). Social media use and social connectedness in adolescents: The positives and potential pitfalls. *Australian Educational and Developmental Psychologist, 31*, 18–31; Li, Q. (2006). Cyberbullying in schools: A research of gender differences. *School Psychology International, 27*, 157–170.

74. Mavin, S. A., Elliott, C., Stead, V., & Williams, J. (2016). Women managers, leaders and the media gaze: Learning from popular culture, autobiographies, broadcast and media press. *Gender in Management: An International Journal, 31*, 314–321.

75. Fiske, S. T. (1998). Stereotyping, prejudice, and discrimination. In D. T. Gilbert, S. T. Fiske, & G. Lindzey (Eds.), *The handbook of social psychology* (4th ed., Vol. 2, pp. 357–411). McGraw-Hill.

76. Choi, N., Fuqua, D. R., & Newman, J. L. (2009). Exploratory and confirmatory studies of the structure of the Bem Sex-Role Inventory short form with two divergent samples. *Educational and Psychological Measurement, 69*, 696–705.

77. These two questions were inspired by James Jones, who posed similar questions about race; see Jones, J. M. (1991). Psychological models of race: What have they been and what should they be? In J. D. Goodchilds (Ed.), *Psychological perspectives on human diversity in America* (pp. 7–46). American Psychological Association.

78. Read, J. G., & Gorman, B. K. (2010). Gender and health inequality. *Annual Review of Sociology*, 36, 371–386; Lyons, A. C. (2009). Masculinities, femininities, behaviour and health. *Social and Personality Psychology Compass, 3*, 394–412; Verbrugge, L. M. (1985). Gender and health: An update of hypotheses and evidence. *Journal of Health and Social Behavior, 26*, 156–182.

79. Russo, N. F., & Tartaro, J. (2008). Women and mental health. In F. L. Denmark & M. A. Paludi (Eds.), *Psychology of women: A handbook of issues and theories* (2nd ed., pp. 440–483). Praeger.

80. American Psychological Association (2018). *APA guidelines for the psychological practice with boys and men.*; McVittie, C., Hepworth, J., & Goodall, K. (2017). Masculinities and health: Whose identities, whose constructions? In M. P. Sánchez-López & R. M. Limiñana-Gras (Eds.), *The psychology of gender and health: Conceptual and applied global concerns* (pp. 119–141). Elsevier; Gough, B., Robertson, S., & Robinson, M.

(2016). Men, "masculinity," and mental health: Critical reflections. In J. Gideon (Ed.), *Handbook on gender and health* (pp. 134–147). Elgar.

81. U.S. Department of Health and Human Services, Centers for Disease Control and Prevention, National Center for Health Statistics. (2022). *Health, United States, 2020–2021*, Tables LExpMort and 21. Retrieved December 19, 2022, from https://www.cdc.gov/nchs/hus/index.htm
82. Smith, D. G. (2022, December 9). How to get more men to try therapy. *New York Times*. Retrieved December 19, 2022, from https://www.nytimes.com/2022/12/09/well/mind/men-mental-health-therapy.html; Sánchez, N. (2020, December 23). Now Bogotá has a listening line for men. *City of Bogotá, Colombia*. Retrieved November 11, 2022, from https://bogota.gov.co/en/international/now-bogota-has-listening-line-men
83. Ghorayshi, A. (2022, January 19). Why are men more likely to die of Covid? It's complicated. *New York Times*. Retrieved January 20, 2022, from https://www.nytimes.com/2022/01/19/health/covid-gender-deaths-men-women.html; Galasso, V., Pons, V., Profeta, P., Becher, M., Brouard, S., & Foucault, M. (2020). Gender differences in COVID-19 attitudes and behavior: Panel evidence from eight countries. *Proceedings of the National Academy of Sciences, 117*, 27285–27291.

CHAPTER 4

1. Uggerslev, K. L., Fassina, N. E., & Kraichy, D. (2012). Recruiting through the stages: A meta-analytic test of predictors of applicant attraction at different stages of the recruiting process. *Personnel Psychology, 65*, 597–660; Hausknecht, J. P., Day, D. V., & Thomas, S. C. (2004). Applicant reactions to selection procedures: An updated model and meta-analysis. *Personnel Psychology, 57*, 639–683.
2. Graves, L. M., & Powell, G. N. (2008). Sex and race discrimination in personnel decisions. In S. Cartwright & C. L. Cooper (Eds.), *The Oxford handbook of personnel psychology* (pp. 438–463). Oxford University Press; Graves. L. M. (1999). Gender bias in interviewers' evaluations of applicants: When and how does it occur? In G. N. Powell (Ed.), *Handbook of gender and work* (pp. 145–164). SAGE.
3. Ferguson, S. (2022, October 31). Understanding America's labor shortage: The most impacted industries. *U.S. Chamber of Commerce*. Retrieved December 26, 2022, from https://www.uschamber.com/workforce/understanding-americas-labor-shortage-the-most-impacted-industries
4. Boswell, W. R., Roehling, M. V., LePine, M. A., & Moynihan, L. M. (2003). Individual job-choice decisions and the impact of job attributes and recruitment practices: A longitudinal field study. *Human Resource Management, 42*, 23–37.
5. Valet, P., Sauer, C., & Tolsma, J. (2021). Preferences for work arrangements: A discrete choice experiment. *PLoS ONE, 16*(7), e0254483; le Barbanchon, T., Rathelot, R., & Roulet, A. (2021). Gender differences in job search: Trading off commute against wage. *Quarterly Journal of Economics, 136*, 381–426; Gilbert, G. R., Burnett, M. F., Phau, I., & Haar, J. (2010). Does gender matter? A review of work-related gender commonalities. *Gender in Management: An International Journal, 25*, 676–699; Konrad, A. M., Ritchie, J. E., Jr., Lieb, P., & Corrigall, E. (2000). Sex differences and similarities in job attribute preferences: A meta-analysis. *Psychological Bulletin, 126*, 593–641.

6. Valet, P., Sauer, C., & Tolsma, J. (2021). Preferences for work arrangements: A discrete choice experiment. *PLoS ONE, 16*(7), e0254483; Corrigall, E. A., & Konrad, A. M. (2006). The relationship of job attribute preferences to employment, hours of paid work, and family responsibilities: An analysis comparing women and men. *Sex Roles, 54*, 95–111; Konrad, A. M. (2003). Family demands and job attribute preferences: A 4-year longitudinal study of women and men. *Sex Roles, 49*, 35–46.

7. Jones, K. S., Newman, D. A., Su, R., & Rounds, J. (2021). Black–White differences in vocational interests: Meta-analysis and boundary conditions. *Journal of Business and Psychology, 36*, 589–607; Morris, M. L. (2016). Vocational interests in the United States: Sex, age, ethnicity and year effects. *Journal of Counseling Psychology, 63*, 604–615; Su, R., Rounds, J., & Armstrong, P. I. (2009). Men and things, women and people: A meta-analysis of sex differences in interests. *Psychological Bulletin, 135*, 859–884.

8. Roos, P. A., & Stevens, L. M. (2018). Integrating occupations: Changing occupational sex segregation in the United States from 2000 to 2014. *Demographic Research, 38*, 127–154; Levanon, A., & Grusky, D. B. (2016). The persistence of extreme gender segregation in the twenty-first century. *American Journal of Sociology, 122*, 573–619; Seron, C., Silbey, S. S., Cech, E., & Rubineau, B. (2016). Persistence is cultural: Professional socialization and the reproduction of sex segregation. *Work and Occupations, 43*, 178–214.

9. Rosette, A. S., Ponce de Leon, R., Koval, C. Z., & Harrison, D. A. (2018). Intersectionality: Connecting experiences of gender with race at work. *Research in Organizational Behavior, 38*, 1–22; Cejka, M. A., & Eagly, A. H. (1999). Gender-stereotypic images of occupations correspond to the sex-segregation of employment. *Personality and Social Psychology Bulletin, 25*, 413–423.

10. Marini, M. M., & Fan, P-L. (1997). The gender gap in earnings at career entry. *American Sociological Review, 62*, 588–604.

11. Jones, K. S., Newman, D. A., Su, R., & Rounds, J. (2021). Black–White differences in vocational interests: Meta-analysis and boundary conditions. *Journal of Business and Psychology, 36*, 589–607; Martinez, A., & Gayfield, A. (2019). *The intersectionality of sex, race, and Hispanic origin in the STEM workforce*. SEHSD Working Paper Number 2018-27. U.S. Census Bureau. Retrieved May 8, 2023, from https://www.census.gov/content/dam/Census/library/working-papers/2019/demo/sehsd-wp2018-27.pdf; Rosette, A. S., Ponce de Leon, R., Koval, C. Z., & Harrison, D. A. (2018). Intersectionality: Connecting experiences of gender with race at work. *Research in Organizational Behavior, 38*, 1–22.

12. Chapman, D. S., Uggerslev, K. L., Carroll, S. A., Piasentin, K. A., & Jones, D. A. (2005). Applicant attraction to organizations and job choice: A meta-analytic review of the correlates of recruiting outcomes. *Journal of Applied Psychology, 90*, 928–944; Bretz, R. D., & Judge, T. A. (1994). The role of human resource systems in job applicant decision processes. *Journal of Management, 20*, 531–551.

13. Kroeper, K. M., Williams, H. E., & Murphy, M. C. (2022). Counterfeit diversity: How strategically misrepresenting gender diversity dampens organizations' perceived sincerity and elevates women's identity threats concerns. *Journal of Personality and Social Psychology, 122*, 399–426; Walker, H. J., Feild, H. S., Bernerth, J. B., & Becton, J. B. (2012). Diversity cues on recruitment websites: Investigating the effects on job seekers' information processing. *Journal of Applied Psychology, 97*, 214–224; Avery, D. R., & McKay, P. F. (2006). Target practice: An organizational impression management approach to attracting minority and female applicants. *Personnel Psychology,*

59, 157–187; McKay, P. F., & Avery, D. R. (2005). Warning! Diversity recruitment could backfire. *Journal of Management Inquiry, 14*, 330–336.

14. Masterson, C. R., Sugiyama, K., & Ladge, J. J. (2021). The value of 21st century work-family supports: Review and cross-level path forward. *Journal of Organizational Behavior, 42*, 118–138.

15. Byrne, D., & Neuman, J. H. (1992). The implications of attraction research for organizational issues. In K. Kelley (Ed.), *Issues, theory, and research in industrial/organizational psychology* (pp. 29–70). Elsevier; Turban, D. B., & Dougherty, T. W. (1992). Influences of campus recruiting on applicant attraction to firms. *Academy of Management Journal, 35*, 739–765; Taylor, M. S., & Bergmann, T. J. (1987). Organizational recruitment activities and applicants' reactions at different stages of the recruitment process. *Personnel Psychology, 40*, 261–285.

16. Rynes, S. L., Bretz, R. D., & Gerhart, B. (1991). The importance of recruitment in job choice: A different way of looking. *Personnel Psychology, 44*, 487–521.

17. Chawla, N., & Gabriel, A. S. (in press). From crude jokes to diminutive terms: Exploring experiences of hostile and benevolent sexism during job search. *Personnel Psychology*; Hildebrand, L. K., Monteith, M. J., Carter, E. R., & Burns, M. D. (2022). Honey, sweetie, dear: Terms of endearment communicate, reflect, and reinforce sexism toward adult women. *Sex Roles, 87*, 185–210; Brands, R. A., & Fernandez-Mateo, I. (2017). Leaning out: How negative recruitment experiences shape women's decisions to compete for executive roles. *Administrative Science Quarterly, 62*, 405–442; Stout, J. G., & Dasgupta, N. (2011). When *he* doesn't mean *you*: Gender-exclusive language as ostracism. *Personality and Social Psychology Bulletin, 36*, 757–769.

18. Figueroa-Armijos, M., Clark, B. B., & da Motta Veiga, S. P. (2023). Ethical perceptions of AI in hiring and organizational trust: The role of performance expectancy and social influence. *Journal of Business Ethics, 186*, 179–197; Jaser, Z., Petrakaki, D., Starr, R., & Oyarbide-Magaña, E. (2022, January 27). Where automated job interviews fall short. *Harvard Business Review*. Retrieved December 27, 2022, from https://hbr.org/2022/01/where-automated-job-interviews-fall-short; Langer, M., Baum. K., König, C. J., Hähne, V., Oster, D., & Spieth, T. (2021). Spare me the details: How the type of information about automated interviews influences applicant reactions. *International Journal of Selection and Assessment, 29*, 154–169; Wesche, J. S., & Sonderegger, A. (2021). Repelled at first sight? Expectations and intentions of job-seekers reading about AI selection in job advertisements. *Computers in Human Behavior, 125*, 106931; Langer, M., König, C. J., & Papathanasiou, M. (2019). Highly automated job interviews: Acceptance under the influence of stakes. *International Journal of Selection and Assessment, 27*, 217–234.

19. Hentschel, T., Braun, S., Peus, C., & Frey, D. (2021). Sounds like a fit! Wording in recruitment advertisements and recruiter gender affect women's pursuit of career development programs via anticipated belongingness. *Human Resource Management, 60*, 581–602; Wille, L., & Derous, E. (2018). When job ads turn you down: How requirements in job ads may stop instead of attract highly qualified women. *Sex Roles, 79*, 464–475; Sylva, H., & Mol, S. T. (2009). E-recruitment: A study into applicant perceptions of an online application system. *International Journal of Selection and Assessment, 17*, 311–323.

20. Boswell, W. R., Zimmerman, R. D., & Swider, B. W. (2012). Employee job search: Toward an understanding of search content and search objectives. *Journal of Management, 38*, 129–163; Kanfer, R., Wanberg, C. R., & Kantrowitz, T. M. (2001). Job

search and employment: A personality-motivational analysis and meta-analytic review. *Journal of Applied Psychology, 86*, 837–855.

21. Huffman, M. L., & Torres, L. (2001). Job search methods: Consequences for gender-based earnings inequality. *Journal of Vocational Behavior, 58*, 127–141; Drentea, P. (1998). Consequences of women's formal and informal job search methods for employment in female-dominated jobs. *Gender & Society, 12*, 321–338; Leicht, K. T., & Marx, J. (1997). The consequences of informal job finding for men and women. *Academy of Management Journal, 40*, 967–987.

22. Woehler, M. L., Cullen-Lester, K. L., Porter, C. M., & Frear, K. A. (2021). Whether, how, and why networks influence men's and women's career success: Review and research agenda. *Journal of Management, 47*, 201–236; Son, J., & Lin, N. (2012). Network diversity, contact diversity, and status attainment. *Social Networks, 34*, 601–613; McDonald, S., Lin, N., & Ao, D. (2009). Networks of opportunity: Gender, race, and job leads. *Social Problems, 56*, 385–402; Petersen, T., Saporta, I., & Seidel, M-D. L. (2000). Offering a job: Meritocracy and social networks. *American Journal of Sociology, 106*, 763–816.

23. Aten, K., DiRenzo, M., & Shatnawi, D. (2017). Gender and professional e-networks: Implications of gender heterophily on job search facilitation and outcomes. *Computers in Human Behavior, 72*, 470–478.

24. Obukhova, E., & Kleinbaum, A. M. (2022). Scouting and schmoozing: A gender difference in networking during job search. *Academy of Management Discoveries, 8*, 203–223.

25. He, J. C., & Kang, S. K. (2021). Covering in cover letters: Gender and self-presentation in job applications. *Academy of Management Journal, 64*, 1097–1126.

26. Dreher, G. F., & Cox, T. H., Jr. (2000). Labor market mobility and cash compensation: The moderating effects of race and gender. *Academy of Management Journal, 43*, 890–900; Keith, K., & McWilliams, A. (1999). The returns to mobility and job search by gender. *Industrial and Labor Relations Review, 52*, 460–477; Lyness, K. S., & Judiesch, M. K. (1999). Are women more likely to be hired or promoted into management positions? *Journal of Vocational Behavior, 54*, 158–173; Brett, J. M., & Stroh, L. K. (1997). Jumping ship: Who benefits from an external labor market career strategy? *Journal of Applied Psychology, 82*, 331–341.

27. Schweitzer, L., Lyons, S., Kuron, L. K. J., & Ng, E. S. W. (2014). The gender gap in pre-career salary expectations: A test of five explanations. *Career Development International, 19*, 404–425; Jackson, L. A., Gardner, P. D., & Sullivan, L. A. (1992). Explaining gender differences in self-pay expectations: Social comparison standards and perceptions of fair pay. *Journal of Applied Psychology, 77*, 631–663; Summers, T. P., Sightler, K. W., & Stahl, M. J. (1992). Gender differences in preference for over-reward and tolerance for over-reward. *Journal of Social Behavior and Personality, 7*, 177–188; Major, B., & Konar, E. (1984). An investigation of sex differences in pay expectations and their possible causes. *Academy of Management Journal, 27*, 777–792.

28. Säve-Söderbergh, J. (2019). Gender gaps in salary negotiations: Salary requests and starting salaries in the field. *Journal of Economic Behavior and Organization, 161*, 35–51; Mazei, J., Hüffmeier, J., Freund, P. A., Stuhlmacher, A. F., Bilke, L., & Hertel, G. (2015). A meta-analysis on gender differences in negotiation outcomes and their moderators. *Psychological Bulletin, 141*, 85–104; Kennedy, J. A., & Kray, L. J. (2015). A pawn in someone else's game? The cognitive, motivational, and paradigmatic barriers to women's excelling in negotiation. *Research in Organizational Behavior, 35*,

3–28; Kulik, C. T., & Olekalns, M. (2012). Negotiating the gender divide: Lessons from the negotiation and organizational behavior literatures. *Journal of Management, 38*, 1387–1415.

29. Lee, S. Y., Pitesa, M., Thau, S., & Pillutla, M. M. (2015). Discrimination in selection decisions: Integrating stereotype fit and interdependence theories. *Academy of Management Journal, 58*, 789–812; Graves, L. M. (1993). Sources of individual differences in interviewer effectiveness: A model and implications for future research. *Journal of Organizational Behavior, 14*, 349–370.

30. Dutz, R., Hubner, S., & Peus, C. (2022). When agency "fits" regardless of gender: Perceptions of applicant fit when job and organization signal male stereotypes. *Personnel Psychology, 75*, 441–483; Heilman, M. E., Manzi, F., & Braun, S. (2015). Presumed incompetent: Perceived lack of fit and gender bias in recruitment and selection. In A. M. Broadbridge & S. L. Fielden (Eds.), *Handbook of gendered careers in management: Getting in, getting on, getting out* (pp. 90–105). Elgar; Perry, E. L., Davis-Blake, A., & Kulik, C. T. (1994). Explaining gender-based selection decisions: A synthesis of contextual and cognitive approaches. *Academy of Management Review, 19*, 786–820; Heilman, M. E. (1983). Sex bias in work settings: The lack of fit model. In L. L. Cummings & B. M. Staw (Eds.), *Research in organizational behavior* (Vol. 5, pp. 269–298). JAI.

31. Koch, A. J., D'Mello, S. D., & Sackett, P. R. (2015). A meta-analysis of gender stereotypes and bias in experimental simulations of employment decision making. *Journal of Applied Psychology, 100*, 128–161; Davison, H. K, & Burke, M. J. (2000). Sex discrimination in simulated employment contexts: A meta-analytic investigation. *Journal of Vocational Behavior, 56*, 225–248; Atwater, L. E., & Van Fleet, D. D. (1997). Another ceiling? Can males compete for traditionally female jobs? *Journal of Management, 23*, 603–626; Perry, E. L., Davis-Blake, A., & Kulik, C. T. (1994). Explaining gender-based selection decisions: A synthesis of contextual and cognitive approaches. *Academy of Management Review, 19*, 786–820.

32. Koch, A. J., D'Mello, S. D., & Sackett, P. R. (2015). A meta-analysis of gender stereotypes and bias in experimental simulations of employment decision making. *Journal of Applied Psychology, 100*, 128–161; Davison, H. K, & Burke, M. J. (2000). Sex discrimination in simulated employment contexts: A meta-analytic investigation. *Journal of Vocational Behavior, 56*, 225–248; Atwater, L. E., & Van Fleet, D. D. (1997). Another ceiling? Can males compete for traditionally female jobs? *Journal of Management, 23*, 603–626; Perry, E. L., Davis-Blake, A., & Kulik, C. T. (1994). Explaining gender-based selection decisions: A synthesis of contextual and cognitive approaches. *Academy of Management Review, 19*, 786–820.

33. U.S. Department of Labor, Bureau of Labor Statistics (2022). *Labor force statistics from the Current Population Survey*, Table 11. Retrieved November 4, 2022, from https://www.bls.gov/cps/tables.htm; Moroney, R. (2007, October 24). Noted female chefs say bias smolders inside the kitchen. *Wall Street Journal*, p. B13; *New York Magazine.* (2007, October 29). A woman's place? Retrieved October 25, 2007, from https://nymag.com/magazine/toc/2007-10-29.html

34. Hall, E. V., Hall, A. V., Galinsky, A. D., & Phillips, K. W. (2019). MOSAIC: A model of stereotyping through associated and intersectional categories. *Academy of Management Review, 44*, 643–672; Rosette, A. S., Ponce de Leon, R., Koval, C. Z., & Harrison, D. A. (2018). Intersectionality: Connecting experiences of gender with race at work. *Research in Organizational Behavior, 38*, 1–22; Hall, E. V., Galinsky, A. D., & Phillips, K. W. (2015). Gender profiling: A gendered race perspective on person-position fit.

Personality and Social Psychology Bulletin, 41, 853–868; Koenig, A. M., & Eagly, A. H. (2014). Evidence for the social role theory of stereotype content: Observations of groups' roles shape stereotypes. *Journal of Personality and Social Psychology, 107,* 371–392.

35. Rosette, A. S., Ponce de Leon, R., Koval, C. Z., & Harrison, D. A. (2018). Intersectionality: Connecting experiences of gender with race at work. *Research in Organizational Behavior, 38,* 1–22; Koenig, A. M., & Eagly, A. H. (2014). Evidence for the social role theory of stereotype content: Observations of groups' roles shape stereotypes. *Journal of Personality and Social Psychology, 107,* 371–392; Ridgeway, C. L., & Kricheli-Katz, T. (2013). Intersecting cultural beliefs in social relations: Gender, race, and class binds and freedoms. *Gender & Society, 27,* 294–318; Ridgeway, C. L., Backor, K., Li, Y. E., Tinkler, J. E., & Erickson, K. G. (2009). How easily does a social difference become a status distinction? Gender matters. *American Sociological Review, 74,* 44–62.

36. Campbell, E. L., & Hahl, O. (2022). He's overqualified, she's highly committed: Qualification signals and gendered assumptions about job candidate commitment. *Organizational Science, 33,* 2451–2476.

37. Hernández, J. C. (2022, November 22). In a "sea change," women of the Philharmonic now outnumber the men. *New York Times.* Retrieved November 22, 2022, from https://www.nytimes.com/2022/11/22/arts/music/women-new-york-philharmonic.html; Goldin, C., & Rouse, C. (2000). Orchestrating impartiality: The impact of blind auditions on female musicians. *American Economic Review, 90,* 715–741.

38. Sergeant, D. C., & Himonides, E. (2019). Orchestrated sex: The representation of male and female musicians in world-class symphony orchestras. *Frontiers in Psychology, 10,* 1760; Fasang, A. (2006). Recruitment in symphony orchestras: Testing a gender neutral recruitment process. *Work, Employment and Society, 20,* 801–809.

39. Latu, I. M., Mast, M. S., & Stewart, T. L. (2015). Gender biases in (inter) action: The role of interviewers' and applicants' implicit and explicit stereotypes in predicting women's job interview outcomes. *Psychology of Women Quarterly, 39,* 539–552; Ridgeway, C. L., & Kricheli-Katz, T. (2013). Intersecting cultural beliefs in social relations: Gender, race, and class binds and freedoms. *Gender & Society, 27,* 294–318; Gallois, C., Callan, V. J., & Palmer, J. M. (1992). The influence of applicant communication style and interviewer characteristics on hiring decisions. *Journal of Applied Social Psychology, 22,* 1041–1060.

40. Friedman, E., & Efrat-Treister, D. (2023). Gender bias in STEM hiring: Implicit in-group gender favoritism among men managers. *Gender & Society, 37,* 32–64.

41. Kazmi, M. A., Spitzmueller, C., Yu, J., Madera, J. M., Tsao, A. S., Dawson, J. F., & Pavlidis, I. (2022). Search committee diversity and applicant pool representation of women and underrepresented minorities: A quasi-experimental field study. *Journal of Applied Psychology, 107,* 1414–1427.

42. McCarthy, J. M., Van Iddekinge, C. H., & Campion, M. A. (2010). Are highly structured job interviews resistant to demographic similarity effects. *Personnel Psychology, 63,* 325–359; Gorman, E. H. (2005). Gender stereotypes, same-gender preferences, and organizational variation in the hiring of women: Evidence from law firms. *American Sociological Review, 70,* 702–728; Graves, L. M., & Powell, G. N. (1996). Sex similarity, quality of the employment interview and recruiters' evaluation of actual applicants. *Journal of Occupational and Organizational Psychology, 69,* 243–261; Graves, L. M., & Powell, G. N. (1995). The effect of sex similarity on recruiters' evaluations of actual

applicants: A test of the similarity-attraction paradigm. *Personnel Psychology, 48*, 85–98.

43. U.S. Department of Labor, Bureau of Labor Statistics (2022). *Labor force statistics from the Current Population Survey*, Table 11. Retrieved November 4, 2022, from https://www.bls.gov/cps/tables.htm; Smith, G., & Rustagi, I. (2021, March 31). When good algorithms go sexist: Why and how to advance AI gender equity. *Stanford Social Innovation Review*. Retrieved January 2, 2023, from https://ssir.org/articles/entry/when_good_algorithms_go_sexist_why_and_how_to_advance_ai_gender_equity; Smith, G., & Rustagi, I. (2020). *Mitigating bias in artificial intelligence: An equity fluent leadership playbook*. Berkeley Haas Center for Equity, Gender, and Leadership. Retrieved January 2, 2023, from https://haas.berkeley.edu/wp-content/uploads/UCB_Playbook_R10_V2_spreads2.pdf

44. Horwitz, J. (2021, April 9). Facebook algorithm shows gender bias in job ads, study finds. *Wall Street Journal*. Retrieved April 14, 2021, from https://www.wsj.com/articles/facebook-shows-men-and-women-different-job-ads-study-finds-11617969600; Imana, B., Korolova, A., & Heidemann, J. (2021). Auditing for discrimination in algorithms delivering job ads. *Proceedings of the Web Conference 2021*, 3767–3778. Lambrecht, A., & Tucker, C. E. (2019). Algorithmic bias? An empirical study of apparent gender-based discrimination in the display of STEM career ads. *Management Science, 65*, 2966–2981; Miller, C. C. (2015, July 9). When algorithms discriminate. *New York Times*. Retrieved July 18, 2017, from https://www.nytimes.com/2015/07/10/upshot/when-algorithms-discriminate.html#:~:text=The%20online%20world%20is%20shaped,%2C%20housing%2C%20education%20and%20policing

45. Hunkenschroer, A. L., & Luetge, C. (2022). Ethics of AI-enabled recruiting and selection: A review and research agenda. *Journal of Business Ethics, 178*, 977–1007; Meyer, D. (2018, October 10). Amazon reportedly killed an AI recruitment system because it couldn't stop the tool from discriminating against women. *Fortune*. Retrieved February 27, 2023, from https://fortune.com/2018/10/10/amazon-ai-recruitment-bias-women-sexist/

46. Tu, M-H., Gilbert, E. K., & Bono, J. E. (2022). Is beauty more than skin deep? Attractiveness, power, and nonverbal presence in evaluations of hirability. *Personnel Psychology, 75*, 119–146; Nault, K. A., Pitesa, M., & Thau, S. (2020). The attractiveness advantage at work: A cross-disciplinary integrative review. *Academy of Management Annals, 14*, 1103–1139; Lee, S., Pitesa, M., Pillutla, M., & Thau, S. (2015). When beauty helps and when it hurts: An organizational context model of attractiveness discrimination in selection decisions. *Organizational Behavior and Human Decision Processes, 128*, 15–28; Behrend, T., Toaddy, S., Thompson, L. F., & Sharek, D. J. (2012). The effects of avatar appearance on interview ratings in virtual employment interviews. *Computers in Human Behavior, 28*, 2128–2133; Eagly, A. H., Ashmore, R. D., Makhijani, M. G., & Longo, L. C. (1991). What is beautiful is good, but . . . A meta-analytic review of research on the physical attractiveness stereotype. *Psychological Bulletin, 110*, 109–128.

47. Kaufmann, M. C., Krings, F., & Sczesny, S. (2016). Looking too old? How an older age appearance reduces chances of being hired. *British Journal of Management, 27*, 727–739; Luxen, M. F., & Van de Vijver, F. J. R. (2006). Facial attractiveness, sexual selection, and personnel selection: When evolved preferences matter. *Journal of Organizational Behavior, 27*, 241–255.

48. De Pater, I. E., Judge, T. A., & Scott, B. A. (2014). Age, gender, and compensation: A study of Hollywood movie stars. *Journal of Management Inquiry, 23*, 407–420, quote on p. 410.

49. Johnson, M. A., & Schminke, M. (2020). Thinking big: An integrative conceptual review of the workplace consequences of obesity and a theoretical extension of the processes that create them. *Journal of Applied Psychology, 105*, 671–692; Rudolph, C. W., Wells, C. L., Weller, M. D., & Baltes, B. B. (2009). A meta-analysis of empirical studies of weight-based bias in the workplace. *Journal of Vocational Behavior, 74*, 1–10; Roehling, M. V., Roehling, P. V., & Odland, L. M. (2008). Investigating the validity of stereotypes about overweight employees: The relationship between body weight and normal personality traits. *Group & Organization Management, 33*, 392–424.

50. Hackney, K. J., Daniels, S. R., Paustian-Underdahl, S. C., Perrewé, P. L., Mandeville, A., & Eaton, A. A. (2021). Examining the effects of perceived pregnancy discrimination on mother and baby health. *Journal of Applied Psychology, 106*, 774–783; Jones, K. P. (2017). To tell or not to tell? Examining the role of discrimination in the pregnancy disclosure process at work. *Journal of Occupational Health Psychology, 22*, 239–250; Gatrell, C. J. (2013). Maternal body work: How women managers and professionals negotiate pregnancy and new motherhood at work. *Human Relations, 66*, 621–644; Cunningham, J., & Macan, T. (2007). Effects of applicant pregnancy on hiring decisions and interview ratings. *Sex Roles, 57*, 497–508.

51. Bolino, M., Long, D., & Turnley, W. (2016). Impression management in organizations: Critical questions, answers, and areas for future research. *Annual Review of Organizational Psychology and Organizational Behavior, 3*, 377–406; Chen, C-C., & Lin, M-M. (2014). The effect of applicant impression management tactics on hiring recommendations: Cognitive and affective processes. *Applied Psychology: An International Review, 63*, 698–724.

52. Powell, G. N. (2011). Consulting analyst wanted. In G. N. Powell, *Managing a diverse workforce: Learning activities* (3rd ed., pp. 25–31). SAGE.

53. Gaucher, D., Friesen, J., & Kay, A. C. (2011). Evidence that gendered wording in job advertisements exists and sustains gender inequality. *Journal of Personality and Social Psychology, 101*, 109–128.

54. Hunkenschroer, A. L., & Luetge, C. (2022). Ethics of AI-enabled recruiting and selection: A review and research agenda. *Journal of Business Ethics, 178*, 977–1007; Chamorro-Premuzic, T., Polli, F., & Dattner, B. (2019, November 21). Building ethical AI for talent management. *Harvard Business Review*. Retrieved February 9, 2023, from https://hbr.org/2019/11/building-ethical-ai-for-talent-management

55. Levashina, J., Hartwell, C. J., Morgeson, F. P., & Campion, M. A. (2014). The structured employment interview: Narrative and quantitative review of the research literature. *Personnel Psychology, 67*, 241–293; McCarthy, J. M., Van Iddekinge, C. H., & Campion, M. A. (2010). Are highly structured job interviews resistant to demographic similarity effects. *Personnel Psychology, 63*, 325–359; Williamson, L. G., Campion, J. E., Malos, S. B., Roehling, M. B., & Campion, M. A. (1997). Employment interview on trial: Linking interview structure with litigation outcomes. *Journal of Applied Psychology, 82*, 900–912.

56. Hunkenschroer, A. L., & Luetge, C. (2022). Ethics of AI-enabled recruiting and selection: A review and research agenda. *Journal of Business Ethics, 178*, 977–1007; Chamorro-Premuzic, T., Polli, F., & Dattner, B. (2019, November 21). Building ethical AI for talent management. *Harvard Business Review*. Retrieved February 9, 2023,

from https://hbr.org/2019/11/building-ethical-ai-for-talent-management; Cox, T. H, Jr., & Blake, S. (1991). Managing cultural diversity: Implications for organizational competitiveness. *Academy of Management Executive, 5*(3), 45–56; Graves, L. M. (1989). College recruitment: Removing personal biases from selection decisions. *Personnel, 66*(3), 48–52.

CHAPTER 5

1. Powell, G. N. (2020). Work–family lockdown: Implications for a post-pandemic research agenda. *Gender in Management: An International Review, 35*, 639–646; Katzenbach, J. R., & Smith, D. K. (2015). *The wisdom of teams: Creating the high-performance organization* (reprint edition). Harvard Business Review Press.
2. Bilefsky, D. (2015, June 11). Women respond to Nobel laureate's "trouble with girls." *New York Times.* Retrieved June 13, 2015, from https://www.nytimes.com/2015/06/12/world/europe/tim-hunt-nobel-laureate-resigns-sexist-women-female-scientists.html
3. Elsbach, K. D., & Bechky, B. A. (2018). How observers assess women who cry in professional work contexts. *Academy of Management Discoveries, 4*, 127–154; Motro, D., & Ellis, A. P. J. (2017). Boys, don't cry: Gender and reactions to negative performance feedback. *Journal of Applied Psychology, 102*, 227–235; Fischer, A. H., Eagly, A. H., & Oosterwijk, S. (2013). The meaning of tears: Which sex seems emotional depends on the social context. *European Journal of Social Psychology, 43*, 505–515.
4. Graves, L. M., & Powell, G. N. (2007). Sex, sex similarity and sex diversity effects in teams: The importance of situational factors. In D. Bilimoria & S. K. Piderit (Eds.), *Handbook of women in business and management* (pp. 217–231). Edward Elgar.
5. Balliet, D., Li, N. P., Macfarlan, S. J., & Van Vugt, M. (2011). Sex differences in cooperation: A meta-analytic review of social dilemmas. *Psychological Bulletin, 137*, 881–909; Carli, L. L., & Bukatko, D. (2000). Gender, communication, and social influence: A developmental perspective. In T. Eckes & H. M. Trautner (Eds.), *The developmental social psychology of gender* (pp. 295–331). Erlbaum.
6. Briggs, C. Q., Gardner, D. M., & Ryan, A. M. (in press). Competence-questioning communication and gender: Exploring mansplaining, ignoring, and interruption behaviors. *Journal of Business and Psychology*; Carli, L. L. (2010). Gender and group behavior. In J. C. Chrisler & D. R. McCreary (Eds.), *Handbook of gender research in psychology* (Vol. 2, pp. 337–358). Springer Science + Business Media.
7. Meyer, B., van Dijk, H., & van Engen, M. (2022). (Mitigating) the self-fulfillment of gender stereotypes in teams: The interplay of competence attributions, behavioral dominance, individual performance, and diversity beliefs. *Journal of Applied Psychology, 107*, 1907–1925; Foschi, M. (2000). Double standards for competence: Theory and research. *Annual Review of Sociology, 26*, 21–42; Foschi, M. (1996). Double standards in the evaluation of men and women. *Social Psychology Quarterly, 59*, 237–254.
8. Sarsons, H. (2017). Recognition for group work: Gender differences in academia. *American Economic Review, 107*, 141–145; Wolfers, J. (2016, January 8). When teamwork doesn't work for women. *New York Times.* Retrieved January 11, 2016, from https://www.nytimes.com/2016/01/10/upshot/when-teamwork-doesnt-work-for-women.html

9. Ridgeway, C. L., Korn, R. M., & Williams, J. C. (2022). Documenting the routine burden of devalued difference in the professional workplace. *Gender and Society, 36*, 627–651.

10. Graves, L. M., & Elsass, P. M. (2005). Sex and sex dissimilarity effects in ongoing teams: Some surprising findings. *Human Relations, 58*, 191–221.

11. Carli, L. L. (2017). Social influence and gender. In S. G. Harkins, K. D. Williams, & J. M. Burger (Eds.), *The Oxford handbook of social influence* (pp. 33–51). Oxford University Press; Smith, A. N., Watkins, M. B., Burke, M. J., Christian, M. S., Smith. C. E., Hall, A., & Simms, S. (2013). Gendered influence: A gender role perspective on the use and effectiveness of influence tactics. *Journal of Management, 39*, 1156–1183; Propp, K. M. (1995). An experimental examination of biological sex as a status cue in decision-making groups and its influence on information use. *Small Group Research, 26*, 451–457.

12. Badura, K. L., Grijalva, E., Newman, D. A., Yan, T. T., & Jeon, G. (2018). Gender and leadership emergence: A meta-analysis and explanatory model. *Personnel Psychology, 71*, 335–367; Ritter, B. A., & Yoder, J. D. (2004). Gender differences in leader emergence persist even for dominant women: An updated confirmation of role congruity theory. *Psychology of Women Quarterly, 28*, 187–193; Carli, L. L., & Eagly, A. H. (1999). Gender effects on social influence and emergent leadership. In G. N. Powell (Ed.), *Handbook of gender and work* (pp. 203–222). SAGE; Eagly, A. H., & Karau, S. J. (1991). Gender and emergence of leaders: A meta-analysis. *Journal of Personality and Social Psychology, 60*, 685–710.

13. Lim, J. Y-K. (2019). Navigating the pathway to leader emergence in self-managed work groups over time: Should I self-promote and try to emerge initially as a leader? *Sex Roles, 80*, 489–502; Rudman, L. A. (1998). Self-promotion as a risk factor for women: The costs and benefits of counterstereotypical impression management. *Journal of Personality and Social Psychology, 74*, 629–645; Carli, L. L., LaFleur, S. J., & Loeber, C. C. (1995). Nonverbal behavior, gender, and influence. *Journal of Personality and Social Psychology, 68*, 1030–1041.

14. Jang, S., Allen, T. D., & Regina, J. (2021). Office housework, burnout, and promotion: Does gender matter? *Journal of Business and Psychology, 36*, 793–805; Babcock, L., Recalde, M. P., & Vesterlund, L. (2018, July 16). Why women volunteer for tasks that don't lead to promotions. *Harvard Business Review.* Retrieved January 12, 2023, from https://hbr.org/2018/07/why-women-volunteer-for-tasks-that-dont-lead-to-promotions; Babcock, L., Recalde, M. P., Vesterlund, L., & Weingart, L. (2017). Gender differences in accepting and receiving requests for tasks with low promotability. *American Economic Review, 107*, 714–747.

15. Tolbert, P. S., Graham, M. E., & Andrews, A. O. (1999). Group gender composition and work group relations: Theories, evidence, and issues. In G. N. Powell (Ed.), *Handbook of gender and work* (pp. 179–202). SAGE.

16. Kanter, R. M. (1977a). *Men and women of the corporation.* Basic; Kanter, R. M. (1977b). Some effects of group proportions on group life: Skewed sex ratios and responses to token women. *American Journal of Sociology, 82*, 965–990.

17. Watkins, M. B., Simmons, A., & Umphress, E. (2019). It's not black and white: Toward a contingency perspective on the consequences of being a token. *Academy of Management Perspectives, 33*, 334–365; King, E. B., Hebl, M. R., George, J. M., & Matusik, S. F. (2010). Understanding tokenism: Antecedents and consequences of a psychological climate of gender inequity. *Journal of Management, 36*, 482–510; Hogue, M. B., &

Yoder, J. D. (2006). Tokenism theory: What happens when few women work with many men. In M. F. Karsten (Ed.), *Gender, race, and ethnicity in the workplace: Issues and challenges for today's organizations* (Vol. 2, pp. 199–216). Praeger.

18. Reinwald, M., & Kunze F. (2020). Being different, being absent? A dynamic perspective on demographic dissimilarity and absenteeism in blue collar teams. *Academy of Management Journal, 63,* 660–684; Veldman, J., Meeussen, L., Van Laar, C., & Phalet, K. (2017). Women (do not) belong here: Gender-work identity conflict among female police officers. *Frontiers in Psychology, 8,* 130; Stichman, A. J., Hassell, K. D., & Archbold, C. A. (2010). Strength in numbers? A test of Kanter's theory of tokenism. *Journal of Criminal Justice, 38,* 633–639; Ott, E. M. (1989). Effects of the male-female ratio at work: Policewomen and male nurses. *Psychology of Women Quarterly, 13,* 41–57.

19. Watkins, M. B., Simmons, A., & Umphress, E. (2019). It's not black and white: Toward a contingency perspective on the consequences of being a token. *Academy of Management Perspectives, 33,* 334–365; Wingfield, A. H. (2009). Racializing the glass escalator: Reconsidering men's experiences with women's work. *Gender & Society, 23,* 5–26.

20. Perez, A. L. U., & Strizhko, T. V. (2018). Minority representation, tokenism, and well-being in army units. *Military Psychology, 30,* 449–463; Chatman, J. A., Polzer, J. T., Barsade, S. G., & Neale, M. A. (1998). Being different yet feeling similar: The influence of demographic composition and organizational culture on work processes and outcomes. *Administrative Science Quarterly, 43,* 749–780.

21. Wood, W. (1987). Meta-analytic review of sex differences in group performance. *Psychological Bulletin, 102,* 53–71.

22. Minbaeva, D., Fitzsimmons, S., & Brewster, C. (2021). Beyond the double-edged sword of cultural diversity in teams: Progress, critique, and next steps. *Journal of International Business Studies, 52,* 45–55; Srikanth, K., Harvey, S., & Peterson, R. (2016). A dynamic perspective on diverse teams: Moving from the dual-process model to a dynamic coordination-based model of diverse team performance. *Academy of Management Annals, 10,* 453–493; Milliken, F. J., & Martins, L. L. (1996). Searching for common threads: Understanding the multiple effects of diversity on occupational groups. *Academy of Management Review, 21,* 402–433.

23. Berle, E. C., Kavajecz, K., & Onozaka, Y. (in press). Effect of gender composition of committees. *Human Relations*; Yang, Y., Tian, T. Y., Woodruff, T. K., Jones, B. F., & Uzzi, B. (2022). Gender-diverse teams produce more novel and higher-impact scientific ideas. *Proceedings of the National Academy of Sciences, 119,* e2200841119.

24. Kelemen, T. K., Matthews, S. H., Zhang, X., Bradley, B. H., & Liu, H. (2020). When does gender diversity enhance team performance? The dual need for visionary leadership and team tenure. *Journal of Applied Social Psychology, 50,* 501–511; Eagly, A. H. (2016). When passionate advocates meet research on diversity, does the honest broker stand a chance? *Journal of Social Issues, 72,* 199–222; Bell, S. T., Villado, A. J., Lukasik, M. A., Belau, L., & Briggs, A. L. (2011). Getting specific about demographic diversity variable and team performance relationships: A meta-analysis. *Journal of Management, 37,* 709–743; Horwitz, S. K., & Horwitz, I. B. (2007). The effects of team diversity on team outcomes: A meta-analytic review of team demography. *Journal of Management, 33,* 987–1015.

25. Kravitz, D. A. (2005). Diversity in teams: A two-edged sword requires careful handling. *Psychological Science in the Public Interest, 6,* i–ii; Milliken, F. J., & Martins, L. L. (1996). Searching for common threads: Understanding the multiple effects of diversity on occupational groups. *Academy of Management Review, 21,* 402–433.

26. Schölmerich, F., Schermuly, C. C., & Deller, J. (2017). To believe or not to believe? The joint impact of faultlines and pro-diversity beliefs on diplomats' performance. *Human Performance, 30*, 99–115; Chung, Y., Liao, H., Jackson, S. E., Subramony, M., Colakoglu, S., & Jiang, Y. (2015). Cracking but not breaking: Joint effects of faultline strength and diversity climate on loyal behavior. *Academy of Management Journal, 58*, 1495–1515; Thatcher, S. M. B., & Patel, P. C. (2012). Group faultlines: A review, integration, and guide to future research. *Journal of Management, 38*, 969–1009; Lau, D. C., & Murnighan, J. K. (1998). Demographic diversity and faultlines: The compositional dynamics of organizational groups. *Academy of Management Review, 23*, 325–340.

27. Reinwald, M., & Kunze F. (2020). Being different, being absent? A dynamic perspective on demographic dissimilarity and absenteeism in blue collar teams. *Academy of Management Journal, 63*, 660–684; Kelemen, T. K., Matthews, S. H., Zhang, X., Bradley, B. H., & Liu, H. (2020). When does gender diversity enhance team performance? The dual need for visionary leadership and team tenure. *Journal of Applied Social Psychology, 50*, 501–511; Schippers, M. C., Den Hartog, D. N., Koopman, P. L., & Wienk, J. A. (2003). Diversity and team outcomes: The moderating effects of outcome interdependence and group longevity and the mediating effect of reflexivity. *Journal of Organizational Behavior, 24*, 779–802; Harrison, D. A., Price, K. H., & Bell, M. P. (1998). Beyond relational demography: Time and the effects of surface- and deep-level diversity on work group cohesion. *Academy of Management Journal, 41*, 96–107.

28. Tasheva, S., & Hillman, A. J. (2019). Integrating diversity at different levels: Multi-level human capital, social capital, and demographic diversity and their implications for team effectiveness. *Academy of Management Review, 44*, 746–765; Schippers, M. C., Den Hartog, D. N., Koopman, P. L., & Wienk, J. A. (2003). Diversity and team outcomes: The moderating effects of outcome interdependence and group longevity and the mediating effect of reflexivity. *Journal of Organizational Behavior, 24*, 779–802; Karakowsky, L., & Siegel, J. P. (1999). The effects of proportional representation and gender orientation of the task on emergent leadership behavior in mixed-sex groups. *Journal of Applied Psychology, 84*, 620–631.

29. Joshi, A., & Roh, H. (2009). The role of context in work team diversity research: A meta-analytic review. *Academy of Management Journal, 52*, 599–627; Elvira, M. M., & Cohen, L. E. (2001). Location matters: A cross-level analysis of the effects of organizational sex composition on turnover. *Academy of Management Journal, 44*, 591–605; Milliken, F. J., & Martins, L. L. (1996). Searching for common threads: Understanding the multiple effects of diversity on occupational groups. *Academy of Management Review, 21*, 402–433.

30. Nielsen, S. (2010). Top management team diversity: A review of theories and methodologies. *International Journal of Management Reviews, 12*, 301–316; Burke, R. J., & McKeen, C. A. (1996). Do women at the top make a difference? Gender proportions and the experiences of managerial and professional women. *Human Relations, 49*, 1093–1104; Ely, R. J. (1995). The power in demography: Women's social constructions of gender identity at work. *Academy of Management Journal, 38*, 589–634; Ely, R. J. (1994). The effects of organizational demographics and social identity on relationships among professional women. *Administrative Science Quarterly, 39*, 203–238.

31. Perez, A. L. U., & Strizhko, T. V. (2018). Minority representation, tokenism, and well-being in army units. *Military Psychology, 30*, 449–463; Chatman, J. A., & Flynn, F. J. (2001). The influence of demographic heterogeneity on the emergence and

consequences of cooperative norms in work teams. *Academy of Management Journal, 44*, 956–974.

32. Nishii, L. H. (2013). The benefits of climate for inclusion for gender-diverse groups. *Academy of Management Journal, 56*, 1754–1774; Shore, L. M., Randel, A. E., Chung, B. G., Dean, M. A., Ehrhart, K. H., & Singh, G. (2011). Inclusion and diversity in work groups: A review and model for future research. *Journal of Management, 37*, 1262–1289; Chatman, J. A. (2010). Norms in mixed sex and mixed race work groups. *Academy of Management Annals, 4*, 447–484; Ely, R. J., & Thomas, D. A. (2001). Cultural diversity at work: The effects of diversity perspectives on work group processes and outcomes. *Administrative Science Quarterly, 46*, 229–273.

33. Villamor, I., Hill, N. S., Kossek, E. E., & Foley, K. O. (2023). Virtuality at work: A double-edged sword for women's career equality? *Academy of Management Annals, 17*, 113–140; Powell, G. N. (2020). Work–family lockdown: Implications for a post-pandemic research agenda. *Gender in Management: An International Review, 35*, 639–646; Raghuram, S., Hill, N. S., Gibbs, J. L., & Maruping, L. M. (2019). Virtual work: Bridging research clusters. *Academy of Management Annals, 13*, 308–341; Dulebohn, J. H., & Hoch, J. E. (2017). Virtual teams in organizations. *Human Resource Management Review, 27*, 569–574.

34. Gilson, L. L., Costa, P., O'Neill, T. A., & Maynard, M. T. (2021). Putting the "TEAM" back into virtual teams. *Organizational Dynamics, 50*, 1–10.

35. Martins, L. L., Gilson, L. L., & Maynard, M. T. (2004). Virtual teams: What do we know and where do we go from here? *Journal of Management, 30*, 805–835.

36. Marlow, S. L., Lacerenza, C. N., & Salas, E. (2017). Communication in virtual teams: A conceptual framework and research agenda. *Human Resource Management Review, 27*, 575–589; Lind, M. (1999). The gender impact of temporary virtual work groups. *IEEE Transactions on Professional Communication, 42*, 276–285; Savicki, V., Kelley, M., & Oesterreich, E. (1998). Effects of instructions on computer-mediated communication in single- or mixed-gender small task groups. *Computers in Human Behavior, 14*, 163–180; Bhappu, A. D., Griffith, T. L., & Northcraft, G. B. (1997). Media effects and communication bias in diverse groups. *Organizational Behavior and Human Decision Processes, 70*, 199–205.

37. Gupta, A. H. (2020, April 14). It's not just you: In online meetings, many women can't get a word in. *New York Times.* Retrieved May 9, 2020, from https://www.nytimes.com/2020/04/14/us/zoom-meetings-gender.html; Powell, G. N. (2020). Work–family lockdown: Implications for a post-pandemic research agenda. *Gender in Management: An International Review, 35*, 639–646.

38. Shockley, K. M., Gabriel, A. S., Robertson, D., Rosen, C. C., Chawla, N., Ganster, M. L., & Ezerins, M. E. (2021). The fatiguing effects of camera use in virtual meetings: A within-person field experiment. *Journal of Applied Psychology, 106*, 1137–1155; Fosslien, L., & Duffy, M. W. (2020, April 29). How to combat Zoom fatigue. *Harvard Business Review.* Retrieved January 20, 2023, from https://hbr.org/2020/04/how-to-combat-zoom-fatigue; Isser, M. (2020, January 2). The grooming gap: What "looking the part" costs women. *In These Times.* Retrieved January 18, 2023, from https://inthesetimes.com/article/grooming-gap-women-economics-wage-gender-sexism-make-up-styling-dress-code

39. Maynard, M. T., & Gilson, L. L. (2021). Getting to know you: The importance of familiarity in virtual teams. *Organizational Dynamics, 50*, 1–6; Graves, L. M., & Karabayeva,

A. (2020). Managing virtual workers: Strategies for success. *IEEE Engineering Management Review, 48*, 166–172.

40. Shockley, K. M., Gabriel, A. S., Robertson, D., Rosen, C. C., Chawla, N., Ganster, M. L., & Ezerins, M. E. (2021). The fatiguing effects of camera use in virtual meetings: A within-person field experiment. *Journal of Applied Psychology, 106*, 1137–1155; Leroy, S., Schmidt, A. M., & Madjar, N. (2021). Working from home during COVID-19: A study of the interruption landscape. *Journal of Applied Psychology, 106*, 1448–1465.

41. Katzenbach, J. R., & Smith, D. K. (2015). *The wisdom of teams: Creating the high-performance organization* (reprint edition). Harvard Business Review Press; Thompson, D. E., & Gooler, L. E. (1996). Capitalizing on the benefits of diversity through work teams. In E. E. Kossek & S. A. Lobel (Eds.), *Managing diversity: Human resource strategies for transforming the workplace* (pp. 392–437). Blackwell.

42. Schölmerich, F., Schermuly, C. C., & Deller, J. (2017). To believe or not to believe? The joint impact of faultlines and pro-diversity beliefs on diplomats' performance. *Human Performance, 30*, 99–115; Chung, Y., Liao, H., Jackson, S. E., Subramony, M., Colakoglu, S., & Jiang, Y. (2015). Cracking but not breaking: Joint effects of faultline strength and diversity climate on loyal behavior. *Academy of Management Journal, 58*, 1495–1515; Lau, D. C., & Murnighan, J. K. (1998). Demographic diversity and faultlines: The compositional dynamics of organizational groups. *Academy of Management Review, 23*, 325–340.

43. Balliet, D., Li, N. P., Macfarlan, S. J., & Van Vugt, M. (2011). Sex differences in cooperation: A meta-analytic review of social dilemmas. *Psychological Bulletin, 137*, 881–909; Goleman, D. (2004). What makes a leader? *Harvard Business Review, 82*(1), 82–91; Tsui, A. S., & Gutek, B. A. (1999). *Demographic differences in organizations: Current research and future directions.* Lexington Books; Northcraft, G. B., Polzer, J. T., Neale, M. A., & Kramer, R. M. (1995). Diversity, social identity, and performance: Emergent social dynamics in cross-functional teams. In S. E. Jackson & M. N. Ruderman (Eds.), *Diversity in work teams: Research paradigms for a changing workplace* (pp. 69–96). American Psychological Association.

44. Williams, J. C., & Mihaylo, S. (2019). How the best bosses interrupt bias on their teams: Strategies to foster equity and inclusion. *Harvard Business Review, 97*(6), 151–155; Williams, J. C., & Multhaup, M. (2018, March 5). For women and minorities to get ahead, managers must assign work fairly. *Harvard Business Review.* Retrieved August 1, 2022, from https://hbr.org/2018/03/for-women-and-minorities-to-get-ahead-managers-must-assign-work-fairly; Babcock, P., Bedard, K., Charness, G., Hartman, J., & Royer, H. (2015). Letting down the team? Social effects of team incentives. *Journal of the European Economic Association, 13*, 841–870; Tsui, A. S., & Gutek, B. A. (1999). *Demographic differences in organizations: Current research and future directions.* Lexington Books; Thompson, D. E., & Gooler, L. E. (1996). Capitalizing on the benefits of diversity through work teams. In E. E. Kossek & S. A. Lobel (Eds.), *Managing diversity: Human resource strategies for transforming the workplace* (pp. 392–437). Blackwell; Sessa, V. I., & Jackson, S. E. (1995). Diversity in decision-making teams: All differences are not created equal. In M. M. Chemers, S. Oskamp, & M. A. Costanzo (Eds.), *Diversity in organizations: New perspectives for a changing workplace* (pp. 133–156). SAGE.

45. Mannix, E., & Neale, M. A. (2005). What differences make a difference? The promise and reality of diverse teams in organizations. *Psychological Science in the Public Interest, 6*, 31–55; Kravitz, D. A. (2005). Diversity in teams: A two-edged sword requires

careful handling. *Psychological Science in the Public Interest, 6*, i–ii; Tsui, A. S., & Gutek, B. A. (1999). *Demographic differences in organizations: Current research and future directions.* Lexington Books; Thompson, D. E., & Gooler, L. E. (1996). Capitalizing on the benefits of diversity through work teams. In E. E. Kossek & S. A. Lobel (Eds.), *Managing diversity: Human resource strategies for transforming the workplace* (pp. 392–437). Blackwell.

46. Hahn, A., & Gawronski, B. (2019). Facing one's implicit biases: From awareness to acknowledgement. *Journal of Personality and Social Psychology: Interpersonal Relations and Group Processes, 116*, 769–794; Soll, J. B., Milkman, K. L., & Payne, J. W. (2015). A user's guide to debiasing. In G. Keren & G. Wu (Eds.), *Wiley Blackwell handbook of judgment and decision making* (Vol. 1, pp. 924–951). Wiley Blackwell; Bazerman, M. H., & Moore, D. A. (2013). *Judgment in managerial decision making* (8th ed.). Wiley; Larrick, R. P. (2004). Debiasing. In D. J. Koehler & N. Harvey (Eds.), *Blackwell handbook of judgment and decision making* (pp. 316–337). Blackwell; Tsui, A. S., & Gutek, B. A. (1999). *Demographic differences in organizations: Current research and future directions.* Lexington Books; Sessa, V. I., & Jackson, S. E. (1995). Diversity in decision-making teams: All differences are not created equal. In M. M. Chemers, S. Oskamp, & M. A. Costanzo (Eds.), *Diversity in organizations: New perspectives for a changing workplace* (pp. 133–156). SAGE.

47. Maynard, M. T., & Gilson, L. L. (2021). Getting to know you: The importance of familiarity in virtual teams. *Organizational Dynamics, 50*, 1–6; Graves, L. M., & Karabayeva, A. (2020). Managing virtual workers: Strategies for success. *IEEE Engineering Management Review, 48*, 166–172.

48. Santos, M., Luna, M., Reyes, D. L., Traylor, A., Lacerenza, C. N., & Salas, E. (2022). How to be an inclusive leader for gender-diverse teams. *Organizational Dynamics, 51*, 100914; Sandberg, S., & Grant, A. (2015, January 12). Speaking while female. *New York Times.* Retrieved February 3, 2015, from https://www.nytimes.com/2015/01/11/opinion/sunday/speaking-while-female.html; Mannix, E., & Neale, M. A. (2005). What differences make a difference? The promise and reality of diverse teams in organizations. *Psychological Science in the Public Interest, 6*, 31–55; Thompson, D. E., & Gooler, L. E. (1996). Capitalizing on the benefits of diversity through work teams. In E. E. Kossek & S. A. Lobel (Eds.), *Managing diversity: Human resource strategies for transforming the workplace* (pp. 392–437). Blackwell; Northcraft, G. B., Polzer, J. T., Neale, M. A., & Kramer, R. M. (1995). Diversity, social identity, and performance: Emergent social dynamics in cross-functional teams. In S. E. Jackson & M. N. Ruderman (Eds.), *Diversity in work teams: Research paradigms for a changing workplace* (pp. 69–96). American Psychological Association.

49. Cox, T., Jr., & Beale, R. L. (1997). *Developing competency to manage diversity: Readings, cases, & activities.* Berrett-Koehler, pp. 53–55.

50. Tsui, A. S., & Gutek, B. A. (1999). *Demographic differences in organizations: Current research and future directions.* Lexington Books.

51. Jang, S., Allen, T. D., & Regina, J. (2021). Office housework, burnout, and promotion: Does gender matter? *Journal of Business and Psychology, 36*, 793–805; Williams, J. C., & Multhaup, M. (2018, March 5). For women and minorities to get ahead, managers must assign work fairly. *Harvard Business Review.* Retrieved August 1, 2022, from https://hbr.org/2018/03/for-women-and-minorities-to-get-ahead-managers-must-assign-work-fairly; Babcock, L., Recalde, M. P., Vesterlund, L., & Weingart,

L. (2017). Gender differences in accepting and receiving requests for tasks with low promotability. *American Economic Review, 107,* 714–747.

52. Hogue, M. B., & Yoder, J. D. (2006). Tokenism theory: What happens when few women work with many men. In M. F. Karsten (Ed.), *Gender, race, and ethnicity in the workplace: Issues and challenges for today's organizations* (Vol. 2, pp. 199–216). Praeger; Kanter, R. M. (1977a). *Men and women of the corporation.* Basic; Kanter, R. M. (1977b). Some effects of group proportions on group life: Skewed sex ratios and responses to token women. *American Journal of Sociology, 82,* 965–990.

53. Tsui, A. S., & Gutek, B. A. (1999). *Demographic differences in organizations: Current research and future directions.* Lexington Books.

CHAPTER 6

1. Hofstede, G. (2001). *Culture's consequences: Comparing values, behaviors, institutions, and organizations across nations* (2nd ed.). SAGE, p. 215.

2. Room for debate: Do women make better bosses? (2009, August 2). *New York Times.* Retrieved August 2, 2009, from https://roomfordebate.blogs.nytimes.com/2009/08/02/do-women-make-better-bosses/

3. Saxe, J. G. (1872). The blind men and the elephant. In *The poems of John Godfrey Saxe.* Retrieved February 1, 2023, from https://en.wikisource.org/wiki/The_poems_of_John_Godfrey_Saxe/The_Blind_Men_and_the_Elephant

4. Powell, G. N. (2020). *Gender and leadership.* SAGE; Powell, G. N. (2012). Six ways of seeing the elephant: The intersection of sex, gender, and leadership. *Gender in Management: An International Journal, 27,* 119–141; Powell, G. N. (2011). The gender and leadership wars. *Organizational Dynamics, 40,* 1–9; Butterfield, D. A., & Grinnell, J. P. (1999). "Re-viewing" gender, leadership, and managerial behavior: Do three decades of research tell us anything? In G. N. Powell (Ed.), *Handbook of gender and work* (pp. 223–238). SAGE.

5. Riffkin, R. (2014, October 14). Americans still prefer a male boss to a female boss. *Gallup News Service.* Retrieved February 12, 2015, from https://news.gallup.com/poll/178484/americans-prefer-male-boss-female-boss.aspx; Newport, F., & Wilke, J. (2013, November 11). Americans still prefer a male boss. *Gallup News Service.* Retrieved November 20, 2017, from https://news.gallup.com/poll/165791/americans-prefer-male-boss.aspx; Newport, F. (2011, September 8). Americans still prefer male bosses; many have no preference. *Gallup News Service.* Retrieved November 20, 2017, from https://news.gallup.com/poll/149360/americans-prefer-male-bosses-no-preference.aspx; Carroll, J. (2006, September 1). Americans prefer male boss to a female boss. *Gallup News Service.* Retrieved May 6, 2009, from https://news.gallup.com/poll/24346/americans-prefer-male-boss-female-boss.aspx; Simmons, W. W. (2001, January 11). When it comes to choosing a boss, Americans still prefer men. *Gallup News Service.* Retrieved September 10, 2001, from https://news.gallup.com/poll/2128/when-comes-choosing-boss-americans-still-prefer-men.aspx

6. Brenan, M. (2017, November 16). Americans no longer prefer male boss to female boss. *Gallup News Service.* Retrieved November 20, 2017, from https://news.gallup.com/poll/222425/americans-no-longer-prefer-male-boss-female-boss.aspx

7. Powell, G. N., & Butterfield, D. A. (2015c). The preference to work for a man or a woman: A matter of sex and gender? *Journal of Vocational Behavior, 86*, 28–37.

8. Schein, V. E. (1975). Relationships between sex role stereotypes and requisite management characteristics among female managers. *Journal of Applied Psychology, 60*, 340–344; Schein, V. E. (1973). The relationship between sex role stereotypes and requisite management characteristics. *Journal of Applied Psychology, 57*, 95–100.

9. Schein, V. E. (2007). Women in management: Reflections and projections. *Women in Management Review, 22*, 6–18; Fullagar, C. J., Sumer, H. C., Sverke, M., & Slick, R. (2003). Managerial sex-role stereotyping: A cross cultural analysis. *International Journal of Cross Cultural Management, 3*, 93–107; Schein, V. E. (2001). A global look at psychological barriers to women's progress in management. *Journal of Social Issues, 57*, 675–688; Schein, V. E., Mueller, R., Lituchy, T., & Liu, J. (1996). Think manager—think male: A global phenomenon? *Journal of Organizational Behavior, 17*, 33–41.

10. Braun, S., Stegmann, S., Bark, A. S. H., Junker, N. M., & van Dick, R. (2017). Think manager—think male, think follower—think female: Gender bias in implicit followership theories. *Journal of Applied Social Psychology, 47*, 377–388.

11. Bem, S. L. (1974). The measurement of psychological androgyny. *Journal of Consulting and Clinical Psychology, 42*, 155–162.

12. Powell, G. N., & Butterfield, D. A. (1979). The "good manager": Masculine or androgynous? *Academy of Management Journal, 22*, 395–403, quote on p. 396.

13. Powell, G. N., & Butterfield, D. A. (2015a). Correspondence between self- and good-manager descriptions: Examining stability and change over four decades. *Journal of Management, 41*, 1745–1773; Powell, G. N., Butterfield, D. A., & Parent, J. D. (2002). Gender and managerial stereotypes: Have the times changed? *Journal of Management, 28*, 177–193; Powell, G. N., & Butterfield, D. A. (1989). The "good manager": Did androgyny fare better in the 1980s? *Group & Organization Studies, 14*, 216–233.

14. Koenig, A. M., Eagly, A. H., Mitchell, A. A., & Ristikari, T. (2011). Are leader stereotypes masculine? A meta-analysis of three research paradigms. *Psychological Bulletin, 137*, 616–642.

15. Powell, G. N., Butterfield, D. A., & Jiang, X. (2021). The "good manager" over five decades: Towards an androgynous profile? *Gender in Management: An International Journal, 36*, 714–730.

16. Feenstra, S., Stoker, J. I., Lammers, J., & Garretsen, H. (2023). Managerial stereotypes over time: The rise of feminine leadership. *Gender in Management: An International Journal, 38*, 770–783.

17. Powell, G. N., Butterfield, D. A., & Jiang, X. (2021). The "good manager" over five decades: Towards an androgynous profile? *Gender in Management: An International Journal, 36*, 714–730; Perry, E. L., Davis-Blake, A., & Kulik, C. T. (1994). Explaining gender-based selection decisions: A synthesis of contextual and cognitive approaches. *Academy of Management Review, 19*, 786–820.

18. Petsko, C. D., & Rosette, A. S. (2023). Are leaders still presumed White by default? Racial bias in leader categorization revisited. *Journal of Applied Psychology, 108*, 330–340; Rosette, A. S., Leonardelli, G. J., & Phillips, K. W. (2008). The White standard: Racial bias in leader categorization. *Journal of Applied Psychology, 93*, 758–777.

19. Petsko, C. D., & Rosette, A. S. (2023). Are leaders still presumed White by default? Racial bias in leader categorization revisited. *Journal of Applied Psychology, 108*,

330–340; Rosette, A. S., Leonardelli, G. J., & Phillips, K. W. (2008). The White standard: Racial bias in leader categorization. *Journal of Applied Psychology, 93*, 758–777.

20. Morgenroth, T., Ryan, M. K., & Sønderlund, A. L. (2021). Think manager—think parent? Investigating the fatherhood advantage and the motherhood penalty using the think manager—think male paradigm. *Journal of Applied Social Psychology, 51*, 237–247; Schein, V. E. (1973). The relationship between sex role stereotypes and requisite management characteristics. *Journal of Applied Psychology, 57*, 95–100.

21. Machiavelli, N. (1532). *The prince* (L, Ricci, Trans, 1903, E.R.P. Vincent, Trans, 1935). New American Library, quote on pp. 89–90.

22. Stogdill, R. M. (1974). *Handbook of leadership: A survey of theory and research.* Free Press.

23. Carli, L. L. (2015). Women and leadership. In A. M. Broadbridge & S. L. Fielden (Eds.), *Handbook of gendered careers in management: Getting in, getting on, getting out* (pp. 290–304). Elgar; van Emmerik, H., Wendt, H., & Euwema, M. C. (2010). Gender ratio, societal culture, and male and female leadership. *Journal of Occupational and Organizational Psychology, 83*, 895–914; Eagly, A. H., & Johannesen-Schmidt, M. C. (2001). The leadership styles of women and men. *Journal of Social Issues, 57*, 781–797; Eagly, A. H., & Johnson, B. T. (1990). Gender and leadership style: A meta-analysis. *Psychological Bulletin, 108*, 233–256.

24. Carli, L. L. (2015). Women and leadership. In A. M. Broadbridge & S. L. Fielden (Eds.), *Handbook of gendered careers in management: Getting in, getting on, getting out* (pp. 290–304). Elgar; Eagly, A. H., & Johannesen-Schmidt, M. C. (2001). The leadership styles of women and men. *Journal of Social Issues, 57*, 781–797; Eagly, A. H., & Johnson, B. T. (1990). Gender and leadership style: A meta-analysis. *Psychological Bulletin, 108*, 233–256.

25. Fischer, T., & Sitkin, S. B. (2023). Leadership styles: A comprehensive assessment and way forward. *Academy of Management Annals, 17*, 331–372; Díaz-Sáenz, H. R. (2011). Transformational leadership. In A. Bryman, D. Collinson, K. Grint, B. Jackson, & M. Uhl-Bien (Eds.), *SAGE handbook of leadership* (pp. 299–310). SAGE; Powell, G. N., Butterfield, D. A., & Bartol, K. M. (2008). Leader evaluations: A new female advantage? *Gender in Management: An International Journal, 23*, 156–174.

26. Bass, B. M., with Bass, R. (2008). Transformational leadership. In *The Bass handbook of leadership: Theory, research, and managerial applications* (4th ed., pp. 618–648). Free Press; Eagly, A. H., Johannesen-Schmidt, M. C., & van Engen, M. L. (2003). Transformational, transactional, and laissez-faire leadership styles: A meta-analysis comparing women and men. *Psychological Bulletin, 129*, 569–591.

27. Eagly, A. H., & Johnson, B. T. (1990). Gender and leadership style: A meta-analysis. *Psychological Bulletin, 108*, 233–256.

28. Bono, J. E., & Judge, T. A. (2004). Personality and transformational and transactional leadership: A meta-analysis. *Journal of Applied Psychology, 89*, 901–910; Eagly, A. H., & Johannesen-Schmidt, M. C. (2001). The leadership styles of women and men. *Journal of Social Issues, 57*, 781–797; Ross, S. M., & Offermann, L. R. (1997). Transformational leaders: Measurement of personality attributes and work group performance. *Personality and Social Psychology Bulletin, 23*, 10781086; Bass, B. M., Avolio, B. J., & Atwater, L. (1996). The transformational and transactional leadership of men and women. *Applied Psychology: An International Review, 45*(1), 5–34.

29. Powell, G. N. (2020). *Gender and leadership*. SAGE; Bass, B. M., with Bass, R. (2008). Women as leaders and followers. In *The Bass handbook of leadership: Theory, research, and managerial applications* (4th ed., pp. 899–942). Free Press.

30. Eagly, A. H., & Johnson, B. T. (1990). Gender and leadership style: A meta-analysis. *Psychological Bulletin, 108*, 233–256.

31. Eagly, A. H., Johannesen-Schmidt, M. C., & van Engen, M. L. (2003). Transformational, transactional, and laissez-faire leadership styles: A meta-analysis comparing women and men. *Psychological Bulletin, 129*, 569–591.

32. Wang, G., Oh, I-S., Courtright, S. H., & Colbert, A. E. (2011). Transformational leadership and performance across criteria and levels: A meta-analytic review of 25 years of research. *Group & Organization Management, 36*, 223–270; Judge, T. A., & Piccolo, R. F. (2004). Transformational and transactional leadership: A meta-analytic test of their relative validity. *Journal of Applied Psychology, 89*, 755–768; Lowe, K. B., Kroeck, K. G., & Sivasubramaniam, N. (1996). Effectiveness correlates of transformational and transactional leadership: A meta-analytic review of the MLQ literature. *Leadership Quarterly, 7*, 385–425.

33. Eagly, A. H., Karau, S. J., & Makhijani, M. G. (1995). Gender and the effectiveness of leaders: A meta-analysis. *Psychological Bulletin, 117*, 125–145.

34. Paustian-Underdahl, S. C., Walker, L. S., & Woehr, D. J. (2014). Gender and perceptions of leader effectiveness: A meta-analysis of contextual moderators. *Journal of Applied Psychology, 99*, 1129–1145; Reuben, E., Rey-Biel, P., Sapienza, P., & Zingales, L. (2012). The emergence of male leadership in competitive environments. *Journal of Economic Behavior and Organization, 83*, 111–117.

35. Berkery, E., Morley, M., & Tiernan, S. (2013). Beyond gender role stereotypes and requisite managerial characteristics: From communal to androgynous, the changing views of women. *Gender in Management: An International Journal, 28*, 278–298; Gartzia, L., & van Engen, M. (2012). Are (male) leaders "feminine" enough? Gendered traits of identity as mediators of sex differences in leadership styles. *Gender in Management: An International Journal, 27*, 292–310; Kark, R., Waismel-Manor, R., & Shamir, B. (2012). Does valuing androgyny and femininity lead to a female advantage? The relationship between gender-role, transformational leadership and identification. *Leadership Quarterly, 23*, 620–640; Kark, R. (2004). The transformational leader: Who is (s)he? A feminist perspective. *Journal of Organizational Change Management, 17*, 160–176; Park, D. (1997). Androgynous leadership style: An integration rather than a polarization. *Leadership and Organization Development Journal, 18*, 166–171; Park, D. (1996). Sex-role identity and leadership style: Looking for an androgynous leadership style. *Journal of Leadership Studies, 3*, 49–59; Blanchard, K. H., & Sargent, A. G. (1984). The one minute manager is an androgynous manager. *Training and Development Journal, 38*(5), 82–85; Sargent, A. G. (1981). *The androgynous manager.* AMACOM.

36. Wilson, S., & Newstead, T. (2022). The virtues of effective crisis leadership: What managers can learn from how women heads of state led in the first wave of COVID-19. *Organizational Dynamics, 51*, 100910; Sergent, K., & Stajkovic, A. D. (2020). Women's leadership is associated with fewer deaths during the COVID-19 crisis: Quantitative and qualitative analyses of United States governors. *Journal of Applied Psychology, 105*, 771–783; Blake-Beard, S., Shapiro, M., & Ingols, C. (2020). Feminine? Masculine? Androgynous leadership as a necessity in COVID-19. *Gender in Management: An International Journal, 35*, 607–617; Bass, B. M., with Bass, R. (2008). Women

as leaders and followers. In *The Bass handbook of leadership: Theory, research, and managerial applications* (4th ed., pp. 899–942). Free Press.

37. Morrison, A. M., White, R. P., Van Velsor, E., & the Center for Creative Leadership. (1987). *Breaking the glass ceiling: Can women reach the top of America's largest corporations?* Addison-Wesley, quote on p. 13.

38. Arifeen, S. R., & Gatrell, G. (2020). Those glass chains that bind you: How British Muslim women professionals experience career, faith and family. *British Journal of Management, 31*, 221–236; Carli, L. L., & Eagly, A. H. (2016). Women face a labyrinth: An examination of metaphors for women leaders. *Gender in Management: An International Journal, 31*, 514–527; Sleek, S. (2015). How brains think. *Observer: Association for Psychological Science, 28*(5), 21; Zimmer, B. (2015, April 3). The phrase "glass ceiling" stretches back decades. *Wall Street Journal.* Retrieved June 5, 2015, from http://www.wsj.com/articles/the-phrase-glass-ceiling-stretches-back-decades-1428089010; Ashcraft, K. L. (2013). The glass slipper: "Incorporating" occupational identity in management studies. *Academy of Management Review, 38*, 6–31; Smith, P., Caputi, P., & Crittenden, N. (2012). A maze of metaphors around glass ceilings. *Gender in Management: An International Journal, 27*, 436–448.

39. Powell, G. N. (2020). *Gender and leadership.* SAGE; Powell, G. N., & Butterfield, D. A. (2015b). The glass ceiling: What have we learned 20 years on? *Journal of Organizational Effectiveness: People and Performance, 2*, 306–326; Powell, G. N. (1999). Reflections on the glass ceiling: Recent trends and future prospects. In G. N. Powell (Ed.), *Handbook of gender and work* (pp. 325–345). SAGE; Powell, G. N., & Butterfield, D. A. (1994). Investigating the "glass ceiling" phenomenon: An empirical study of actual promotions to top management. *Academy of Management Journal, 37*, 68–86.

40. Calás, M. B., Smircich, L., & Holvino, E. (2014). Theorizing gender-and-organization: Changing times . . . changing theories? In S. Kumra, R. Simpson, & R. J. Burke (Eds.), *The Oxford handbook of gender in organizations* (pp. 17–52). Oxford University Press; Alvesson, M., & Due Billing, Y. (2009). *Understanding gender and organizations* (2nd ed.). SAGE; Maier, M. (1999). On the gendered substructure of organization. Dimensions and dilemmas of corporate masculinity. In G. N. Powell (Ed.), *Handbook of gender and work* (pp. 69–93). SAGE.

41. Powell, G. N. (2020). *Gender and leadership.* SAGE; Marshall, J. (1984). *Women managers: Travellers in a male world.* Wiley; Riger, S., & Galligan, P. (1980). Women in management: An exploration of competing paradigms. *American Psychologist, 35*, 902–910.

42. Kuperberg, A., & Stone, P. (2008). The media depiction of women who opt out. *Gender & Society, 22*, 497–517; Belkin, L. (2003, October 26). The opt-out revolution. *New York Times.* Retrieved September 9, 2010, from https://www.nytimes.com/2003/10/26/magazine/the-opt-out-revolution.html

43. Netchaeva, E., Sheppard, L. D., & Balushkina, T. (2022). A meta-analytic review of the gender difference in leadership aspirations. *Journal of Vocational Behavior, 137*, 103744; Kossek, E. E., Su, R., & Wu, L. (2017). "Opting out" or "pushed out"? Integrating perspectives on women's career equality for gender inclusion and interventions. *Journal of Management, 43*, 228–254; Hoobler, J. M., Lemmon, G., & Wayne, S. J. (2014). Women's managerial aspirations: An organizational development perspective. *Journal of Management, 40*, 703–730.

44. Powell, G. N., & Butterfield, D. A. (2022). Aspirations to top management over five decades: A shifting role of gender? *Gender in Management: An International Journal, 37*, 953–968.

45. Singh, V., Kumra, S., & Vinnicombe, S. (2002). Gender and impression management: Playing the promotion game. *Journal of Business Ethics, 37*, 77–89; Leeming, A., & Baruch, Y. (1998). The MBA as a bridge over the troubled waters of discrimination. *Women in Management Review, 13*, 95–104.

46. Adamson, M., & Kelan, E. K. (2019). "Female heroes": Celebrity executives as post-feminist role models. *British Journal of Management, 30*, 981–996; Metz, I., & Kumra, S. (2019). Why are self-help books with career advice for women popular? *Academy of Management Perspectives, 33*, 82–93; Sandberg, S. (2013). *Lean in: Women, work, and the will to lead*. Knopf, quote on p. 12.

47. Goldberg, G. (2022, June 2). What Sheryl Sandberg's "lean in" has meant to women. *New York Times*. Retrieved June 2, 2022, from https://www.nytimes.com/2022/06/02/business/sheryl-sandberg-lean-in.html; Chrobot-Mason, D., Hoobler, J. M., & Burno, J. (2019). *Lean In* versus the literature: An evidence-based examination. *Academy of Management Perspectives, 33*, 110–130; Whippman, R. (2019, October 10). Enough leaning in. Let's tell men to lean out. *New York Times*. Retrieved October 17, 2019, from https://www.nytimes.com/2019/10/10/opinion/sunday/feminism-lean-in.html

48. Flores, L. Y., Settles, I., McGillen, G. G., & Davis, T. M. (2021). Critical contributions to scholarship on women and work: Celebrating 50 years of progress and looking ahead to a new decade. *Journal of Vocational Behavior, 126*, 103490; Offermann, L. R., Thomas, K. R., Lanzo, L. A., & Smith, L. N. (2020). Achieving leadership and success: A 28-year follow-up of college women leaders. *Leadership Quarterly, 31*, 101345.

49. Antal, A. B., & Krebsbach-Gnath, C. (1988). Women in management: Unused resources in the Federal Republic of Germany. In N. J. Adler & D. N. Izraeli (Eds.), *Women in management worldwide* (pp. 141–156). Sharpe.

50. Kanter, R. M. (1977). *Men and women of the corporation.* Basic.

51. Lawrence, T. B., Schlindwein, E., Jalan, R., & Heaphy, E. D. (2023). Organizational body work: Efforts to shape human bodies in organizations. *Academy of Management Annals, 17*, 37–73; Grandey, A. A., Gabriel, A. S., & King, E. B. (2020). Tackling taboo topics: A review of the three *Ms* in working women's lives. *Journal of Management, 46*, 7–35; Gatrell, C. J. (2019). Boundary creatures? Employed, breastfeeding mothers and "abjection as practice." *Organization Studies, 40*, 421–442; Gatrell, C. J., Cooper, C. L., CBE, & Kossek, E. E. (2017). Maternal bodies as taboo at work: New perspectives on the marginalizing of senior-level women in organizations. *Academy of Management Perspectives, 31*, 239–252; Sherman, G. D., Lerner, J. S., Josephs, R. A., Renshon, J., & Gross, J. J. (2016). The interaction of testosterone and cortisol is associated with attained status in male executives. *Journal of Personality and Social Psychology, 110*, 921–929; Gatrell, C. J. (2013). Maternal body work: How women managers and professionals negotiate pregnancy and new motherhood at work. *Human Relations, 66*, 621–644.

52. Biggerstaff, L. E., Campbell, J. T., & Goldie, B. A. (in press). Hitting the "grass ceiling": Golfing CEOs, exclusionary schema, and career outcomes for female executives. *Journal of Management*; Crouse, K. (2021, April 6). At Augusta National, not talking about race is tradition. *New York Times*. Retrieved May 24, 2023, from https://www.nytimes.com/2020/11/10/sports/golf/lee-elder-masters-augusta-national.

html#:~:text=A%20plan%20to%20honor%20Lee,that%20hosts%20golf's%20marquee%20event.; Perkins, C., Mincyte, D., & Cole, C. L. (2010). Making the critical links and the links critical in golf studies: Introduction to special issue. *Journal of Sport and Social Issues, 34*, 267–271.

53. Reinwald, M., Zaia, J., & Kunze, F. (2023). Shine bright like a diamond: When signaling creates glass cliffs for female executives. *Journal of Management, 49*, 1005–1036; Morgenroth, T., Kirby, T. A., Ryan, M. K., & Sudkämper, A. (2020). The who, when, and why of the glass cliff phenomenon: A meta-analysis of appointments to precarious leadership positions. *Psychological Bulletin, 146*, 797–829; Gupta, V. K., Mortal, S. C, Silveri, S. D., Sun, M., & Turban, D. B. (2020). You're fired! Gender disparities in CEO dismissal. *Journal of Management, 46*, 560–582; Gupta, V. K., Han, S., Mortal, S. C., Silveri, S. D., & Turban, D. B. (2018). Do women CEOs face greater threat of shareholder activism compared to male CEOs? A role congruity perspective. *Journal of Applied Psychology, 103*, 228–236; Glass, C., & Cook, A. (2016). Leading at the top: Understanding women's challenges above the glass ceiling. *Leadership Quarterly, 27*, 51–63; Ryan, M. K., Haslam, S. A., Hersby, M. D., & Bongiorno, R. (2011). Think crisis—think female: The glass cliff and contextual variation in the think manager—think male stereotype. *Journal of Applied Psychology, 96*, 470–484.

54. Morgenroth, T., Kirby, T. A., Ryan, M. K., & Sudkämper, A. (2020). The who, when, and why of the glass cliff phenomenon: A meta-analysis of appointments to precarious leadership positions. *Psychological Bulletin, 146*, 797–829; Cook, A., & Glass, C. (2014). Above the glass ceiling: When are women and racial/ethnic minorities promoted to CEO? *Strategic Management Journal, 35*, 1080–1089.

55. Kark, R., Yakobovitz, N., Segal-Caspi, L., & Kalker-Zimmerman, S. (in press). Catty, bitchy, queen bee, or sister? A review of competition among women in organizations from a paradoxical-coopetition perspective. *Journal of Organizational Behavior*; Sheppard, L. D., & Aquino, K. (2017). Sisters at arms: A theory of female same-sex conflict and its problematization in organizations. *Journal of Management, 43*, 691–715; Derks, B., Van Laar, C., & Ellemers, N. (2016). The queen bee phenomenon: Why women leaders distance themselves from junior women. *Leadership Quarterly, 27*, 456–469; Mavin, S., Grandy, G., & Williams, J. (2014). Experiences of women elite leaders doing gender: Intra-gender micro-violence between women. *British Journal of Management, 25*, 439–455, quote on p. 441; Ellemers, N., Rink, F., Derks, B., & Ryan, M. K. (2012). Women in high places: When and why promoting women into top positions can harm them individually or as a group (and how to prevent this). *Research in Organizational Behavior, 32*, 163–187; Staines, G., Tavris, C., & Jayaratne, T. E. (1974). The queen bee syndrome. *Psychology Today, 7*(8), 55–60.

56. Kark, R., Yakobovitz, N., Segal-Caspi, L., & Kalker-Zimmerman, S. (in press). Catty, bitchy, queen bee, or sister? A review of competition among women in organizations from a paradoxical-coopetition perspective. *Journal of Organizational* Behavior; Lublin, J. S. (2014, November 11). Female CEOs make room for female directors. *Wall Street Journal.* Retrieved June 19, 2015, from http://online.wsj.com/articles/female-ceos-make-room-for-female-directors-1415732625; Wang, M., & Kelan, E. (2013). The gender quota and female leadership: Effects of the Norwegian gender quota on board chairs and CEOs. *Journal of Business Ethics, 117*, 449–466; Kurtulus, F. A., & Tomaskovic-Devey, D. (2012). Do female managers help women to advance? A panel study using EEO-1 records. *Annals of the American Academy of Political and Social Science, 639*, 173–197; Elsaid, E., & Ursel, N. D. (2011). CEO succession, gender and risk taking. *Gender in Management: An International Journal, 26*, 499–512; Matsa, D. A., &

Miller, A. R. (2011). Chipping away at the glass ceiling: Gender spillovers in corporate leadership. *American Economic Review: Papers and Proceedings, 101*, 635–639; Ely, R. J. (1994). The effects of organizational demographics and social identity on relationships among professional women. *Administrative Science Quarterly, 39*, 203–238.

57. Rosette, A. S., Ponce de Leon, R., Koval, C. Z., & Harrison, D. A. (2018). Intersectionality: Connecting experiences of gender with race at work. *Research in Organizational Behavior, 38*, 1–22; Rosette, A. S., Koval, C. Z., Ma, A., & Livingston, R. (2016). Race matters for women leaders: Intersectional effects on agentic deficiencies and penalties. *Leadership Quarterly, 27*, 429–445; Sanchez-Hucles, J. V., & Davis, D. D. (2010). Women and women of color in leadership. *American Psychologist, 65*, 171–181; Ospina, S., & Foldy, E. (2009). A critical review of race and ethnicity in the leadership literature: Surfacing context, power and the collective dimensions of leadership. *Leadership Quarterly, 20*, 876–896; Parker, P. S., & ogilvie, d. t. (1996). Gender, culture, and leadership: Toward a culturally distinct model of African-American women executives' leadership strategies. *Leadership Quarterly, 7*, 189–214.

58. Carter, J. T., & Ponce de Leon, R. (2022). Double jeopardy or intersectional invisibility? Reconciling (seemingly) opposing perspectives. In E. B. King, Q. M. Roberson, & M. R. Hebl (Eds.), *The future of scholarship on race in organizations* (pp. 233–258). Information Age Publishing; Smith, A. N., Watkins, M. B., Ladge, J. J., & Carlton, P. (2019). Making the invisible visible: Paradoxical effects of intersectional invisibility on the career experiences of executive Black women in the workplace. *Academy of Management Journal, 62*, 1705–1734.

59. Bem, S. L. (1978). Beyond androgyny: Some presumptuous prescriptions for a liberated sexual identity. In J. A. Sherman & F. L. Denmark (Ed.), *The psychology of women: Future directions in research* (pp. 1–23). Psychological Dimensions, quote on p. 19.

60. Powell, G. N. (2020). *Gender and leadership*. SAGE; Yoder, J. D. (2001). Making leadership work more effectively for women. *Journal of Social Issues, 57*, 815–828.

61. Hogue, M. B., Yoder, J. D., & Ludwig, J. (2002). Increasing initial leadership effectiveness: Assisting both women and men. *Sex Roles, 46*, 377–384; Falkenberg, L. (1990). Improving the accuracy of stereotypes within the workplace. *Journal of Management, 16*, 107–118.

62. Powell, G. N. (2020). *Gender and leadership*. SAGE; Chang, E. H., & Milkman, K. L. (2020). Improving decisions that affect gender equality in the workplace. *Organizational Dynamics, 49*, 100709; Hahn, A., & Gawronski, B. (2019). Facing one's implicit biases: From awareness to acknowledgement. *Journal of Personality and Social Psychology: Interpersonal Relations and Group Processes, 116*, 769–794; Soll, J. B., Milkman, K. L., & Payne, J. W. (2015). A user's guide to debiasing. In G. Keren & G. Wu (Eds.), *Wiley Blackwell handbook of judgment and decision making* (Vol. 1, pp. 924–951). Wiley Blackwell; Bazerman, M. H., & Moore, D. A. (2013). *Judgment in managerial decision making* (8th ed.). Wiley; Larrick, R. P. (2004). Debiasing. In D. J. Koehler & N. Harvey (Eds.), *Blackwell handbook of judgment and decision making* (pp. 316–337). Blackwell.

63. White, E. (2007, August 28). Advice for women on developing a leadership style. *Wall Street Journal.* Retrieved September 5, 2007, from https://www.wsj.com/articles/SB118825040976910243; Hymowitz, C. (2005, October 24). Too many women fall for stereotypes of selves, study says. *Wall Street Journal*, B1.

64. Adler, N. J., & Osland, J. S. (2016). Women leading globally: What we know, thought we knew, and need to know about leadership in the 21st century. *Advances in Global*

Leadership, 9, 15–56; Adler, N. J. (2002). Women joining men as global leaders in the new economy. In M. J. Gannon & K. L. Newman (Eds.), *Blackwell handbook of cross-cultural management* (pp. 236–249). Basil Blackwell; Adler, N. J. (1999). Global leaders: Women of influence. In G. N. Powell (Ed.), *Handbook of gender and work* (pp. 239–261). SAGE.

65. Dwivedi, P., Joshi, A., & Misangyi, V. F. (2018). Gender-inclusive gatekeeping: How (mostly male) predecessors influence the success of female CEOs. *Academy of Management Journal, 61*, 379–404.

66. Powell, G. N. (2020). *Gender and leadership*. SAGE; Powell, G. N., & Butterfield, D. A. (2015b). The glass ceiling: What have we learned 20 years on? *Journal of Organizational Effectiveness: People and Performance, 2*, 306–326; Powell, G. N., & Butterfield, D. A. (2002). Exploring the influence of decision makers' race and gender on actual promotions to top management. *Personnel Psychology, 55*, 397–428; Powell, G. N., & Butterfield, D. A. (1997). Effect of race on promotions to top management in a federal department. *Academy of Management Journal, 40*, 112–128; Powell, G. N., & Butterfield, D. A. (1994). Investigating the "glass ceiling" phenomenon: An empirical study of actual promotions to top management. *Academy of Management Journal, 37*, 68–86.

67. Wilson, S., & Newstead, T. (2022). The virtues of effective crisis leadership: What managers can learn from how women heads of state led in the first wave of COVID-19. *Organizational Dynamics, 51*, 100910; Powell, G. N., Butterfield, D. A., & Jiang, X. (2021). The "good manager" over five decades: Towards an androgynous profile? *Gender in Management: An International Journal, 36*, 714–730; Sergent, K., & Stajkovic, A. D. (2020). Women's leadership is associated with fewer deaths during the COVID-19 crisis: Quantitative and qualitative analyses of United States governors. *Journal of Applied Psychology, 105*, 771–783; Blake-Beard, S., Shapiro, M., & Ingols, C. (2020). Feminine? Masculine? Androgynous leadership as a necessity in COVID-19. *Gender in Management: An International Journal, 35*, 607–617.

68. Powell, G. N. (2012). Six ways of seeing the elephant: The intersection of sex, gender, and leadership. *Gender in Management: An International Journal, 27*, 119–141.

69. Room for debate: Do women make better bosses? (2009, August 2). *New York Times*. Retrieved August 2, 2009, from https://roomfordebate.blogs.nytimes.com/2009/08/02/do-women-make-better-bosses/

CHAPTER 7

1. Rawski, S. L., O'Leary-Kelly, A. M., & Breaux-Soignet, D. (2022). It's all fun and games until someone gets hurt: An interactional framing theory of work social sexual behavior. *Academy of Management Review, 47*, 617–636; Kray, L. J., Kennedy, J. A., & Rosenblum, M. (2022). Who do they think they are? A social-cognitive account of gender differences in social sexual identity and behavior at work. *Organizational Behavior and Human Decision Processes, 172*, 104186; Aquino, K., Sheppard, L., Watkins, M. B., O'Reilly, J., & Smith, A. (2014). Social sexual behavior at work. *Research in Organizational Behavior, 34*, 217–236; Berdahl, J. L., & Aquino, K. (2009). Sexual behavior at work: Fun or folly? *Journal of Applied Psychology, 94*, 34–47.

2. Cortina, L. M., & Areguin, M. A. (2021). Putting people down and pushing them out: Sexual harassment in the workplace. *Annual Review of Organizational Psychology and Organizational Behavior, 8*, 285–309; Sears, B., Mallory, C., Flores, A. R., & Conron,

K. J. (2021). *LGBT people's experiences of workplace discrimination and harassment.* Williams Institute, UCLA School of Law. Retrieved February 21, 2022, from https://williamsinstitute.law.ucla.edu/publications/lgbt-workplace-discrimination/; Quick, J, C., & McFadyen, M. A. (2017). Sexual harassment: Have we made any progress? *Journal of Occupational Health Psychology, 22*, 286–298; Ilies, R., Hauserman, N., Schwochau, S., & Stibal, J. (2003). Reported incidence rates of work-related sexual harassment in the United States: Using meta-analysis to explain reported rate disparities. *Personnel Psychology, 56*, 607–631.

3. Herstik, L. (2023, February 23). Harvey Weinstein sentenced to 16 years for Los Angeles sex crimes. *New York Times.* Retrieved March 25, 2023, from https://www.nytimes.com/2023/02/23/us/harvey-weinstein-sentence-los-angeles.html; Ransom, J. (2020, March 11). Harvey Weinstein's stunning downfall: 23 years in prison. *New York Times.* Retrieved March 25, 2023, from https://www.nytimes.com/2020/03/11/nyregion/harvey-weinstein-sentencing.html; Kantor, J., & Twohey, M. (2019). *She said: Breaking the sexual harassment story that helped ignite a movement.* Penguin Press; Kantor, J., & Twohey, M. (2017, October 5). Harvey Weinstein paid off sexual harassment accusers for decades. *New York Times.* Retrieved December 8, 2017, from https://www.nytimes.com/2017/10/05/us/harvey-weinstein-harassment-allegations.html

4. Leopold, J., Lambert, J. R., Ogunyomi, I. O., & Bell, M. P. (2021). The hashtag heard round the world: How #MeToo did what laws did not. *Equality, Diversity and Inclusion: An International Journal, 40*, 461–476; Bogen, K. W., Bleiweiss, K. K., Leach, N. R., & Orchowski, L. M. (2021). #MeToo: Disclosure and response to sexual victimization on Twitter. *Journal of Interpersonal Violence, 36*, 8257–8288; Gill, R., & Orgad, S. (2018). The shifting terrain of sex and power: From the "sexualization of culture" to #MeToo. *Sexualities, 21*, 1313–1324; Carlsen, A., Salam, M., Miller, C. C., Lu, D., Ngu, A., Patel, J. K., & Wichter, Z. (2018, October 29). #MeToo brought down 201 powerful men. Nearly half of their replacements are women. *New York Times.* Retrieved March 16, 2020, from https://www.nytimes.com/interactive/2018/10/23/us/metoo-replacements.html

5. Anand, A., Doll, J. L., Centobelli, P., Singh, S. K., & Cerchione, R. (2023). Struck by a cupid's arrow: The conjuring bliss and sinister shades of employee workplace romance. *Journal of Business Research, 154*, 113304; Milligan, S. (2022, June 7). Workplace romance is on the rise. *HR Magazine.* Retrieved February 22, 2023, from https://www.shrm.org/hr-today/news/hr-magazine/summer2022/pages/workplace-romance-is-on-the-rise.aspx; Society for Human Resource Management. (2013, September 24). *SHRM survey findings: Workplace romance.* Retrieved December 1, 2017, from https://www.shrm.org/hr-today/trends-and-forecasting/research-and-surveys/pages/shrm-workplace-romance-findings.aspx

6. Baker. A. N., King, D., Nalick, M., Tempio, M., Gupta, V. K., Pierce, C. A. (2021). Managers' sexually oriented behavior and firm performance: Linking media reports to stock market reactions and legal risk. *Journal of Strategy and Management, 14*, 562–581; Soergel, A. (2020, January 8). #MeToo contributes to 2019's "staggering" CEO departures. *U.S. News and World Report.* Retrieved April 19, 2020, from https://www.usnews.com/news/economy/articles/2020-01-08/metoo-contributes-to-2019s-staggering-ceo-departures; Morgan, R. (2016, May 5). The bosses who got screwed for boning in the corner office. *New York Post.* Retrieved July 24, 2017, from https://nypost.com/2016/05/05/the-bosses-who-got-screwed-for-boning-in-the-corner-office/

7. Watkins, M. B., Smith, A. N., & Aquino, K. (2013). The use and consequences of strategic sexual performances. *Academy of Management Perspectives, 27*, 173–186; Philaretou, A. G., & Young, C. L. (2007). The social construction of female sexuality in a sexualized work environment (SWE): The case of a comedy club. *Sexual Addiction and Compulsivity, 14*, 41–62.

8. Saguy, A. C., & Rees, M. E. (2021). Gender, power, and harassment: Sociology in the #MeToo era. *Annual Review of Sociology, 47*, 417–435; Cortina, L. M., & Areguin, M. A. (2021). Putting people down and pushing them out: Sexual harassment in the workplace. *Annual Review of Organizational Psychology and Organizational Behavior, 8*, 285–309; O'Leary-Kelly, A. M., Bowes-Sperry, L., Bates, C. A., & Lean, E. R. (2009). Sexual harassment at work: A decade (plus) of progress. *Journal of Management, 35*, 503–536; Bowes-Sperry, L., & Tata, J. (1999). A multiperspective framework of sexual harassment: Reviewing two decades of research. In G. N. Powell (Ed.), *Handbook of gender and work* (pp. 263–280). SAGE.

9. U.S. Equal Employment Opportunity Commission. (2023). *Code of Federal Regulations, Title 29—Labor, Subtitle B, Part 1604—Guidelines on discrimination because of sex, Section 1604.11—Sexual harassment.* Retrieved February 23, 2023, from https://www.ecfr.gov/current/title-29/subtitle-B/chapter-XIV/part-1604?toc=1

10. European Institute for Gender Equality (2023). *What is sexual harassment*? European Institute for Gender Equality. Retrieved February 23, 2023, from https://eige.europa.eu/publications/sexism-at-work-handbook/part-1-understand/what-sexual-harassment; Saguy, A. C. (2018). Europeanization or national specificity? Legal approaches to sexual harassment in France, 2002–2012. *Law & Society Review, 52*, 140–171; Zippel, K. (2009). The European Union 2002 directive on sexual harassment: A feminist success? *Comparative European Politics, 7*, 139–157.

11. Mainiero, L. (2020). Workplace romance versus sexual harassment: A call to action regarding sexual hubris and sexploitation in the #MeToo era. *Gender in Management: An International Journal, 35*, 329–347; McDonald, P. (2012). Workplace sexual harassment 30 years on: A review of the literature. *International Journal of Management Reviews, 14*, 1–17; O'Leary-Kelly, A. M., Bowes-Sperry, L., Bates, C. A., & Lean, E. R. (2009). Sexual harassment at work: A decade (plus) of progress. *Journal of Management, 35*, 503–536.

12. Pierce, C. A., Muslin, I. S., Dudley, C. M., & Aguinis, H. (2008). From charm to harm: A content-analytic review of sexual harassment court cases involving workplace romance. *Management Research, 6*, 27–45; Terpstra, D. E., & Baker, D. D. (1992). Outcomes of federal court decisions on sexual harassment. *Academy of Management Journal, 35*, 181–190.

13. Fielden, S. L., & Hunt, C. (2014). Sexual harassment in the workplace. In S. Kumra, R. Simpson, & R. J. Burke (Eds.), *Oxford handbook of gender in organizations* (pp. 353–370). Oxford University Press; Cortina, L. M., & Berdahl, J. L. (2008). Sexual harassment in organizations: A decade of research in review. In J. Barling & C. L. Cooper, *The SAGE handbook of organizational behavior* (Vol. 1, pp. 469–497). SAGE; Gruber, J. E., Smith, M., & Kauppinen-Toropainen, K. (1996). Sexual harassment types and severity: Linking research and policy. In M. S. Stockdale (Ed.), *Sexual harassment in the workplace: Perspectives, frontiers, and response strategies* (pp. 151–173). SAGE.

14. Mainiero, L. A., & Jones, K. J. (2013a). Sexual harassment versus workplace romance: Social media spillover and textual harassment in the workplace. *Academy of Management Perspectives, 27*, 187–203; Mainiero, L. A., & Jones, K. J. (2013b).

Workplace romance 2.0: Developing a communication ethics model to address potential sexual harassment from inappropriate social media contacts between coworkers. *Journal of Business Ethics, 114*, 367–379.

15. Saguy, A. C., & Rees, M. E. (2021). Gender, power, and harassment: Sociology in the #MeToo era. *Annual Review of Sociology, 47*, 417–435; McDonald, P. (2012). Workplace sexual harassment 30 years on: A review of the literature. *International Journal of Management Reviews, 14*, 1–17; Cortina, L. M., & Berdahl, J. L. (2008). Sexual harassment in organizations: A decade of research in review. In J. Barling & C. L. Cooper, *The SAGE handbook of organizational behavior* (Vol. 1, pp. 469–497). SAGE; O'Connor, M., Gutek, B. A., Stockdale, M., Geer, T. M., & Melançon, R. (2004). Explaining sexual harassment judgments: Looking beyond gender of the rater. *Law and Human Behavior, 28*, 69–95; Rotundo, M., Nguyen, D-H., & Sackett, P. R. (2001). A meta-analytic review of gender differences in perceptions of sexual harassment. *Journal of Applied Psychology, 86*, 914–922.
16. Strom, P., Collins, C. J., Avgar, A. C., & Ryan, K. (2023). Drawing the line: How the workplace shapes the naming of sexual harassment. *Personnel Psychology, 76*, 113–139; Collins, E. G. C., & Blodgett, T. B. (1981). Sexual harassment: Some see it . . . some won't. *Harvard Business Review, 59*(2), 76–95.
17. Powell, G. N. (2020). *Gender and leadership*. SAGE; Cortina, L. M., & Areguin, M. A. (2021). Putting people down and pushing them out: Sexual harassment in the workplace. *Annual Review of Organizational Psychology and Organizational Behavior, 8*, 285–309; McDonald, P. (2012). Workplace sexual harassment 30 years on: A review of the literature. *International Journal of Management Reviews, 14*, 1–17; O'Leary-Kelly, A. M., Bowes-Sperry, L., Bates, C. A., & Lean, E. R. (2009). Sexual harassment at work: A decade (plus) of progress. *Journal of Management, 35*, 503–536.
18. Cortina, L. M., & Areguin, M. A. (2021). Putting people down and pushing them out: Sexual harassment in the workplace. *Annual Review of Organizational Psychology and Organizational Behavior, 8*, 285–309; Powell, G. N. (2020). *Gender and leadership*. SAGE; McDonald, P. (2012). Workplace sexual harassment 30 years on: A review of the literature. *International Journal of Management Reviews, 14*, 1–17; Tangri, S. S., Burt, M. R., & Johnson, L. B. (1982). Sexual harassment at work: Three explanatory models. *Journal of Social Issues, 38*(4), 33–54.
19. Pina, A., Gannon, T. A., & Saunders, B. (2009). An overview of the literature on sexual harassment: Perpetrator, theory, and treatment issues. *Aggression and Violent Behavior, 14*, 126–138; O'Leary-Kelly, A. M., Bowes-Sperry, L., Bates, C. A., & Lean, E. R. (2009). Sexual harassment at work: A decade (plus) of progress. *Journal of Management, 35*, 503–536; Perry, E. L., Schmidtke, J. M., & Kulik, C. T. (1998). Propensity to sexually harass: An exploration of gender differences. *Sex Roles, 38*, 443–460.
20. Fiske, S. T., & Glick, P. (1995). Ambivalence and stereotypes cause sexual harassment: A theory with implications for organizational change. *Journal of Social Issues, 51*(1), 97–115.
21. O'Leary-Kelly, A. M., Paetzold, R. L., & Griffin, R. W. (2000). Sexual harassment as aggressive behavior: An actor-based perspective. *Academy of Management Review, 25*, 372–388; Malamuth, N. M., Linz, D., Heavey, C. L., Barnes, G., & Acker, M. (1995). Using the confluence model of sexual aggression to predict men's conflict with women: A 10-year follow-up study. *Journal of Personality and Social Psychology, 69*, 353–369.

22. Berdahl, J. L. (2007). The sexual harassment of uppity women. *Journal of Applied Psychology, 92*, 425–437.

23. Berdahl, J. L. (2007). The sexual harassment of uppity women. *Journal of Applied Psychology, 92*, 425–437.

24. Powell, G. N. (2020). *Gender and leadership*. SAGE; Chamberlain, L. J., Crowley, M., Tope, D., & Hodson, R. (2008). Sexual harassment in organizational context. *Work and Occupations, 35*, 262–295; Tangri, S. S., Burt, M. R., & Johnson, L. B. (1982). Sexual harassment at work: Three explanatory models. *Journal of Social Issues, 38*(4), 33–54.

25. Saguy, A. C., & Rees, M. E. (2021). Gender, power, and harassment: Sociology in the #MeToo era. *Annual Review of Sociology, 47*, 417–435; McLaughlin, H., Uggen, C., & Blackstone, A. (2012). Sexual harassment, workplace authority, and the paradox of power. *American Sociological Review, 77*, 625–647; Ilies, R., Hauserman, N., Schwochau, S., & Stibal, J. (2003). Reported incidence rates of work-related sexual harassment in the United States: Using meta-analysis to explain reported rate disparities. *Personnel Psychology, 56*, 607–631.

26. Cortina, L. M., & Areguin, M. A. (2021). Putting people down and pushing them out: Sexual harassment in the workplace. *Annual Review of Organizational Psychology and Organizational Behavior, 8*, 285–309; Willness, C. R., Steel, P., & Lee, K. (2007). A meta-analysis of the antecedents and consequences of workplace sexual harassment. *Personnel Psychology, 60*, 127–162; Hulin, C. L., Fitzgerald, L. F., & Drasgow, F. (1996). Organizational influences on sexual harassment. In M. S. Stockdale (Ed.), *Sexual harassment in the workplace: Perspectives, frontiers, and response strategies* (pp. 127–150). SAGE.

27. Bowes-Sperry, L., & O'Leary-Kelly, A. M. (2005). To act or not to act: The dilemma faced by observers of sexual harassment. *Academy of Management Review, 30*, 288–306; Bowes-Sperry, L., & Powell, G. N. (1999). Observers' reactions to social-sexual behavior at work: An ethical decision making perspective. *Journal of Management, 25*, 779–802.

28. Calás, M. B., Smircich, L., & Holvino, E. (2014). Theorizing gender-and-organization: Changing times . . . changing theories? In S. Kumra, R. Simpson, & R. J. Burke (Eds.), *The Oxford handbook of gender in organizations* (pp. 17–52). Oxford University Press; Berdahl, J. L. (2007). Harassment based on sex: Protecting social status in the context of gender hierarchy. *Academy of Management Review, 32*, 641–658; Marshall, J. (1984). *Women managers: Travellers in a male world*. Wiley; Tangri, S. S., Burt, M. R., & Johnson, L. B. (1982). Sexual harassment at work: Three explanatory models. *Journal of Social Issues, 38*(4), 33–54.

29. Cassino, D., & Besen-Cassino, Y. (2019). Race, threat, and workplace sexual harassment: The dynamics of harassment in the United States, 1997–2016. *Gender, Work, and Organization, 26*, 1221–1240; Berdahl, J. L., & Moore, C. (2006). Workplace harassment: Double jeopardy for minority women. *Journal of Applied Psychology, 91*, 426–436.

30. McDonald, P. (2012). Workplace sexual harassment 30 years on: A review of the literature. *International Journal of Management Reviews, 14*, 1–17; Gutek, B. A., & Done, R. S. (2001). Sexual harassment. In R. K. Unger (Ed.), *Handbook of the psychology of women and gender* (pp. 367–387). Wiley; Gutek, B. A. (1985). *Sex and the workplace: The impact of sexual behavior and harassment on women, men, and organizations*. Jossey-Bass.

31. Cortina, L. M., & Areguin, M. A. (2021). Putting people down and pushing them out: Sexual harassment in the workplace. *Annual Review of Organizational Psychology and Organizational Behavior, 8*, 285–309; U.S. Merit Systems Protection Board. (2018). *Research brief: Update on sexual harassment in the federal workplace*. Retrieved February 20, 2023, from https://mspbpublic.azurewebsites.net/studies/studies/Sexual_Harassment_in_the_Federal_Workplace_Trends_Progress_Continuing_Challenges_253661.pdf; Fielden, S. L., & Hunt, C. (2014). Sexual harassment in the workplace. In S. Kumra, R. Simpson, & R. J. Burke (Eds.), *Oxford handbook of gender in organizations* (pp. 353–370). Oxford University Press; McDonald, P. (2012). Workplace sexual harassment 30 years on: A review of the literature. *International Journal of Management Reviews, 14*, 1–17; Cortina, L. M., & Berdahl, J. L. (2008). Sexual harassment in organizations: A decade of research in review. In J. Barling & C. L. Cooper, *The SAGE handbook of organizational behavior* (Vol. 1, pp. 469–497). SAGE; U.S. Merit Systems Protection Board. (1995). *Sexual harassment in the federal workplace: Trends, progress, and continuing challenges.* Government Printing Office.

32. Sears, B., Mallory, C., Flores, A. R., & Conron, K. J. (2021). *LGBT people's experiences of workplace discrimination and harassment*. Williams Institute, UCLA School of Law. Retrieved February 21, 2022, from https://williamsinstitute.law.ucla.edu/publications/lgbt-workplace-discrimination/; McDonald, P., & Charlesworth, S. (2016). Workplace sexual harassment at the margins. *Work, Employment and Society, 30*, 118–134.

33. Dewan, S. (2017, November 30). She didn't fight back: 5 (misguided) reasons people doubt sexual harassment victims. *New York Times.* Retrieved November 30, 2017, from https://www.nytimes.com/2017/11/30/us/sexual-harassment-weinstein-women.html; Carlson, G. (2016, November 12). Gretchen Carlson: My fight against sexual harassment. *New York Times.* Retrieved November 14, 2016, from https://www.nytimes.com/2016/11/13/opinion/sunday/gretchen-carlson-my-fight-against-sexual-harassment.html

34. Cortina, L. M., & Areguin, M. A. (2021). Putting people down and pushing them out: Sexual harassment in the workplace. *Annual Review of Organizational Psychology and Organizational Behavior, 8*, 285–309; Willness, C. R., Steel, P., & Lee, K. (2007). A meta-analysis of the antecedents and consequences of workplace sexual harassment. *Personnel Psychology, 60*, 127–162; Bergman, M. E., Langhout, R. D., Palmieri, P. A., Cortina, L. M., & Fitzgerald, L. F. (2002). The (un)reasonableness of reporting: Antecedents and consequences of reporting sexual harassment. *Journal of Applied Psychology, 87*, 230–242; Hulin, C. L., Fitzgerald, L. F., & Drasgow, F. (1996). Organizational influences on sexual harassment. In M. S. Stockdale (Ed.), *Sexual harassment in the workplace: Perspectives, frontiers, and response strategies* (pp. 127–150). SAGE.

35. Cortina, L. M., & Areguin, M. A. (2021). Putting people down and pushing them out: Sexual harassment in the workplace. *Annual Review of Organizational Psychology and Organizational Behavior, 8*, 285–309; McLaughlin, H., Uggen, C., & Blackstone, A. (2017). The economic and career effects of sexual harassment on working women. *Gender and Society, 31*, 333–358; McDonald, P. (2012). Workplace sexual harassment 30 years on: A review of the literature. *International Journal of Management Reviews, 14*, 1–17; Willness, C. R., Steel, P., & Lee, K. (2007). A meta-analysis of the antecedents and consequences of workplace sexual harassment. *Personnel Psychology, 60*, 127–162; Bowling, N. A., & Beehr, T. A. (2006). Workplace harassment from the victim's perspective: A theoretical model and meta-analysis. *Journal of Applied Psychology, 91*, 998–1012; Raver, J. A., & Gelfand, M. J. (2005). Beyond the individual victim:

Linking sexual harassment, team processes, and team performance. *Academy of Management Journal, 48*, 387–400.

36. Bowes-Sperry, L., & O'Leary-Kelly, A. M. (2005). To act or not to act: The dilemma faced by observers of sexual harassment. *Academy of Management Review, 30*, 288–306; Bowes-Sperry, L., & Powell, G. N. (1999). Observers' reactions to social-sexual behavior at work: An ethical decision making perspective. *Journal of Management, 25*, 779–802; Bowes-Sperry, L., & Powell, G. N. (1996). Sexual harassment as a moral issue: An ethical decision-making perspective. In M. S. Stockdale (Ed.), *Sexual harassment in the workplace: Perspectives, frontiers, and response strategies* (pp. 105–124). SAGE.

37. Kundro, T. G., Burke, V., Grandey, A. A., & Sayre, G. M. (2022). A perfect storm: Customer sexual harassment as a joint function of financial dependence and emotional labor. *Journal of Applied Psychology, 107*, 1385–1396; Liang, Y., & Park, Y. (2022). Because I know how it hurts: Employee bystander intervention in customer sexual harassment through empathy and its moderating factors. *Journal of Occupational Health Psychology, 27*, 339–348; Gettman, H. J., & Gelfand, M. J. (2007). When the customer shouldn't be king: Antecedents and consequences of sexual harassment by clients and customers. *Journal of Applied Psychology, 92*, 757–770.

38. Kantor, J., & Twohey, M. (2022, October 3). How to measure the impact of #MeToo? *New York Times*. Retrieved October 4, 2022, from https://www.nytimes.com/interactive/2022/10/03/us/me-too-five-years.html; Leopold, J., Lambert, J. R., Ogunyomi, I. O., & Bell, M. P. (2021). The hashtag heard round the world: How #MeToo did what laws did not. *Equality, Diversity and Inclusion: An International Journal, 40*, 461–476; Johnson, S. K., Keplinger, K., Kirk, J. F., & Barnes, L. (2019, July 18). Has sexual harassment at work decreased since #MeToo? *Harvard Business Review*. Retrieved April 21, 2020, from https://hbr.org/2019/07/has-sexual-harassment-at-work-decreased-since-metoo; Mendes, K., Ringrose, J., & Keller, J. (2018). #MeToo and the promise and pitfalls of challenging rape culture through digital feminist activism. *European Journal of Women's Studies, 25*, 236–246; Carlsen, A., Salam, M., Miller, C. C., Lu, D., Ngu, A., Patel, J. K., & Wichter, Z. (2018, October 29). #MeToo brought down 201 powerful men. Nearly half of their replacements are women. *New York Times*. Retrieved March 16, 2020, from https://www.nytimes.com/interactive/2018/10/23/us/metoo-replacements.html

39. Leopold, J., Lambert, J. R., Ogunyomi, I. O., & Bell, M. P. (2021). The hashtag heard round the world: How #MeToo did what laws did not. *Equality, Diversity and Inclusion: An International Journal, 40*, 461–476; MacKinnon, C. A. (2018, February 4). #MeToo has done what the law could not. *New York Times*. Retrieved September 16, 2021, from https://www.nytimes.com/2018/02/04/opinion/metoo-law-legal-system.html; MacKinnon, C. A. (1979). *Sexual harassment of working women: A case of sex discrimination*. Yale University Press.

40. Conger, K., & Wakabayashi, D. (2018, November 8). Google overhauls sexual misconduct policy after employee walkout. *New York Times*. Retrieved November 9, 2018, from https://www.nytimes.com/2018/11/08/technology/google-arbitration-sexual-harassment.html; Wakabayashi, D., & Benner, K. (2018, October 25). How Google protected Andy Rubin, the "father of Android." *New York Times*. Retrieved November 9, 2018, from https://www.nytimes.com/2018/10/25/technology/google-sexual-harassment-andy-rubin.html.

41. Draper, K., & Creswell, J. (2018, May 5). Nike's CEO vows changes after claims of workplace harassment and bias. *New York Times*. Retrieved May 8, 2018, from https://www.nytimes.com/2018/05/05/business/mark-parker-nike.html; Creswell, J., Draper, K., & Abrams, R. (2018, April 28). At Nike, revolt led by women leads to exodus of male executives. *New York Times*. Retrieved May 8, 2018, from https://www.nytimes.com/2018/04/28/business/nike-women.html

42. Bennhold, K. (2019, January 27). Another side of #MeToo: Male managers fearful of mentoring women. *New York Times*. Retrieved January 28, 2019, from https://www.nytimes.com/2019/01/27/world/europe/metoo-backlash-gender-equality-davos-men.html; Atwater, L. E., Tringale, A. M., Sturm, R. E., Taylor, S. N., & Braddy, P. W. (2019). Looking ahead: How what we know about sexual harassment now informs us of the future. *Organizational Dynamics, 48*, 100677; The #MeToo backlash (2019). *Harvard Business Review, 97*(5), 19–22.

43. Onwuachi-Willig, A. (2018). What about #UsToo? The invisibility of race in the #MeToo movement. *Yale Law Journal Forum, 128*, 105–120.

44. Varagur, K. (2020, November 22). Workplace romance? Many millennials and Gen Zers would never. *Wall Street Journal*. Retrieved November 23, 2020, from https://www.wsj.com/articles/workplace-romance-many-millennials-and-gen-zers-would-never-11606093201; Furhmans, V., & Feintzeig, R. (2019, December 5). Want to date a colleague? Think carefully. *Wall Street Journal*. Retrieved December 6, 2019, from https://www.wsj.com/articles/want-to-date-a-colleague-think-carefully-11575588567

45. This section is primarily based on Powell, G. N., & Foley, S. (1999). Romantic relationships in organizational settings: Something to talk about. In G. N. Powell (Ed.), *Handbook of gender and work* (pp. 281–304). SAGE; Powell, G. N., & Foley, S. (1998). Something to talk about: Romantic relationships in organizational settings. *Journal of Management, 24*, 421–448.

46. Ferguson, M., Carlson, D., Boswell, W., Whitten, D., Butts, M. M., & Kacmar, K. M. (2016). Tethered to work: A family systems approach linking mobile device use to turnover intentions. *Journal of Applied Psychology, 101*, 520–534; Burke, R. J., & Cooper, C. L. (Eds.). (2008). *The long work hours culture: Causes, consequences and choices*. Emerald; Cooper, C. L., & Lewis, S. (1999). Gender and the changing nature of work. In G. N. Powell (Ed.), *Handbook of gender and work* (pp. 37–46). SAGE.

47. Sternberg, R. J. (1998). *Cupid's arrow: The course of love through time*. Cambridge University Press; Sternberg, R. J. (1986). A triangular theory of love. *Psychological Review, 93*, 119–135.

48. Sternberg, R. J. (1998). *Cupid's arrow: The course of love through time*. Cambridge University Press; Pierce, C. A., Byrne, D., & Aguinis, H. (1996). Attraction in organizations: A model of workplace romance. *Journal of Organizational Behavior, 17*, 5–32.

49. Anand, A., Doll, J. L., Centobelli, P., Singh, S. K., & Cerchione, R. (2023). Struck by a cupid's arrow: The conjuring bliss and sinister shades of employee workplace romance. *Journal of Business Research, 154*, 113304; Pierce, C. A., Byrne, D., & Aguinis, H. (1996). Attraction in organizations: A model of workplace romance. *Journal of Organizational Behavior, 17*, 5–32; Dillard, J. P., & Miller, K. I. (1988). Intimate relationships in task environments. In S. Duck (Ed.), *Handbook of personal relationships: Theory, research and interventions* (pp. 449–465). Wiley; Quinn, R. (1977). Coping with cupid: The formation, impact, and management of romantic relationships in organizations. *Administrative Science Quarterly, 22*, 30–45.

50. Anand, A., Doll, J. L., Centobelli, P., Singh, S. K., & Cerchione, R. (2023). Struck by a cupid's arrow: The conjuring bliss and sinister shades of employee workplace romance. *Journal of Business Research, 154*, 113304; Pierce, C. A., Byrne, D., & Aguinis, H. (1996). Attraction in organizations: A model of workplace romance. *Journal of Organizational Behavior, 17*, 5–32; Quinn, R. (1977). Coping with cupid: The formation, impact, and management of romantic relationships in organizations. *Administrative Science Quarterly, 22*, 30–45.

51. Anand, A., Doll, J. L., Centobelli, P., Singh, S. K., & Cerchione, R. (2023). Struck by a cupid's arrow: The conjuring bliss and sinister shades of employee workplace romance. *Journal of Business Research, 154*, 113304; Chory, R. M., & Hoke, H. G. G. (2019). Young love at work: Perceived effects of workplace romance among millennial generation organizational members. *Journal of Psychology, 153*, 575–598; Wilson, F. (2015). Romantic relationships at work: Why love can hurt. *International Journal of Management Reviews, 17*, 1–19; Powell, G. N. (1986). What do tomorrow's managers think about sexual intimacy in the workplace? *Business Horizons, 29*(4), 30–35.

52. Pierce, C. A., & Aguinis, H. (2003). Romantic relationships in organizations: A test of a model of formation and impact factors. *Management Research, 1*, 161–169; Pierce, C. A., Byrne, D., & Aguinis, H. (1996). Attraction in organizations: A model of workplace romance. *Journal of Organizational Behavior, 17*, 5–32.

53. Chory, R. M., Mainiero, L. A., & Horan, S. M. (in press). Workplace romance and career reputation effects across industries. *International Journal of Business Communication*; Anand, A., Doll, J. L., Centobelli, P., Singh, S. K., & Cerchione, R. (2023). Struck by a cupid's arrow: The conjuring bliss and sinister shades of employee workplace romance. *Journal of Business Research, 154*, 113304; Salvaggio, A. N., Streich, M., Hopper, J. E., & Pierce, C. A. (2011). Why do fools fall in love (at work)? Factors associated with the incidence of workplace romance. *Journal of Applied Social Psychology, 41*, 906–937; Riach, K., & Wilson, F. (2007). Don't screw the crew: Exploring the rules of engagement in organizational romance. *British Journal of Management, 18*, 79–92; Mainiero, L. A. (1989). *Office romance: Love, power, and sex in the workplace.* Rawson Associates; Gutek, B. A. (1985). *Sex and the workplace: The impact of sexual behavior and harassment on women, men, and organizations.* Jossey-Bass.

54. Anand, A., Doll, J. L., Centobelli, P., Singh, S. K., & Cerchione, R. (2023). Struck by a cupid's arrow: The conjuring bliss and sinister shades of employee workplace romance. *Journal of Business Research, 154*, 113304; Cowan, R. L., & Horan, S. M. (2021). Understanding information and communication technology use in workplace romance escalation and de-escalation. *International Journal of Business Communication, 58*, 55–78; Mainiero, L. A., & Jones, K. J. (2013a). Sexual harassment versus workplace romance: Social media spillover and textual harassment in the workplace. *Academy of Management Perspectives, 27*, 187–203; Mainiero, L. A., & Jones, K. J. (2013b). Workplace romance 2.0: Developing a communication ethics model to address potential sexual harassment from inappropriate social media contacts between coworkers. *Journal of Business Ethics, 114*, 367–379.

55. Guzzo, K. B. (2014). Trends in cohabitation outcomes: Compositional changes and engagement among never-married young adults. *Journal of Marriage and Family, 76*, 826–842; Dillard, J. P. (1987). Close relationships at work: Perceptions of the motives and performance of relational participants. *Journal of Social and Personal Relationships, 4*, 179–193.

56. Mainiero, L. (2020). Workplace romance versus sexual harassment: A call to action regarding sexual hubris and sexploitation in the #MeToo era. *Gender in Management: An International Journal, 35*, 329–347; Salvaggio, A. N., Streich, M., Hopper, J. E., & Pierce, C. A. (2011). Why do fools fall in love (at work)? Factors associated with the incidence of workplace romance. *Journal of Applied Social Psychology, 41*, 906–937; Mainiero, L. A. (1986). A review and analysis of power dynamics in organizational romances. *Academy of Management Review, 11*, 750–762.

57. Anand, A., Doll, J. L., Centobelli, P., Singh, S. K., & Cerchione, R. (2023). Struck by a cupid's arrow: The conjuring bliss and sinister shades of employee workplace romance. *Journal of Business Research, 154*, 113304; Mainiero, L. (2020). Workplace romance versus sexual harassment: A call to action regarding sexual hubris and sexploitation in the #MeToo era. *Gender in Management: An International Journal, 35*, 329–347.

58. Berscheid, E. (2010). Love in the fourth dimension. *Annual Review of Psychology, 61*, 1–25.

59. Mainiero, L. (2020). Workplace romance versus sexual harassment: A call to action regarding sexual hubris and sexploitation in the #MeToo era. *Gender in Management: An International Journal, 35*, 329–347; Pierce, C. A., Muslin, I. S., Dudley, C. M., & Aguinis, H. (2008). From charm to harm: A content-analytic review of sexual harassment court cases involving workplace romance. *Management Research, 6*, 27–45; Pierce, C. A., & Aguinis, H. (2005). Legal standards, ethical standards, and responses to social-sexual conduct at work. *Journal of Organizational Behavior*, 26, 727–732; Pierce, C. A., Broberg, B. J., McClure, J. R., & Aguinis, H. (2004). Responding to sexual harassment complaints: Effects of a dissolved workplace romance on decision-making standards. *Organizational Behavior and Human Decision Processes, 95*, 66–82; Pierce, C. A., Aguinis, H., & Adams, S. K. R. (2000). Effects of a dissolved workplace romance and rater characteristics on responses to a sexual harassment accusation. *Academy of Management Journal, 43*, 869–880; Pierce, C. A., & Aguinis, H. (1997). Bridging the gap between romantic relationships and sexual harassment in organizations. *Journal of Organizational Behavior, 18*, 197–200.

60. Peel, E., Ellis, S. J., & Riggs, D. W. (2022). Lesbian, gay, bisexual and transgender people: Prejudice, stereotyping, discrimination and social change. In C. Tileagă, M. Augoustinis, & K. Durrheim (Eds.), *The Routledge handbook of discrimination, prejudice, and stereotyping* (pp. 104–117). Routledge; Sears, B., Mallory, C., Flores, A. R., & Conron, K. J. (2021). *LGBT people's experiences of workplace discrimination and harassment*. Williams Institute, UCLA School of Law. Retrieved February 21, 2022, from https://williamsinstitute.law.ucla.edu/publications/lgbt-workplace-discrimination/; Priola, V., Lasio, D., De Simone, S., & Serri, F. (2014). The sound of silence: Lesbian, gay, bisexual and transgender discrimination in "inclusive organizations." *British Journal of Management, 25*, 488–502; Herek, G. M., & McLemore, K. A. (2013). Sexual prejudice. *Annual Review of Psychology, 64*, 309–333; Ragins, B. R., Singh, R., & Cornwell, J. M. (2007). Making the invisible visible: Fear and disclosure of sexual orientation at work. *Journal of Applied Psychology, 92*, 1103–1118; Ragins, B. R., & Cornwell, J. M. (2001). Pink triangles: Antecedents and consequences of perceived workplace discrimination against gay and lesbian employees. *Journal of Applied Psychology, 86*, 1244–1261.

61. Anand, A., Doll, J. L., Centobelli, P., Singh, S. K., & Cerchione, R. (2023). Struck by a cupid's arrow: The conjuring bliss and sinister shades of employee workplace romance. *Journal of Business Research, 154*, 113304; Kleindienst, I., Abreha, K. G.,

Schweizer, D., Proelss, J., & Cserpes, T. (2022). CEO divorce and firm operating performance. *Academy of Management Discoveries, 8*, 561–584; Sheppard, L. D., O'Reilly, J., van Dijke, M., Restubog, S. L. D., & Aquino, K. (2020). The stress-relieving benefits of positively experienced social sexual behavior in the workplace. *Organizational Behavior and Human Decision Processes, 156*, 38–52; Wilson, F. (2015). Romantic relationships at work: Why love can hurt. *International Journal of Management Reviews, 17*, 1–19; Pierce, C. A., Byrne, D., & Aguinis, H. (1996). Attraction in organizations: A model of workplace romance. *Journal of Organizational Behavior, 17*, 5–32; Dillard, J. P., & Miller, K. I. (1988). Intimate relationships in task environments. In S. Duck (Ed.), *Handbook of personal relationships: Theory, research and interventions* (pp. 449–465). Wiley.

62. Morgan, L. M., & Davidson, M. J. (2008). Sexual dynamics in mentoring relationships: A critical review. *British Journal of Management, 19*, S120–S129; Clawson, J. G., & Kram, K. E. (1984). Managing cross-gender mentoring. *Business Horizons, 27*(3), 22–32.

63. Anand, A., Doll, J. L., Centobelli, P., Singh, S. K., & Cerchione, R. (2023). Struck by a cupid's arrow: The conjuring bliss and sinister shades of employee workplace romance. *Journal of Business Research, 154*, 113304; Pierce, C. A., Byrne, D., & Aguinis, H. (1996). Attraction in organizations: A model of workplace romance. *Journal of Organizational Behavior, 17*, 5–32; Dillard, J. P., & Miller, K. I. (1988). Intimate relationships in task environments. In S. Duck (Ed.), *Handbook of personal relationships: Theory, research and interventions* (pp. 449–465). Wiley; Quinn, R. (1977). Coping with cupid: The formation, impact, and management of romantic relationships in organizations. *Administrative Science Quarterly, 22*, 30–45.

64. Anand, A., Doll, J. L., Centobelli, P., Singh, S. K., & Cerchione, R. (2023). Struck by a cupid's arrow: The conjuring bliss and sinister shades of employee workplace romance. *Journal of Business Research, 154*, 113304; Powell, G. N. (2001). Workplace romances between senior-level executives and lower-level employees: An issue of work disruption and gender. *Human Relations, 54*, 1519–1544; Anderson, C. J., & Fisher, C. (1991). Male–female relationships in the workplace: Perceived motivations in office romances. *Sex Roles, 25*, 163–180; Quinn, R. (1977). Coping with cupid: The formation, impact, and management of romantic relationships in organizations. *Administrative Science Quarterly, 22*, 30–45.

65. Cole, N. (2009). Workplace romance: A justice analysis. *Journal of Business and Psychology, 24*, 363–372; Powell, G. N. (2001). Workplace romances between senior-level executives and lower-level employees: An issue of work disruption and gender. *Human Relations, 54*, 1519–1544; Foley, S., & Powell, G. N. (1999). Not all is fair in love and work: Coworkers' preferences for and responses to managerial interventions regarding workplace romances. *Journal of Organizational Behavior, 20*, 1043–1056.

66. U.S. Equal Employment Opportunity Commission. Available at https://www.law.cornell.edu/cfr/text/29/1604.11

67. Roehling, M. V., Wu, D., Choi, M. G., & Dulebohn, J. H. (2022). The effects of sexual harassment training on proximal and transfer training outcomes: A meta-analytic investigation. *Personnel Psychology, 75*, 3–31; Cortina, L. M., & Areguin, M. A. (2021). Putting people down and pushing them out: Sexual harassment in the workplace. *Annual Review of Organizational Psychology and Organizational Behavior, 8*, 285–309; Saguy, A. C., & Rees, M. E. (2021). Gender, power, and harassment: Sociology in the #MeToo era. *Annual Review of Sociology, 47*, 417–435; Dobbin, F., & Kalev, A. (2020).

Why sexual harassment programs backfire and what to do about it. *Harvard Business Review, 98*(3), 44–52; Mainiero, L. (2020). Workplace romance versus sexual harassment: A call to action regarding sexual hubris and sexploitation in the #MeToo era. *Gender in Management: An International Journal, 35*, 329–347; Atwater, L. E., Tringale, A. M., Sturm, R. E., Taylor, S. N., & Braddy, P. W. (2019). Looking ahead: How what we know about sexual harassment now informs us of the future. *Organizational Dynamics, 48*, 100677; Roehling, M. V., & Huang, J. (2018). Sexual harassment training effectiveness: An interdisciplinary review and call for research. *Journal of Organizational Behavior, 39*, 134–150; Quick, J, C., & McFadyen, M. A. (2017). Sexual harassment: Have we made any progress? *Journal of Occupational Health Psychology, 22*, 286–298; Fielden, S. L., & Hunt, C. (2014). Sexual harassment in the workplace. In S. Kumra, R. Simpson, & R. J. Burke (Eds.), *Oxford handbook of gender in organizations* (pp. 353–370). Oxford University Press; McDonald, P. (2012). Workplace sexual harassment 30 years on: A review of the literature. *International Journal of Management Reviews, 14*, 1–17.

68. This procedure is primarily based on Powell, G. N. (1983). Sexual harassment: Confronting the issue of definition. *Business Horizons, 26*(4), 24–28.

69. Cortina, L. M., & Areguin, M. A. (2021). Putting people down and pushing them out: Sexual harassment in the workplace. *Annual Review of Organizational Psychology and Organizational Behavior, 8*, 285–309; Atwater, L. E., Tringale, A. M., Sturm, R. E., Taylor, S. N., & Braddy, P. W. (2019). Looking ahead: How what we know about sexual harassment now informs us of the future. *Organizational Dynamics, 48*, 100677; The #MeToo backlash (2019). *Harvard Business Review, 97*(5), 19–22; Rubino, C., Avery, D. R., McKay, P. F., Moore, B. L., Wilson, D. C., Van Driel, M. S., Witt, L. A., & McDonald, D. P. (2018). And justice for all: How organizational justice climate deters sexual harassment. *Personnel Psychology, 71*, 519–544.

70. Powell, G. N. (2020). *Gender and leadership*. SAGE; Hall, C., & Powell, G. N. (2017, October 20). Men at the top play by different rules. *UConn Today.* University of Connecticut. Retrieved October 20, 2017, from https://today.uconn.edu/2017/10/men-top-play-different-rules/

71. Powell, G. N. (2020). *Gender and leadership*. SAGE; Morrissey, E. M. (2018). #MeToo spells trouble for them too: Sexual harassment scandals and the corporate board. *Tulane Law Review, 93*, 177–205.

72. Yagil, D., Karnieli-Miller, O., Eisikovits, Z., & Enosh, G. (2006). Is that a "no"? The interpretation of responses to unwanted sexual attention. *Sex Roles, 54*, 251–260; Bowes-Sperry, L., & O'Leary-Kelly, A. M. (2005). To act or not to act: The dilemma faced by observers of sexual harassment. *Academy of Management Review, 30*, 288–306; Malamut, A. B., & Offermann, L. R. (2001). Coping with sexual harassment: Personal, environmental, and cognitive determinants. *Journal of Applied Psychology, 86*, 1152–1166; Knapp, D. E., Faley, R. H., Ekeberg, S. E., & Dubois, C. L. Z. (1997). Determinants of target responses to sexual harassment: A conceptual framework. *Academy of Management Review, 22*, 687–729; Bowes-Sperry, L., & Powell, G. N. (1996). Sexual harassment as a moral issue: An ethical decision-making perspective. In M. S. Stockdale (Ed.), *Sexual harassment in the workplace: Perspectives, frontiers, and response strategies* (pp. 105–124). SAGE; Rowe, M. P. (1996). Dealing with harassment: A systems approach. In M. S. Stockdale (Ed.), *Sexual harassment in the workplace: Perspectives, frontiers, and coping strategies* (pp. 241–271). SAGE; U.S. Merit Systems Protection Board. (1995). *Sexual harassment in the federal workplace: Trends, progress, and continuing challenges.* Government Printing Office.

73. Hall, C., & Powell, G. N. (2017, October 20). Men at the top play by different rules. *UConn Today.* University of Connecticut. Retrieved October 20, 2017, from https://today.uconn.edu/2017/10/men-top-play-different-rules/

74. Quest Martial Arts; see https://questmartialarts.us.

75. Rowe, M. P. (1996). Dealing with harassment: A systems approach. In M. S. Stockdale (Ed.), *Sexual harassment in the workplace: Perspectives, frontiers, and coping strategies* (pp. 241–271). SAGE.

76. Mead, M. (1980). A proposal: We need taboos on sex at work. In D. A. Neugarten & J. M. Shafritz (Eds.), *Sexuality in organizations: Romantic and coercive behaviors at work* (pp. 53–56). Moore Publishing; MacKinnon, C. A. (1979). *Sexual harassment of working women: A case of sex discrimination.* Yale University Press.

77. Society for Human Resource Management. (2013, September 24). *SHRM survey findings: Workplace romance.* Retrieved December 1, 2017, from https://www.shrm.org/hr-today/trends-and-forecasting/research-and-surveys/pages/shrm-workplace-romance-findings.aspx

78. Anand, A., Doll, J. L., Centobelli, P., Singh, S. K., & Cerchione, R. (2023). Struck by a cupid's arrow: The conjuring bliss and sinister shades of employee workplace romance. *Journal of Business Research, 154*, 113304; Lickey, N. C., Berry, G. R., & Whelan-Berry, K. S. (2009). Responding to workplace romance: A proactive and pragmatic approach. *Journal of Business Inquiry, 8*, 100–119; Pierce, C. A., & Aguinis, H. (2009). Moving beyond a legal-centric approach to managing workplace romances: Organizationally sensible recommendations for HR leaders. *Human Resource Management*, 48, 447–464.

79. Powell, G. N. (2001). Workplace romances between senior-level executives and lower-level employees: An issue of work disruption and gender. *Human Relations, 54*, 1519–1544; Quinn, R. (1977). Coping with cupid: The formation, impact, and management of romantic relationships in organizations. *Administrative Science Quarterly, 22*, 30–45.

80. Mainiero, L. A. (1989). *Office romance: Love, power, and sex in the workplace.* Rawson Associates; Mainiero, L. A. (1986). A review and analysis of power dynamics in organizational romances. *Academy of Management Review, 11*, 750–762; Quinn, R. (1977). Coping with cupid: The formation, impact, and management of romantic relationships in organizations. *Administrative Science Quarterly, 22*, 30–45.

CHAPTER 8

1. Greenhaus, J. H., & Powell, G. N. (2017). *Making work and family work: From hard choices to smart choices.* Routledge.

2. Allen, T. D., & French, K. A. (2023). Work–family research: A review and next steps. *Personnel Psychology, 76*, 437–471; Vaziri, H., Wayne, J. H., Casper, W. J., Lapierre, L. M., Greenhaus, J. H., Amirkamali, F., & Li, Y. (2022). A meta-analytic investigation of the personal and work-related antecedents of work–family balance. *Journal of Organizational Behavior, 43*, 662–692; Rothbard, N. P., Beetz, A. M., & Harari, D. (2021). Balancing the scales: A configurational approach to work–life balance. *Annual Review of Organizational Psychology and Organizational Behavior, 8*, 73–103; Hirschi, A., Shockley, K. M., & Zacher, H. (2019). Achieving work–family balance: An action regulation

model. *Academy of Management Review, 44*, 150–171; Casper, W. J., Vaziri, H., Wayne, J. H., DeHauw, S., & Greenhaus, J. H. (2018). The jingle-jangle of work–nonwork balance: A comprehensive and meta-analytic review of its meaning and measurement. *Journal of Applied Psychology, 103*, 182–214; Wayne, J. H., Butts, M. M., Casper, W. J., & Allen, T. D. (2017). In search of balance: A conceptual and empirical integration of multiple meanings of work–family balance. *Personnel Psychology, 70*, 167–210; Greenhaus, J. H., & Allen, T. D. (2011). Work–family balance: A review and extension of the literature. In J. C. Quick & L. E. Tetrick (Eds.), *Handbook of occupational health psychology* (2nd ed., pp. 165–183). American Psychological Association.

3. Miller, C. C. (2023, March 13). Fathers gained family time in the pandemic. Many don't want to give it back. *New York Times.* Retrieved March 13, 2023, from https://www.nytimes.com/2023/03/12/upshot/fathers-pandemic-remote-work.html; Alsop, R. (2017, November 28). Millennials see paternity leave as a priority. *New York Times.* Retrieved December 12, 2017, from https://www.nytimes.com/2017/11/28/well/family/millennials-see-paternity-leave-as-a-priority.html; Ernst & Young (2015). *Global generations: A global study on work-life challenges across generations.* Retrieved December 15, 2017, from https://cs-wordpress.s3.amazonaws.com/crowdsource-v4/uploads/2015/06/Generations-Globally-work-life-challenges-EY-5-15.pdf; Galinsky, E., Aumann, K., & Bond, J. T. (2011). *Times are changing: Gender and generation at work and at home.* Families and Work Institute. Retrieved December 18, 2017, from https://www.familiesandwork.org/research/2009/times-are-changing-gender-and-generation-at-work-and-at-home/

4. Bellafante, G. (2022, February 4). Why Wall Street is suddenly bullish on work–life balance. *New York Times.* Retrieved February 4, 2022, from https://www.nytimes.com/2022/02/04/nyregion/wall-street-toxic-work-place-culture.html; Feintzeig, R. (2022, October 31). Can you get ahead and still have a life? Younger women are trying to find out. *New York Times.* Retrieved October 31, 2022, from https://www.wsj.com/articles/can-you-get-ahead-and-still-have-a-life-younger-women-are-trying-to-find-out-11667163773; Needelman, J. (2022, August 15). How quitting a job changed my work–life balance. *New York Times.* Retrieved August 15, 2022, from https://www.nytimes.com/2022/08/15/style/quitting-work-life-balance-career.html; Hennekam, S., Ladge, J. J., & Powell, G. N. (2021). Confinement during the COVID-19 pandemic: How multi-domain work–life shock events may result in positive identity change. *Journal of Vocational Behavior, 130*, 103261; Powell, G. N. (2020). Work–family lockdown: Implications for a post-pandemic research agenda. *Gender in Management: An International Review, 35*, 639–646.

5. Bellafante, G. (2022, February 4). Why Wall Street is suddenly bullish on work–life balance. *New York Times.* Retrieved February 4, 2022, from https://www.nytimes.com/2022/02/04/nyregion/wall-street-toxic-work-place-culture.html; Feintzeig, R. (2022, October 31). Can you get ahead and still have a life? Younger women are trying to find out. *New York Times.* Retrieved October 31, 2022, from https://www.wsj.com/articles/can-you-get-ahead-and-still-have-a-life-younger-women-are-trying-to-find-out-11667163773; Needelman, J. (2022, August 15). How quitting a job changed my work–life balance. *New York Times.* Retrieved August 15, 2022, from https://www.nytimes.com/2022/08/15/style/quitting-work-life-balance-career.html; Hennekam, S., Ladge, J. J., & Powell, G. N. (2021). Confinement during the COVID-19 pandemic: How multi-domain work–life shock events may result in positive identity change. *Journal of Vocational Behavior, 130*, 103261; Powell, G. N. (2020). Work–family lockdown: Implications for a post-pandemic research agenda. *Gender in Management: An International Review, 35*, 639–646.

6. Powell, G. N., Greenhaus, J. H., Allen, T. D., & Johnson, R. E. (2019). Advancing and expanding work–life theory from multiple perspectives. *Academy of Management Review, 44*, 54–71; Leslie, L., Manchester, C. F., & Kim, Y. (2016). Gender and the work–family domain: A social role-based perspective. In T. D. Allen & L. T. Eby (Eds.), *Oxford handbook of work and family* (pp. 53–67). Oxford University Press; Greenhaus, J. H., & Parasuraman, S. (1999). Research on work, family, and gender. In G. N. Powell (Ed.), *Handbook of gender and work* (pp. 391–412). SAGE.

7. Ng, T. W. H., Eby, L. T., Sorenson, K. L., & Feldman, D. C. (2005). Predictors of objective and subjective career success: A meta-analysis. *Personnel Psychology, 58*, 367–408; Judge, T. A., Cable, D. M., Boudreau, J. W., & Bretz, R. D., Jr. (1995). An empirical investigation of the predictors of executive career success. *Personnel Psychology, 48*, 485–519.

8. Terpstra-Tong, J., Ralston, D. A., Treviño, L., Karam, C., Furrer, O., Froese, F., Tjemkes, B., Darder, F. L., Richards, M., Dabic, M., Li, Y., Fu, P., Molteni, M., Palmer, I., Tučková, Z., Szabo, E., Poeschl, G., Hemmert, M., Butt, A., de la Garza, T., . . . & Crowley-Henry, M. (2022). The impact of gender-role-orientations on subjective career success: A multilevel study of 36 societies. *Journal of Vocational Behavior, 138*, 103773; Briscoe, J. P., Kaše, R., Dries, N., Dysvik, A., Unite, J. A., Adeleye, I., Andresen, M., Apospori, E., Babaloa, O., Bagdadli, S., Çakmak-Otluoglu, K. Ö., Casado, T., Cerdin, J-L., Cha, J-S., Chudzikowski, K., Russo, S. D., Eggenhofer-Rehart, P., Fei, Z., Gianecchini, M., Gubler, M., . . . & Zikic, J. (2021). Here, there, and everywhere: Development and validation of a cross-culturally representative measure of subjective career success. *Journal of Vocational Behavior, 130*, 203612; Shockley, K. M., Ureksoy, H., Rodopman, O. B., Poteat, L. F., & Dullaghan, T. R. (2016). Development of a new scale to measure subjective career success: A mixed-methods study. *Journal of Organizational Behavior, 37*, 128–153.

9. Spurk, D., Hirschi, A., & Dries, N. (2019). Antecedents and outcomes of objective versus subjective career success: Competing perspectives and future directions. *Journal of Management, 45*, 35–69; Abele, A. E., & Spurk, D. (2009). How do objective and career success interrelate over time? *Journal of Organizational and Occupational Psychology, 82*, 803–824; Ng, T. W. H., Eby, L. T., Sorenson, K. L., & Feldman, D. C. (2005). Predictors of objective and subjective career success: A meta-analysis. *Personnel Psychology, 58*, 367–408.

10. Eddleston, K. A., Veiga, J. F., & Powell, G. N. (2006). Explaining sex differences in managerial career satisfier preferences: The role of gender self-schema. *Journal of Applied Psychology, 91*, 437–445.

11. Powell, G. N., & Mainiero, L. A. (1992). Cross-currents in the river of time: Conceptualizing the complexities of women's careers. *Journal of Management, 18*, 215–237.

12. Frear, K. A., Paustian-Underdahl, S. C., Heggestad, E. D., & Walker, L. S. (2019). Gender and career success: A typology and analysis of dual paradigms. *Journal of Organizational Behavior, 40*, 400–416; Kirchmeyer, C. (2002). Gender differences in managerial careers: Yesterday, today, and tomorrow. *Journal of Business Ethics, 37*, 5–24; Stroh, L. K., & Reilly, A. H. (1999). Gender and careers: Present experiences and emerging trends. In G. N. Powell (Ed.), *Handbook of gender and work* (pp. 307–324). SAGE; Kirchmeyer, C. (1998). Determinants of managerial career success: Evidence and explanation of male/female differences. *Journal of Management, 24*, 673–692; Schneer, J. A., & Reitman, F. (1995). The impact of gender as managerial careers unfold. *Journal of Vocational Behavior, 47*, 290–315; Cox, T. H., & Harquail, C.

V. (1991). Career paths and career success in the early career stages of male and female MBAs. *Journal of Vocational Behavior, 39*, 54–75.

13. Abele, A. E. (2014). How gender influences objective career success and subjective career satisfaction: The impact of self-concept and of parenthood. In I. Schoon & J. S. Eccles (Eds.), *Gender differences in aspirations and achievement: A life course perspective* (pp. 412–426). Cambridge University Press; Miller, C. C. (2014, September 6). The motherhood penalty vs. the fatherhood bonus: A child helps your career, if you're a man. *New York Times.* Retrieved October 29, 2015, from https://www.nytimes.com/2014/09/07/upshot/a-child-helps-your-career-if-youre-a-man.html; Johnson, C. D., & Eby, L. T. (2011). Evaluating career success of African American males: It's what you know and who you are that matters. *Journal of Vocational Behavior, 79*, 699–709; Kirchmeyer, C. (2006). The different effects of family on objective career success across gender: A test of alternative explanations. *Journal of Vocational Behavior, 68*, 323–346; Kirchmeyer, C. (2002). Gender differences in managerial careers: Yesterday, today, and tomorrow. *Journal of Business Ethics, 37*, 5–24.

14. Valet, P. (2018). Social structure and the paradox of the contented female worker: How occupational gender segregation biases justice perceptions of wages. *Work and Occupations, 45*, 168–193; Davison, H. K. (2014). The paradox of the contented female worker: Are women satisfied with lower pay? *Employee Responsibilities and Rights Journal, 26*, 195–216; Crosby, F. J. (1982). *Relative deprivation and working women.* Oxford University Press.

15. Powell, G. N., & Eddleston, K. A. (2008). The paradox of the contented female business owner. *Journal of Vocational Behavior, 73*, 24–36; Eddleston, K. A., & Powell, G. N. (2008). The role of gender identity in explaining sex differences in business owners' career satisfier preferences. *Journal of Business Venturing, 23*, 244–256.

16. Choi, J., Kim, A., Han, K., Ryu, S., Park, J. G., & Kwon, B. (2018). Antecedents and consequences of satisfaction with work–family balance: A moderating role of perceived insider status. *Journal of Organizational Behavior, 39*, 1–11; Eddleston, K. A., & Powell, G. N. (2012). Nurturing entrepreneurs' work–family balance: A gendered perspective. *Entrepreneurship Theory and Practice, 36*, 513–541.

17. Seltzer, J. A (2019). Family change and changing family demography. *Demography, 56*, 405–426; Zaidi, B., & Morgan, S. P. (2017). The second demographic transition theory: A review and appraisal. *Annual Review of Sociology, 43*, 473–492; Goldscheider, F., Bernhardt, E., & Lappegård, T. (2015). The gender revolution: A framework for understanding changing family and demographic behavior. *Population and Development Review, 41*, 207–239; Marks, S. R. (2006). Understanding diversity of families in the 21st century and its impact on the work–family area of study. In M. Pitt-Catsouphes, E. E. Kossek, & S. Sweet (Eds.), *The work and family handbook: Multi-disciplinary perspectives, methods, and approaches* (pp. 41–65). Erlbaum.

18. U.S. Department of Labor, Bureau of Labor Statistics. (2023a). *Employment characteristics of families—2022* (computed from data in Table 4). Retrieved May 27, 2023, from https://www.bls.gov/news.release/pdf/famee.pdf

19. Zaidi, B., & Morgan, S. P. (2017). The second demographic transition theory: A review and appraisal. *Annual Review of Sociology, 43*, 473–492; Guzzo, K. B. (2014). Trends in cohabitation outcomes: Compositional changes and engagement among never-married young adults. *Journal of Marriage and Family, 76*, 826–842; Copen, C. E., Daniels, K., & Mosher, W. D. (2013). First premarital cohabitation in the United States: 2006–2010 national survey of family growth. *National Health Statistics Reports* (No. 64). U.S.

Department of Health and Human Services, Centers for Disease Control and Prevention, National Center for Health Statistics. Retrieved October 15, 2015, from https://www.cdc.gov/nchs/data/nhsr/nhsr064.pdf

20. Scherer, Z. (2022, November 22). Number of same-sex couple households exceeded 1 million in 2021. *U.S. Census Bureau*. Retrieved March 26, 2023, from https://www.census.gov/library/stories/2022/11/same-sex-couple-households-exceeded-one-million.html; Walker, L., & Taylor, D. (2021). Same-sex couple households: 2019. *U.S. Census Bureau*. Retrieved March 26, 2023, from https://www.census.gov/library/publications/2021/acs/acsbr-005.html; Murphy, L. D., Thomas, C. L., Cobb, H. R., & Hartman, A. E. (2021). A review of the LGBTQ+ work-family interface: What do we know and where do we go from here? *Journal of Organizational Behavior, 42*, 139–161; Gates, G. J. (2015). Marriage and family: LGBT individuals and same-sex couples. *The Future of Family, 25*(2), 67–87.

21. Greenhaus, J. H., & Powell, G. N. (2017). *Making work and family work: From hard choices to smart choices*. Routledge.

22. Greenhaus, J. H., & Powell, G. N. (2017). *Making work and family work: From hard choices to smart choices*. Routledge.

23. ten Brummelhuis, L. L., & Greenhaus, J. H. (2018). How role jugglers maintain relationships at home and at work: A gender comparison. *Journal of Applied Psychology, 103*, 1265–1282; Young, E. (2018, August 14). Preliminary evidence suggests women may be better role jugglers than men. *Research Digest*. Retrieved August 16, 2018, from https://www.bps.org.uk/research-digest/preliminary-evidence-suggests-women-may-be-better-role-jugglers-men; Ruderman, M. N., Ohlott, P. J., Panzer, K., & King, S. N. (2002). Benefits of multiple roles for professional women. *Academy of Management Journal, 45*, 369–386.

24. Allen, T. D., & French, K. A. (2023). Work–family research: A review and next steps. *Personnel Psychology, 76*, 437–471; Allen, T. D., French, K. A., Dumani, S., & Shockley, K. M. (2020). A cross-national meta-analytic examination of predictors and outcomes associated with work–family conflict. *Journal of Applied Psychology, 105*, 539–576; Eby, L. T., Casper, W. J., Lockwood, A., Bordeaux, C., & Brinley, A. (2005). Work and family research in IO/OB: Content analysis and review of the literature (1980–2002). *Journal of Vocational Behavior, 66*, 124–197; Allen, T. D., Herst, D. E. L., Bruck, C. S., & Sutton, M. (2000). Consequences associated with work-to-family conflict: A review and agenda for future research. *Journal of Occupational Health Psychology, 5*, 278–308.

25. Shockley, K. M., Shen, W., DeNunzio, M. M., Arvan, M. L., & Knudsen, E. A. (2017). Disentangling the relationship between gender and work–family conflict: An integration of theoretical perspectives using meta-analytic methods. *Journal of Applied Psychology*, 102, 1601–1635; Carlson, D. S., Kacmar, K. M., & Williams, L. J. (2000). Construction and initial validation of a multidimensional measure of work–family conflict. *Journal of Vocational Behavior, 56*, 249–276; Greenhaus, J. H., & Beutell, N. J. (1985). Sources of conflict between work and family roles. *Academy of Management Review, 10*, 76–88.

26. Liu, C., Peng, Y., & Rubenstein, K. (2022). Challenge job demands, time-based work–family conflict, and family well-being outcomes: The moderating effect of conscientiousness. *International Journal of Stress Management, 29*, 182–192; Greenhaus, J. H., & Beutell, N. J. (1985). Sources of conflict between work and family roles. *Academy of Management Review, 10*, 76–88.

27. Thompson. M. J., Carlson, D. S., Kacmar, K. M., & Vogel, R. M. (2020). The cost of being ignored: Emotional exhaustion in the work and family domains. *Journal of Applied Psychology, 105*, 186–195; Greenhaus, J. H., & Beutell, N. J. (1985). Sources of conflict between work and family roles. *Academy of Management Review, 10*, 76–88.

28. Pluut, H., Ilies, R., Su, R., Weng, Q., & Liang, A. X. (2022). How social stressors at work influence marital behaviors at home: An interpersonal model of work–family spillover. *Journal of Occupational Health Psychology, 27*, 74–88; Greenhaus, J. H., & Beutell, N. J. (1985). Sources of conflict between work and family roles. *Academy of Management Review, 10*, 76–88.

29. Murphy, L. D., Thomas, C. L., Cobb, H. R., & Hartman, A. E. (2021). A review of the LGBTQ+ work–family interface: What do we know and where do we go from here? *Journal of Organizational Behavior, 42*, 139–161; Sawyer, K. B., Thoroughgood, C., & Ladge, J. J. (2017). Invisible families, invisible conflicts: Examining the added layer of work–family conflict for employees with LGB families. *Journal of Vocational Behavior, 103*, 23–39.

30. Grose, J. (2023, April 26). Dads still get extra leisure time. Moms are still subsidizing it. *New York Times*. Retrieved April 26, 2023, from https://www.nytimes.com/2023/04/26/opinion/remote-work-moms-dads.html; Allen, T. D., & French, K. A. (2023). Work–family research: A review and next steps. *Personnel Psychology, 76*, 437–471; Collins, C., Landivar, L. C., Ruppanner, L., & Scarborough, W. J. (2021). COVID-19 and the gender gap in work hours. *Gender, Work, and Organization, 28*(S1), 101–112; Murphy, L. D., Thomas, C. L., Cobb, H. R., & Hartman, A. E. (2021). A review of the LGBTQ+ work–family interface: What do we know and where do we go from here? *Journal of Organizational Behavior, 42*, 139–161; Shockley, K. M., Shen, W., DeNunzio, M. M., Arvan, M. L., & Knudsen, E. A. (2017). Disentangling the relationship between gender and work–family conflict: An integration of theoretical perspectives using meta-analytic methods. *Journal of Applied Psychology, 102*, 1601–1635.

31. Allen, T. D., & French, K. A. (2023). Work–family research: A review and next steps. *Personnel Psychology, 76*, 437–471; Michel, J. S., Kotrba, L. M., Mitchelson, J. K., Clark, M. A., & Baltes, B. B. (2011). Antecedents of work–family conflict: A meta-analytic review. *Journal of Organizational Behavior, 32*, 689–725; Greenhaus, J. H., & Powell, G. N. (2003). When work and family collide: Deciding between competing role demands. *Organizational Behavior and Human Decision Processes, 90*, 291–303.

32. Powell, G. N. (1998). The abusive organization. *Academy of Management Executive, 12*(2), 95–96.

33. Allen, T. D., & French, K. A. (2023). Work–family research: A review and next steps. *Personnel Psychology, 76*, 437–471; French, K. A., & Shockley, K. M. (2020). Formal and informal supports for managing work and family. *Current Directions in Psychological Science, 29*, 207–216; Pluut, H., Ilies, R., Curşeu, P. L., & Liu, Y. (2018). Social support at work and at home: Dual-buffering effects in the work–family conflict process. *Organizational Behavior and Human Decision Processes, 146*, 1–13; French, K. A., Dumani, S., Allen, T. D., & Shockley, K. M. (2018). A meta-analysis of work–family conflict and social support. *Psychological Bulletin, 144*, 284–314; Powell, G. N., & Greenhaus, J. H. (2006). Managing incidents of work–family conflict: A decision-making perspective. *Human Relations, 59*, 1179–1212; Greenhaus, J. H., & Parasuraman, S. (1994). Work–family conflict, social support and well-being. In M. J. Davidson

& R. J. Burke (Eds.), *Women in management: Current research issues* (pp. 213–229). Chapman.

34. Allen, T. D., French, K. A., Dumani, S., & Shockley, K. M. (2020). A cross-national meta-analytic examination of predictors and outcomes associated with work–family conflict. *Journal of Applied Psychology, 105*, 539–576; Rajadhyaksha, U., Korabik, K., Lero, D. S., Zugec, L., Hammer, L. B., & Beham, B. (2020). The work–family interface around the world: Implications and recommendations for policy and practice. *Organizational Dynamics, 49*, 1–11; Ollier-Malaterre, A., & Foucreault, A. (2017). Cross-national work–life research: Cultural and structural impacts for individuals and organizations. *Journal of Management, 43*, 111–136; Shockley, K. M., Douek, J., Smith, C. R., Yu, P. P., Dumani, S., & French, K. A. (2017). Cross-cultural work and family research: A review of the literature. *Journal of Vocational Behavior, 101*, 1–20; Powell, G. N., Francesco, A. M., & Ling, Y. (2009). Toward culture-sensitive theories of the work–family interface. *Journal of Organizational Behavior, 30*, 597–616; Ling, Y., & Powell, G. N. (2001). Work–family conflict in contemporary China: Beyond an American-based model. *International Journal of Cross Cultural Management, 1*, 357–373.

35. Allen, T. D., & French, K. A. (2023). Work–family research: A review and next steps. *Personnel Psychology, 76*, 437–471; McClean, S. T., Yim, J., Courtright, S. H., & Dunford, B. B. (2021). Transformed by the family: An episodic, attachment theory perspective on family–work enrichment and transformational leadership. *Journal of Applied Psychology, 106*, 1848–1866; Lin, S-H. (J.), Chang, C-H. (D.), Lee, H. W., & Johnson, R. E. (2021). Positive family events facilitate effective leader behaviors at work: A within-individual investigation of family–work enrichment. *Journal of Applied Psychology, 106*, 1412–1434; Lapierre, L. M., Li, Y., Kwan, H. K., Greenhaus, J. H., DiRenzo, M. S., & Shao, P. (2018). A meta-analysis of the antecedents of work–family enrichment. *Journal of Organizational Behavior, 39*, 385–401; Zhang, Y., Xu, S., Jin, J., & Ford, M. T. (2018). The within and cross domain effects of work–family enrichment: A meta-analysis. *Journal of Vocational Behavior, 104*, 210–227; McNall, L. A., Nicklin, J. M., & Masuda, A. D. (2010). A meta-analytic review of the consequences associated with work–family enrichment. *Journal of Business and Psychology, 25*, 381–396; Graves, L. M., Ohlott, P. J., & Ruderman, M. N. (2007). Commitment to family roles: Effects on managers' attitudes and performance. *Journal of Applied Psychology, 92*, 44–56.

36. Greenhaus, J. H., & Powell, G. N. (2006). When work and family are allies: A theory of work–family enrichment. *Academy of Management Review, 31*, 72–92.

37. Allen, T. D., French, K. A., Dumani, S., & Shockley, K. M. (2020). A cross-national meta-analytic examination of predictors and outcomes associated with work–family conflict. *Journal of Applied Psychology, 105*, 539–576; Ollier-Malaterre, A., & Foucreault, A. (2017). Cross-national work–life research: Cultural and structural impacts for individuals and organizations. *Journal of Management, 43*, 111–136; Shockley, K. M., Douek, J., Smith, C. R., Yu, P. P., Dumani, S., & French, K. A. (2017). Cross-cultural work and family research: A review of the literature. *Journal of Vocational Behavior, 101*, 1–20; Powell, G. N., Francesco, A. M., & Ling, Y. (2009). Toward culture-sensitive theories of the work–family interface. *Journal of Organizational Behavior, 30*, 597–616.

38. Rothbard, N. P., & Ollier-Malaterre, A. (2016). Boundary management. In T. D. Allen & L. T. Eby (Eds.), *Oxford handbook of work and family* (pp. 109–122). Oxford University Press; Allen, T. D., Cho, E., & Meier, L. L. (2014). Work–family boundary dynamics. *Annual Review of Organizational Psychology and Organizational Behavior, 1*, 99–121;

Kreiner, G. E. (2006). Consequences of work–home segmentation or integration: A person–environment fit perspective. *Journal of Organizational Behavior, 27*, 485–507; Ashforth, B. E., Kreiner, G. E., & Fugate, M. (2000). All in a day's work: Boundaries and micro role transitions. *Academy of Management Review, 25*, 472–491.

39. Powell, G. N. (2020). Work–family lockdown: Implications for a post-pandemic research agenda. *Gender in Management: An International Review, 35*, 639–646; Rothbard, N. P., & Ollier-Malaterre, A. (2016). Boundary management. In T. D. Allen & L. T. Eby (Eds.), *Oxford handbook of work and family* (pp. 109–122). Oxford University Press; Allen, T. D., Cho, E., & Meier, L. L. (2014). Work–family boundary dynamics. *Annual Review of Organizational Psychology and Organizational Behavior, 1*, 99–121; Kreiner, G. E. (2006). Consequences of work–home segmentation or integration: A person–environment fit perspective. *Journal of Organizational Behavior, 27*, 485–507.

40. Hughes, K. D., & Silver, W. A. (2020). Beyond time-binds: Rethinking work–family dynamics for a mobile world. *Human Relations, 73*, 924–952; Ollier-Malaterre, A., Jacobs, J. A., & Rothbard, N. P. (2019). Technology, work, and family: Digital cultural capital and boundary management. *Annual Review of Sociology, 45*, 425–447; Kossek, E. E. (2016). Managing work–life boundaries in the digital age. *Organizational Dynamics, 45*, 258–270; Rothbard, N. P., & Ollier-Malaterre, A. (2016). Boundary management. In T. D. Allen & L. T. Eby (Eds.), *Oxford handbook of work and family* (pp. 109–122). Oxford University Press.

41. Powell, G. N., & Greenhaus, J. H. (2010b). Sex, gender, and the work-to-family interface: Exploring negative and positive interdependencies. *Academy of Management Journal, 53*, 513–534.

42. Shockley, K. M., Shen, W., DeNunzio, M. M., Arvan, M. L., & Knudsen, E. A. (2017). Disentangling the relationship between gender and work–family conflict: An integration of theoretical perspectives using meta-analytic methods. *Journal of Applied Psychology, 102*, 1601–1635.

43. Greenhaus, J. H., & Powell, G. N. (2017). *Making work and family work: From hard choices to smart choices*. Routledge; Greenhaus, J. H., & Powell, G. N. (2012). The family-relatedness of work decisions: A framework and agenda for theory and research. *Journal of Vocational Behavior, 80*, 246–255; Powell, G. N., & Greenhaus, J. H. (2012). When family considerations influence work decisions: Decision-making processes. *Journal of Vocational Behavior, 81*, 322–329.

44. Wanberg, C. R., Csillag, B., & Duffy, M. K. (2023). After the break-up: How divorcing affects individuals at work. *Personnel Psychology, 76*, 77–112.

45. Powell, G. N., & Greenhaus, J. H. (2010a). Sex, gender, and decisions at the family–work interface. *Journal of Management, 36*, 1011–1039.

46. U.S. Department of Labor, Bureau of Labor Statistics. (2023b). *Labor force statistics from the Current Population Survey*, computed from Table 8. Retrieved March 30, 2023, from https://www.bls.gov/cps/cps_over.htm

47. Campion, E. D., Caza, B. B., & Moss, S. E. (2020). Multiple jobholding: An integrative systematic review and future research agenda. *Journal of Management, 46*, 165–191; Lyonette, C. (2015). Part-time work, work–life balance and gender equality. *Journal of Social Welfare and Family Law, 37*, 321–333; Booth, A. L., & van Ours, J. C. (2013). Part-time jobs: What women want? *Journal of Population Economics, 26*, 263–283; van Rijswijk, K., Bekker, M. H. J., Rutte, C. G., & Croon, M. A. (2004). The relationships among part-time work, work–family interference, and well-being. *Journal of*

Occupational Health Psychology, 9, 286–295; Higgins, C., Duxbury, L., & Johnson, K. L. (2000). Part-time work for women: Does it really help balance work and family? *Human Resource Management, 39*, 17–32.

48. U.S. Department of Labor, Bureau of Labor Statistics. (2023b). *Labor force statistics from the Current Population Survey*, computed from Table 8. Retrieved March 30, 2023, from https://www.bls.gov/cps/cps_over.htm

49. Powell, G. N. (2020). Work–family lockdown: Implications for a post-pandemic research agenda. *Gender in Management: An International Review, 35*, 639–646.

50. Krugman, P. (2023, May 22). Working from home and realizing what matters. *New York Times*. Retrieved May 22, 2023, from https://www.nytimes.com/2023/05/22/opinion/work-from-home-commuting-gdp.html; Huyghebaert-Zouaghi, T., Morin, A. J. S., Fernet, C., Austin, S., & Gillet, N. (2022). Longitudinal profiles of work–family interface: Their individual and organizational predictors, personal and work outcomes, and implications for onsite and remote workers. *Journal of Vocational Behavior, 134*, 103695; Jachimowicz, J. M., Cunningham, J. L., Staats, B. R., Gino, F., & Menges, J. I. (2021). Between home and work: Commuting as an opportunity for role transitions. *Organization Science, 32*, 64–85; Wang, Y., & Yang, M. (2019). Long commutes to work during pregnancy and infant health at birth. *Economics and Human Biology, 35*, 1–17.

51. Goldberg, E., & Casselman, B. (2023, April 24). What young workers miss without the "power of proximity." *New York Times*. Retrieved May 22, 2023, from https://www.nytimes.com/2023/04/24/business/remote-work-feedback.html; Rattner, S. (2023, March 22). Is working from home really working? *New York Times*. Retrieved March 22, 2023, from https://www.nytimes.com/2023/03/22/opinion/remote-work-salesforce-meta-working-from-home.html; Huyghebaert-Zouaghi, T., Morin, A. J. S., Fernet, C., Austin, S., & Gillet, N. (2022). Longitudinal profiles of work–family interface: Their individual and organizational predictors, personal and work outcomes, and implications for onsite and remote workers. *Journal of Vocational Behavior, 134*, 103695; Torry, H. (2022, March 13). Women embrace flexible working, but economists say it could hurt their careers. *Wall Street Journal*. Retrieved March 13, 2022, from https://www.wsj.com/articles/women-embrace-flexible-working-but-economists-say-it-could-hinder-their-careers-11647180001; Hickok, H. (2021, May 6). Are men-dominated offices the future of the workplace? *BBC*. Retrieved August 11, 2021, from https://www.bbc.com/worklife/article/20210503-are-men-dominated-offices-the-future-of-the-workplace

52. Reitman, F., & Schneer, J. A. (2005). The long-term negative impacts of managerial career interruptions: A longitudinal study of men and women MBAs. *Group & Organization Management, 30*, 243–262; Schneer, J. A., & Reitman, F. (1997). The interrupted managerial career path: A longitudinal study of MBAs. *Journal of Vocational Behavior, 51*, 411–434.

53. Parks-Stamm, E. J., & Tharp, D. T. (2023). But what do they *do* on leave? Differing evaluations of men and women's completion of work tasks on parental leave. *Journal of Occupational and Organizational Psychology, 96*, 235–241; Gatrell, C., Ladge, J. J., & Powell, G. N. (2022). A review of fatherhood and employment: Introducing new perspectives for management research. *Journal of Management Studies, 59*, 1198–1226; Harrington, B., Humberd, B. K., & Van Deusen, F. (2016). Work–family issues for men. In T. D. Allen & L. T. Eby (Eds.), *Oxford handbook of work and family* (pp. 441–452). Oxford University Press; Rudman, L. A., & Mescher, K. (2013). Penalizing men who

request a family leave: Is flexibility stigma a femininity stigma? *Journal of Social Issues, 69*, 322–340; Powell, G. N. (1997). The sex difference in employee inclinations regarding work–family programs: Why does it exist, should we care, and what should be done about it (if anything)? In S. Parasuraman & J. H. Greenhaus (Eds.), *Integrating work and family: Challenges and choices for a changing world* (pp. 167–174). Quorum.

54. Ernst & Young (2015). *Global generations: A global study on work–life challenges across generations*. Retrieved December 15, 2017, from https://cs-wordpress.s3.amazonaws.com/crowdsource-v4/uploads/2015/06/Generations-Globally-work-life-challenges-EY-5-15.pdf; Galinsky, E., Aumann, K., & Bond, J. T. (2011). *Times are changing: Gender and generation at work and at home*. Families and Work Institute. Retrieved December 18, 2017, from https://www.familiesandwork.org/research/2009/times-are-changing-gender-and-generation-at-work-and-at-home/; Powell, G. N., & Greenhaus, J. H. (2010a). Sex, gender, and decisions at the family–work interface. *Journal of Management, 36*, 1011–1039.

55. This section is largely based on Chapter 6, Greenhaus, J. H., & Powell, G. N. (2017). *Making work and family work: From hard choices to smart choices*. Routledge.

56. Cluley, H., & Hecht, T. D. (2020). Micro work–family decision-making of dual-income couples with young children: What does a couple like us do in a situation like this? *Journal of Occupational and Organizational Psychology, 93*, 45–72; Crawford, W. S., Thompson, M. J., & Ashforth, B. E. (2019). Work–life events theory: Making sense of shock events in dual-earner couples. *Academy of Management Review, 44*, 194–212; Radcliffe, L. S., & Cassell, C. (2014). Resolving couples' work–family conflicts: The complexity of decision making and the introduction of a new framework. *Human Relations, 67*, 793–819.

57. Ullrich, J., Pluut, H., & Büttgen, M. (2015). Gender differences in the family-relatedness of relocation decisions. *Journal of Vocational Behavior, 90*, 1–12; Benson, A. (2015). A theory of dual job search and sex-based occupational clustering. *Industrial Relations, 54*, 367–400; Benson, A. (2014). Rethinking the two-body problem: The segregation of women into geographically dispersed occupations. *Demography, 51*, 1619–1639; Wallston, B. S., Foster, M. A., & Berger, M. (1978). I will follow him: Myth, reality, or forced choice—Job-seeking experiences of dual-career couples. *Psychology of Women Quarterly, 3*, 9–21.

58. Bear, J. B. (2019). The caregiving ambition framework. *Academy of Management Review, 44*, 99–125; Masterson, C. R., & Hoobler, J. M. (2015). Care and career: A family identity-based typology of dual-earner couples. *Journal of Organizational Behavior, 36*, 75–93.

59. Greenhaus, J. H., & Powell, G. N. (2017). *Making work and family work: From hard choices to smart choices*. Routledge; Masterson, C. R., & Hoobler, J. M. (2015). Care and career: A family identity-based typology of dual-earner couples. *Journal of Organizational Behavior, 36*, 75–93.

60. This section is largely based on Chapter 4, Greenhaus, J. H., & Powell, G. N. (2017). *Making work and family work: From hard choices to smart choices*. Routledge.

61. Allen, T. D., & French, K. A. (2023). Work–family research: A review and next steps. *Personnel Psychology, 76*, 437–471; Masterson, C. R., Sugiyama, K., & Ladge, J. J. (2021). The value of 21st century work–family supports: Review and cross-level path forward. *Journal of Organizational Behavior, 42*, 118–138; Sprung, J. M., Toumbeva, T. H., & Matthews, R. A. (2015). Family-friendly organizational policies, practices, and benefits through the gender lens. In M. J. Mills (Ed.), *Gender and the work–family*

experience: An intersection of two domains (pp. 227–249). Springer; Butts, M. M., Casper, W. J., & Yang, T. S. (2013). How important are work–family support policies? A meta-analytic investigation of their effects on employee outcomes. *Journal of Applied Psychology, 98*, 1–25.

62. U.S. Department of Labor, Bureau of Labor Statistics. (2023c). *What data does the BLS publish on family leave?* Retrieved April 4, 2023, from https://www.bls.gov/ebs/publications/pdf/family-leave-benefits-fact-sheet.pdf; Wheelwright, T. (2022, May 3). Paid maternity leave across the world in 2022. *Business.org*. Retrieved April 4, 2023, from https://www.business.org/hr/workforce-management/paid-maternity-leave-across-the-world/; International Labour Office. (2014). *Maternity and paternity at work: Law and practice across the world*. Retrieved May 13, 2014, from https://www.ilo.org/global/topics/equality-and-discrimination/maternity-protection/publications/maternity-paternity-at-work-2014/lang--en/index.htm

63. Allen, T. D., & French, K. A. (2023). Work–family research: A review and next steps. *Personnel Psychology, 76*, 437–471; Modestino, A. S., Ladge, J. J., Swartz, A., & Lincoln, A. (2021, April 29). Childcare is a business issue. *Harvard Business Review*. Retrieved August 10, 2021, from https://hbr.org/2021/04/childcare-is-a-business-issue; Masterson, C. R., Sugiyama, K., & Ladge, J. J. (2021). The value of 21st century work–family supports: Review and cross-level path forward. *Journal of Organizational Behavior, 42*, 118–138

64. Kossek, E. E., Perrigino, M. B., & Lautsch, B. A. (2023). Work–life flexibility policies from a boundary control and implementation perspective: A review and research framework. *Journal of Management, 49*, 2062–2108; Allen, T. D., & French, K. A. (2023). Work–family research: A review and next steps. *Personnel Psychology, 76*, 437–471; Masterson, C. R., Sugiyama, K., & Ladge, J. J. (2021). The value of 21st century work–family supports: Review and cross-level path forward. *Journal of Organizational Behavior, 42*, 118–138; Spreitzer, G. M., Cameron, L., & Garrett, L. (2017). Alternative work arrangements: Two images of the new world of work. *Annual Review of Organizational Psychology and Organizational Behavior, 4*, 473–499.

65. Bolino, M. C., Kelemen, T. K., & Matthews, S. H. (2021). Working 9-to-5? A review of research on nonstandard work schedules. *Journal of Organizational Behavior, 42*, 188–211; Spreitzer, G. M., Cameron, L., & Garrett, L. (2017). Alternative work arrangements: Two images of the new world of work. *Annual Review of Organizational Psychology and Organizational Behavior, 4*, 473–499; Thompson, R. J., Payne, S. C., & Taylor, A. B. (2015). Applicant attraction to flexible work arrangements: Separating the influence of flextime and flexplace. *Journal of Occupational and Organizational Psychology, 88*, 726–749; Kossek, E. E., & Michel, J. S. (2011). Flexible work schedules. In S. Zedeck (Ed.), *APA handbook of industrial and organizational psychology* (Vol. 1, pp. 535–572). American Psychological Association.

66. Allen, T. D., & French, K. A. (2023). Work–family research: A review and next steps. *Personnel Psychology, 76*, 437–471; Spreitzer, G. M., Cameron, L., & Garrett, L. (2017). Alternative work arrangements: Two images of the new world of work. *Annual Review of Organizational Psychology and Organizational Behavior, 4*, 473–499; Thompson, R. J., Payne, S. C., & Taylor, A. B. (2015). Applicant attraction to flexible work arrangements: Separating the influence of flextime and flexplace. *Journal of Occupational and Organizational Psychology, 88*, 726–749; Allen, T. D., Golden, T. D., & Shockley, K. M. (2015). How effective is telecommuting? Assessing the status of our scientific findings. *Psychological Science in the Public Interest, 16*(2), 40–68; Golden, T. D., Veiga, J.

F., & Simsek, Z. (2006). Telecommuting's differential impact on work–family conflict: Is there no place like home? *Journal of Applied Psychology, 91*, 1340–1350.

67. Joseph, B., Walker, A., & Fuller-Tyszkiewicz, M. (2018). Evaluating the effectiveness of employee assistance programmes: A systematic review. *European Journal of Work and Organizational Psychology, 27*, 1–15; Compton, R-L., & McManus, J. G. (2015). Employee assistance programs in Australia: Evaluating success. *Journal of Workplace Behavioral Health, 30*, 32–45; Cooper, C. L., Dewe, P. J., & O'Driscoll, M. P. (2011). Employee assistance programs: Strengths, challenges, and future roles. In J. C. Quick & L. E. Tetrick (Eds.), *Handbook of occupational health psychology* (2nd ed., pp. 337–356). American Psychological Association; Chaker, A. M. (2007, October 4). Employers offer help on college admissions. *Wall Street Journal*. Retrieved October 4, 2007, from https://www.wsj.com/articles/SB119146374898648587

68. Kossek, E. E., Lautsch, B. A., Perrigino, M. B., Greenhaus, J. H., & Merriweather, T. J. (2023). Work–life flexibility policies: Moving from traditional views toward work–life intersectionality considerations. *Research in Personnel and Human Resources Management, 41*, 199–243; Greenhaus, J. H., & Powell, G. N. (2017). *Making work and family work: From hard choices to smart choices*. Routledge.

69. Allen, T. D., & French, K. A. (2023). Work–family research: A review and next steps. *Personnel Psychology, 76*, 437–471; Bourdeau, S., Ollier-Malaterre, A., & Houlfort, N. (2019). Not all work–life policies are created equal: Career consequences of using enabling versus enclosing work–life policies. *Academy of Management Review, 44*, 172–193; Perrigino, M. B., Dunford, B. B., & Wilson, K. S. (2018). Work–family backlash: The "dark side" of work–life balance (WLB) policies. *Academy of Management Annals, 12*, 600–630.

70. Brady, J. M., Hammer, L. B., Mohr, C. D., & Bodner, T. E. (2021). Supportive supervisor training improves family relationships among employee and spouse dyads. *Journal of Occupational Health Psychology, 26*, 31–48; Crain, T. L., & Stevens, S. C. (2018). Family-supportive supervisor behaviors: A review and recommendations for research and practice. *Journal of Organizational Behavior, 39*, 869–888; Rofcanin, Y., Las Heras, M., & Bakker, A. B. (2017). Family supportive supervisor behaviors and organizational culture: Effects on work engagement and performance. *Journal of Occupational Health Psychology, 22*, 207–217; Odle-Dusseau, H. N., Hammer, L. B., Crain, T. L., & Bodner, T. E. (2016). The influence of family-supportive supervisor training on employee job performance and attitudes: An organizational work–family intervention. *Journal of Occupational Health Psychology, 21*, 296–308.

71. Powell, G. N., & Mainiero, L. A. (1999). Managerial decision making regarding alternative work arrangements. *Journal of Occupational and Organizational Psychology, 72*, 41–56.

72. Perrigino, M. B., Dunford, B. B., & Wilson, K. S. (2018). Work–family backlash: The "dark side" of work–life balance (WLB) policies. *Academy of Management Annals, 12*, 600–630; Casper, W. J., Marquardt, D. J., Roberto, K. J., & Buss, C. (2016). The hidden family lives of single adults without dependent children. In T. D. Allen & L. T. Eby (Eds.), *Oxford handbook of work and family* (pp. 182–195). Oxford University Press; Casper, W. J., & DePaulo, B. (2012). A new layer to inclusion: Creating singles-friendly work environments. In N. P. Reilly, M. J. Sirgy, & C. A. Gorman (Eds.), *Work and quality of life: Ethical practices in organizations* (pp. 217–234). Springer; Casper, W. J., Weltman, D., & Kwesiga, E. (2007). Beyond family-friendly: The construct and measurement of singles-friendly work culture. *Journal of Vocational Behavior, 70*,

478–501; DePaulo, B. M. (2006). *Singled out: How singles are stereotyped, singled, and ignored and still live happily ever after.* St. Martin's Press.

73. Murphy, L. D., Thomas, C. L., Cobb, H. R., & Hartman, A. E. (2021). A review of the LGBTQ+ work–family interface: What do we know and where do we go from here? *Journal of Organizational Behavior, 42*, 139–161; Dixon, J. (2018). Looking out from the family closet: Discourse dependence and queer family identity in workplace conversation. *Management Communication Quarterly, 32*, 271–275.

74. Nsair, V., & Piszczek, M. (2021). Gender matters: The effects of gender and segmentation preferences on work-to-family conflict in family sacrifice climates. *Journal of Occupational and Organizational Psychology, 94*, 509–530; Greenhaus, J. H., & Kossek, E. E. (2014). The contemporary career: A work–home perspective. *Annual Review of Organizational Psychology and Organizational Behavior, 1*, 361–388.

75. Padavic, I., Ely, R. J., & Reid, E. M. (2020). Explaining the persistence of gender inequality: The work–family narrative as a social defense against the 24/7 work culture. *Administrative Science Quarterly, 65*, 61–111; Ely, R. J., & Padavic, I. (2020). What's really holding women back? *Harvard Business Review, 98*(2), 58–67; Miller, C. C. (2019, April 26). Women did everything right. Then work got "greedy." *New York Times.* Retrieved May 1, 2019, from https://www.nytimes.com/2019/04/26/upshot/women-long-hours-greedy-professions.html; Powell, G. N. (1998). The abusive organization. *Academy of Management Executive, 12*(2), 95–96.

76. Greenhaus, J. H., & Powell, G. N. (2017). *Making work and family work: From hard choices to smart choices.* Routledge.

77. French, K. A., & Shockley, K. M. (2020). Formal and informal supports for managing work and family. *Current Directions in Psychological Science, 29*, 207–216; Pluut, H., Ilies, R., Curşeu, P. L., & Liu, Y. (2018). Social support at work and at home: Dual-buffering effects in the work–family conflict process. *Organizational Behavior and Human Decision Processes, 146*, 1–13; French, K. A., Dumani, S., Allen, T. D., & Shockley, K. M. (2018). A meta-analysis of work-family conflict and social support. *Psychological Bulletin, 144*, 284–314; Powell, G. N., & Greenhaus, J. H. (2006). Managing incidents of work-family conflict: A decision-making perspective. *Human Relations, 59*, 1179–1212; Greenhaus, J. H., & Parasuraman, S. (1994). Work–family conflict, social support and well-being. In M. J. Davidson & R. J. Burke (Eds.), *Women in management: Current research issues* (pp. 213–229). Chapman.

78. Franczak, J., & Margolis, J. (2022). Women and great places to work: Gender diversity in leadership and how to get there. *Organizational Dynamics, 51*, 100913; Ragins, B. R. (2020). What the research tells us: Glass-ceiling chisels. In E. E. Kossek & K-Y. Lee (Eds.), *Creating gender-inclusive organizations: Lessons from research and practice* (pp. 53–66). University of Toronto Press; Janssen, S., van Vuuren, M., & de Jong, M. D. T. (2016). Informal mentoring at work: A review and suggestions for future research. *International Journal of Management Reviews, 18*, 498–517; Greenhaus, J. H., & Singh, R. (2007). Mentoring and the work–family interface. In B. R. Ragins & K. E. Kram (Eds.), *The handbook of mentoring at work: Theory, research, and practice* (pp. 519–544). SAGE; McKeen, C., & Bujaki, M. (2007). Gender and mentoring: Issues, effects, and opportunities. In B. R. Ragins & K. E. Kram (Eds.), *The handbook of mentoring at work: Theory, research, and practice* (pp. 197–222). SAGE; Ragins, B. R. (1999). Gender and mentoring relationships: A review and research agenda for the next decade. In G. N. Powell (Ed.), *Handbook of gender and work* (pp. 347–370). SAGE.

79. U.S. Department of Labor (2023). *Vacation leave*. Retrieved May 28, 2023, from https://www.dol.gov/general/topic/workhours/vacation_leave; Maye, A. (2019). *No vacation nation, revised*. Center for Economic Policy and Research. Retrieved May 23, 2023, from https://cepr.net/images/stories/reports/no-vacation-nation-2019-05.pdf

80. Kuykendall, L., Craig, L., Stiksma, M., & Guarino, K. (2021). Understanding employees' unused vacation days: A social cognitive approach. *Journal of Occupational Health Psychology, 26*, 69–85; Greenhaus, J. H., & Powell, G. N. (2017). *Making work and family work: From hard choices to smart choices*. Routledge; Maume, D. L. (2006). Gender differences in taking vacation time. *Work and Occupations, 33*, 161–190.

81. Poelmans, S. A. Y., & Stepanova, E. O. (2016). A neuroscience perspective of the work–family–life interface. In T. D. Allen & L. T. Eby (Eds.), *Oxford handbook of work and family* (pp. 401–416). Oxford University Press; Davidson, M. J., & Fielden, S. (1999). Stress and the working woman. In G. N. Powell (Ed.), *Handbook of gender and work* (pp. 413–426). SAGE; Edwards, J. R., & Rothbard, N. P. (1999). Work and family stress and well-being: An examination of person–environment fit in the work and family domains. *Organizational Behavior and Human Decision Processes, 77*, 85–129.

82. Powell, G. N., & Greenhaus, J. H. (2010b). Sex, gender, and the work-to-family interface: Exploring negative and positive interdependencies. *Academy of Management Journal, 53*, 513–534.

83. Greenhaus, J. H., & Powell, G. N. (2017). *Making work and family work: From hard choices to smart choices*. Routledge.

CHAPTER 9

1. Walmart. (2023). *Culture, diversity, equity & inclusion*. Retrieved April 13, 2023, from https://corporate.walmart.com/purpose/culture-diversity-equity-inclusion; Amazon. (2023). *Diversity, equity, and inclusion*. Retrieved April 13, 2023, from https://www.aboutamazon.com/workplace/diversity-inclusion; CVS Health. (2023). *Diversity, equity and inclusion*. Retrieved April 13, 2023, from https://www.cvshealth.com/about/our-strategy/diversity.html; Apple. (2023). *Careers at Apple*. Retrieved April 13, 2023, from https://www.apple.com/careers/us/; UnitedHealth Group. (2023). *Advancing diversity, equity and inclusion*. Retrieved April 13, 2023, from https://sustainability.uhg.com/people-culture/inclusion-diversity.html.

2. Largest U.S. corporations. (2023). *Fortune, 185*(3), F1–F20. Retrieved May 29, 2023, from https://fortune.com/ranking/fortune500/

3. Wang, W., Dinh, J. V., Jones, K. S., Upadhyay, S., & Yang, J. (2023). Corporate diversity statements and employees' online DEI ratings: An unsupervised machine-learning text-mining analysis. *Journal of Business and Psychology, 38*, 45–61; Corrington, A., Fa-Kaji, N. M., Hebl, M. R., King, E. B., Stewart, D., & Alao, T. (2022). The impact of organizational statements of support for the black community in the wake of a racial mega-threat on organizational attraction and revenue. *Human Resource Management, 61*, 699–722; Moore, E., & Philip, A. (2022). Black Lives Matter: True commitment or tokenism? In E. B. King, Q. M. Roberson, & M. R. Hebl (Eds.), *The future of scholarship on race in organizations* (pp. 137–177). Information Age Publishing; Callaham, S. (2020, August 23). Does "Black Lives Matter" hinder or help universal equity? Three diversity executives speak out. *Forbes*. Retrieved April 13, 2023, from

https://www.forbes.com/sites/sheilacallaham/2020/08/23/does-black-lives-matter-hinder-or-help-universal-equity-three-diversity-executives-speak-out/

4. Leslie, L. M., Flynn, E., Foster-Gimbel, O. A., & Manchester, C. F. (in press). Happy talk: Is common diversity rhetoric effective diversity rhetoric? *Academy of Management Journal*; Nkomo, S. M., Bell, M. P., Roberts, L. M., Joshi, A., & Thatcher, S. M. B. (2019). Diversity at a critical juncture: New theories for a complex phenomenon. *Academy of Management Review, 44*, 498–517; Windscheid, L., Bowes-Sperry, L., Kidder, D. L., Cheung, H. K., Morner, M., & Lievens, F. (2016). Actions speak louder than words: Outsiders' perceptions of diversity mixed messages. *Journal of Applied Psychology, 101*, 1329–1341; Bell, J. M., & Hartmann, D. (2007). Diversity in everyday discourse: The cultural ambiguities and consequences of "happy talk." *American Sociological Review, 72*, 895–914.

5. Mor Barak, M. E. (2022). *Managing diversity: Toward a globally inclusive workplace* (5th ed.). SAGE; Dunleavy, E. M., Engelsted, L., & Morris, A. (2018). A primer on equal employment opportunity law and contemporary enforcement. In A. J. Colella & E. B. King (Eds.), *The Oxford handbook of workplace discrimination* (pp. 253–263). Oxford University Press; Sedmak, N. J., & Vidas, C. (1994). *Primer of equal employment opportunity* (6th ed.). Bureau of National Affairs; Gamble, B. S. (Ed.). (1992). *Sex discrimination handbook*. Bureau of National Affairs.

6. U. S. Equal Employment Opportunity Commission. (2023). *Sexual orientation and gender identity (SOGI) discrimination*. Retrieved April 13, 2023, from https://www.eeoc.gov/sexual-orientation-and-gender-identity-sogi-discrimination; U. S. Equal Employment Opportunity Commission. (2021). *Protection against employment discrimination based on sexual orientation or gender identity*. Retrieved April 13, 2023, from https://www.eeoc.gov/laws/guidance/protections-against-employment-discrimination-based-sexual-orientation-or-gender

7. Sedmak, N. J., & Vidas, C. (1994). *Primer of equal employment opportunity* (6th ed.). Bureau of National Affairs, p. 39.

8. Sedmak, N. J., & Vidas, C. (1994). *Primer of equal employment opportunity* (6th ed.). Bureau of National Affairs, p. 44; Ledvinka, J., & Scarpello, V. G. (1991). *Federal regulation of personnel and human resource management* (2nd ed.). PWS-Kent, p. 60.

9. Hooters. (2023). *Careers*. Retrieved April 14, 2023, from https://jobs.hooters.com/; Thornton, J. (1997, October 1). Hoots greet the settlement of Hooters sex-bias lawsuit. *Chicago Tribune*. Retrieved December 29, 2017, from https://www.chicagotribune.com/news/ct-xpm-1997-10-01-9710010254-story.html; Bovard, J. (1995, November 17). The EEOC's war on Hooters. *Wall Street Journal*, p. A18.

10. Crosby, F. J., Iyer, A., & Sincharoen, S. (2006). Understanding affirmative action. *Annual Review of Psychology, 57*, 585–611; Konrad, A. M., & Linnehan, F. (2003). Affirmative action as a means of increasing workforce diversity. In M. J. Davidson & S. L. Fielden (Eds.), *Individual diversity and psychology in organizations* (pp. 95–111). Wiley; Konrad, A. M., & Linnehan, F. (1999). Affirmative action: History, effects, and attitudes. In G. N. Powell (Ed.), *Handbook of gender and work* (pp. 429–452). SAGE.

11. Brown, N. D., & Jacoby-Senghor, D. S. (2022). Majority members misperceive even "win–win" diversity policies as unbeneficial to them. *Journal of Personality and Social Psychology, 122*, 1075–1097; Konrad, A. M., Richard, O. C., & Yang, Y. (2021). *Both* diversity *and* meritocracy: Managing the diversity–meritocracy paradox with organizational ambidexterity. *Journal of Management Studies, 58*, 2180–2206; Livingston, R. (2020). How to promote racial equity in the workplace. *Harvard Business Review,*

98(5), 64–72; Leslie, L. M. (2019). Diversity initiative effectiveness: A typological theory of unintended consequences. *Academy of Management Review, 44*, 538–563.

12. Bhatia, A., Miller, C. C., & Katz, J. (2023, July 24). Study of elite college admissions data suggests being very rich is its own qualification. *New York Times*. Retrieved July 24, 2023, from https://www.nytimes.com/interactive/2023/07/24/upshot/ivy-league-elite-college-admissions.html; Saul, S. (2022, July 13). The quiet fight to keep legacy admissions. *New York Times*. Retrieved July 13, 2022, from http://nytimes.com/2022/07/13/us/legacy-admissions-colleges-universities.html; McWhorter, J. (2022, February 1). End affirmative action for rich White students, too. *New York Times*. Retrieved February 1, 2022, from https://www.nytimes.com/2022/02/01/opinion/affirmative-action.html; Golden, D. (2007). *The price of admission: How America's ruling class buys its way into elite colleges—and who gets left outside the gates*. Three Rivers Press; Golden, D. (2003, February 20). Many colleges bend rules to admit rich applicants. *Wall Street Journal*. Retrieved January 5, 2018, from https://www.wsj.com/public/resources/documents/Polk_Rich_Applicants.htm
13. Hughes, M. M., Paxton, P., & Krook, M. L. (2017). Gender quotas for legislatures and corporate boards. *Annual Review of Sociology, 43*, 331–352; Sojo, V. E., Wood, R. E., Wood, S. A., & Wheeler, M. A. (2016). Reporting requirements, targets, and quotas for women in leadership. *Leadership Quarterly, 27*, 519–536; Wang, M., & Kelan, E. (2013). The gender quota and female leadership: Effects of the Norwegian gender quota on board chairs and CEOs. *Journal of Business Ethics, 117*, 449–466.
14. Tost, L. P., Hardin, A. E., Roberson, J. W., & Gino, F. (2022). Different roots, different fruits: Gender-based differences in cultural narratives about perceived discrimination produce divergent psychological consequences. *Academy of Management Journal, 65*, 1804–1834; Triana, M. d. C., Jayasinghe, M., Pieper, J. R., Delgado, D. M., & Li, M. (2019). Perceived workplace gender discrimination and employee consequences: A meta-analysis and complementary studies considering country context. *Journal of Management, 45*, 2419–2447; Jones, K. P., Peddie, C. I., Gilrane, V. L., King, E. B., & Gray, A. L. (2016). Not so subtle: A meta-analytic investigation of the correlates of subtle and overt discrimination. *Journal of Management, 42*, 1588–1613; Pascoe, E. A., & Richman, L. S. (2009). Perceived discrimination and health: A meta-analytic review. *Psychological Bulletin, 135*, 531–554; Goldman, B. M., Gutek, B. A., Stein, J. H., & Lewis, K. (2006). Employment discrimination in organizations: Antecedents and consequences. *Journal of Management, 32*, 786–830.
15. Dixon, A. R., & Telles, E. E. (2017). Skin color and colorism: Global research, concepts, and measurement. *Annual Review of Sociology, 43*, 405–424; Gebert, D., Boerner, S., Kearney, E., King, J. E., Jr., Zhang, K., & Song, L. J. (2014). Expressing religious identities in the workplace: Analyzing a neglected diversity dimension. *Human Relations, 67*, 543–563; Binggeli, S., Dietz, J., & Krings, F. (2013). Immigrants: A forgotten minority. *Industrial and Organizational Psychology, 6*, 107–113; Ruggs, E. N., Hebl, M. R., Law, C., Cox, C. B., Roehling, M. V., Wiener, R. L., & Barron, L. (2013). Gone fishing: I-O psychologists' missed opportunities to understand marginalized employees' experiences with discrimination. *Industrial and Organizational Psychology, 6*, 39–60.
16. Ponce de Leon, R., & Rosette, A. S. (2022). "Invisible" discrimination: Divergent outcomes for the nonprototypicality of Black women. *Academy of Management Journal, 65*, 784–812; Summerville, K. M., & Ruggs, E. N. (2022). The authenticity paradox: A double consciousness perspective of race, gender, and authenticity at work for Black

women. In E. B. King, Q. M. Roberson, & M. R. Hebl (Eds.), *The future of scholarship on race in organizations* (pp. 201–232). Information Age Publishing; Phillips, L. T., Jun, S., & Shakeri, A. (2022). Barriers and boosts: Using inequity frames theory to expand understanding of mechanisms of race and gender inequity. *Academy of Management Annals, 16*, 547–587.

17. Apfelbaum, E. P., & Sommers, S. R. (2013). Law and diversity: The legal-behavioral science divide in how define, assess, and counteract bias. In Q. M. Roberson (Ed.), *Oxford handbook of diversity and work* (pp. 442–459). Oxford University Press.

18. James, E. H., & Wooten, L. P. (2006). Diversity crises: How firms manage discrimination lawsuits. *Academy of Management Journal, 49*, 1103–1118 Goldman, B. M., Gutek, B. A., Stein, J. H., & Lewis, K. (2006). Employment discrimination in organizations: Antecedents and consequences. *Journal of Management, 32*, 786–830; Baucus, M. S., & Baucus, D. A. (1997). Paying the piper: An empirical examination of longer-term financial consequences of illegal corporate behavior. *Academy of Management Journal, 40*, 129–151.

19. Mor Barak, M. E. (2022). *Managing diversity: Toward a globally inclusive workplace* (5th ed.). SAGE; Post, C., Muzio, D., Sarala, R., Wei, L., & Faems, D. (2021). Theorizing diversity in management studies: New perspectives and future directions. *Journal of Management Studies, 58*, 2003–2023; Roberson, Q. M. (2019). Diversity in the workplace: A review, synthesis, and future research agenda. *Annual Review of Organizational Psychology and Organizational Behavior, 6*, 69–88; Mor Barak, M. E., & Travis, D. J. (2013). Socioeconomic trends: Broadening the diversity ecosystem. In Q. M. Roberson (Ed.), *Oxford handbook of diversity and work* (pp. 394–419). Oxford University Press.

20. Ngai, L. R., & Petrongolo, B. (2017). Gender gaps and the rise of the service economy. *American Economic Journal: Macroeconomics, 9*(4), 1–44; Gutek, B. A., Cherry, B., & Groth, M. (1999). Gender and service delivery. In G. N. Powell (Ed.), *Handbook of gender and work* (pp. 47–68). SAGE.

21. Maddux, W. W., Lu, J. G., Affinito, S. J., & Galinsky, A. D. (2021). Multicultural experiences: A systematic review and new theoretical framework. *Academy of Management Annals, 15*, 345–376; Özbilgin, M., Jonsen, K., Tatli, A., Vassilopoulou, J., & Surgevil, O. (2013). Global diversity management. In Q. M. Roberson (Ed.), *Oxford handbook of diversity and work* (pp. 419–441). Oxford University Press.

22. Post, C., Lokshin, B., & Boone, C. (2022). What changes after women enter top management teams? A gender-based model of strategic renewal. *Academy of Management Journal, 65*, 273–303; Post, C., Lokshin, B., & Boone, C. (2021, April 6). Adding women to the C-suite changes how companies think. *Harvard Business Review*. Retrieved June 1, 2021, from https://hbr.org/2021/04/research-adding-women-to-the-c-suite-changes-how-companies-think; Hoobler, J. M., Masterson, C. R., Nkomo, S. M., & Michel, E. J. (2018). The business case for women leaders: Meta-analysis, research critique, and path forward. *Journal of Management, 44*, 2473–2499; Roberson, Q., Holmes, O., IV, & Perry, J. L. (2017). Transforming research on diversity and firm performance: A dynamic capabilities perspective. *Academy of Management Annals, 11*, 189–216; Post, C., & Byron, K. (2015). Women on boards and firm financial performance: A meta-analysis. *Academy of Management Journal, 58*, 1546–1571.

23. Post, C., Ketchen, D. J., Jr., & Wowak, K. D. (2021). Should governments mandate more female board representation? Possible intended and unintended

consequences. *Business Horizons, 64*, 379–384; Graham, M. E., Walia, B., & Robinson, C. (2020). Women executives and off-the-job misconduct by high-profile employees: A study of National Football League team organizations. *Journal of Organizational Behavior, 41*, 815–829; Torchia, M., Calabrò, A., & Huse, M. (2011). Women directors on corporate boards: From tokenism to critical mass. *Journal of Business Ethics, 102*, 299–317; Kanter, R. M. (1977). *Men and women of the corporation*. Basic.

24. Chang, E. H., Milkman, K. L., Chugh, D., & Akinola, M. (2019). Diversity thresholds: How social norms, visibility, and scrutiny relate to group composition. *Academy of Management Journal, 62*, 144–171.

25. Kravitz, D. A. (2005). Diversity in teams: A two-edged sword requires careful handling. *Psychological Science in the Public Interest, 6*, i–ii; Milliken, F. J., & Martins, L. L. (1996). Searching for common threads: Understanding the multiple effects of diversity in organizational groups. *Academy of Management Review, 21*, 402–433.

26. Cox, T., Jr. (1993). *Cultural diversity in organizations: Theory, research and practice*. Berrett-Koehler; Cox, T., Jr. (1991). The multicultural organization. *Academy of Management Executive, 5*(2), 34–47.

27. Nishii, L. H. (2020). What the research tells us: The role of inclusive climates in closing the gender gap. In E. E. Kossek & K-Y. Lee (Eds.), *Creating gender-inclusive organizations: Lessons from research and practice* (pp. 15–26). University of Toronto Press; Nishii, L. H. (2013). The benefits of climate for inclusion for gender-diverse groups. *Academy of Management Journal, 56*, 1754–1774; Fitzsimmons, S. R. (2013). Multicultural employees: A framework for understanding how they contribute to organizations. *Academy of Management Review, 38*, 525–549.

28. Gilbert, J. A., & Ivancevich, J. M. (2000). Valuing diversity: A tale of two organizations. *Academy of Management Executive, 14*(1), 93–105.

29. Gutierrez, L. J., & Kellar, S. J. (2022). The business and employee cases for inclusion: Implications for organizations. In E. B. King, Q. M. Roberson, & M. R. Hebl (Eds.), *The future of scholarship on diversity and inclusion in organizations* (pp. 1–22). Information Age Publishing; Holmes, O., IV, Jiang, K., Avery, D. R., McKay, P. F., Oh, I-S., & Tillman, C. J. (2021). A meta-analysis integrating 25 years of diversity climate research. *Journal of Management, 47*, 1357–1382; Reinwald, M., Huettermann, H., & Bruch, H. (2019). Beyond the mean: Understanding firm-level consequences of variability in diversity climate perceptions. *Journal of Organizational Behavior, 40*, 472–491; Shore, L. M., Cleveland, J. N., & Sanchez, D. (2018). Inclusive workplaces: A review and model. *Human Resource Management Review, 28*, 176–189; Dwertmann, D. J. G., Nishii, L. H., & van Knippenberg, D. (2016). Disentangling the fairness & discrimination and synergy perspectives on diversity climate: Moving the field forward. *Journal of Management, 42*, 1136–1168; McKay, P. F., & Avery, D. R. (2015). Diversity climate in organizations: Current wisdom and domains of uncertainty. *Research in Personnel and Human Resources Management, 33*, 191–233.

30. Mor Barak, M. E. (2022). *Managing diversity: Toward a globally inclusive workplace* (5th ed.). SAGE; Franczak, J., & Margolis, J. (2022). Women and great places to work: Gender diversity in leadership and how to get there. *Organizational Dynamics, 51*, 100913; Kossek, E. E., & Lee, K-Y. (Eds.). (2020a). *Creating gender-inclusive organizations: Lessons from research and practice*. University of Toronto Press; Dobbin, F., & Kalev, A. (2013). The origins and effects of corporate diversity programs. In Q. M. Roberson (Ed.), *Oxford handbook of diversity and work* (pp. 253–281). Oxford University Press; Lobel, S. A. (1999). Impacts of diversity and work–life initiatives

in organizations. In G. N. Powell (Ed.), *Handbook of gender and work* (pp. 453–474). SAGE; Cox, T. H., Jr., & Blake, S. (1991). Managing cultural diversity: Implications for organizational competitiveness. *Academy of Management Executive, 5*(3), 45–56.

31. Gutierrez, L. J., & Kellar, S. J. (2022). The business and employee cases for inclusion: Implications for organizations. In E. B. King, Q. M. Roberson, & M. R. Hebl (Eds.), *The future of scholarship on diversity and inclusion in organizations* (pp. 1–22). Information Age Publishing; Franczak, J., & Margolis, J. (2022). Women and great places to work: Gender diversity in leadership and how to get there. *Organizational Dynamics, 51*, 100913; Hoobler, J. M., Masterson, C. R., Nkomo, S. M., & Michel, E. J. (2018). The business case for women leaders: Meta-analysis, research critique, and path forward. *Journal of Management, 44*, 2473–2499; Olsen, J. E., & Martins, L. L. (2012). Understanding organizational diversity management programs: A theoretical framework and directions for future research. *Journal of Organizational Behavior, 33*, 1168–1187; Cox, T., Jr. (1993). *Cultural diversity in organizations: Theory, research and practice.* Berrett-Koehler.

32. Leslie, L. M., Flynn, E., Foster-Gimbel, O. A., & Manchester, C. F. (in press). Happy talk: Is common diversity rhetoric effective diversity rhetoric? *Academy of Management Journal.*

33. Hayes, T. L., Oltman, K. A., Kaylor, L. E., & Belgudri, A. (2020). How leaders can become more committed to diversity management. *Consulting Psychology Journal, 72*, 247–262; Rice, J. (2012). Why make diversity so hard to achieve? *Harvard Business Review, 90*(6), 40; Gilbert, J. A., & Ivancevich, J. M. (2000). Valuing diversity: A tale of two organizations. *Academy of Management Executive, 14*(1), 93–105.

34. Jourdan, L. (2023, May 4). 7 metrics to measure your organization's DEI progress. *Harvard Business Review.* Retrieved May 28, 2023, from https://hbr.org/2023/05/7-metrics-to-measure-your-organizations-dei-progress

35. Kossek, E. E., & Lee, K-Y. (2020b). Managerial and organizational actions for creating inclusive climates. In E. E. Kossek & K-Y. Lee (Eds.), *Creating gender-inclusive organizations: Lessons from research and practice* (pp. 36–52). University of Toronto Press; Cox, T. H., Jr., & Blake, S. (1991). Managing cultural diversity: Implications for organizational competitiveness. *Academy of Management Executive, 5*(3), 45–56.

36. PQ Corporation. (2023). *LinkedIn.* Retrieved April 26, 2023, from https://www.linkedin.com/company/pq-corporation; Poole, J. C., & Kautz, E. T. (1987). An EEO/AA program that exceeds quotas—It targets biases. *Personnel Journal, 66*(1), 103–105.

37. Nordell, J. (2017, January 11). A fix for gender bias in health care? Check. *New York Times.* Retrieved January 13, 2017, from https://www.nytimes.com/2017/01/11/opinion/a-fix-for-gender-bias-in-health-care-check.html

38. Koh, Y. (2018, October 29). Intel hits an internal goal for workforce diversity. *Wall Street Journal.* Retrieved October 31, 2018, from https://www.wsj.com/articles/intel-hits-a-novel-diversity-target-it-calls-full-representation-1540818005

39. Konrad, A. M., Richard, O. C., & Yang, Y. (2021). *Both* diversity *and* meritocracy: Managing the diversity–meritocracy paradox with organizational ambidexterity. *Journal of Management Studies, 58*, 2180–2206; Livingston, R. (2020). How to promote racial equity in the workplace. *Harvard Business Review, 98*(5), 64–72.

40. Microsoft Corporation. (2023). *Inside Microsoft.* Retrieved April 27, 2023, from https://www.microsoft.com/en-us/diversity/inside-microsoft/default.aspx; Microsoft Corporation. (2023). *Global diversity and inclusion report 2022.* Retrieved April 27,

2023, from https://blogs.microsoft.com/blog/2022/10/27/2022-diversity-inclusion-report-driving-progress-through-greater-accountability-and-transparency/

41. Microsoft Corporation. (2023). *Inside Microsoft.* Retrieved April 27, 2023, from https://www.microsoft.com/en-us/diversity/inside-microsoft/default.aspx; Microsoft Corporation. (2023). *Global diversity and inclusion report 2022.* Retrieved April 27, 2023, from https://blogs.microsoft.com/blog/2022/10/27/2022-diversity-inclusion-report-driving-progress-through-greater-accountability-and-transparency/

42. Melaku, T. M., Beeman, A., Smith, D. G., & Johnson, W. B. (2020). Be a better ally: How White men can help their marginalized colleagues advance. *Harvard Business Review, 98*(6), 135–139; Sawyer, K., & Valerio, A. M. (2018). Making the case for male champions for gender inclusiveness at work. *Organizational Dynamics, 47*, 1–7; Men Advocating Real Change. (2017). *Actions men can take to create an inclusive workplace.* Retrieved January 4, 2018, from https://www.catalyst.org/wp-content/uploads/2019/01/actions_men_can_take_2018.pdf; Prime, J., & Moss-Racusin, C. A. (2009). *Engaging men in gender initiatives: What change agents need to know.* Catalyst. Retrieved January 4, 2018, from https://www.catalyst.org/research/engaging-men-in-gender-initiatives-what-change-agents-need-to-know/

43. Bezrukova, K., Spell, C. S., Perry, J. L., & Jehn, K. A. (2016). A meta-analytical integration of over 40 years of research on diversity training evaluation. *Psychological Bulletin, 142*, 1227–1274; Kalinoski, Z. T., Steele-Johnson, D., Peyton, E. J., Leas, K. A., Steinke, J., & Bowling, N. A. (2013). A meta-analytic evaluation of diversity training outcomes. *Journal of Organizational Behavior, 34*, 1076–1104.

44. Roberson, L., Kulik, C. T., & Tan, R. Y. (2013). Effective diversity training. In Q. M. Roberson (Ed.), *Oxford handbook of diversity and work* (pp. 341–365). Oxford University Press; Arredondo, P. (1996). The role of education and training. *Successful diversity management initiatives: A blueprint for planning and implementation* (pp. 125–145). SAGE.

45. Devine, P. G., & Ash, T. L. (2022). Diversity training goals, limitations, and promise: A review of the multidisciplinary literature. *Annual Review of Psychology, 73*, 403–429; Arredondo, P. (1996). The role of education and training. *Successful diversity management initiatives: A blueprint for planning and implementation* (pp. 125–145). SAGE.

46. Roberson, L., Kulik, C. T., & Tan, R. Y. (2013). Effective diversity training. In Q. M. Roberson (Ed.), *Oxford handbook of diversity and work* (pp. 341–365). Oxford University Press; Kulik, C. T., & Roberson, L. (2008). Common goals and golden opportunities: Evaluations of diversity education in academic and organizational settings. *Academy of Management Learning & Education, 7*, 309–331; Kulik, C. T., Pepper, M. B., Roberson, L., & Parker, S. K. (2007). The rich get richer: Predicting participation in voluntary diversity training. *Journal of Organizational Behavior, 28*, 753–769.

47. Browning, K. (2023, May 21). Uber's diversity chief put on leave after complaints of insensitivity. *New York Times.* Retrieved May 22, 2023, from https://www.nytimes.com/2023/05/21/business/uber-bo-young-lee-suspended.html; Koopman, J., Lanaj, K., Lee, Y. E., Alterman, V., Bradley, C., & Stoverink, A. C. (2023). Walking on eggshells: A self-control perspective on workplace political correctness. *Journal of Applied Psychology, 108*, 425–445; Cheng, S., Corrington, A., Dinh, J., Hebl, M., King, E., Ng, L., Reyes, D., Salas, E., & Traylor, A. (2019). Challenging diversity training myths: Changing the conversation about diversity training to shape science and practice. *Organizational Dynamics, 48*, 100678.

48. Johnson, W. B., Smith, D. G., & Christensen, H. (2023, March 8). Where women's leadership development programs fall short. *Harvard Business Review.* Retrieved March 9, 2023, from https://hbr.org/2023/03/where-womens-leadership-development-programs-fall-short; Loumpourdi, M. (2023). Leadership development programmes: Part of the solution or part of the problem of women's underrepresentation in leadership? *Gender in Management: An International Journal, 38*, 619–633; Vinnicombe, S., Moore, L. L., & Anderson, D. (2014). Women's leadership programmes are still important. In S. Vinnecombe, OBE, R. J. Burke, S. Blake-Beard, & L. L. Moore (Eds.), *Handbook of research on promoting women's careers* (pp. 406–419). Elgar; Ely, R. J., Ibarra, H., & Kolb, D. M. (2011). Taking gender into account: Theory and design for women's leadership development programs. *Academy of Management Learning & Education, 10*, 474–493.

49. Kossek, E. E., & Lee, K-Y. (Eds.). (2020a). *Creating gender-inclusive organizations: Lessons from research and practice.* University of Toronto Press; Bryer, A. (2020). Making organizations more inclusive: The work of belonging. *Organization Studies, 41*, 641–660; Pless, N. M., & Maak, T. (2004). Building an inclusive diversity culture: Principles, processes and practice. *Journal of Business Ethics, 54*, 129–147; Kossek, E. E., & Zonia, S. C. (1993). Assessing diversity climate: A field study of reactions to employer efforts to promote diversity. *Journal of Organizational Behavior, 14*, 61–81.

50. Buengeler, C., Leroy, H., & De Stobbeleir, K. (2018). How leaders shape the impact of HR's diversity practices on employee inclusion. *Human Resource Management Review, 28*, 289–303.

51. Özbilgin, M., Jonsen, K., Tatli, A., Vassilopoulou, J., & Surgevil, O. (2013). Global diversity management. In Q. M. Roberson (Ed.), *Oxford handbook of diversity and work* (pp. 419–441). Oxford University Press.

INDEX

ABOUT THE AUTHOR

Gary N. Powell, PhD, is professor emeritus of management at the University of Connecticut. He is author of *Gender in Management* (6th ed.), *Gender and Leadership, Making Work and Family Work: From Hard Choices to Smart Choices*, and *Managing a Diverse Workforce: Learning Activities* (3rd ed.) and the editor of *Handbook of Gender and Work*. He is an internationally recognized scholar and educator on gender, diversity, and work–family issues in the workplace. His graduate course on women and men in management won an award on innovation in education from the Committee on Equal Opportunity for Women of the Association to Advance Collegiate Schools of Business (AACSB). He has won the University of Connecticut School of Business Outstanding Graduate Teaching Award four times and the Outstanding Undergraduate Teaching Award. He has received the University of Connecticut President's Award for Promoting Multiculturalism.

He has served as chair of the Women in Management Division (now Diversity, Equity, and Inclusion Division) of the Academy of Management and received both the Janet Chusmir Service Award for his contributions to the division and the SAGE Scholarship Award for his contributions to research on gender in organizations. He has received the Richard Whipp Lifetime Achievement Award of the British Academy of Management for his contributions to business and management research in the United Kingdom (UK). He has received the Ellen Galinsky Generative Researcher Award of the Work and Family Researchers Network and was also named as a top ten extraordinary contributor for his contributions to work and family research. He has served as distinguished scholar at Lancaster University Management School in Lancaster, UK. He has published over 120 articles in journals such as *Academy of Management Journal, Academy of Management Review, Journal of Applied Psychology, Journal of Management, Journal of Management Studies, Personnel Psychology, Organizational Behavior and Human Decision Processes, Journal of Business Venturing, Journal of Vocational Behavior, Journal of Organizational Behavior, Journal of Occupational and Organizational Psychology, Entrepreneurship Theory and Practice,* and *Human Relations*; contributed over 30 chapters to edited volumes; and made over 180 presentations at professional conferences. He is a Fellow of the British Academy of Management, Academy of Social Sciences, and Eastern Academy of Management. He has served on the board of governors of the Academy of Management and as president of the Eastern Academy of Management. He has served as co-editor of a special issue of *Academy of Management Review* on work–life theory and on the editorial board of *Academy of Management*

Review, Journal of Management, Journal of Management Studies, Human Relations, and *Academy of Management Executive.*

Prior to joining the faculty at the University of Connecticut, he worked at General Electric (GE), graduating from its manufacturing management program. At GE, he designed and implemented automated project scheduling systems as well as systems for inventory control, materials procurement, and so on. He has provided management training and development for many companies, including Webster Financial Corporation, The Hartford Financial Services Group, The Implementation Partners (TIP), GE Capital, General Signal, Apple Computer, Monroe Auto Equipment, Allstate, and CIGNA and has conducted numerous other workshops.

He holds a doctorate in organizational behavior and a master's degree in management science from the University of Massachusetts and a bachelor's degree in management from the Massachusetts Institute of Technology (MIT).

ABOUT THE CONTRIBUTOR

Laura M. Graves, PhD, is professor emerita of management at Clark University. She is a recognized scholar on diversity in the workplace. Her work has examined gender and race effects in organizations, particularly gender bias in employment interviewers' decision processes and the effects of demographic diversity on work teams. She has also explored issues related to work–life integration, well-being, and motivation. She has served as chair of the Gender and Diversity in Organizations Division (now Diversity, Equity, and Inclusion Division) of the Academy of Management and received the SAGE Scholarship Award for her contributions to research on gender and diversity in organizations. Her research has appeared in leading academic journals, including *Academy of Management Review, Journal of Applied Psychology*, and *Journal of Management.* She has contributed chapters to many books and presented numerous papers at academic meetings. She has served on the editorial board of the *Academy of Management Journal.* She has also held several positions in the Eastern Academy of Management.

Prior to joining the faculty at Clark University, she was a member of the management faculty at the University of Connecticut. She also worked as an internal consultant in corporate human resources at Aetna. She holds a doctorate and a master's degree in social psychology from the University of Connecticut and a bachelor's degree in psychology from the College of William and Mary.

If you are based in the European Union and have safety concerns related to physical Sage products, in compliance with GPSR, please contact our Authorized Representative:

EC REP

International Associates Auditing & Certification Limited
The Black Church, St Mary's Place,
Dublin 7, D07 P4AX Ireland
EUAR@ie.ia-net.com